NOISE

Also by DANIEL KAHNEMAN

Thinking, Fast and Slow

Also by OLIVIER SIBONY

You're About to Make a Terrible Mistake!: How Biases Distort Decision-Making — and What You Can Do to Fight Them

Also by CASS R. SUNSTEIN

Too Much Information: Understanding What You Don't Want to Know

Nudge: Improving Decisions About Health, Wealth, and Happiness (with Richard H. Thaler)

NOISE

A Flaw in Human Judgment

DANIEL KAHNEMAN
OLIVIER SIBONY
CASS R. SUNSTEIN

WILLIAM
COLLINS

William Collins
An imprint of HarperCollins*Publishers*
1 London Bridge Street
London SE1 9GF

WilliamCollinsBooks.com

HarperCollins*Publishers*
1st Floor, Watermarque Building, Ringsend Road
Dublin 4, Ireland

First published in Great Britain in 2021 by William Collins
First published in the United States in 2021 by Little, Brown Spark

2

Copyright © Daniel Kahneman, Olivier Sibony and Cass R. Sunstein 2021

Daniel Kahneman, Olivier Sibony and Cass R. Sunstein
assert the moral right to be identified as the authors of this work in
accordance with the Copyright, Designs and Patents Act 1988

A catalogue record for this book is available from the British Library

ISBN 978-0-00-830899-5 (hardback)
ISBN 978-0-00-830900-8 (trade paperback)
ISBN 978-0-00-847256-6 (limited edition hardback)
ISBN 978-0-00-848016-5 (limited edition trade paperback)

Typeset in Sabon LT Std by Palimpsest Book Production Ltd, Falkirk, Stirlingshire

Printed and bound in Great Britain by CPI Group (UK) Ltd, Croydon CR0 4YY

MIX
Paper from
responsible sources
FSC™ C007454

This book is produced from independently certified FSC™ paper
to ensure responsible forest management.

For more information visit: www.harpercollins.co.uk/green

For Noga, Ori and Gili — DK
For Fantin and Lélia — OS
For Samantha — CRS

Contents

Introduction: Two Kinds of Error   3

Part I: Finding Noise   11

  1. Crime and Noisy Punishment   13

  2. A Noisy System   23

  3. Singular Decisions   34

Part II: Your Mind Is a Measuring Instrument   39

  4. Matters of Judgment   43

  5. Measuring Error   55

  6. The Analysis of Noise   69

  7. Occasion Noise   79

  8. How Groups Amplify Noise   94

Part III: Noise in Predictive Judgments   107

  9. Judgments and Models   111

  10. Noiseless Rules   123

11. Objective Ignorance   137

12. The Valley of the Normal   148

Part IV: How Noise Happens   159

13. Heuristics, Biases, and Noise   161

14. The Matching Operation   176

15. Scales   187

16. Patterns   200

17. The Sources of Noise   210

Part V: Improving Judgments   221

18. Better Judges for Better Judgments   225

19. Debiasing and Decision Hygiene   236

20. Sequencing Information in Forensic Science   245

21. Selection and Aggregation in Forecasting   259

22. Guidelines in Medicine   273

23. Defining the Scale in Performance Ratings   287

24. Structure in Hiring   300

25. The Mediating Assessments Protocol   312

Part VI: Optimal Noise   325

26. The Costs of Noise Reduction   329

27. Dignity   339

28. Rules or Standards?   350

Review and Conclusion: Taking Noise Seriously   361

Epilogue: A Less Noisy World   377

Appendix A: How to Conduct a Noise Audit   379

Appendix B: A Checklist for a Decision Observer   387

CONTENTS

Appendix C: Correcting Predictions   391

Acknowledgments   397

Notes   399

Index   439

NOISE

INTRODUCTION

Two Kinds of Error

I magine that four teams of friends have gone to a shooting arcade. Each team consists of five people; they share one rifle, and each person fires one shot. Figure 1 shows their results.

In an ideal world, every shot would hit the bull's-eye.

TEAM A

TEAM B

TEAM C

TEAM D

FIGURE 1: *Four teams*

That is nearly the case for Team A. The team's shots are tightly clustered around the bull's-eye, close to a perfect pattern.

We call Team B *biased* because its shots are systematically off target. As the figure illustrates, the consistency of the bias supports a prediction. If one of the team's members were to take another shot, we would bet on its landing in the same area as the first five. The consistency of the bias also invites a causal explanation: perhaps the gunsight on the team's rifle was bent.

We call Team C *noisy* because its shots are widely scattered. There is no obvious bias, because the impacts are roughly centered on the bull's-eye. If one of the team's members took another shot, we would know very little about where it is likely to hit. Furthermore, no interesting hypothesis comes to mind to explain the results of Team C. We know that its members are poor shots. We do not know why they are so noisy.

Team D is both biased and noisy. Like Team B, its shots are systematically off target; like Team C, its shots are widely scattered.

But this is not a book about target shooting. Our topic is human error. Bias and noise — systematic deviation and random scatter — are different components of error. The targets illustrate the difference.

The shooting range is a metaphor for what can go wrong in human judgment, especially in the diverse decisions that people make on behalf of organizations. In these situations, we will find the two types of error illustrated in figure 1. Some judgments are biased; they are systematically off target. Other judgments are noisy, as people who are expected to agree end up at very different points around the target. Many organizations, unfortunately, are afflicted by both bias and noise.

Figure 2 illustrates an important difference between bias and noise. It shows what you would see at the shooting range if you were shown only the backs of the targets at which the teams were shooting, without any indication of the bull's-eye they were aiming at.

From the back of the target, you cannot tell whether Team A or Team B is closer to the bull's-eye. But you can tell at a glance that

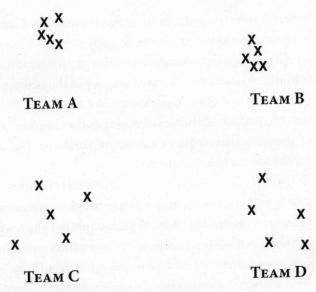

FIGURE 2: *Looking at the back of the target*

Teams C and D are noisy and that Teams A and B are not. Indeed, you know just as much about scatter as you did in figure 1. A general property of noise is that you can recognize and measure it while knowing nothing about the target or bias.

The general property of noise just mentioned is essential for our purposes in this book, because many of our conclusions are drawn from judgments whose true answer is unknown or even unknowable. When physicians offer different diagnoses for the same patient, we can study their disagreement without knowing what ails the patient. When film executives estimate the market for a movie, we can study the variability of their answers without knowing how much the film eventually made or even if it was produced at all. We don't need to know who is right to measure how much the judgments of the same case vary. All we have to do to measure noise is look at the back of the target.

To understand error in judgment, we must understand both bias and noise. Sometimes, as we will see, noise is the more important problem. But in public conversations about human error and in

5

organizations all over the world, noise is rarely recognized. Bias is the star of the show. Noise is a bit player, usually offstage. The topic of bias has been discussed in thousands of scientific articles and dozens of popular books, few of which even mention the issue of noise. This book is our attempt to redress the balance.

In real-world decisions, the amount of noise is often scandalously high. Here are a few examples of the alarming amount of noise in situations in which accuracy matters:

- *Medicine is noisy.* Faced with the same patient, different doctors make different judgments about whether patients have skin cancer, breast cancer, heart disease, tuberculosis, pneumonia, depression, and a host of other conditions. Noise is especially high in psychiatry, where subjective judgment is obviously important. However, considerable noise is also found in areas where it might not be expected, such as in the reading of X-rays.

- *Child custody decisions are noisy.* Case managers in child protection agencies must assess whether children are at risk of abuse and, if so, whether to place them in foster care. The system is noisy, given that some managers are much more likely than others to send a child to foster care. Years later, more of the unlucky children who have been assigned to foster care by these heavy-handed managers have poor life outcomes: higher delinquency rates, higher teen birth rates, and lower earnings.

- *Forecasts are noisy.* Professional forecasters offer highly variable predictions about likely sales of a new product, likely growth in the unemployment rate, the likelihood of bankruptcy for troubled companies, and just about everything else. Not only do they disagree with each other, but they also disagree with themselves. For example, when the same software developers were asked on two separate days to estimate the completion time for the same task, the hours they projected differed by 71%, on average.

- *Asylum decisions are noisy.* Whether an asylum seeker will be admitted into the United States depends on something like a lottery. A study of cases that were randomly allotted to different judges found that one judge admitted 5% of applicants, while another admitted 88%. The title of the study says it all: "Refugee Roulette." (We are going to see a lot of roulette.)

• *Personnel decisions are noisy.* Interviewers of job candidates make widely different assessments of the same people. Performance ratings of the same employees are also highly variable and depend more on the person doing the assessment than on the performance being assessed.

• *Bail decisions are noisy.* Whether an accused person will be granted bail or instead sent to jail pending trial depends partly on the identity of the judge who ends up hearing the case. Some judges are far more lenient than others. Judges also differ markedly in their assessment of which defendants present the highest risk of flight or reoffending.

• *Forensic science is noisy.* We have been trained to think of fingerprint identification as infallible. But fingerprint examiners sometimes differ in deciding whether a print found at a crime scene matches that of a suspect. Not only do experts disagree, but the same experts sometimes make inconsistent decisions when presented with the same print on different occasions. Similar variability has been documented in other forensic science disciplines, even DNA analysis.

• *Decisions to grant patents are noisy.* The authors of a leading study on patent applications emphasize the noise involved: "Whether the patent office grants or rejects a patent is significantly related to the happenstance of which examiner is assigned the application." This variability is obviously troublesome from the standpoint of equity.

All these noisy situations are the tip of a large iceberg. Wherever you look at human judgments, you are likely to find noise. To improve the quality of our judgments, we need to overcome noise as well as bias.

This book comes in six parts. In part 1, we explore the difference between noise and bias, and we show that both public and private organizations can be noisy, sometimes shockingly so. To appreciate the problem, we begin with judgments in two areas. The first involves criminal sentencing (and hence the public sector). The second involves insurance (and hence the private sector). At first glance, the two areas could not be more different. But with respect to noise, they have much in common. To establish that point, we introduce the idea of a noise audit, designed to measure how much disagreement there is among professionals considering the same cases within an organization.

In part 2, we investigate the nature of human judgment and explore how to measure accuracy and error. Judgments are susceptible to both bias and noise. We describe a striking equivalence in the roles of the two types of error. Occasion noise is the variability in judgments of the same case by the same person or group on different occasions. A surprising amount of occasion noise arises in group discussion because of seemingly irrelevant factors, such as who speaks first.

Part 3 takes a deeper look at one type of judgment that has been researched extensively: predictive judgment. We explore the key advantage of rules, formulas, and algorithms over humans when it comes to making predictions: contrary to popular belief, it is not so much the superior insight of rules but their noiselessness. We discuss the ultimate limit on the quality of predictive judgment — objective ignorance of the future — and how it conspires with noise to limit the quality of prediction. Finally, we address a question that you will almost certainly have asked yourself by then: if noise is so ubiquitous, then why had you not noticed it before?

Part 4 turns to human psychology. We explain the central causes of noise. These include interpersonal differences arising from a variety of factors, including personality and cognitive style; idiosyncratic variations in the weighting of different considerations; and the different uses that people make of the very same scales. We explore why people are oblivious to noise and are frequently unsurprised by events and judgments they could not possibly have predicted.

Part 5 explores the practical question of how you can improve your judgments and prevent error. (Readers who are primarily interested in practical applications of noise reduction might skip the discussion of the challenges of prediction and of the psychology of judgment in parts 3 and 4 and move directly to this part.) We investigate efforts to tackle noise in medicine, business, education, government, and elsewhere. We introduce several noise-reduction techniques that we collect under the label of *decision hygiene*. We present five case studies of domains in which there is much documented noise and in which people have made sustained efforts to reduce it, with instructively varying degrees of success. The case studies include unreliable medical diagnoses, performance ratings, forensic science, hiring decisions, and forecasting in general. We conclude by offering a system we call the *mediating assessments protocol:* a general-purpose approach to the evaluation of options that incorporates several key practices of decision hygiene and aims to produce less noisy and more reliable judgments.

What is the right level of noise? Part 6 turns to this question. Perhaps counterintuitively, the right level is not zero. In some areas, it just isn't feasible to eliminate noise. In other areas, it is too expensive to do so. In still other areas, efforts to reduce noise would compromise important competing values. For example, efforts to eliminate noise could undermine morale and give people a sense that they are being treated like cogs in a machine. When algorithms are part of the answer, they raise an assortment of objections; we address some of them here. Still, the current level of noise is unacceptable. We urge both private and public organizations to conduct noise audits and to undertake, with unprecedented seriousness, stronger efforts to reduce noise. Should they do so, organizations could reduce widespread unfairness — and reduce costs in many areas.

With that aspiration in mind, we end each chapter with a few brief propositions in the form of quotations. You can use these statements as they are or adapt them for any issues that matter to you, whether they involve health, safety, education, money, employment, entertainment, or something else. Understanding the problem of noise, and trying to solve it, is a work in progress and a collective endeavor. All of us have opportunities to contribute to this work. This book is written in the hope that we can seize those opportunities.

PART I

Finding Noise

It is not acceptable for similar people, convicted of the same offense, to end up with dramatically different sentences — say, five years in jail for one and probation for another. And yet in many places, something like that happens. To be sure, the criminal justice system is pervaded by bias as well. But our focus in chapter 1 is on noise — and in particular, on what happened when a famous judge drew attention to it, found it scandalous, and launched a crusade that in a sense changed the world (but not enough). Our tale involves the United States, but we are confident that similar stories can be (and will be) told about many other nations. In some of those nations, the problem of noise is likely to be even worse than it is in the United States. We use the example of sentencing in part to show that noise can produce great unfairness.

Criminal sentencing has especially high drama, but we are also concerned with the private sector, where the stakes can be large, too. To illustrate the point, we turn in chapter 2 to a large insurance company. There, underwriters have the task of setting insurance premiums for potential clients, and claims adjusters must judge the value of claims. You might predict that these tasks would be simple and mechanical and that different professionals would come up with roughly the same amounts. We conducted a carefully designed experiment — a noise audit — to test that prediction. The results surprised us, but more importantly they astonished and dismayed the company's leadership. As we learned, the sheer volume of noise is costing the company a great deal of money. We use this example to show that noise can produce large economic losses.

Both of these examples involve studies of a large number of people making a large number of judgments. But many important judgments are *singular* rather than repeated: how to handle an apparently unique business opportunity, whether to launch a whole new product, how to deal with a pandemic, whether to hire someone who just doesn't meet the standard profile. Can noise be found in decisions about unique situations like these? It is tempting to think that it is absent there. After all, noise is unwanted variability, and how can you have variability with singular decisions? In chapter 3, we try to answer this question. The judgment that you make, even in a seemingly unique situation, is one in a cloud of possibilities. You will find a lot of noise there as well.

The theme that emerges from these three chapters can be summarized in one sentence, which will be a key theme of this book: *wherever there is judgment, there is noise — and more of it than you think.* Let's start to find out how much.

CHAPTER 1

Crime and Noisy Punishment

Suppose that someone has been convicted of a crime — shoplifting, possession of heroin, assault, or armed robbery. What is the sentence likely to be?

The answer should not depend on the particular judge to whom the case happens to be assigned, on whether it is hot or cold outside, or on whether a local sports team won the day before. It would be outrageous if three similar people, convicted of the same crime, received radically different penalties: probation for one, two years in jail for another, and ten years in jail for another. And yet that outrage can be found in many nations — not only in the distant past but also today.

All over the world, judges have long had a great deal of discretion in deciding on appropriate sentences. In many nations, experts have celebrated this discretion and have seen it as both just and humane. They have insisted that criminal sentences should be based on a host of factors involving not only the crime but also the defendant's character and circumstances. Individualized tailoring was the order of the day. If judges were constrained by rules, criminals would be treated in a dehumanized way; they would not be seen as unique individuals entitled to draw attention to the details of their situation. The very idea of due process of law seemed, to many, to call for open-ended judicial discretion.

In the 1970s, the universal enthusiasm for judicial discretion started to collapse for one simple reason: startling evidence of noise. In 1973, a famous judge, Marvin Frankel, drew public attention to the problem. Before he became a judge, Frankel was a defender of freedom of speech and a passionate human rights advocate who helped found the Lawyers' Committee for Human Rights (an organization now known as Human Rights First).

Frankel could be fierce. And with respect to noise in the criminal justice system, he was outraged. Here is how he describes his motivation:

> *If a federal bank robbery defendant was convicted, he or she could receive a maximum of 25 years. That meant anything from 0 to 25 years. And where the number was set, I soon realized, depended less on the case or the individual defendant than on the individual judge, i.e., on the views, predilections, and biases of the judge. So the same defendant in the same case could get widely different sentences depending on which judge got the case.*

Frankel did not provide any kind of statistical analysis to support his argument. But he did offer a series of powerful anecdotes, showing unjustified disparities in the treatment of similar people. Two men, neither of whom had a criminal record, were convicted for cashing counterfeit checks in the amounts of $58.40 and $35.20, respectively. The first man was sentenced to fifteen *years*, the second to 30 *days*. For embezzlement actions that were similar to one another, one man was sentenced to 117 *days* in prison, while another was sentenced to 20 *years*. Pointing to numerous cases of this kind, Frankel deplored what he called the "almost wholly unchecked and sweeping powers" of federal judges, resulting in "arbitrary cruelties perpetrated daily," which he deemed unacceptable in a "government of laws, not of men."

Frankel called on Congress to end this "discrimination," as he described those arbitrary cruelties. By that term, he mainly meant noise, in the form of inexplicable variations in sentencing. But he was also concerned about bias, in the form of racial and socioeconomic disparities. To combat both noise and bias, he urged that differences in treatment of criminal defendants should not be allowed unless the differences could be "justified by relevant tests capable of formulation and application with sufficient objectivity to ensure that the results will be more than the idiosyncratic ukases of particular officials, justices, or others." (The term *idiosyncratic ukases* is a bit esoteric; by it, Frankel meant personal edicts.) Much more than that, Frankel argued for a reduction in noise through a "detailed profile or checklist of factors that would include, wherever possible, some form of numerical or other objective grading."

Writing in the early 1970s, he did not go quite so far as to defend what he called "displacement of people by machines." But startlingly, he came close. He believed that "the rule of law calls for a body of impersonal rules, applicable across the board, binding on judges as well as everyone else." He explicitly argued for the use of "computers as an aid toward orderly thought in sentencing." He also recommended the creation of a commission on sentencing.

Frankel's book became one of the most influential in the entire history of criminal law — not only in the United States but also throughout the world. His work did suffer from a degree of informality. It was devastating but impressionistic. To test for the reality of noise, several people immediately followed up by exploring the level of noise in criminal sentencing.

An early large-scale study of this kind, chaired by Judge Frankel himself, took place in 1974. Fifty judges from various districts were asked to set sentences for defendants in hypothetical cases summarized in identical pre-sentence reports. The basic finding was that "absence of consensus was the norm" and that the variations across punishments were "astounding." A heroin dealer could be incarcerated for one to ten years, depending on the judge. Punishments for a bank robber ranged from five to eighteen years in prison. The study found that in an extortion case, sentences varied from a whopping twenty years imprisonment and a $65,000 fine to a mere three years imprisonment and no fine. Most startling of all, in sixteen of twenty cases, there was no unanimity on whether any incarceration was appropriate.

This study was followed by a series of others, all of which found similarly shocking levels of noise. In 1977, for example, William Austin and Thomas Williams conducted a survey of forty-seven judges, asking them to respond to the same five cases, each involving low-level offenses. All the descriptions of the cases included summaries of the information used by judges in actual sentencing, such as the charge, the testimony, the previous criminal record (if any), social background, and evidence relating to character. The key finding was "substantial disparity." In a case involving burglary, for example, the recommended sentences ranged from five years in prison to a mere thirty days (alongside a fine of $100). In a case involving possession of marijuana, some judges recommended prison terms; others recommended probation.

A much larger study, conducted in 1981, involved 208 federal judges who were exposed to the same sixteen hypothetical cases. Its central findings were stunning:

> In only 3 of the 16 cases was there a unanimous agreement to impose a prison term. Even where most judges agreed that a prison term was appropriate, there was a substantial variation in the lengths of prison terms recommended. In one fraud case in which the mean prison term was 8.5 years, the longest term was life in prison. In another case the mean prison term was 1.1 years, yet the longest prison term recommended was 15 years.

As revealing as they are, these studies, which involve tightly controlled experiments, almost certainly understate the magnitude of noise in the real world of criminal justice. Real-life judges are exposed to far more information than what the study participants received in the carefully specified vignettes of these experiments. Some of this additional information is relevant, of course, but there is also ample evidence that irrelevant information, in the form of small and seemingly random factors, can produce major differences in outcomes. For example, judges have been found more likely to grant parole at the beginning of the day or after a food break than immediately before such a break. If judges are hungry, they are tougher.

A study of thousands of juvenile court decisions found that when the local football team loses a game on the weekend, the judges make harsher decisions on the Monday (and, to a lesser extent, for the rest of the week). Black defendants disproportionately bear the brunt of that increased harshness. A different study looked at 1.5 million judicial decisions over three decades and similarly found that judges are more severe on days that follow a loss by the local city's football team than they are on days that follow a win.

A study of six million decisions made by judges in France over twelve years found that defendants are given more leniency on their birthday. (The defendant's birthday, that is; we suspect that judges might be more lenient on their own birthdays as well, but as far as we know, that hypothesis has not been tested.) Even something as irrelevant as outside temperature can influence judges. A review of 207,000 immigration court decisions over four years found a significant effect of daily temperature variations: when it is hot outside, people are less likely to get asylum. If you are suffering political persecution in your home country and want asylum elsewhere, you should hope and maybe even pray that your hearing falls on a cool day.

Reducing Noise in Sentencing

In the 1970s, Frankel's arguments, and the empirical findings supporting them, came to the attention of Edward M. Kennedy, brother of the slain president John F. Kennedy, and one of the most influential members of the US Senate. Kennedy was shocked and appalled. As early as 1975, he introduced sentencing reform legislation; it didn't go anywhere. But Kennedy was relentless. Pointing to the evidence, he continued to press for the enactment of that legislation, year after year. In 1984, he succeeded. Responding to the evidence of unjustified variability, Congress enacted the Sentencing Reform Act of 1984.

The new law was intended to reduce noise in the system by reducing "the unfettered discretion the law confers on those judges and parole authorities responsible for imposing and implementing the sentences." In particular, members of Congress referred to "unjustifiably wide" sentencing disparity, specifically citing findings that in the New York area, punishments for identical actual cases could range from three years to twenty years of imprisonment. Just as Judge Frankel had recommended, the law created the US Sentencing Commission, whose principal job was clear: to issue sentencing guidelines that were meant to be mandatory and that would establish a restricted range for criminal sentences.

In the following year, the commission established those guidelines, which were generally based on average sentences for similar crimes in an analysis of ten thousand actual cases. Supreme Court Justice Stephen Breyer, who was heavily involved in the process, defended the use of past practice by pointing to the intractable disagreement within the commission: "Why didn't the Commission sit down and really go and rationalize this thing and not just take history? The short answer to that is: we couldn't. We couldn't because there are such good arguments all over the place pointing in opposite directions.... Try listing all the crimes that there are in rank order of punishable merit.... Then collect results from your friends and see if they all match. I will tell you they won't."

Under the guidelines, judges have to consider two factors to establish sentences: the crime and the defendant's criminal history. Crimes are assigned one of forty-three "offense levels," depending on their seriousness. The defendant's criminal history refers principally to the number and severity of a defendant's previous convictions. Once the crime and the criminal history are put together, the guidelines offer a relatively narrow range of sentencing, with the top of the range authorized to exceed the bottom by the greater of six months or 25%. Judges are permitted to depart from the range altogether by reference to what they see as aggravating or mitigating circumstances, but departures must be justified to an appellate court.

Even though the guidelines are mandatory, they are not entirely rigid. They do not go nearly as far as Judge Frankel wanted. They offer judges significant room to maneuver. Nonetheless, several studies, using a variety of methods and focused on a range of historical periods, reach the same conclusion: the guidelines cut the noise. More technically, they "reduced the net variation in sentence attributable to the happenstance of the identity of the sentencing judge."

The most elaborate study came from the commission itself. It compared sentences in bank robbery, cocaine distribution, heroin distribution, and bank embezzlement cases in 1985 (before the guidelines went into effect) with the sentences imposed between January 19, 1989, and September 30, 1990. Offenders were matched with respect to the factors deemed relevant to sentencing under the guidelines. For every offense, variations across judges were much smaller in the later period, after the Sentencing Reform Act had been implemented.

According to another study, the expected difference in sentence length between judges was 17%, or 4.9 months, in 1986 and 1987. That number fell to 11%, or 3.9 months, between 1988 and 1993. An independent study covering different periods found similar success in reducing interjudge disparities, which were defined as the differences in average sentences among judges with similar caseloads.

Despite these findings, the guidelines ran into a firestorm of criticism. Some people, including many judges, thought that some sentences were too severe — a point about bias, not noise. For our purposes, a much more interesting objection, which came from numerous judges, was that guidelines were deeply unfair because they prohibited judges from taking adequate account of the particulars of the case. The price of reducing noise was to make decisions unacceptably mechanical. Yale law professor Kate Stith and federal judge José Cabranes wrote that "the need is not for blindness, but for insight, for equity," which "can only occur in a judgment that takes account of the complexities of the individual case."

This objection led to vigorous challenges to the guidelines, some of them based on law, others based on policy. Those challenges failed until, for technical reasons entirely unrelated to the debate summarized here, the Supreme Court struck the guidelines down in 2005. As a result of the court's ruling, the guidelines became merely advisory. Notably, most federal judges were much happier after the Supreme Court decision. Seventy-five percent preferred the advisory regime, whereas just 3% thought the mandatory regime was better.

What have been the effects of changing the guidelines from mandatory to advisory? Harvard law professor Crystal Yang investigated this question, not with an experiment or a survey but with a massive data set of actual sentences, involving nearly four hundred thousand criminal defendants. Her central finding is that by multiple measures, interjudge disparities increased significantly after 2005. When the guidelines were mandatory, defendants who had been sentenced by a relatively harsh judge were sentenced to 2.8 months longer than if they had been sentenced by an average judge. When the guidelines became merely advisory, the disparity was doubled. Sounding much like Judge Frankel from forty years before, Yang writes that her "findings raise large equity concerns because the identity of the assigned sentencing judge contributes significantly to the disparate treatment of similar offenders convicted of similar crimes."

After the guidelines became advisory, judges became more likely to base their sentencing decisions on their personal values. Mandatory guidelines reduce bias as well as noise. After the Supreme Court's decision, there was a significant increase in the disparity between the sentences of African American defendants and white people convicted of the same crimes. At the same time, female judges became more likely than male judges were to exercise their increased discretion in favor of leniency. The same is true of judges appointed by Democratic presidents.

Three years after Frankel's death in 2002, striking down the mandatory guidelines produced a return to something more like his nightmare: law without order.

———

The story of Judge Frankel's fight for sentencing guidelines offers a glimpse of several of the key points we will cover in this book. First, judgment is difficult because the world is a complicated, uncertain place. This complexity is obvious in the judiciary and holds in most other situations requiring professional judgment. Broadly, these situations include judgments made by doctors, nurses, lawyers, engineers, teachers, architects, Hollywood executives, members of hiring committees, book publishers, corporate executives of all kinds, and managers of sports teams. Disagreement is unavoidable wherever judgment is involved.

Second, the extent of these disagreements is much greater than we expect. While few people object to the principle of judicial discretion, almost everyone disapproves of the magnitude of the disparities it produces. *System noise,* that is, unwanted variability in judgments that should ideally be identical, can create rampant injustice, high economic costs, and errors of many kinds.

Third, noise can be reduced. The approach advocated by Frankel and implemented by the US Sentencing Commission — rules and guidelines — is one of several approaches that successfully reduce noise. Other approaches are better suited to other types of judgment. Some methods adopted to reduce noise can simultaneously reduce bias as well.

Fourth, efforts at noise reduction often raise objections and run into serious difficulties. These issues must be addressed, too, or the fight against noise will fail.

Speaking of Noise in Sentencing

"Experiments show large disparities among judges in the sentences they recommend for identical cases. This variability cannot be fair. A defendant's sentence should not depend on which judge the case happens to be assigned to."

"Criminal sentences should not depend on the judge's mood during the hearing, or on the outside temperature."

"Guidelines are one way to address this issue. But many people don't like them, because they limit judicial discretion, which might be necessary to ensure fairness and accuracy. After all, each case is unique, isn't it?"

CHAPTER 2

A Noisy System

Our initial encounter with noise, and what first triggered our interest in the topic, was not nearly so dramatic as a brush with the criminal justice system. Actually, the encounter was a kind of accident, involving an insurance company that had engaged the consulting firm with which two of us were affiliated.

Of course, the topic of insurance is not everyone's cup of tea. But our findings show the magnitude of the problem of noise in a for-profit organization that stands to lose a lot from noisy decisions. Our experience with the insurance company helps explain why the problem is so often unseen and what might be done about it.

The insurance company's executives were weighing the potential value of an effort to increase consistency — to reduce noise — in the judgments of people who made significant financial decisions on the firm's behalf. Everyone agreed that consistency is desirable. Everyone also agreed that these judgments could never be entirely consistent, because they are informal and partly subjective. Some noise is inevitable.

Disagreement emerged when it came to its magnitude. The executives doubted that noise could be a substantial problem for their

23

company. Much to their credit, however, they agreed to settle the question by a kind of simple experiment that we will call a *noise audit*. The result surprised them. It also turned out to be a perfect illustration of the problem of noise.

A Lottery That Creates Noise

Many professionals in any large company are authorized to make judgments that bind the company. For example, this insurance company employs numerous underwriters who quote premiums for financial risks, such as insuring a bank against losses due to fraud or rogue trading. It also employs many claims adjusters who forecast the cost of future claims and also negotiate with claimants if disputes arise.

Every large branch of the company has several qualified underwriters. When a quote is requested, anyone who happens to be available may be assigned to prepare it. In effect, the particular underwriter who will determine a quote is selected by a lottery.

The exact value of the quote has significant consequences for the company. A high premium is advantageous if the quote is accepted, but such a premium risks losing the business to a competitor. A low premium is more likely to be accepted, but it is less advantageous to the company. For any risk, there is a Goldilocks price that is just right — neither too high nor too low — and there is a good chance that the average judgment of a large group of professionals is not too far from this Goldilocks number. Prices that are higher or lower than this number are costly — this is how the variability of noisy judgments hurts the bottom line.

The job of claims adjusters also affects the finances of the company. For example, suppose that a claim is submitted on behalf of a worker (the claimant) who permanently lost the use of his right hand in an industrial accident. An adjuster is assigned to the claim — just as the underwriter was assigned, because she happens to be available. The adjuster gathers the facts of the case and provides an estimate of its ultimate cost to the company. The same adjuster then takes charge of negotiating with the claimant's representative to ensure that the claimant receives the benefits promised in the policy while also protecting the company from making excessive payments.

The early estimate matters because it sets an implicit goal for the adjuster in future negotiations with the claimant. The insurance company is also legally obligated to reserve the predicted cost of each claim (i.e., to have enough cash to be able to pay it). Here again, there is a Goldilocks value from the perspective of the company. A settlement is not guaranteed, as there is an attorney for the claimant on the other side, who may choose to go to court if the offer is miserly. On the other hand, an overly generous reserve may allow the adjuster too much latitude to agree to frivolous demands. The adjuster's judgment is consequential for the company — and even more consequential for the claimant.

We use the word *lottery* to emphasize the role of chance in the selection of one underwriter or adjuster. In the normal operation of the company, a single professional is assigned to a case, and no one can ever know what would have happened if another colleague had been selected instead.

Lotteries have their place, and they need not be unjust. Acceptable lotteries are used to allocate "goods," like courses in some universities, or "bads," like the draft in the military. They serve a purpose. But the judgment lotteries we talk about allocate nothing. They just produce uncertainty. Imagine an insurance company whose underwriters are noiseless and set the optimal premium, but a chance device then intervenes to modify the quote that the client actually sees. Evidently, there would be no justification for such a lottery. Neither is there any justification for a system in which the outcome depends on the identity of the person randomly chosen to make a professional judgment.

Noise Audits Reveal System Noise

The lottery that picks a particular judge to establish a criminal sentence or a single shooter to represent a team creates variability, but this variability remains unseen. A noise audit — like the one conducted on federal judges with respect to sentencing — is a way to reveal noise. In such an audit, the same case is evaluated by many individuals, and the variability of their responses is made visible.

The judgments of underwriters and claims adjusters lend themselves especially well to this exercise because their decisions are based on written information. To prepare for the noise audit, executives of the company constructed detailed descriptions of five representative cases for each group (underwriters and adjusters). Employees were asked to evaluate two or three cases each, working independently. They were not told that the purpose of the study was to examine the variability of their judgments.

Before reading on, you may want to think of your own answer to the following questions: In a well-run insurance company, if you randomly selected two qualified underwriters or claims adjusters, how different would you expect their estimates for the same case to be? Specifically, what would be the difference between the two estimates, as a percentage of their average?

We asked numerous executives in the company for their answers, and in subsequent years, we have obtained estimates from a wide variety of people in different professions. Surprisingly, one answer is clearly more popular than all others. Most executives of the insurance company guessed 10% or less. When we asked 828 CEOs and senior executives from a variety of industries how much variation they expected to find in similar expert judgments, 10% was also the median answer and the most frequent one (the second most popular was 15%). A 10% difference would mean, for instance, that one of the two underwriters set a premium of $9,500 while the other quoted $10,500. Not a negligible difference, but one that an organization can be expected to tolerate.

Our noise audit found much greater differences. By our measure, the median difference in underwriting was 55%, about five times as large as was expected by most people, including the company's executives. This result means, for instance, that when one underwriter sets a premium at $9,500, the other does not set it at $10,500 — but instead quotes $16,700. For claims adjusters, the median ratio was 43%. We stress that these results are medians: in half the pairs of cases, the difference between the two judgments was even larger.

The executives to whom we reported the results of the noise audit were quick to realize that the sheer volume of noise presented an expensive problem. One senior executive estimated that the company's annual cost of noise in underwriting — counting both the loss of business from excessive quotes and the losses incurred on under-priced contracts — was in the hundreds of millions of dollars.

No one could say precisely how much error (or how much bias) there was, because no one could know for sure the Goldilocks value for each case. But no one needed to see the bull's-eye to measure the scatter on the back of the target and to realize that the variability was a problem. The data showed that the price a customer is asked to pay depends to an uncomfortable extent on the lottery that picks the employee who will deal with that transaction. To say the least, customers would not be pleased to hear that they were signed up for such a lottery without their consent. More generally, people who deal with organizations expect a system that reliably delivers consistent judgments. They do not expect system noise.

Unwanted Variability Versus Wanted Diversity

A defining feature of system noise is that it is *unwanted,* and we should stress right here that variability in judgments is not always unwanted.

Consider matters of preference or taste. If ten film critics watch the same movie, if ten wine tasters rate the same wine, or if ten people read the same novel, we do not expect them to have the same opinion. Diversity of tastes is welcome and entirely expected. No one would want to live in a world in which everyone has exactly the same likes and dislikes. (Well, almost no one.) But diversity of tastes can help account for errors if a personal taste is mistaken for a professional judgment. If a film producer decides to go forward with an unusual project (about, say, the rise and fall of the rotary phone) because she personally likes the script, she might have made a major mistake if no one else likes it.

Variability in judgments is also expected and welcome in a competitive situation in which the best judgments will be rewarded. When several companies (or several teams in the same organization) compete to generate innovative solutions to the same customer problem, we don't want them to focus on the same approach. The same is true when multiple teams of researchers attack a scientific problem, such as the development of a vaccine: we very much want them to look at it from different angles. Even forecasters sometimes behave like competitive players. The analyst who correctly calls a recession that no one else has anticipated is sure to gain fame, whereas the one who never strays from the consensus remains obscure. In such settings, variability in ideas and judgments is again welcome, because variation is only the first step. In a second phase, the results of these judgments will be pitted against one another, and the best will triumph. In a market as in nature, selection cannot work without variation.

Matters of taste and competitive settings all pose interesting problems of judgment. But our focus is on judgments in which variability is undesirable. System noise is a problem of systems, which are organizations, not markets. When traders make different assessments of the value of a stock, some of them will make money, and others will not. Disagreements make markets. But if one of those traders is randomly chosen to make that assessment on behalf of her firm, and if we find out that her colleagues in the same firm would produce very different assessments, then the firm faces system noise, and that is a problem.

An elegant illustration of the issue arose when we presented our findings to the senior managers of an asset management firm, prompting them to run their own exploratory noise audit. They asked forty-two experienced investors in the firm to estimate the fair value of a stock (the price at which the investors would be indifferent to buying or selling). The investors based their analysis on a one-page description of the business; the data included simplified profit and loss, balance sheet, and cash flow statements for the past three years and projections for the next two. Median noise, measured in the same way as in the insurance company, was 41%. Such large differences among investors in the same firm, using the same valuation methods, cannot be good news.

Wherever the person making a judgment is randomly selected from a pool of equally qualified individuals, as is the case in this asset management firm, in the criminal justice system, and in the insurance company discussed earlier, noise is a problem. System noise plagues many organizations: an assignment process that is effectively random often decides which doctor sees you in a hospital, which judge hears your case in a courtroom, which patent examiner reviews your application, which customer service representative hears your complaint, and so on. Unwanted variability in these judgments can cause serious problems, including a loss of money and rampant unfairness.

A frequent misconception about unwanted variability in judgments is that it doesn't matter, because random errors supposedly cancel one another out. Certainly, positive and negative errors in a judgment about the same case will tend to cancel one another out, and we will discuss in detail how this property can be used to reduce noise. But noisy systems do not make multiple judgments of the same case. They make noisy judgments of different cases. If one insurance policy is overpriced and another is underpriced, pricing may on average look right, but the insurance company has made two costly errors. If two felons who both should be sentenced to five years in prison receive sentences of three years and seven years, justice has not, on average, been done. In noisy systems, errors do not cancel out. They add up.

The Illusion of Agreement

A large literature going back several decades has documented noise in professional judgment. Because we were aware of this literature, the results of the insurance company's noise audit did not surprise us. What did surprise us, however, was the reaction of the executives to whom we reported our findings: no one at the company had expected anything like the amount of noise we had observed. No one questioned the validity of the audit, and no one claimed that the observed amount of noise was acceptable. Yet the problem of noise — and its large cost — seemed like a new one for the organization. Noise was like a leak in the basement. It was tolerated not because it was thought acceptable but because it had remained unnoticed.

How could that be? How could professionals in the same role and in the same office differ so much from one another without becoming aware of it? How could executives fail to make this observation, which they understood to be a significant threat to the performance and reputation of their company? We came to see that the problem of system noise often goes unrecognized in organizations and that the common inattention to noise is as interesting as its prevalence. The noise audits suggested that respected professionals — and the organizations that employ them — maintained an *illusion of agreement* while in fact disagreeing in their daily professional judgments.

To begin to understand how the illusion of agreement arises, put yourself in the shoes of an underwriter on a normal working day. You have more than five years of experience, you know that you are well regarded among your colleagues, and you respect and like them. You know you are good at your job. After thoroughly analyzing the complex risks faced by a financial firm, you conclude that a premium of $200,000 is appropriate. The problem is complex but not much different from those you solve every day of the week.

Now imagine being told that your colleagues at the office have been given the same information and assessed the same risk. Could you believe that at least half of them have set a premium that is either higher than $255,000 or lower than $145,000? The thought is hard to accept. Indeed, we suspect that underwriters who heard about the noise audit and accepted its validity never truly believed that its conclusions applied to them personally.

Most of us, most of the time, live with the unquestioned belief that the world looks as it does because that's the way it is. There is one small step from this belief to another: "Other people view the world much the way I do." These beliefs, which have been called *naive realism,* are essential to the sense of a reality we share with other people. We rarely question these beliefs. We hold a single interpretation of the world around us at any one time, and we normally invest little effort in generating plausible alternatives to it. One interpretation is enough, and we experience it as true. We do not go through life imagining alternative ways of seeing what we see.

In the case of professional judgments, the belief that others see the world much as we do is reinforced every day in multiple ways. First, we share with our colleagues a common language and set of rules about the considerations that should matter in our decisions. We also have the reassuring experience of agreeing with others on the absurdity of judgments that violate these rules. We view the occasional disagreements with colleagues as lapses of judgment on their part. We have little opportunity to notice that our agreed-on rules are vague, sufficient to eliminate some possibilities but not to specify a shared positive response to a particular case. We can live comfortably with colleagues without ever noticing that they actually do not see the world as we do.

One underwriter we interviewed described her experience in becoming a veteran in her department: "When I was new, I would discuss seventy-five percent of cases with my supervisor.... After a few years, I didn't need to — I am now regarded as an expert.... Over time, I became more and more confident in my judgment." Like many of us, this person had developed confidence in her judgment mainly by exercising it.

The psychology of this process is well understood. Confidence is nurtured by the subjective experience of judgments that are made with increasing fluency and ease, in part because they resemble judgments made in similar cases in the past. Over time, as this underwriter learned to agree with her past self, her confidence in her judgments increased. She gave no indication that — after the initial apprenticeship phase — she had learned to agree with others, had checked to what extent she did agree with them, or had even tried to prevent her practices from drifting away from those of her colleagues.

For the insurance company, the illusion of agreement was shattered only by the noise audit. How had the leaders of the company remained unaware of their noise problem? There are several possible answers here, but one that seems to play a large role in many settings is simply the discomfort of disagreement. Most organizations prefer consensus and harmony over dissent and conflict. The procedures in place often seem expressly designed to minimize the frequency of exposure to actual disagreements and, when such disagreements happen, to explain them away.

Nathan Kuncel, a professor of psychology at the University of Minnesota and a leading researcher on the prediction of performance, shared with us a story that illustrates this problem. Kuncel was helping a school's admissions office review its decision process. First a person read an application file, rated it, and then handed it off with ratings to a second reader, who then also rated it. Kuncel suggested — for reasons that will become obvious throughout this book — that it would be preferable to mask the first reader's ratings so as not to influence the second reader. The school's reply: "We used to do that, but it resulted in so many disagreements that we switched to the current system." This school is not the only organization that considers conflict avoidance at least as important as making the right decision.

Consider another mechanism that many companies resort to: postmortems of unfortunate judgments. As a learning mechanism, postmortems are useful. But if a mistake has truly been made — in the sense that a judgment strayed far from professional norms — discussing it will not be challenging. Experts will easily conclude that the judgment was way off the consensus. (They might also write it off as a rare exception.) Bad judgment is much easier to identify than good judgment. The calling out of egregious mistakes and the marginalization of bad colleagues will not help professionals become aware of how much they disagree when making broadly acceptable judgments. On the contrary, the easy consensus about bad judgments may even reinforce the illusion of agreement. The true lesson, about the ubiquity of system noise, will never be learned.

We hope you are starting to share our view that system noise is a serious problem. Its existence is not a surprise; noise is a consequence of the informal nature of judgment. However, as we will see throughout this book, the amount of noise observed when an organization takes a serious look almost always comes as a shock. Our conclusion is simple: wherever there is judgment, there is noise, and more of it than you think.

Speaking of System Noise in the Insurance Company

"We depend on the quality of professional judgments, by underwriters, claims adjusters, and others. We assign each case to one expert, but we operate under the wrong assumption that another expert would produce a similar judgment."

"System noise is five times larger than we thought — or than we can tolerate. Without a noise audit, we would never have realized that. The noise audit shattered the illusion of agreement."

"System noise is a serious problem: it costs us hundreds of millions."

"Wherever there is judgment, there is noise — and more of it than we think."

CHAPTER 3

Singular Decisions

The case studies we have discussed thus far involve judgments that are made repeatedly. What is the right sentence for someone convicted of theft? What is the right premium for a particular risk? While each case is in some sense unique, judgments like these are *recurrent decisions*. Doctors diagnosing patients, judges hearing parole cases, admissions officers reviewing applications, accountants preparing tax forms — these are all examples of recurrent decisions.

Noise in recurrent decisions is demonstrated by a noise audit, such as those we introduced in the previous chapter. Unwanted variability is easy to define and measure when interchangeable professionals make decisions in similar cases. It seems much harder, or perhaps even impossible, to apply the idea of noise to a category of judgments that we call *singular decisions*.

Consider, for instance, the crisis the world faced in 2014. In West Africa, numerous people were dying from Ebola. Because the world is interconnected, projections suggested that infections would rapidly spread all over the world and hit Europe and North America particularly hard. In the United States, there were insistent calls to shut down air travel from affected regions and to take aggressive steps to close the borders. The political pressure to move in that direction was intense, and prominent and well-informed people favored those steps.

President Barack Obama was faced with one of the most difficult decisions of his presidency — one that he had not encountered before and never encountered again. He chose not to close any borders. Instead he sent three thousand people — health workers and soldiers — to West Africa. He led a diverse, international coalition of nations that did not always work well together, using their resources and expertise to tackle the problem at its source.

Singular Versus Recurrent

Decisions that are made only once, like the president's Ebola response, are singular because they are not made recurrently by the same individual or team, they lack a prepackaged response, and they are marked by genuinely unique features. In dealing with Ebola, President Obama and his team had no real precedents on which to draw. Important political decisions are often good examples of singular decisions, as are the most fateful choices of military commanders.

In the private realm, decisions you make when choosing a job, buying a house, or proposing marriage have the same characteristics. Even if this is not your first job, house, or marriage, and despite the fact that countless people have faced these decisions before, the decision feels unique to you. In business, heads of companies are often called on to make what seem like unique decisions to them: whether to launch a potentially game-changing innovation, how much to close down during a pandemic, whether to open an office in a foreign country, or whether to capitulate to a government that seeks to regulate them.

Arguably, there is a continuum, not a category difference, between singular and recurrent decisions. Underwriters may deal with some cases that strike them as very much out of the ordinary. Conversely, if you are buying a house for the fourth time in your life, you have probably started to think of home buying as a recurrent decision. But extreme examples clearly suggest that the difference is meaningful. Going to war is one thing; going through annual budget reviews is another.

Noise in Singular Decisions

Singular decisions have traditionally been treated as quite separate from the recurrent judgments that interchangeable employees routinely make in large organizations. While social scientists have dealt with recurrent decisions, high-stakes singular decisions have been the province of historians and management gurus. The approaches to the two types of decisions have been quite different. Analyses of recurrent decisions have often taken a statistical bent, with social scientists assessing many similar decisions to discern patterns, identify regularities, and measure accuracy. In contrast, discussions of singular decisions typically adopt a causal view; they are conducted in hindsight and are focused on identifying the causes of what happened. Historical analyses, like case studies of management successes and failures, aim to understand how an essentially unique judgment was made.

The nature of singular decisions raises an important question for the study of noise. We have defined noise as undesirable variability in judgments of the same problem. Since singular problems are never exactly repeated, this definition does not apply to them. After all, history is only run once. You will never be able to compare Obama's decision to send health workers and soldiers to West Africa in 2014 with the decisions other American presidents made about how to handle that particular problem at that particular time (though you can speculate). You may agree to compare your decision to marry that special someone with the decisions of other people like you, but that comparison will not be as relevant to you as the one we made between the quotes of underwriters on the same case. You and your spouse are unique. There is no direct way to observe the presence of noise in singular decisions.

Yet singular decisions are not free from the factors that produce noise in recurrent decisions. At the shooting range, the shooters on Team C (the noisy team) may be adjusting the gunsight on their rifle in different directions, or their hands may just be unsteady. If we observed only the first shooter on the team, we would have no idea how noisy the team is, but the sources of noise would still be there. Similarly, when you make a singular decision, you have to imagine that another decision maker, even one just as competent as you and sharing the same goals and values, would not reach the same conclusion from the same facts. And as the decision maker, you should recognize that you might have made a different decision if some irrelevant aspects of the situation or of the decision-making process had been different.

In other words, we cannot measure noise in a singular decision, but if we think counterfactually, we know for sure that noise is there. Just as the shooter's unsteady hand implies that a single shot *could* have landed somewhere else, noise in the decision makers and in the decision-making process implies that the singular decision *could* have been different.

Consider all the factors that affect a singular decision. If the experts in charge of analyzing the Ebola threat and preparing response plans had been different people, with different backgrounds and life experiences, would their proposals to President Obama have been the same? If the same facts had been presented in a slightly different manner, would the conversation have unfolded the same way? If the key players had been in a different mood or had been meeting during a snowstorm, would the final decision have been identical? Seen in this light, the singular decision does not seem so determined. Depending on many factors that we are not even aware of, the decision could plausibly have been different.

For another exercise in counterfactual thinking, consider how different countries and regions responded to the COVID-19 crisis. Even when the virus hit them roughly at the same time and in a similar manner, there were wide differences in responses. This variation provides clear evidence of noise in different countries' decision making. But what if the epidemic had struck a single country? In that case, we wouldn't have observed any variability. But our inability to observe variability would not make the decision less noisy.

Controlling Noise in Singular Decisions

This theoretical discussion matters. If singular decisions are just as noisy as recurrent ones, then the strategies that reduce noise in recurrent decisions should also improve the quality of singular decisions.

This is a more counterintuitive prescription than it seems. When you have a one-of-a-kind decision to make, your instinct is probably to treat it as, well, one of a kind. Some even claim that the rules of probabilistic thinking are entirely irrelevant to singular decisions made under uncertainty and that such decisions call for a radically different approach.

Our observations here suggest the opposite advice. From the perspective of noise reduction, *a singular decision is a recurrent decision that happens only once.* Whether you make a decision only once or a hundred times, your goal should be to make it in a way that reduces both bias and noise. And practices that reduce error should be just as effective in your one-of-a-kind decisions as in your repeated ones.

Speaking of Singular Decisions

"The way you approach this unusual opportunity exposes you to noise."

"Remember: a singular decision is a recurrent decision that is made only once."

"The personal experiences that made you who you are are not truly relevant to this decision."

PART II

Your Mind Is a Measuring Instrument

Measurement, in everyday life as in science, is the act of using an instrument to assign a value on a scale to an object or event. You measure the length of a carpet in inches, using a tape measure. You measure the temperature in degrees Fahrenheit or Celsius by consulting a thermometer.

The act of making a judgment is similar. When judges determine the appropriate prison term for a crime, they assign a value on a scale. So do underwriters when they set a dollar value to insure a risk, or doctors when they make a diagnosis. (The scale need not be numerical: "guilty beyond a reasonable doubt," "advanced melanoma," and "surgery is recommended" are judgments, too.)

Judgment can therefore be described as *measurement in which the instrument is a human mind*. Implicit in the notion of measurement is the goal of accuracy — to approach truth and minimize error. The goal of judgment is not to impress, not to take a stand, not to persuade. It is important to note that the concept of judgment as we use it here is borrowed from the technical psychological literature, and that it is a much narrower concept than the same word has in everyday language. *Judgment* is not a synonym for *thinking,* and *making accurate judgments* is not a synonym for *having good judgment.*

As we define it, a judgment is a conclusion that can be summarized in a word or phrase. If an intelligence analyst writes a long report leading to the conclusion that a regime is unstable, only the conclusion is a judgment. *Judgment,* like *measurement,* refers both to the mental activity of making a judgment and to its product. And we will sometimes use *judge* as a technical term to describe people who make judgments, even when they have nothing to do with the judiciary.

Although accuracy is the goal, perfection in achieving this goal is never achieved even in scientific measurement, much less in judgment. There is always some error, some of which is bias and some of which is noise.

To experience how noise and bias contribute to error, we invite you to play a game that will take you less than one minute. If you have a smartphone with a stopwatch, it probably has a lap function, which enables you to measure consecutive time intervals without stopping the stopwatch or even looking at the display. Your goal is to produce five consecutive laps of exactly ten seconds without looking at the phone. You may want to observe a ten-second interval a few times before you begin. Go.

Now look at the lap durations recorded on your phone. (The phone itself was not free from noise, but there was very little of it.) You will see that the laps are not all exactly ten seconds and that they vary over a substantial range. You tried to reproduce the same timing exactly, but you were unable to do so. The variability you could not control is an instance of noise.

This finding is hardly surprising, because noise is universal in physiology and psychology. Variability across individuals is a biological given; no two peas in a pod are truly identical. Within the same person, there is variability, too. Your heartbeat is not exactly regular. You cannot repeat the same gesture with perfect precision. And when you have your hearing examined by an audiologist, there will be some sounds so soft you never hear them, and others so loud you always do. But there will also be some sounds that you will sometimes hear and sometimes miss.

Now look at the five numbers on your phone. Do you see a pattern? For instance, are all five laps shorter than ten seconds, a pattern suggesting that your internal clock is running fast? In this simple task, the bias is the difference, positive or negative, between the mean of your laps and ten seconds. Noise constitutes the variability of your results, analogous to the scatter of shots we saw earlier. In statistics, the most common measure of variability is *standard deviation*, and we will use it to measure noise in judgments.

We can think of most judgments, specifically *predictive* judgments, as similar to the measurements you just made. When we make a prediction, we attempt to come close to a true value. An economic forecaster aims to be as close as possible to the true value of the growth in next year's gross domestic product; a doctor aims to make the correct diagnosis. (Note that the term *prediction*, in the technical sense used in this book, does not imply predicting the future: for our purposes, the diagnosis of an existing medical condition is a prediction.)

We will rely extensively on the analogy between judgment and measurement because it helps explain the role of noise in error. People who make predictive judgments are just like the shooter who aims at the bull's-eye or the physicist who strives to measure the true weight of a particle. Noise in their judgments implies error. Simply put, when a judgment aims at a true value, two different judgments cannot both be right. Like measuring instruments, some people generally show more error than others in a particular task — perhaps because of deficiencies in skill or training. But, like measuring instruments, the people who make judgments are never perfect. We need to understand and measure their errors.

Of course, most professional judgments are far more complex than the measurement of a time interval. In chapter 4, we define different types of professional judgments and explore what they aim at. In chapter 5, we discuss how to measure error and how to quantify the contribution of system noise to it. Chapter 6 dives deeper into system noise and identifies its components, which are different types of noise. In chapter 7, we explore one of these components: occasion noise. Finally, in chapter 8, we show how groups often amplify noise in judgments.

A simple conclusion emerges from these chapters: like a measuring instrument, the human mind is imperfect — it is both biased and noisy. Why, and by how much? Let's find out.

CHAPTER 4

Matters of Judgment

T his book is about professional judgments, broadly understood, and it assumes that whoever makes such a judgment is competent and aiming to get it right. However, the very concept of judgment involves a reluctant acknowledgment that you can never be certain that a judgment is right.

Consider the phrases "matter of judgment" or "it's a judgment call." We do not consider the proposition that the sun will rise tomorrow or that the formula of sodium chloride is NaCl to be matters of judgment, because reasonable people are expected to agree perfectly on them. A matter of judgment is one with some uncertainty about the answer and where we allow for the possibility that reasonable and competent people might disagree.

But there is a limit to how much disagreement is admissible. Indeed, the word *judgment* is used mainly where people believe they should agree. Matters of judgment differ from matters of opinion or taste, in which unresolved differences are entirely acceptable. The insurance executives who were shocked by the result of the noise audit would have no problem if claims adjusters were sharply divided over the relative merits of the Beatles and the Rolling Stones, or of salmon and tuna.

Matters of judgment, including professional judgments, occupy a space between questions of fact or computation on the one hand and matters of taste or opinion on the other. They are defined by the *expectation of bounded disagreement.*

Exactly how much disagreement is acceptable in a judgment is itself a judgment call and depends on the difficulty of the problem. Agreement is especially easy when a judgment is absurd. Judges who differ widely in the sentences they set in a run-of-the-mill fraud case will concur that a fine of one dollar and a life sentence are both unreasonable. Judges at wine competitions differ greatly on which wines should get medals, but are often unanimous in their contempt for the rejects.

The Experience of Judgment: An Example

Before we further discuss the experience of judgment, we now ask you to make one yourself. You will absorb more from the rest of this chapter if you do this exercise and carry it out to completion.

> *Imagine that you are a member of a team charged with evaluating candidates for the position of chief executive in a moderately successful regional financial firm that faces increasing competition. You are asked to assess the probability that the following candidate will be successful after two years on the job.* Successful *is defined simply as the candidate's having kept the CEO job at the end of the two years. Express the probability on a scale from 0 (impossible) to 100 (certain).*
>
> *Michael Gambardi is thirty-seven years old. He has held several positions since he graduated from Harvard Business School twelve years ago. Early on, he was a founder and an investor in two start-ups that failed without attracting much financial support. He then joined a large insurance company and quickly rose to the position of regional chief operating officer for Europe. In that post, he initiated and managed an important*

improvement in the timely resolution of claims. He was described by colleagues and subordinates as effective but also as domineering and abrasive, and there was significant turnover of executives during his tenure. Colleagues and subordinates also attest to his integrity and willingness to take responsibility for failures. For the last two years, he has served as CEO of a medium-sized financial company that was initially at risk of failing. He stabilized the company, where he is considered successful though difficult to work with. He has indicated an interest in moving on. Human resources specialists who interviewed him a few years ago gave him superior grades for creativity and energy but also described him as arrogant and sometimes tyrannical.

Recall that Michael is a candidate for a CEO position in a regional financial firm that is moderately successful and that faces increasing competition. What is the probability that Michael, if hired, will still be in his job after two years? Please decide on a specific number in the range of 0 to 100 before reading on. Read the description again if you need to.

If you engaged in the task seriously, you probably found it difficult. There is a mass of information, much of it seemingly inconsistent. You had to struggle to form the coherent impression that you needed to produce a judgment. In constructing that impression, you focused on some details that appeared important and you very likely ignored others. If asked to explain your choice of a number, you would mention a few salient facts but not enough of them for a full accounting of your judgment.

The thought process you went through illustrates several features of the mental operation we call judgment:

- Of all the cues provided by the description (which are only a subset of what you might need to know), you attended to some more than others without being fully aware of the choices you made. Did you notice that Gambardi is an Italian name? Do you remember the school he attended? This exercise was designed to overload you so that you could not easily recover all the details of the case. Most likely, your recollection of what we presented would be different from that of other readers. Selective attention and selective recall are a source of variability across people.

- Then, you informally integrated these cues into an overall impression of Gambardi's prospects. The key word here is *informally*. You did not construct a plan for answering the question. Without being fully aware of what you were doing, your mind worked to construct a coherent impression of Michael's strengths and weaknesses and of the challenges he faces. The informality allowed you to work quickly. It also produces variability: a formal process such as adding a column of numbers guarantees identical results, but some noise is inevitable in an informal operation.

- Finally, you converted this overall impression into a number on a probability scale of success. Matching a number between 0 and 100 to an impression is a remarkable process, to which we will return in chapter 14. Again, you do not know exactly why you responded as you did. Why did you choose, say, 65 rather than 61 or 69? Most likely, at some point, a number came to your mind. You checked whether that number felt right, and if it did not, another number came to mind. This part of the process is also a source of variability across people.

Since each of these three steps in a complex judgment process entails some variability, we should not be surprised to find a lot of noise in answers about Michael Gambardi. If you ask a few friends to read the case, you will probably find that your estimates of his probability of success are scattered widely. When we showed the case to

115 MBA students, their estimates of Gambardi's probability of success ranged from 10 to 95. That is a great deal of noise.

Incidentally, you may have noticed that the stopwatch exercise and the Gambardi problem illustrate two types of noise. The variability of judgments over successive trials with the stopwatch is noise within a single judge (yourself), whereas the variability of judgments of the Gambardi case is noise between different judges. In measurement terms, the first problem illustrates *within-person* reliability, and the second illustrates *between-person* reliability.

What Judgment Aims to Achieve: The Internal Signal

Your answer to the Gambardi question is a predictive judgment, as we have defined the term. However, it differs in important ways from other judgments that we call predictive, including tomorrow's peak temperature in Bangkok, the result of tonight's football game, or the outcome of the next presidential election. If you disagree with a friend about these problems, you will, at some point, find out who is right. But if you disagree about Gambardi, time will *not* tell who was right, for a simple reason: Gambardi does not exist.

Even if the question referred to a real person and we knew the outcome, a single probability judgment (other than 0 or 100%) cannot be confirmed or disconfirmed. The outcome does not reveal what the ex ante probability was. If an event that was assigned a probability of 90% fails to happen, the judgment of probability was not necessarily a bad one. After all, outcomes that are just 10% likely to happen end up happening 10% of the time. The Gambardi exercise is an example of a *nonverifiable* predictive judgment, for two separate reasons: Gambardi is fictitious and the answer is probabilistic.

Many professional judgments are nonverifiable. Barring egregious errors, underwriters will never know, for instance, whether a particular policy was overpriced or underpriced. Other forecasts may be nonverifiable because they are conditional. "If we go to war, we will be crushed" is an important prediction, but it is likely to remain untested (we hope). Or forecasts may be too long term for the professionals who make them to be brought to account — like, for instance, an estimate of mean temperatures by the end of the twenty-first century.

Did the nonverifiable nature of the Gambardi task change how you approached it? Did you, for instance, ask yourself whether Gambardi was real or fictitious? Did you wonder whether the outcome would be revealed later in the text? Did you reflect on the fact that, even if that were the case, the revelation would not give you the answer to the question you were facing? Probably not, because these considerations did not seem relevant when you answered the question.

Verifiability does not change the experience of judgment. To some degree, you might perhaps think harder about a problem whose answer will be revealed soon, because the fear of being exposed concentrates the mind. Conversely, you might refuse to give much thought to a problem so hypothetical as to be absurd ("If Gambardi had three legs and could fly, would he be a better CEO?"). But, by and large, you address a plausible, hypothetical problem in much the same way that you tackle a real one. This similarity is important to psychological research, much of which uses made-up problems.

Since there is no outcome — and you probably did not even ask yourself whether there would ever be one — you were not trying to minimize error relative to that outcome. You tried to get the judgment right, to land on a number in which you had enough confidence to make it your answer. Of course, you were not perfectly confident in that answer, in the way you would be perfectly confident that four times six is twenty-four. You were aware of some uncertainty (and, as we will see, there is probably more of it than you recognized). But at some point, you decided that you were no longer making progress and settled for an answer.

What made you feel you got the judgment right, or at least right enough to be your answer? We suggest this feeling is an *internal signal of judgment completion,* unrelated to any outside information.

Your answer felt right if it seemed to fit comfortably enough with the evidence. An answer of 0 or 100 would not give you that sense of fit: the confidence it implies is inconsistent with the messy, ambiguous, conflicting evidence provided. But the number on which you settled, whatever it is, gave you the sense of coherence you needed. The aim of judgment, as you experienced it, was the achievement of a coherent solution.

The essential feature of this internal signal is that the sense of coherence is part of the experience of judgment. It is not contingent on a real outcome. As a result, the internal signal is just as available for nonverifiable judgments as it is for real, verifiable ones. This explains why making a judgment about a fictitious character like Gambardi feels very much the same as does making a judgment about the real world.

How Judgment Is Evaluated: The Outcome and the Process

Verifiability does not change the experience of judgment as it takes place. It does, however, change its evaluation after the fact.

Verifiable judgments can be scored by an objective observer on a simple measure of error: the difference between the judgment and the outcome. If a weather forecaster said today's high temperature would be seventy degrees Fahrenheit and it is sixty-five degrees, the forecaster made an error of plus five degrees. Evidently, this approach does not work for nonverifiable judgments like the Gambardi problem, which have no true outcome. How, then, are we to decide what constitutes good judgment?

The answer is that there is a second way to evaluate judgments. This approach applies both to verifiable and nonverifiable ones. It consists in evaluating the *process* of judgment. When we speak of good or bad judgments, we may be speaking either about the output (e.g., the number you produced in the Gambardi case) or about the process — what you did to arrive at that number.

One approach to the evaluation of the process of judgment is to observe how that process performs when it is applied to a large number of cases. For instance, consider a political forecaster who has assigned probabilities of winning to a large number of candidates in local elections. He described one hundred of these candidates as being 70% likely to win. If seventy of them are eventually elected, we have a good indication of the forecaster's skill in using the probability scale. The judgments are verifiable as an ensemble, although no single probability judgment can be declared right or wrong. Similarly, bias for or against a particular group can best be established by examining statistical results for a substantial number of cases.

Another question that can be asked about the process of judgment is whether it conforms to the principles of logic or probability theory. A large body of research on cognitive biases of judgment has been in this vein.

Focusing on the process of judgment, rather than its outcome, makes it possible to evaluate the quality of judgments that are not verifiable, such as judgments about fictitious problems or long-term forecasts. We may not be able to compare them to a known outcome, but we can still tell whether they have been made incorrectly. And when we turn to the question of *improving* judgments rather than just evaluating them, we will focus on process, too. All the procedures we recommend in this book to reduce bias and noise aim to adopt the judgment process that would minimize error over an ensemble of similar cases.

We have contrasted two ways of evaluating a judgment: by comparing it to an *outcome* and by assessing the quality of the *process* that led to it. Note that when the judgment is verifiable, the two ways of evaluating it may reach different conclusions in a single case. A skilled and careful forecaster using the best possible tools and techniques will often miss the correct number in making a quarterly inflation forecast. Meanwhile, in a single quarter, a dart-throwing chimpanzee will sometimes be right.

Scholars of decision-making offer clear advice to resolve this tension: focus on the process, not on the outcome of a single case. We recognize, however, that this is not standard practice in real life. Professionals are usually evaluated on how closely their judgments match verifiable outcomes, and if you ask them what they aim for in their judgments, a close match is what they will answer.

In summary, what people usually claim to strive for in verifiable judgments is a prediction that matches the outcome. What they are effectively trying to achieve, regardless of verifiability, is the internal signal of completion provided by the coherence between the facts of the case and the judgment. And what they should be trying to achieve, normatively speaking, is the judgment process that would produce the best judgment over an ensemble of similar cases.

Evaluative Judgments

So far in this chapter, we have focused on predictive judgment tasks, and most of the judgments we will discuss are of that type. But chapter 1, which discusses Judge Frankel and noise in sentencing by federal judges, examines another type of judgment. Sentencing a felon is not a prediction. It is an *evaluative judgment* that seeks to match the sentence to the severity of the crime. Judges at a wine fair and restaurant critics make evaluative judgments. Professors who grade essays, judges at ice-skating competitions, and committees that award grants to research projects make evaluative judgments.

A different kind of evaluative judgment is made in decisions that involve multiple options and trade-offs between them. Consider managers who choose among candidates for hiring, management teams that must decide on strategic options, or even presidents choosing how to respond to an epidemic in Africa. To be sure, all these decisions rely on predictive judgments that provide input — for instance, how a candidate will perform in her first year, how the stock market will respond to a given strategic move, or how quickly the epidemic will spread if left unchecked. But the final decisions entail trade-offs between the pros and cons of various options, and these trade-offs are resolved by evaluative judgments.

Like predictive judgments, evaluative judgments entail an expectation of bounded disagreement. No self-respecting federal judge is likely to say, "This is the punishment I like best, and I don't care a bit if my colleagues think otherwise." And decision makers who choose from several strategic options expect colleagues and observers who have the same information and share the same goals to agree with them, or at least not to disagree too much. Evaluative judgments partly depend on the values and preferences of those making them, but they are not mere matters of taste or opinion.

For that reason, the boundary between predictive and evaluative judgments is fuzzy and people who make judgments are often unaware of it. Judges who set sentences or professors who grade essays think hard about their task and strive to find the "right" answer. They develop confidence in their judgments and in the justifications they have for them. Professionals feel much the same, act much the same, and speak much the same to justify themselves when their judgments are predictive ("How well will this new product sell?") and when they are evaluative ("How well did my assistant perform this year?").

What's Wrong with Noise

The observation of noise in predictive judgments always indicates that something is wrong. If two doctors disagree on a diagnosis or two forecasters disagree about the next quarter's sales, at least one of them must be in error. The error may happen because one of them is less skilled, and therefore more likely to be wrong, or because of some other source of noise. Regardless of the cause, failing to make the correct judgment can have serious consequences for those who rely on the diagnoses and forecasts of these individuals.

Noise in evaluative judgments is problematic for a different reason. In any system in which judges are assumed to be interchangeable and assigned quasi-randomly, large disagreements about the same case violate expectations of fairness and consistency. If there are large differences in sentences given to the same defendant, we are in the domain of the "arbitrary cruelties" that Judge Frankel denounced. Even judges who believe in the value of individualized sentencing and who disagree on a robber's sentence will agree that a level of disagreement that turns a judgment into a lottery is problematic. The same is true (if less dramatically so) when vastly different grades are given to the same essay, different safety ratings to the same restaurant, or different scores to the same ice-skater — or when one person, suffering from depression, gets social security disability benefits, while another person with the same condition gets nothing.

Even when unfairness is only a minor concern, system noise poses another problem. People who are affected by evaluative judgments expect the values these judgments reflect to be those of the system, not of the individual judges. Something must have gone badly wrong if one customer, complaining of a defective laptop, gets fully reimbursed, and another gets a mere apology; or if one employee who has been with a firm for five years asks for a promotion and gets exactly that, while another employee, whose performance is otherwise identical, is politely turned down. System noise is inconsistency, and inconsistency damages the credibility of the system.

Undesirable but Measurable

All we need to measure noise is multiple judgments of the same problem. We do not need to know a true value. As the shooting-range story in the introduction illustrates, when we look at the back of the target, the bull's-eye is invisible, but we can see the scatter of the shots. As soon as we know that all the shooters were aiming at the same bull's-eye, we can measure noise. This is what a noise audit does. If we ask all our forecasters to estimate next quarter's sales, the scatter in their forecasts is noise.

This difference between bias and noise is essential for the practical purpose of improving judgments. It may seem paradoxical to claim that we can improve judgments when we cannot verify whether they are right. But we can — if we start by measuring noise.

Regardless of whether the goal of judgment is just accuracy or a more complex trade-off between values, noise is undesirable and often measurable. And once noise is measured, as we will discuss in part 5, it is often possible to reduce it.

Speaking of Professional Judgment

"This is a matter of judgment. You can't expect people to agree perfectly."

"Yes, this is a matter of judgment, but some judgments are so far out that they are wrong."

"Your choice between the candidates was just an expression of taste, not a serious judgment."

"A decision requires both predictive and evaluative judgments."

CHAPTER 5

Measuring Error

I t is obvious that a consistent bias can produce costly errors. If a scale adds a constant amount to your weight, if an enthusiastic manager routinely predicts that projects will take half the time they end up taking, or if a timid executive is unduly pessimistic about future sales year after year, the result will be numerous serious mistakes.

We have now seen that noise can produce costly errors as well. If a manager most often predicts that projects will take half the time they ultimately take, and occasionally predicts they will take twice their actual time, it is unhelpful to say that the manager is "on average" right. The different errors add up; they do not cancel out.

An important question, therefore, is how, and how much, bias and noise contribute to error. This chapter aims to answer that question. Its basic message is straightforward: in professional judgments of all kinds, whenever accuracy is the goal, *bias and noise play the same role in the calculation of overall error*. In some cases, the larger contributor will be bias; in other cases it will be noise (and these cases are more common than one might expect). But in every case, a reduction of noise has the same impact on overall error as does a reduction of bias by the same amount. For that reason, the measurement and reduction of noise should have the same high priority as the measurement and reduction of bias.

This conclusion rests on a particular approach to the measurement of error, which has a long history and is generally accepted in science and in statistics. In this chapter, we provide an introductory overview of that history and a sketch of the underlying reasoning.

Should GoodSell Reduce Noise?

Begin by imagining a large retail company named GoodSell, which employs many sales forecasters. Their job is to predict GoodSell's market share in various regions. Perhaps after reading a book on the topic of noise, Amy Simkin, head of the forecasting department at GoodSell, has conducted a noise audit. All forecasters produced independent estimates of the market share in the same region.

Figure 3 shows the (implausibly smooth) results of the noise audit. Amy can see that the forecasts were distributed in the familiar bell-shaped curve, also known as the normal or Gaussian distribution.

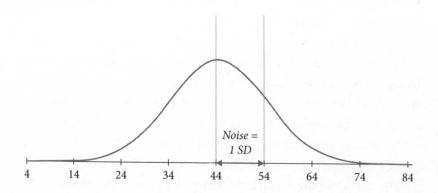

FIGURE 3: *Distribution of GoodSell's market share forecasts for one region*

The most frequent forecast, represented by the peak of the bell curve, is 44%. Amy can also see that the forecasting system of the company is quite noisy: the forecasts, which would be identical if all were accurate, vary over a considerable range.

We can attach a number to the amount of noise in GoodSell's forecasting system. Just as we did when you used your stopwatch to measure laps, we can compute the *standard deviation* of the forecasts. As its name indicates, the standard deviation represents a typical distance from the mean. In this example, it is 10 percentage points. As is true for every normal distribution, about two-thirds of the forecasts are contained within one standard deviation on either side of the mean — in this example, between a 34% and a 54% market share. Amy now has an estimate of the amount of system noise in the forecasts of market share. (A better noise audit would use several forecasting problems for a more robust estimate, but one is enough for our purpose here.)

As was the case with the executives of the real insurance company of chapter 2, Amy is shocked by the results and wants to take action. The unacceptable amount of noise indicates that the forecasters are not disciplined in implementing the procedures they are expected to follow. Amy asks for authority to hire a noise consultant to achieve more uniformity and discipline in her forecasters' work. Unfortunately, she does not get approval. Her boss's reply seems sensible enough: how, he asks, could we reduce errors when we don't know if our forecasts are right or wrong? Surely, he says, if there is a large average error in the forecasts (i.e., a large bias), addressing it should be the priority. Before undertaking anything to improve its forecasts, he concludes, GoodSell must wait and find out if they are correct.

One year after the original noise audit, the outcome that the forecasters were trying to predict is known. Market share in the target region turned out to be 34%. Now we also know each forecaster's error, which is simply the difference between the forecast and the outcome. The error is 0 for a forecast of 34%, it is 10% for the mean forecast of 44%, and it is –10% for a lowball forecast of 24%.

Figure 4 shows the distribution of errors. It is the same as the distribution of forecasts in figure 3, but the true value (34%) has been subtracted from each forecast. The shape of the distribution has not changed, and the standard deviation (our measure of noise) is still 10%.

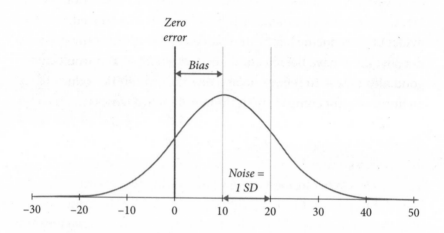

FIGURE 4: *Distribution of errors in GoodSell's forecasts for one region*

The difference between figures 3 and 4 is analogous to the difference between a pattern of shots seen from the back and the front of the target in figures 1 and 2 (see the introduction). Knowing the position of the target was not necessary to observe noise in shooting; similarly, knowing the true outcome adds nothing at all to what was already known about noise in forecasting.

Amy Simkin and her boss now know something they did not know earlier: the amount of bias in the forecasts. Bias is simply the average of errors, which in this case is also 10%. Bias and noise, therefore, happen to be numerically identical in this set of data. (To be clear, this equality of noise and bias is by no means a general rule, but a case in which bias and noise are equal makes it easier to understand their roles.) We can see that most forecasters had made an optimistic error — that is, they overestimated the market share that would be achieved: most of them erred on the right-hand side of the zero-error vertical bar. (In fact, using the properties of the normal distribution, we know that is the case for 84% of the forecasts.)

As Amy's boss notes with barely concealed satisfaction, he was right. There was a lot of bias in the forecasts! And indeed, it is now evident that reducing bias would be a good thing. But, Amy still wonders, would it have been a good idea a year ago — and would it be a good idea now — to reduce noise, too? How would the value of such an improvement compare with the value of reducing bias?

Mean Squares

To answer Amy's question, we need a "scoring rule" for errors, a way to weight and combine individual errors into a single measure of overall error. Fortunately, such a tool exists. It is the *method of least squares,* invented in 1795 by Carl Friedrich Gauss, a famous mathematical prodigy born in 1777, who began a career of major discoveries in his teens.

Gauss proposed a rule for scoring the contribution of individual errors to overall error. His measure of overall error — called *mean squared error* (MSE) — is the average of the squares of the individual errors of measurement.

Gauss's detailed arguments for his approach to the measurement of overall error are far beyond the scope of this book, and his solution is not immediately obvious. Why use the squares of errors? The idea seems arbitrary, even bizarre. Yet, as you will see, it builds on an intuition that you almost certainly share.

To see why, let us turn to what appears to be a completely different problem but turns out to be the same one. Imagine that you are given a ruler and asked to measure the length of a line to the nearest millimeter. You are allowed to make five measurements. They are represented by the downward-pointing triangles on the line in figure 5.

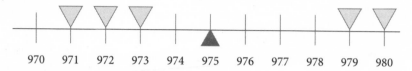

FIGURE 5: *Five measurements of the same length*

As you can see, the five measurements are all between 971 and 980 millimeters. What is your best estimate of the true length of the line? There are two obvious contenders. One possibility is the median number, the measurement that sits between the two shorter measurements and the two longer ones. It is 973 millimeters. The other possibility is the arithmetic mean, known in common parlance as the average, which in this example is 975 millimeters and shown here as an upward-pointing arrow. Your intuition probably favors the mean, and your intuition is correct. The mean contains more information; it is affected by the size of the numbers, while the median is affected only by their order.

There is a tight link between this problem of estimation, about which you have a clear intuition, and the problem of overall error measurement that concerns us here. They are, in fact, two sides of the same coin. That is because the best estimate is one that minimizes the overall error of the available measurements. Accordingly, if your intuition about the mean being the best estimate is correct, the formula you use to measure overall error should be one that yields the arithmetic mean as the value for which error is minimized.

MSE has that property — and it is the only definition of overall error that has it. In figure 6, we have computed the value of MSE in the set of five measurements for ten possible integer values of the line's true length. For instance, if the true value was 971, the errors in the five measurements would be 0, 1, 2, 8, and 9. The squares of these errors add up to 150, and their mean is 30. This is a large number, reflecting the fact that some measurements are far from the true value. You can see that MSE decreases as we get closer to 975 — the mean — and increases again beyond that point. The mean is our best estimate because it is the value that minimizes overall error.

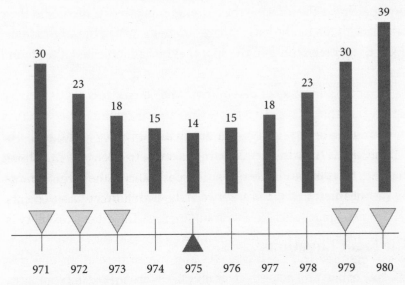

FIGURE 6: *Mean squared error (MSE) for ten possible values of the true length*

You can also see that the overall error increases rapidly when your estimate diverges from the mean. When your estimate increases by just 3 millimeters, from 976 to 979, for instance, MSE doubles. This is a key feature of MSE: squaring gives large errors a far greater weight than it gives small ones.

You now see why Gauss's formula to measure overall error is called mean squared error and why his approach to estimation is called the least squares method. The squaring of errors is its central idea, and no other formula would be compatible with your intuition that the mean is the best estimate.

The advantages of Gauss's approach were quickly recognized by other mathematicians. Among his many feats, Gauss used MSE (and other mathematical innovations) to solve a puzzle that had defeated the best astronomers of Europe: the rediscovery of Ceres, an asteroid that had been traced only briefly before it disappeared into the glare of the sun in 1801. The astronomers had been trying to estimate Ceres's trajectory, but the way they accounted for the measurement error of their telescopes was wrong, and the planet did not reappear anywhere near the location their results suggested. Gauss redid their calculations, using the least squares method. When the astronomers trained their telescopes to the spot that he had indicated, they found Ceres!

Scientists in diverse disciplines were quick to adopt the least squares method. Over two centuries later, it remains the standard way to evaluate errors wherever achieving accuracy is the goal. The weighting of errors by their square is central to statistics. In the vast majority of applications across all scientific disciplines, MSE rules. As we are about to see, the approach has surprising implications.

The Error Equations

The role of bias and noise in error is easily summarized in two expressions that we will call *the error equations*. The first of these equations decomposes the error in a single measurement into the two components with which you are now familiar: bias — the average error — and a residual "noisy error." The noisy error is positive when the error is larger than the bias, negative when it is smaller. The average of noisy errors is zero. Nothing new in the first error equation.

Error in a single measurement = Bias + Noisy Error

The second error equation is a decomposition of MSE, the measure of overall error we have now introduced. Using some simple algebra, MSE can be shown to be equal to the sum of the squares of bias and noise. (Recall that noise is the standard deviation of measurements, which is identical to the standard deviation of noisy errors.) Therefore:

Overall Error (MSE) = Bias^2 + Noise^2

The form of this equation — a sum of two squares — may remind you of a high-school favorite, the Pythagorean theorem. As you might remember, in a right triangle, the sum of the squares of the two shorter sides equals the square of the longest one. This suggests a simple visualization of the error equation, in which MSE, Bias^2, and Noise^2 are the areas of three squares on the sides of a right triangle. Figure 7 shows how MSE (the area of the darker square) equals the sum of the areas of the other two squares. In the left panel, there is more noise than bias; in the right panel, more bias than noise. But MSE is the same, and the error equation holds in both cases.

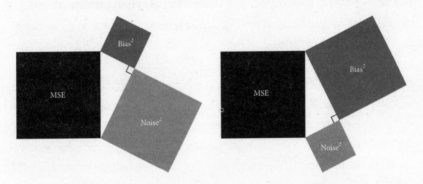

FIGURE 7: *Two decompositions of MSE*

As the mathematical expression and its visual representation both suggest, bias and noise play identical roles in the error equation. They are independent of each other and equally weighted in the determination of overall error. (Note that we will use a similar decomposition into a sum of squares when we analyze the components of noise in later chapters.)

The error equation provides an answer to the practical question that Amy raised: how will reductions in either noise or bias by the same amount affect overall error? The answer is straightforward: bias and noise are interchangeable in the error equation, and the decrease in overall error will be the same, regardless of which of the two is reduced. In figure 4, in which bias and noise happen to be equal (both are 10%), their contributions to overall error are equal.

The error equation also provides unequivocal support for Amy Simkin's initial impulse to try to reduce noise. Whenever you observe noise, you should work to reduce it! The equation shows that Amy's boss was wrong when he suggested that GoodSell wait to measure the bias in its forecasts and only then decide what to do. In terms of overall error, noise and bias are independent: the benefit of reducing noise is the same, regardless of the amount of bias.

This notion is highly counterintuitive but crucial. To illustrate it, figure 8 shows the effect of reducing bias and noise by the same amount. To help you appreciate what has been accomplished in both panels, the original distribution of errors (from figure 4) is represented by a broken line.

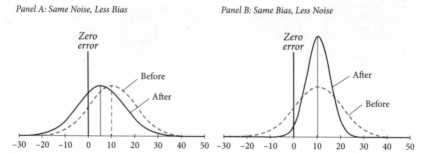

FIGURE 8: *Distribution of errors with bias reduced by half vs. noise reduced by half*

In panel A, we assume that Amy's boss decided to do things his way: he found out what the bias was, then somehow managed to reduce it by half (perhaps by providing feedback to the overoptimistic forecasters). Nothing was done about noise. The improvement is visible: the whole distribution of forecasts has shifted closer to the true value.

In panel B, we show what would have happened if Amy had won the argument. Bias is unchanged, but noise is reduced by half. The paradox here is that noise reduction seems to have made things worse. The forecasts are now more concentrated (less noisy) but not more accurate (not less biased). Whereas 84% of forecasts were on one side of the true value, almost all (98%) now err in the direction of overshooting the true value. Noise reduction seems to have made the forecasts more precisely wrong — hardly the sort of improvement for which Amy hoped!

Despite appearances, however, overall error has been reduced just as much in panel B as in panel A. The illusion of deterioration in panel B arises from an erroneous intuition about bias. The relevant measure of bias is not the imbalance of positive and negative errors. It is average error, which is the distance between the peak of the bell curve and the true value. In panel B, this average error has not changed from the original situation — it is still high, at 10%, but not worse. True, the presence of bias is now more striking, because it accounts for a larger proportion of overall error (80% rather than 50%). But that is because noise has been reduced. Conversely, in panel A, bias has been reduced, but noise has not. The net result is that MSE is the same in both panels: reducing noise or reducing bias by the same amount has the same effect on MSE.

As this example illustrates, MSE conflicts with common intuitions about the scoring of predictive judgments. To minimize MSE, you must concentrate on avoiding large errors. If you measure length, for example, the effect of reducing an error from 11cm to 10cm is 21 times as large as the effect of going from an error of 1cm to a perfect hit. Unfortunately, people's intuitions in this regard are almost the mirror image of what they should be: people are very keen to get perfect hits and highly sensitive to small errors, but they hardly care at all about the difference between two large errors. Even if you sincerely believe that your goal is to make accurate judgments, your emotional reaction to results may be incompatible with the achievement of accuracy as science defines it.

Of course, the best solution here would be to reduce both noise and bias. Since bias and noise are independent, there is no reason to choose between Amy Simkin and her boss. In that regard, if Good-Sell decides to reduce noise, the fact that noise reduction makes bias more visible — indeed, impossible to miss — may turn out to be a blessing. Achieving noise reduction will ensure that bias reduction is next on the company's agenda.

Admittedly, reducing noise would be less of a priority if bias were much larger than noise. But the GoodSell example offers another lesson worth highlighting. In this simplified model, we have assumed that noise and bias are equal. Given the form of the error equation, their contributions to total error are equal, too: bias accounts for 50% of overall error, and so does noise. Yet, as we have noted, 84% of the forecasters err in the same direction. It takes a bias this large (six out of seven people making mistakes in the same direction!) to have as much effect as noise has. We should not be surprised, therefore, to find situations in which there is more noise than bias.

We illustrated the application of the error equation to a single case, one particular region of GoodSell's territory. Of course, it is always desirable to carry out a noise audit on multiple cases at once. Nothing changes. The error equation is applied to the separate cases; and an overall equation is obtained by taking the averages of MSE, bias squared and noise squared over the cases. It would have been better for Amy Simkin to obtain multiple forecasts for several regions, either from the same or from different forecasters. Averaging results would give her a more accurate picture of bias and noise in the forecasting system of GoodSell.

The Cost of Noise

The error equation is the intellectual foundation of this book. It provides the rationale for the goal of reducing system noise in predictive judgments, a goal that is in principle as important as the reduction of statistical bias. (We should emphasize that statistical bias is not a synonym for social discrimination; it is simply the average error in a set of judgments.)

The error equation and the conclusions we have drawn from it depend on the use of MSE as the measure of overall error. The rule is appropriate for purely predictive judgments, including forecasts and estimates, all of which aim to approach a true value with maximum accuracy (the least bias) and precision (the least noise).

The error equation does not apply to evaluative judgments, however, because the concept of error, which depends on the existence of a true value, is far more difficult to apply. Furthermore, even if errors could be specified, their costs would rarely be symmetrical and would be unlikely to be precisely proportional to their square.

For a company that makes elevators, for example, the consequences of errors in estimating the maximum load of an elevator are obviously asymmetrical: underestimation is costly, but overestimation could be catastrophic. Squared error is similarly irrelevant to the decision of when to leave home to catch a train. For that decision, the consequences of being either one minute late or five minutes late are the same. And when the insurance company of chapter 2 prices policies or estimates the value of claims, errors in both directions are costly, but there is no reason to assume that their costs are equivalent.

These examples highlight the need to specify the roles of predictive and evaluative judgments in decisions. A widely accepted maxim of good decision making is that you should not mix your values and your facts. Good decision making must be based on objective and accurate predictive judgments that are completely unaffected by hopes and fears, or by preferences and values. For the elevator company, the first step would be a neutral calculation of the maximum technical load of the elevator under different engineering solutions. Safety becomes a dominant consideration only in the second step, when an evaluative judgment determines the choice of an acceptable safety margin to set the maximum capacity. (To be sure, that choice will also greatly depend on factual judgments involving, for example, the costs and benefits of that safety margin.) Similarly, the first step in deciding when to leave for the station should be an objective determination of the probabilities of different travel times. The respective costs of missing your train and of wasting time at the station become relevant only in your choice of the risk you are willing to accept.

The same logic applies to much more consequential decisions. A military commander must weigh many considerations when deciding whether to launch an offensive, but much of the intelligence on which the leader relies is a matter of predictive judgment. A government responding to a health crisis, such as a pandemic, must weigh the pros and cons of various options, but no evaluation is possible without accurate predictions about the likely consequences of each option (including the decision to do nothing).

In all these examples, the final decisions require evaluative judgments. The decision makers must consider multiple options and apply their values to make the optimal choice. But the decisions depend on underlying predictions, which should be value-neutral. Their goal is accuracy — hitting as close as possible to the bull's-eye — and MSE is the appropriate measure of error. Predictive judgments will be improved by procedures that reduce noise, as long as they do not increase bias to a larger extent.

Speaking of the Error Equation

"Oddly, reducing bias and noise by the same amount has the same effect on accuracy."

"Reducing noise in predictive judgment is always useful, regardless of what you know about bias."

"When judgments are split 84 to 16 between those that are above and below the true value, there is a large bias — that's when bias and noise are equal."

"Predictive judgments are involved in every decision, and accuracy should be their only goal. Keep your values and your facts separate."

CHAPTER 6

The Analysis of Noise

The previous chapter discussed variability in the measurement or judgment of a single case. When we focus on a single case, all variability of judgment is error, and the two constituents of error are bias and noise. Of course, the judgment systems we are examining, including those involving courts and insurance companies, are designed to deal with different cases and to discriminate among them. Federal judges and claims adjusters would be of little use if they returned the same judgment for all the cases that come their way. Much of the variability in judgments of different cases is intentional.

However, variability in judgments of the same case is still undesirable — it is system noise. As we will show, a noise audit in which the same people make judgments about several cases permits a more detailed analysis of system noise.

A Noise Audit of Sentencing

To illustrate the analysis of noise with multiple cases, we turn to an exceptionally detailed noise audit of sentencing by federal judges. The analysis was published in 1981 as part of the movement toward sentencing reform that we described in chapter 1. The study narrowly focused on sentencing decisions, but the lessons it offers are general and bear on other professional judgments. The goal of the noise audit was to go beyond the vivid but anecdotal evidence of noise assembled by Judge Frankel and others and to "determine the extent of sentencing disparity" more systematically.

The study's authors developed sixteen hypothetical cases in which the defendant had been found guilty and was to be sentenced. The vignettes depicted either robberies or cases of fraud and differed on six other dimensions, including whether the defendant was a principal or an accomplice in the crime, whether he had a criminal record, whether (for the robbery cases) a weapon had been used, and so on.

The researchers organized carefully structured interviews with a national sample of 208 active federal judges. In the course of ninety minutes, the judges were presented with all sixteen cases and asked to set a sentence.

To appreciate what can be learned from this study, you will find an exercise in visualization helpful. Picture a large table with sixteen columns for the crimes, labeled from A to P, and 208 rows for the judges, labeled 1 to 208. Each cell, from A1 to P208, shows the prison term set for a particular case by a particular judge. Figure 9 illustrates what this 3,328-cell table would look like. To study noise, we will want to focus on the sixteen columns, each of which is a separate noise audit.

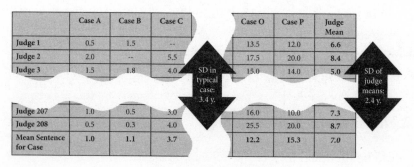

	Case A	Case B	Case C		Case O	Case P	Judge Mean	
Judge 1	0.5	1.5	--		13.5	12.0	6.6	
Judge 2	2.0	--	5.5		17.5	20.0	8.4	
Judge 3	1.5	1.8	4.0	SD in typical case: 3.4 y.	15.0	14.0	5.0	SD of judge means: 2.4 y.
Judge 207	1.0	0.5	3.0		16.0	10.0	7.3	
Judge 208	0.5	0.3	4.0		25.5	20.0	8.7	
Mean Sentence for Case	1.0	1.1	3.7		12.2	15.3	7.0	

FIGURE 9: *A representation of the sentencing study*

Mean Sentences

There is no objective way to determine what the "true value" of a sentence is for a particular case. In what follows, we treat the average of the 208 sentences for each case (mean sentence) as if it were the "just" sentence for that case. As we noted in chapter 1, the US Sentencing Commission made the same assumption when it used the average practice in past cases as the foundation for establishing sentencing guidelines. This label assumes zero bias in the mean judgment of each case.

We are fully aware that, in reality, this assumption is wrong: the average judgment of some cases is quite likely to be biased relative to the average judgment of other, highly similar cases, for example because of racial discrimination. The variance of biases across cases — some positive, some negative — is an important source of error and unfairness. Confusingly, this variance is what is often referred to as "bias." Our analysis in this chapter — and in this book — is focused on noise, which is a distinct source of error. Judge Frankel emphasized the injustice of noise, but also drew attention to bias (including racial discrimination). Similarly, our focus on noise should not be taken to diminish the importance of measuring and combating shared biases.

For convenience, the mean sentence for each case is indicated in the bottom row of the table. The cases are arranged in increasing order of severity: the mean sentence in Case A is 1 year; in Case P it is 15.3 years. The average prison term for all sixteen cases is 7 years.

Now imagine a perfect world in which all judges are flawless measuring instruments of justice, and sentencing is noise-free. What would figure 9 look like in such a world? Evidently, all the cells in the Case A column would be identical, because all judges would give the defendant in case A the same sentence of exactly one year. The same would be true in all the other columns. The numbers in each row, of course, would still vary, because the cases are different. But each row would be identical to the one above it and below it. The differences between the cases would be the only source of variability in the table.

Unfortunately, the world of federal justice is not perfect. The judges are not identical, and variability within columns is large, indicating noise in the judgments of each case. There is more variability in sentences than there should be, and the study's aim is to analyze it.

The Sentencing Lottery

Start from the picture of the perfect world we described above, in which all cases receive the same punishment from every judge. Each column is a series of 208 identical numbers. Now, add noise by going down each column and changing some numbers here and there — sometimes by adding prison time to the mean sentence, sometimes by subtracting from it. Because the changes you make are not all the same, they create variability within the column. This variability is noise.

The essential result of this study is the large amount of noise observed *within the judgments of each case*. The measure of noise within each case is the standard deviation of the prison terms assigned to that case. For the average case, the mean sentence was 7.0 years, and the standard deviation around that mean was 3.4 years.

While you may well be familiar with the term *standard deviation*, you may find a concrete description useful. Imagine that you randomly pick two judges and compute the difference between their judgments of a case. Now repeat, for all pairs of judges and all cases, and average the results. This measure, the *mean absolute difference*, should give you a sense of the lottery that faces the defendant in a federal courtroom. Assuming that the judgments are normally distributed, it is 1.128 times the standard deviation, which implies that the average difference between two randomly chosen sentences of the same case will be 3.8 years. In chapter 3, we spoke of the lottery that faces the client who needs specialized underwriting from an insurance company. The criminal defendant's lottery is, to say the least, more consequential.

A mean absolute difference of 3.8 years between judges when the average sentence is 7.0 years is a disturbing and, in our view, unacceptable result. Yet there are good reasons to suspect that there is even more noise in the actual administration of justice. First, the participants in the noise audit dealt with artificial cases, which were unusually easy to compare and were presented in immediate succession. Real life does not provide nearly as much support for the maintenance of consistency. Second, judges in a courtroom have much more information than they had here. New information, unless it is decisive, provides more opportunities for judges to differ from one another. For these reasons, we suspect that the amount of noise defendants face in actual courtrooms is even larger than what we see here.

Some Judges Are Severe: Level Noise

In the next step of the analysis, the authors broke down noise into separate components. The first interpretation of noise that probably came to your mind — as it did to Judge Frankel's mind — is that noise is due to variation among judges in their disposition to set severe sentences. As any defense lawyer will tell you, judges have reputations, some for being harsh "hanging judges," who are more severe than the average judge, and others for being "bleeding-heart judges," who are more lenient than the average judge. We refer to these deviations as *level errors*. (Again: error is defined here as a deviation from the average; an error may in fact correct an injustice, if the average judge is wrong.)

Variability in level errors will be found in any judgment task. Examples are evaluations of performance where some supervisors are more generous than others, predictions of market share where some forecasters are more optimistic than others, or recommendations for back surgery where some orthopedists are more aggressive than others.

Each row in figure 9 shows the sentences set by one judge. The mean sentence set by each judge, shown in the rightmost column of the table, is a measure of the judge's level of severity. As it turns out, judges vary widely on this dimension. The standard deviation of the values in the rightmost column was 2.4 years. This variability has nothing to do with justice. Instead, as you might suspect, differences in average sentencing reflect variation among judges in other characteristics — their backgrounds, life experiences, political opinions, biases, and so on. The researchers examined the judges' attitudes to sentencing in general — for example, whether they think the main goal of sentencing is incapacitation (removing the criminal from society), rehabilitation, or deterrence. They found that judges who think that the main goal is rehabilitation tend to assign shorter prison sentences and more supervised time than do judges who pointed to deterrence or incapacitation. Separately, judges located in the American South assigned significantly longer sentences than did their counterparts in other parts of the country. Not surprisingly, conservative ideology was also related to severity of sentences.

The general conclusion is that the average level of sentencing functions like a personality trait. You could use this study to arrange judges on a scale that ranges from very harsh to very lenient, just as a personality test might measure their degree of extraversion or agreeableness. Like other traits, we would expect severity of sentencing to be correlated with genetic factors, with life experiences, and with other aspects of personality. None of these has anything to do with the case or the defendant. We use the term *level noise* for the variability of the judges' average judgments, which is identical to the variability of level errors.

Judges Differ: Pattern Noise

As the black arrows show in figure 9, level noise is 2.4 years and system noise is 3.4 years. This difference indicates that there is more to system noise than differences in average severity across individual judges. We will call this other component of noise *pattern noise*.

To understand pattern noise, consider again figure 9, and focus on one randomly chosen cell — say, cell C3. The mean sentence in Case C is shown at the bottom of the column; as you can see, it is 3.7 years. Now, look at the rightmost column to find the mean sentence given by Judge 3 across all cases. It is 5.0 years, just 2.0 years less than the grand mean. If the variation in judges' severity were the only source of noise in column 3, you would predict that the sentence in cell C3 is 3.7 − 2.0 = 1.7 years. But the actual entry in cell C3 is 4 years, indicating that Judge 3 was especially harsh in sentencing that case.

The same simple, additive logic would let you predict every sentence in every column of the table, but in fact you would find deviations from the simple model in most cells. Looking across a row, you will find that judges are not equally severe in their sentencing of all cases: they are harsher than their personal average in some and more lenient in others. We call these residual deviations *pattern errors.* If you wrote down these pattern errors in each cell of the table, you would find that they add up to zero for every judge (row) and that they also add up to zero for every case (column). However, the pattern errors do not cancel out in their contribution to noise, because the values in all cells are squared for the computation of noise.

There is an easier way to confirm that the simple additive model of sentencing does not hold. You can see in the table that the mean sentences at the bottom of each column increase steadily from left to right, but the same is not true within the rows. Judge 208, for example, set a much higher sentence to the defendant in Case O than to the defendant in Case P. If individual judges ranked the cases by the prison time they thought appropriate, their rankings would not be the same.

We use the term *pattern noise* for the variability we just identified, because that variability reflects a complex pattern in the attitudes of judges to particular cases. One judge, for instance, may be harsher than average in general but relatively more lenient toward white-collar criminals. Another may be inclined to punish lightly but more severely when the offender is a recidivist. A third may be close to the average severity but sympathetic when the offender is merely an accomplice and tough when the victim is an older person. (We use the term *pattern noise* in the interest of readability. The proper statistical term for pattern noise is *judge × case interaction* — pronounced "judge-by-case." We apologize to people with statistical training for imposing the burden of translation on them.)

In the context of criminal justice, some of the idiosyncratic reactions to cases may reflect the judge's personal philosophy of sentencing. Other responses may result from associations of which the judge is barely aware, such as a defendant who reminds him of a particularly hateful criminal or who perhaps looks like his daughter. Whatever their origin, these patterns are not mere chance: we would expect them to recur if the judge saw the same case again. But because pattern noise is, in practice, difficult to predict, it adds uncertainty to the already-unpredictable lottery of sentencing. As the study's authors noted, "Patterned differences between judges in the influence of offense/offender characteristics" are "an additional form of sentence disparity."

You may have noticed that the decomposition of system noise into level noise and pattern noise follows the same logic as the error equation in the previous chapter, which decomposed error into bias and noise. This time, the equation can be written as follows:

$$\textbf{System Noise}^2 = \textbf{Level Noise}^2 + \textbf{Pattern Noise}^2$$

This expression can be represented visually in the same manner as the original Error Equation (Figure 10). We have represented the two sides of the triangle as equal. That is because, in the study of sentencing, pattern noise and level noise contribute approximately equally to system noise.

Pattern noise is pervasive. Suppose that doctors are deciding whether to admit people for hospitalization, that companies are deciding whom to hire, that lawyers are deciding which cases to bring, or that Hollywood executives are deciding which television shows to produce. In all these cases, there will be pattern noise, with different judges producing different rankings of the cases.

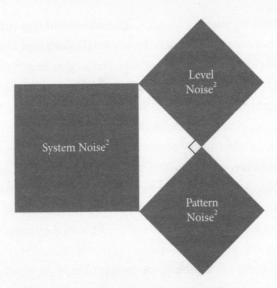

FIGURE 10: *Decomposing system noise*

The Components of Noise

Our treatment of pattern noise glossed over a significant complexity: the possible contribution of random error.

Recall the stopwatch exercise. When you tried to measure ten seconds repeatedly, your results varied from one lap to the next; you showed within-person variability. By the same token, the judges would not have set precisely the same sentences to the sixteen cases if they had been asked to judge them again on another occasion. Indeed, as we will see, they would not have set the same sentences if the original study had been conducted on another day of the same week. If a judge is in a good mood because something nice happened to her daughter, or because a favorite sports team won yesterday, or because it is a beautiful day, her judgment might be more lenient than it would otherwise be. This within-person variability is conceptually distinct from the stable between-person differences that we have just discussed — but it is difficult to tell these sources of variability apart. Our name for the variability that is due to transient effects is *occasion noise*.

We effectively ignored occasion noise in this study and chose to interpret the judges' idiosyncratic patterns of sentencing in the noise audit as indicating stable attitudes. This assumption is certainly optimistic, but there are independent reasons to believe that occasion noise did not play a large role in this study. The highly experienced judges who participated in it surely brought with them some set ideas about the significance of various features of offenses and of defendants. In the next chapter, we discuss occasion noise in greater detail and show how it can be separated from the stable component of pattern noise.

To summarize, we discussed several types of noise. *System noise* is undesirable variability in the judgments of the same case by multiple individuals. We have identified its two major components, which can be separated when the same individuals evaluate multiple cases:

- ❑ *Level noise* is variability in the average level of judgments by different judges.
- ❑ *Pattern noise* is variability in judges' responses to particular cases.

In the present study, the amounts of level noise and pattern noise were approximately equal. However, the component that we identified as pattern noise certainly contains some *occasion noise*, which can be treated as random error.

We have used a noise audit in the judicial system as an illustration, but the same analysis can be applied to any noise audit — in business, medicine, government, or elsewhere. Level noise and pattern noise (which includes occasion noise) both contribute to system noise, and we will encounter them repeatedly as we proceed.

Speaking of Analyzing Noise

"Level noise is when judges show different levels of severity. Pattern noise is when they disagree with one another on which defendants deserve more severe or more lenient treatment. And part of pattern noise is occasion noise — when judges disagree with themselves."

"In a perfect world, defendants would face justice; in our world, they face a noisy system."

CHAPTER 7

Occasion Noise

A professional basketball player is preparing for a free throw. He stands at the foul line. He concentrates — and shoots. This is a precise sequence of moves he has practiced countless times. Will he make the shot?

We don't know, and neither does he. In the National Basketball Association, players typically make about three-quarters of their attempts. Some players, obviously, are better than others, but no player scores 100% of the time. The all-time best make a little over 90% of their free throws. (At the time of this writing, they are Stephen "Steph" Curry, Steve Nash, and Mark Price.) The all-time worst are around 50%. (The great Shaquille O'Neal, for example, made only about 53% of his shots.) Although the hoop is always exactly ten feet high and fifteen feet away, and the ball always weighs twenty-two ounces, the ability to repeat the precise sequence of gestures required to score does not come easily. Variability is expected, not just between players but within players. The free throw is a form of lottery, with a much higher chance of success if the shooter is Curry than if he is O'Neal, but it is a lottery nonetheless.

Where does this variability come from? We know that countless factors can influence the player at the foul line: the fatigue of a long game, the mental pressure of a tight score, the cheers of the home court, or the boos of the opposing team's fans. If someone like Curry or Nash misses, we will invoke one of these explanations. But in truth, we are unlikely to know the exact role these factors play. The variability in a shooter's performance is a form of noise.

The Second Lottery

Variability in free throws or in other physical processes comes as no surprise. We are used to variability in our bodies: our heart rate, our blood pressure, our reflexes, the tone of our voice, and the trembling of our hands are different at different times. And however hard we try to produce the same signature, it is still slightly different on every check.

It is less easy to observe the variability of our minds. Of course, we have all had the experience of changing our minds, even without new information. The film that made us laugh out loud last night now seems mediocre and forgettable. The person we judged severely yesterday now seems to deserve our indulgence. An argument that we had not liked or understood sinks in and now appears essential. But as these examples suggest, we usually associate such changes with relatively minor and largely subjective matters.

In reality, our opinions do change without apparent reason. This point holds even for matters of careful, considered judgment by professional experts. For instance, it is common to obtain significantly different diagnoses from the same physicians when they are presented twice with the same case (see chapter 22). When wine experts at a major US wine competition tasted the same wines twice, they scored only 18% of the wines identically (usually, the very worst ones). A forensic expert can reach different conclusions when examining the same fingerprints twice, just a few weeks apart (see chapter 20). Experienced software consultants can offer markedly different estimates of the completion time for the same task on two occasions. Simply put, just like a basketball player who never throws the ball twice in exactly the same way, we do not always produce identical judgments when faced with the same facts on two occasions.

We have described the process that picks an underwriter, a judge, or a doctor as a lottery that creates system noise. Occasion noise is the product of a second lottery. This lottery picks the moment when the professional makes a judgment, the professional's mood, the sequence of cases that are fresh in mind, and countless other features of the occasion. This second lottery usually remains much more abstract than the first. We can see how the first lottery could have selected a different underwriter, for instance, but the alternatives to the actual responses of the selected underwriter are abstract counterfactuals. We know only that the judgment that did occur was picked from a cloud of possibilities. Occasion noise is the variability among these unseen possibilities.

Measuring Occasion Noise

Measuring occasion noise is not easy — for much the same reason that its existence, once established, often surprises us. When people form a carefully considered professional opinion, they associate it with the reasons that justify their point of view. If pressed to explain their judgment, they will usually defend it with arguments that they find convincing. And if they are presented with the same problem a second time and recognize it, they will reproduce the earlier answer both to minimize effort and maintain consistency. Consider this example from the teaching profession: if a teacher gives an excellent grade to a student essay and then rereads the same essay a week later after seeing the original grade, he will be unlikely to give it a very different grade.

For this reason, direct measurements of occasion noise are hard to obtain whenever cases are easily memorable. If, for example, you show an underwriter or a criminal judge a case that they previously decided, they will probably recognize the case and just repeat their previous judgment. One review of research on variability in professional judgment (technically known as *test-retest reliability,* or *reliability* for short) included many studies in which the experts made the same judgment twice in the same session. Not surprisingly, they tended to agree with themselves.

The experiments we mentioned above bypassed this issue by using stimuli that the experts would not recognize. The wine judges took part in a blind tasting. The fingerprint examiners were shown pairs of prints they had already seen, and the software experts were asked about tasks they had already worked on — but some weeks or months later and without being told that these were cases they had already examined.

There is another, less direct way to confirm the existence of occasion noise: by using big data and econometric methods. When a large sample of past professional decisions is available, analysts can sometimes check whether these decisions were influenced by occasion-specific, irrelevant factors, such as time of day or outside temperature. Statistically significant effects of such irrelevant factors on judgments are evidence of occasion noise. Realistically speaking, there is no hope of discovering all the extraneous sources of occasion noise, but those that can be found illustrate the great variety of these sources. If we are to control occasion noise, we must try to understand the mechanisms that produce it.

One Is a Crowd

Think of this question: what percentage of the world's airports are in the United States? As you thought about it, an answer probably came to your mind. But it did not occur to you in the same way that you would remember your age or your phone number. You are aware that the number you just produced is an estimate. It is not a random number — 1% or 99% would clearly be wrong answers. But the number you came up with is just one in a range of possibilities that you would not rule out. If someone added or subtracted 1 percentage point from your answer, you would probably not find the resulting guess much less plausible than yours. (The correct answer, in case you wonder, is 32%.)

Two researchers, Edward Vul and Harold Pashler, had the idea of asking people to answer this question (and many similar ones) not once but twice. The subjects were not told the first time that they would have to guess again. Vul and Pashler's hypothesis was that the average of the two answers would be more accurate than either of the answers on its own.

The data proved them right. In general, the first guess was closer to the truth than the second, but the best estimate came from averaging the two guesses.

Vul and Pashler drew inspiration from the well-known phenomenon known as the *wisdom-of-crowds effect:* averaging the independent judgments of different people generally improves accuracy. In 1907, Francis Galton, a cousin of Darwin and a famous polymath, asked 787 villagers at a country fair to estimate the weight of a prize ox. None of the villagers guessed the actual weight of the ox, which was 1,198 pounds, but the mean of their guesses was 1,200, just 2 pounds off, and the median (1,207) was also very close. The villagers were a "wise crowd" in the sense that although their individual estimates were quite noisy, they were unbiased. Galton's demonstration surprised him: he had little respect for the judgment of ordinary people, and despite himself, he urged that his results were "more creditable to the trustworthiness of a democratic judgment than might have been expected."

Similar results have been found in hundreds of situations. Of course, if questions are so difficult that only experts can come close to the answer, crowds will not necessarily be very accurate. But when, for instance, people are asked to guess the number of jelly beans in a transparent jar, to predict the temperature in their city one week out, or to estimate the distance between two cities in a state, the average answer of a large number of people is likely to be close to the truth.

The reason is basic statistics: averaging several independent judgments (or measurements) yields a new judgment, which is less noisy, albeit not less biased, than the individual judgments.

Vul and Pashler wanted to find out if the same effect extends to occasion noise: can you get closer to the truth by combining two guesses from the same person, just as you do when you combine the guesses of different people? As they discovered, the answer is yes. Vul and Pashler gave this finding an evocative name: *the crowd within.*

Averaging two guesses by the same person does not improve judgments as much as does seeking out an independent second opinion. As Vul and Pashler put it, "You can gain about 1/10th as much from asking yourself the same question twice as you can from getting a second opinion from someone else." This is not a large improvement. But you can make the effect much larger by waiting to make a second guess. When Vul and Pashler let three weeks pass before asking their subjects the same question again, the benefit rose to one-third the value of a second opinion. Not bad for a technique that does not require any additional information or outside help. And this result certainly provides a rationale for the age-old advice to decision makers: "Sleep on it, and think again in the morning."

Working independently of Vul and Pashler but at about the same time, two German researchers, Stefan Herzog and Ralph Hertwig, came up with a different implementation of the same principle. Instead of merely asking their subjects to produce a second estimate, they encouraged people to generate an estimate that — while still plausible — was as different as possible from the first one. This request required the subjects to think actively of information they had not considered the first time. The instructions to participants read as follows:

> *First, assume that your first estimate is off the mark. Second, think about a few reasons why that could be. Which assumptions and considerations could have been wrong? Third, what do these new considerations imply? Was the first estimate*

rather too high or too low? Fourth, based on this new perspective, make a second, alternative estimate.

Like Vul and Pashler, Herzog and Hertwig then averaged the two estimates thus produced. Their technique, which they named *dialectical bootstrapping*, produced larger improvements in accuracy than did a simple request for a second estimate immediately following the first. Because the participants forced themselves to consider the question in a new light, they sampled another, more different version of themselves — two "members" of the "crowd within" who were further apart. As a result, their average produced a more accurate estimate of the truth. The gain in accuracy with two immediately consecutive "dialectical" estimates was about half the value of a second opinion.

The upshot for decision makers, as summarized by Herzog and Hertwig, is a simple choice between procedures: if you can get independent opinions from others, do it — this real wisdom of crowds is highly likely to improve your judgment. If you cannot, make the same judgment yourself a second time to create an "inner crowd." You can do this either after some time has passed — giving yourself distance from your first opinion — or by actively trying to argue against yourself to find another perspective on the problem. Finally, regardless of the type of crowd, unless you have very strong reasons to put more weight on one of the estimates, your best bet is to average them.

Beyond practical advice, this line of research confirms an essential insight about judgment. As Vul and Pashler put it, "Responses made by a subject are sampled from an internal probability distribution, rather than deterministically selected on the basis of all the knowledge a subject has." This observation echoes the experience you had when answering the question about airports in the United States: Your first answer did not capture all your knowledge or even the best of it. The answer was just one point in the cloud of possible answers that your mind could have generated. The variability we observe in judgments of the same problem by the same person is not a fluke observed in a few highly specialized problems: occasion noise affects all our judgments, all the time.

Sources of Occasion Noise

There is at least one source of occasion noise that we have all noticed: mood. We've all experienced how our own judgments can depend on how we feel — and we are certainly aware that the judgments of others vary with their moods, too.

The effect of moods on judgment has been the subject of a vast amount of psychological research. It is remarkably easy to make people temporarily happy or sad and to measure the variability of their judgments and decisions after these moods have been induced. Researchers use a variety of techniques to do this. For example, participants are sometimes asked to write a paragraph recalling either a happy memory or a sad one. Sometimes they simply view a video segment taken either from a funny movie or from a tearjerker.

Several psychologists have spent decades investigating the effects of mood manipulation. Perhaps the most prolific is Australian psychologist Joseph Forgas. He has published around a hundred scientific papers on the subject of mood.

Some of Forgas's research confirms what you already think: People who are in a good mood are generally more positive. They find it easier to recall happy memories than sad ones, they are more approving of people, they are more generous and helpful, and so on. Negative mood has the opposite effects. As Forgas writes, "The same smile that is seen as friendly by a person in a good mood may be judged as awkward when the observer is in a negative mood; discussing the weather could be seen as poised when the person is in a good mood but boring when that person is in a bad mood."

In other words, mood has a measurable influence on what you think: what you notice in your environment, what you retrieve from your memory, how you make sense of these signals. But mood has another, more surprising effect: it also changes *how* you think. And here, the effects are not those you might imagine. Being in a good mood is a mixed blessing, and bad moods have a silver lining. The costs and benefits of different moods are situation-specific.

In a negotiation situation, for instance, good mood helps. People in a good mood are more cooperative and elicit reciprocation. They tend to end up with better results than do unhappy negotiators. Of course, successful negotiations make people happy, too, but in these experiments, the mood is not caused by what is going on in the negotiation; it is induced before people negotiate. Also, negotiators who shift from a good mood to an angry one during the negotiation often achieve good results — something to remember when you're facing a stubborn counterpart!

On the other hand, a good mood makes us more likely to accept our first impressions as true without challenging them. In one of Forgas's studies, participants read a short philosophical essay, to which a picture of the author was appended. Some readers saw a stereotypical philosophy professor — male, middle-aged, and wearing glasses. Others saw a young woman. As you can guess, this is a test of the readers' vulnerability to stereotypes: do people rate the essay more favorably when it is attributed to a middle-aged man than they do when they believe that a young woman wrote it? They do, of course. But importantly, the difference is larger in the good-mood condition. People who are in a good mood are more likely to let their biases affect their thinking.

Other studies tested the effect of mood on gullibility. Gordon Pennycook and colleagues have conducted many studies of people's reactions to meaningless, pseudo-profound statements generated by assembling randomly selected nouns and verbs from the sayings of popular gurus into grammatically correct sentences, such as "Wholeness quiets infinite phenomena" or "Hidden meaning transforms unparalleled abstract beauty." The propensity to agree with such statements is a trait known as *bullshit receptivity*. (*Bullshit* has become something of a technical term since Harry Frankfurt, a philosopher at Princeton University, published an insightful book, *On*

Bullshit, in which he distinguished bullshit from other types of misrepresentation.)

Sure enough, some people are more receptive than others to bullshit. They can be impressed by "seemingly impressive assertions that are presented as true and meaningful but are actually vacuous." But here again, this gullibility is not merely a function of permanent, unchanging dispositions. Inducing good moods makes people more receptive to bullshit and more gullible in general; they are less apt to detect deception or identify misleading information. Conversely, eyewitnesses who are exposed to misleading information are better able to disregard it — and to avoid false testimony — when they are in a bad mood.

Even moral judgments are strongly influenced by mood. In one study, researchers exposed subjects to the footbridge problem, a classic problem in moral philosophy. In this thought experiment, five people are about to be killed by a runaway trolley. Subjects are to imagine themselves standing on a footbridge, underneath which the trolley will soon pass. They must decide whether to push a large man off the footbridge and onto the tracks so that his body will stop the trolley. If they do so, they are told, the large man will die, but the five people will be saved.

The footbridge problem illustrates the conflict between approaches to moral reasoning. Utilitarian calculation, associated with English philosopher Jeremy Bentham, suggests that the loss of one life is preferable to the loss of five. Deontological ethics, associated with Immanuel Kant, prohibits killing someone, even in the service of saving several others. The footbridge problem clearly contains a salient element of personal emotion: physically pushing a man off a bridge into the path of an oncoming trolley is a particularly repugnant act. Making the utilitarian choice to push the man off the bridge requires people to overcome their aversion to a physically violent act against a stranger. Only a minority of people (in this study, fewer than one in ten) usually say they would do so.

However, when the subjects were placed in a positive mood — induced by watching a five-minute video segment — they became three times more likely to say that they would push the man off the bridge. Whether we regard "Thou shalt not kill" as an absolute principle or are willing to kill one stranger to save five should reflect our deepest values. Yet our choice seems to depend on what video clip we have just watched.

We have described these studies of mood in some detail because we need to emphasize an important truth: *you are not the same person at all times.* As your mood varies (something you are, of course, aware of), some features of your cognitive machinery vary with it (something you are *not* fully aware of). If you are shown a complex judgment problem, your mood in the moment may influence your approach to the problem and the conclusions you reach, even when you believe that your mood has no such influence and even when you can confidently justify the answer you found. In short, you are noisy.

Many other incidental factors induce occasion noise in judgments. Among the extraneous factors that should not influence professional judgments, but do, are two prime suspects: stress and fatigue. A study of nearly seven hundred thousand primary care visits, for instance, showed that physicians are significantly more likely to prescribe opioids at the end of a long day. Surely, there is no reason why a patient with a 4 pm appointment should be in greater pain than one who shows up at 9 am. Nor should the fact that the doctor is running behind schedule influence prescription decisions. And indeed, prescriptions of other pain treatments, such as nonsteroidal antiinflammatory drugs and referrals to physical therapy, do not display similar patterns. When physicians are under time pressure, they are apparently more inclined to choose a quick-fix solution, despite its serious downsides. Other studies showed that, toward the end of the day, physicians are more likely to prescribe antibiotics and less likely to prescribe flu shots.

Even the weather has a measurable influence on professional judgments. Since these judgments are often made in air-conditioned rooms, the effect of weather is probably "mediated" by mood (that is, the weather does not directly affect decisions but modifies the decision maker's mood, which in turn does change how they decide). Bad weather is associated with improved memory; judicial sentences tend to be more severe when it is hot outside; and stock market performance is affected by sunshine. In some cases, the effect of the weather is less obvious. Uri Simonsohn showed that college admissions officers pay more attention to the academic attributes of candidates on cloudier days and are more sensitive to nonacademic attributes on sunnier days. The title of the article in which he reported these findings is memorable enough: "Clouds Make Nerds Look Good."

Another source of random variability in judgment is the order in which cases are examined. When a person is considering a case, the decisions that immediately preceded it serve as an implicit frame of reference. Professionals who make a series of decisions in sequence, including judges, loan officers, and baseball umpires, lean toward restoring a form of balance: after a streak, or a series of decisions that go in the same direction, they are more likely to decide in the opposite direction than would be strictly justified. As a result, errors (and unfairness) are inevitable. Asylum judges in the United States, for instance, are 19% less likely to grant asylum to an applicant when the previous two cases were approved. A person might be approved for a loan if the previous two applications were denied, but the same person might have been rejected if the previous two applications had been granted. This behavior reflects a cognitive bias known as the *gambler's fallacy:* we tend to underestimate the likelihood that streaks will occur by chance.

Sizing Occasion Noise

How large is occasion noise relative to total system noise? Although no single number applies to all situations, a general rule emerges. In terms of their size, the effects we have described in this chapter are smaller than stable differences between individuals in their levels and patterns of judgments.

As noted, for instance, the chance that an asylum applicant will be admitted in the United States drops by 19% if the hearing follows two successful ones by the same judge. This variability is certainly troubling. But it pales in comparison with the variability between judges: in one Miami courthouse, Jaya Ramji-Nogales and her co-authors found that one judge would grant asylum to 88% of applicants and another to only 5%. (This is real data, not a noise audit, so the applicants were different, but they were quasi-randomly assigned, and the authors checked that differences in country of origin did not explain the discrepancies.) Given such disparities, reducing one of these numbers by 19% does not seem like such a big deal.

Similarly, fingerprint examiners and physicians sometimes disagree with themselves, but they do so less often than they disagree with others. In every case we reviewed in which the share of occasion noise in total system noise could be measured, occasion noise was a smaller contributor than were differences among individuals.

Or to put it differently, you are not always the same person, and you are less consistent over time than you think. But somewhat reassuringly, you are more similar to yourself yesterday than you are to another person today.

Occasion Noise, Inner Causes

Mood, fatigue, weather, sequence effects: many factors may trigger unwanted variations in the judgment of the same case by the same person. We might hope to construct a setting in which all the extraneous factors bearing on decisions are known and controlled. In theory at least, such a setting should reduce occasion noise. But even this setting would probably not be sufficient to eliminate occasion noise entirely.

Michael Kahana and his University of Pennsylvania colleagues study memory performance. (Memory is not a judgment task by our definition, but it is a cognitive task for which conditions can be rigorously controlled and variations in performance easily measured.) In one study, they asked seventy-nine subjects to participate in an exceptionally thorough analysis of their memory performance. The subjects sat through twenty-three sessions on separate days, during each of which they had to recall words from twenty-four different lists of twenty-four words each. The percentage of words recalled defines memory performance.

Kahana and his colleagues were not interested in the differences between subjects but rather in the predictors of variability in the performance of each subject. Would performance be driven by how alert the subjects felt? By how much sleep they got the previous night? By the time of day? Would their performance increase with practice from one session to the next? Would it deteriorate within each session as they got tired or bored? Would some lists of words prove easier to memorize than others?

The answer to all these questions was yes, but not by very much. A model that incorporated all these predictors explained only 11% of the variation in the performance of a given subject. As the researchers put it, "We were struck by how much variability remained after removing the effects of our predictor variables." Even in this tightly controlled setting, exactly what factors drive occasion noise was a mystery.

Of all the variables the researchers studied, the most powerful predictor of a subject's performance on a particular list was not an external factor. Performance on one list of words was best predicted by how well a subject had performed on the list that immediately preceded it. A successful list was likely to be followed by another relatively successful one, and a mediocre one by another mediocre one. Performance did not vary randomly from list to list: within each session, it ebbed and flowed over time, with no obvious external cause.

These findings suggest that memory performance is driven in large part by, in Kahana and coauthors' words, "the efficiency of endogenous neural processes that govern memory function." In other words, the moment-to-moment variability in the efficacy of the brain is not just driven by external influences, like the weather or a distracting intervention. It is a characteristic of the way our brain itself functions.

It is very likely that intrinsic variability in the functioning of the brain also affects the quality of our judgments in ways that we cannot possibly hope to control. This variability in brain function should give pause to anyone who thinks occasion noise can be eliminated. The analogy with the basketball player at the free-throw line was not as simplistic as it may have initially appeared: just as the player's muscles never execute exactly the same gesture, our neurons never operate in exactly the same way. If our mind is a measuring instrument, it will never be a perfect one.

We can, however, strive to control those undue influences that can be controlled. Doing so is especially important when judgments are made in groups, as we will see in chapter 8.

Speaking of Occasion Noise

"Judgment is like a free throw: however hard we try to repeat it precisely, it is never exactly identical."

"Your judgment depends on what mood you are in, what cases you have just discussed, and even what the weather is. You are not the same person at all times."

"Although you may not be the same person you were last week, you are less different from the 'you' of last week than you are from someone else today. Occasion noise is not the largest source of system noise."

CHAPTER 8

How Groups Amplify Noise

Noise in individual judgment is bad enough. But group decision making adds another layer to the problem. Groups can go in all sorts of directions, depending in part on factors that should be irrelevant. Who speaks first, who speaks last, who speaks with confidence, who is wearing black, who is seated next to whom, who smiles or frowns or gestures at the right moment — all these factors, and many more, affect outcomes. Every day, similar groups make very different decisions, whether the question involves hiring, promotion, office closings, communications strategies, environmental regulations, national security, university admissions, or new product launches.

It might seem odd to emphasize this point, since we noted in the previous chapter that aggregating the judgments of multiple individuals reduces noise. But because of group dynamics, groups can add noise, too. There are "wise crowds," whose mean judgment is close to the correct answer, but there are also crowds that follow tyrants, that fuel market bubbles, that believe in magic, or that are under the sway of a shared illusion. Minor differences can lead one group toward a firm yes and an essentially identical group toward an emphatic no. And because of the dynamics among group members — our emphasis here — the level of noise can be high. That proposition holds whether we are speaking of noise across similar groups or of a single group whose firm judgment on an important matter should be seen as merely one in a cloud of possibilities.

Noise in the Music

For evidence, we begin in what might seem to be an unlikely place: a large-scale study of music downloads by Matthew Salganik and his coauthors. As the study was designed, the experimenters created a control group of thousands of people (visitors to a moderately popular website). Members of the control group could hear and download one or more of seventy-two songs by new bands. The songs were vividly named: "Trapped in an Orange Peel," "Gnaw," "Eye Patch," "Baseball Warlock v1," and "Pink Aggression." (Some of the titles sound directly related to our concerns here: "Best Mistakes," "I Am Error," "The Belief Above the Answer," "Life's Mystery," "Wish Me Luck," and "Out of the Woods.")

In the control group, the participants were told nothing about what anyone else had said or done. They were left to make their own independent judgments about which songs they liked and wished to download. But Salganik and his colleagues also created eight other groups, to which thousands of other website visitors were randomly assigned. For members of those groups, everything was the same, with just one exception: people could see how many people in their particular group had previously downloaded every individual song. For example, if "Best Mistakes" was immensely popular in one group, its members would see that, and so too if no one was downloading it.

Because the various groups did not differ along any important dimension, the study was essentially running history eight times. You might well predict that in the end, the good songs would always rise to the top and the bad ones would always sink to the bottom. If so, the various groups would end up with identical or at least similar rankings. Across groups, there would be no noise. And indeed, that was the precise question that Salganik and his coauthors meant to explore. They were testing for a particular driver of noise: *social influence.*

The key finding was that group rankings were wildly disparate: across different groups, there was a great deal of noise. In one group, "Best Mistakes" could be a spectacular success, while "I Am Error" could flop. In another group, "I Am Error" could do exceedingly well, and "Best Mistakes" could be a disaster. If a song benefited from early popularity, it could do really well. If it did not get that benefit, the outcome could be very different.

To be sure, the very worst songs (as established by the control group) never ended up at the very top, and the very best songs never ended up at the very bottom. But otherwise, almost anything could happen. As the authors emphasize, "The level of success in the social influence condition was more unpredictable than in the independent condition." In short, social influences create significant noise across groups. And if you think about it, you can see that individual groups were noisy, too, in the sense that their judgment in favor of one song, or against it, could easily have been different, depending on whether it attracted early popularity.

As Salganik and his coauthors later demonstrated, group out-comes can be manipulated fairly easily, because popularity is self-reinforcing. In a somewhat fiendish follow-up experiment, they inverted the rankings in the control group (in other words, they lied about how popular songs were), which meant that people saw the least popular songs as the most popular, and vice versa. The research-ers then tested what the website's visitors would do. The result was that most of the unpopular songs became quite popular, and most of the popular songs did very poorly. Within very large groups, popular-ity and unpopularity bred more of the same, even when the research-ers misled people about which songs were popular. The single exception is that the very most popular song in the control group did rise in popularity over time, which means that the inverted ranking could not keep the best song down. For the most part, however, the inverted ranking helped determine the ultimate ranking.

It should be easy to see how these studies bear on group judgments in general. Suppose that a small group consisting of, say, ten people is deciding whether to adopt some bold new initiative. If one or two advocates speak first, they might well shift the entire room in their preferred direction. The same is true if skeptics speak first. At least this is so if people are influenced by one another — and they usually are. For this reason, otherwise similar groups might end up making very different judgments simply because of who spoke first and initiated the equivalent of early downloads. The popularity of "Best Mistakes" and "I Am Error" have close analogues in professional judgments of all kinds. And if groups do not hear the analogue to the popularity rankings of such songs — loud enthusiasm, say, for that bold initiative — the initiative might not go anywhere, simply because those who supported it did not voice their opinion.

Beyond Music Downloads

If you are skeptical, you might be thinking that the case of music downloads is unique or at least distinctive and that it tells us little about judgments by other groups. But similar observations have been made in many other areas as well. Consider, for example, the popularity of proposals for referenda in the United Kingdom. In deciding whether to support a referendum, people must of course judge whether it is a good idea, all things considered. The patterns are similar to those observed by Salganik and his coauthors: an initial burst of popularity is self-reinforcing, and if a proposal attracts little support on the first day, it is essentially doomed. In politics, as in music, a great deal depends on social influences and, in particular, on whether people see that other people are attracted or repelled.

Building directly on the music downloads experiment, sociologist Michael Macy of Cornell University and his collaborators asked whether the visible views of other people could suddenly make identifiable political positions popular among Democrats and unpopular among Republicans — or vice versa. The short answer is yes. If

Democrats in an online group saw that a particular point of view was obtaining initial popularity among Democrats, they would endorse that point of view, ultimately leading most Democrats, in the relevant group, to favor it. But if Democrats in a different online group saw that the very same point of view was obtaining initial popularity among Republicans, they would reject that point of view, ultimately leading most Democrats, in the relevant group, to reject it. Republicans behaved similarly. In short, political positions can be just like songs, in the sense that their ultimate fate can depend on initial popularity. As the researchers put it, "chance variation in a small number of early movers" can have major effects in tipping large populations — and in getting both Republicans and Democrats to embrace a cluster of views that actually have nothing to do with each other.

Or consider a question that bears directly on group decisions in general: how people judge comments on websites. Lev Muchnik, a professor at the Hebrew University of Jerusalem, and his colleagues carried out an experiment on a website that displays diverse stories and allows people to post comments, which can in turn be voted up or down. The researchers automatically and artificially gave certain comments on stories an immediate up vote — the first vote that a comment would receive. You might well think that after hundreds or thousands of visitors and ratings, a single initial vote on a comment could not possibly matter. That is a sensible thought, but it is wrong. After seeing an initial up vote (and recall that it was entirely artificial), the next viewer became 32% more likely to give an up vote.

Remarkably, this effect persisted over time. After five months, a single positive initial vote artificially increased the mean rating of comments by 25%. The effect of a single positive early vote is a recipe for noise. Whatever the reason for that vote, it can produce a large-scale shift in overall popularity.

This study offers a clue about how groups shift and why they are noisy (again in the sense that similar groups can make very different judgments, and single groups can make judgments that are merely one in a cloud of possibilities). Members are often in a position to offer the functional equivalent of an early up vote (or down vote) by indicating agreement, neutrality, or dissent. If a group member has given immediate approval, other members have reason to do so as well. There is no question that when groups move in the direction of some products, people, movements, and ideas, it may not be because of their intrinsic merits but instead because of the functional equivalent of early up votes. Of course Muchnik's own study involved very large groups. But the same thing can happen in small ones, in fact even more dramatically, because an initial up vote — in favor of some plan, product, or verdict — often has a large effect on others.

There is a related point. We have pointed to the wisdom of crowds: if you take a large group of people and ask them a question, there is a good chance that the average answer will be close to the target. Aggregating judgments can be an excellent way of reducing noise, and therefore error. But what happens if people are listening to one another? You might well think that their doing so is likely to help. After all, people can learn from one another and thus figure out what is right. Under favorable circumstances, in which people share what they know, deliberating groups can indeed do well. But independence is a prerequisite for the wisdom of crowds. If people are not making their own judgments and are relying instead on what other people think, crowds might not be so wise after all.

Research has revealed exactly that problem. In simple estimation tasks — the number of crimes in a city, population increases over specified periods, the length of a border between nations — crowds were indeed wise as long as they registered their views independently. But if they learned the estimates of other people — for example, the average estimate of a group of twelve — the crowd did worse. As the authors put it, social influences are a problem because they reduce "group diversity without diminishing the collective error." The irony is that while multiple independent opinions, properly aggregated, can be strikingly accurate, even a little social influence can produce a kind of herding that undermines the wisdom of crowds.

Cascades

Some of the studies we are describing involve *informational cascades*. Such cascades are pervasive. They help explain why similar groups in business, government, and elsewhere can go in multiple directions and why small changes can produce such different outcomes and hence noise. We are able to see history only as it was actually run, but for many groups and group decisions, there are clouds of possibilities, only one of which is realized.

To see how informational cascades work, imagine that ten people are in a large office, deciding whom to hire for an important position. There are three main candidates: Thomas, Sam, and Julie. Assume that the group members are announcing their views in sequence. Each person attends, reasonably enough, to the judgments of others. Arthur is the first to speak. He suggests that the best choice is Thomas. Barbara now knows Arthur's judgment; she should certainly go along with his view if she is also enthusiastic about Thomas. But suppose she isn't sure about who is the best candidate. If she trusts Arthur, she might simply agree: Thomas is the best. Because she trusts Arthur well enough, she supports his judgment.

Now turn to a third person, Charles. Both Arthur and Barbara have said that they want to hire Thomas, but Charles's own view, based on what he knows to be limited information, is that Thomas is not the right person for the job and that Julie is the best candidate. Even though Charles has that view, he might well ignore what he knows and simply follow Arthur and Barbara. If so, the reason is not that Charles is a coward. Instead it is because he is a respectful listener. He may simply think that both Arthur and Barbara have evidence for their enthusiasm.

Unless David thinks that his own information is really better than that of those who preceded him, he should and will follow their lead. If he does that, David is in a cascade. True, he will resist if he has very strong grounds to think that Arthur, Barbara, and Charles are wrong. But if he lacks those grounds, he will likely go along with them.

Importantly, Charles or David may have information or insights about Thomas (or the other candidates) — information or insights of which Arthur and Barbara are unaware. If it had been shared, this private information might have changed Arthur's or Barbara's views. If Charles and David had spoken first, they would not only have expressed their views about the candidates but also contributed information that might have swayed the other participants. But since they speak last, their private information might well remain private.

Now suppose that Erica, Frank, and George are expected to express their views. If Arthur, Barbara, Charles, and David have previously said that Thomas is best, each of them might well say the same thing even if they have good reason to think that another choice would be better. Sure, they might oppose the growing consensus if it is clearly wrong. But what if the decision isn't clear? The trick in this example is that Arthur's initial judgment has started a process by which several people are led to participate in a cascade, leading the group to opt unanimously for Thomas — even if some of those who support him actually have no view and even if others think he is not the best choice at all.

This example, of course, is highly artificial. But within groups of all kinds, something like it happens all the time. People learn from others, and if early speakers seem to like something or want to do something, others might assent. At least this is so if they do not have reason to distrust them and if they lack a good reason to think that they are wrong.

For our purposes, the most important point is that informational cascades make noise across groups possible and even likely. In the example we have given, Arthur spoke first and favored Thomas. But suppose that Barbara had spoken first and favored Sam. Or suppose that Arthur had felt slightly differently and preferred Julie. On plausible assumptions, the group would have turned to Sam or Julie, not because they are better but because that is how the cascade would have worked itself out. That is the central finding of the music download experiment (and its cousins).

Note that it is not necessarily irrational for people to participate in informational cascades. If people are unsure about whom to hire, they might be smart to follow others. As the number of people who share the same view gets larger, relying on them becomes smarter still. Nonetheless, there are two problems. First, people tend to neglect the possibility that most of the people in the crowd are in a cascade, too — and are not making independent judgments of their own. When we see three, ten, or twenty people embracing some conclusion, we might well underestimate the extent to which they are all following their predecessors. We might think that their shared agreement reflects collective wisdom, even if it reflects the initial views of just a few people. Second, informational cascades can lead groups of people in truly terrible directions. After all, Arthur might have been wrong about Thomas.

Information is not, of course, the only reason that group members are influenced by one another. Social pressures also matter. At a company or in government, people might silence themselves so as not to appear uncongenial, truculent, obtuse, or stupid. They want to be team players. That is why they follow the views and actions of others. People think that they know what is right or probably right, but they nonetheless go along with the apparent consensus of the group, or the views of early speakers, to stay in the group's good graces.

With minor variations, the hiring tale just told can proceed in the same way, not because people are learning from one another about the merits of Thomas but because they do not want to look disagreeable or silly. Arthur's early judgment in favor of Thomas might start a kind of bandwagon effect, ultimately imposing strong social pressure on Erica, Frank, or George, simply because everyone else has favored Thomas. And as with informational cascades, so with social pressure cascades: people might well exaggerate the conviction of those who have spoken before them. If people are endorsing Thomas, they might be doing so not because they really prefer Thomas but because an early speaker, or a powerful one, endorsed him. And yet group members end up adding their voice to the consensus and thus increasing the level of social pressure. This is a familiar phenomenon in companies and government offices, and it can lead to confidence about, and unanimous support for, a judgment that is quite wrong.

Across groups, social influences also produce noise. If someone starts a meeting by favoring a major change in the company's direction, that person might initiate a discussion that leads a group unanimously to support the change. Their agreement might be a product of social pressures, not of conviction. If someone else had started the meeting by indicating a different view, or if the initial speaker had decided to be silent, the discussion might have headed in an altogether different direction — and for the same reason. Very similar groups can end up in divergent places because of social pressures.

Group Polarization

In the United States and in many other countries, criminal cases (and many civil cases) are generally tried by a jury. One would hope that, through their deliberations, juries make wiser decisions than do the individuals who constitute these deliberative bodies. However, the study of juries uncovers a distinct kind of social influence that is also a source of noise: *group polarization*. The basic idea is that when people speak with one another, they often end up at a more extreme point in line with their original inclinations. If, for example, most people in a seven-person group tend to think that opening a new office in Paris would be a pretty good idea, the group is likely to conclude, after discussion, that opening that office would be a terrific idea. Internal discussions often create greater confidence, greater unity, and greater extremism, frequently in the form of increased enthusiasm. As it happens, group polarization does not only occur in juries; teams that make professional judgments often become polarized, too.

In a series of experiments, we studied the decisions of juries that award punitive damages in product liability cases. Each jury's decision is a monetary amount, which is intended to punish the company for its wrongdoing and be a deterrent to others. (We will return to these studies and describe them in greater detail in chapter 15.) For our purposes here, consider an experiment that compares real-world deliberating juries and "statistical juries." First, we presented the 899 participants in our study with case vignettes and asked them to make their own independent judgments about them, using a seven-degree scale to express their outrage and punitive intent and a dollar scale for monetary awards (if any). Then, with the aid of the computer, we used these individual responses to create millions of statistical juries, that is, virtual six-person groups (assembled randomly). In each statistical jury, we took the median of the six individual judgments as the verdict.

We found, in short, that the judgments of these statistical juries were much more consistent. Noise was substantially reduced. The low noise was a mechanical effect of statistical aggregation: the noise present in the independent, individual judgments is always reduced by averaging them.

Real-world juries are not, however, statistical juries; they meet and discuss their views of the case. You could reasonably wonder whether deliberating juries would, in fact, tend to arrive at the judgment of their median members. To find out, we followed up the first experiment with another, this one involving more than three thousand jury-eligible citizens and more than five hundred six-person juries.

The results were straightforward. Looking at the same case, deliberating juries were far noisier than statistical juries — a clear reflection of social influence noise. Deliberation had the effect of increasing noise.

There was another intriguing finding. When the median member of a six-person group was only moderately outraged and favored a lenient punishment, the verdict of the deliberating jury typically ended up more lenient still. When, on the contrary, the median member of a six-person group was quite outraged and expressed a severe punitive intent, the deliberating jury typically ended up more outraged and more severe still. And when this outrage was expressed as a monetary award, there was a systematic tendency to come up with monetary awards that were higher than that of the jury's median member. Indeed, 27% of juries chose an award as high as, or even higher than, that of their most severe member. Not only were deliberating juries noisier than statistical juries, but they also accentuated the opinions of the individuals composing them.

Recall the basic finding of group polarization: after people talk with one another, they typically end up at a more extreme point in line with their original inclinations. Our experiment illustrates this effect. Deliberating juries experienced a shift toward greater leniency (when the median member was lenient) and a shift toward greater severity (when the median member was severe). Similarly, juries that were inclined to impose monetary punishments ended up imposing more severe punishments than what their median members had favored.

The explanations for group polarization are, in turn, similar to the explanations for cascade effects. Information plays a major role. If most people favor a severe punishment, then the group will hear many arguments in favor of severe punishment — and fewer arguments the other way. If group members are listening to one another, they will shift in the direction of the dominant tendency, rendering the group more unified, more confident, and more extreme. And if people care about their reputation within the group, they will shift in the direction of the dominant tendency, which will also produce polarization.

Group polarization can, of course, produce errors. And it often does. But our main focus here is on variability. As we have seen, an aggregation of judgments will reduce noise, and for those purposes, the more judgments, the better. This is why statistical juries are less noisy than individual jurors. At the same time, we found that deliberating juries are noisier than statistical juries. When similarly situated groups end up differing, group polarization is often the reason. And the resulting noise can be very loud.

In business, in government, and everywhere else, cascades and polarization can lead to wide disparities between groups looking at the same problem. The potential dependence of outcomes on the judgments of a few individuals — those who speak first or who have the largest influence — should be especially worrisome now that we have explored how noisy individual judgments can be. We have seen that level noise and pattern noise make differences between the opinions of group members larger than they should be (and larger than we would expect). We have also seen that occasion noise — fatigue, mood, comparison points — may affect the judgment of the first person who speaks. Group dynamics can amplify this noise. As a result, deliberating groups tend to be noisier than statistical groups that merely average individual judgments.

Since many of the most important decisions in business and government are made after some sort of deliberative process, it is especially important to be alert to this risk. Organizations and their leaders should take steps to control noise in the judgments of their individual members. They should also manage deliberating groups in a way that is likely to reduce noise, not amplify it. The noise-reduction strategies we will propose aim to achieve that goal.

Speaking of Group Decisions

"Everything seems to depend on early popularity. We'd better work hard to make sure that our new release has a terrific first week."

"As I always suspected, ideas about politics and economics are a lot like movie stars. If people think that other people like them, such ideas can go far."

"I've always been worried that when my team gets together, we end up confident and unified — and firmly committed to the course of action that we choose. I guess there's something in our internal processes that isn't going all that well!"

PART III

Noise in Predictive Judgments

Many judgments are predictions, and since verifiable predictions can be evaluated, we can learn a lot about noise and bias by studying them. In this part of the book, we focus on predictive judgments.

Chapter 9 compares the accuracy of predictions made by professionals, by machines, and by simple rules. You will not be surprised by our conclusion that the professionals come third in this competition. In chapter 10, we explore the reasons for this outcome and show that noise is a major factor in the inferiority of human judgment.

To reach these conclusions, we must evaluate the quality of predictions, and to do that, we need a measure of predictive accuracy, a way to answer this question: How closely do the predictions *co-vary* with the outcomes? If the HR department routinely rates the potential of new hires, for example, we can wait a few years to find out how employees perform and see how closely ratings of potential co-vary with evaluations of performance. Predictions are accurate to the extent that the employees whose potential was rated high when they were hired also earn high evaluations for their work.

A measure that captures this intuition is the *percent concordant (PC)*, which answers a more specific question: Suppose you take a pair of employees at random. What is the probability that the one who scored higher on an evaluation of potential also performs better on the job? If the accuracy of the early ratings were perfect, the PC would be 100%: the ranking of two employees by potential would be a perfect prediction of their eventual ranking by performance. If the predictions were entirely useless, concordance would occur by chance only, and the "higher-potential" employee would be just as likely as not to perform better: PC would be 50%. We will discuss this example, which has been studied extensively, in chapter 9. For a simpler example, PC for foot length and height in adult men is 71%. If you look at two people, first at their head and then at their feet, there is a 71% chance that the taller of the two also has the larger feet.

PC is an immediately intuitive measure of covariation, which is a large advantage, but it is not the standard measure that social scientists use. The standard measure is the *correlation coefficient (r)*, which varies between 0 and 1 when two variables are positively related. In the preceding example, the correlation between height and foot size is about .60.

There are many ways to think about the correlation coefficient. Here is one that is intuitive enough: the correlation between two variables is their percentage of shared determinants. Imagine, for instance, that some trait is entirely genetically determined. We would expect to find a .50 correlation on that trait between siblings, who have 50% of their genes in common, and a .25 correlation between first cousins, who have 25% of their genes in common. We can also read the .60 correlation between height and foot size as suggesting that 60% of the causal factors that determine height also determine shoe size.

The two measures of covariation we have described are directly related to each other. Table 1 presents the PC for various values of the correlation coefficient. In the rest of this book, we always present the two measures together when we discuss the performance of humans and models.

Table 1: *Correlation coefficient and percentage concordant (PC)*

Correlation coefficient	Percentage concordant (PC)
.00	50%
.10	53%
.20	56%
.30	60%
.40	63%
.60	71%
.80	79%
1.00	100%

In chapter 11, we discuss an important limit on predictive accuracy: the fact that most judgments are made in a state of what we call *objective ignorance,* because many things on which the future depends can simply not be known. Strikingly, we manage, most of the time, to remain oblivious to this limitation and make predictions with confidence (or, indeed, overconfidence). Finally, in chapter 12, we show that objective ignorance affects not just our ability to predict events but even our capacity to understand them—an important part of the answer to the puzzle of why noise tends to be invisible.

CHAPTER 9

Judgments and Models

M any people are interested in forecasting people's future performance on the job — their own and that of others. The forecasting of performance is therefore a useful example of predictive professional judgment. Consider, for instance, two executives in a large company. Monica and Nathalie were assessed by a specialized consulting firm when they were hired and received ratings on a 1-to-10 scale for leadership, communication, interpersonal skills, job-related technical skills, and motivation for the next position (table 2). Your task is to predict their performance evaluations two years after they were hired, also using a 1-to-10 scale.

Table 2: *Two candidates for an executive position*

	Leader- ship	Communi- cation	Interpersonal skills	Technical skills	Motiva- tion	Your prediction
Monica	4	6	4	8	8	
Nathalie	8	10	6	7	6	

Most people, when faced with this type of problem, simply eyeball each line and produce a quick judgment, sometimes after mentally computing the average of the scores. If you just did that, you probably concluded that Nathalie was the stronger candidate and that the difference between her and Monica was 1 or 2 points.

Judgment or Formula?

The informal approach you took to this problem is known as *clinical judgment*. You consider the information, perhaps engage in a quick computation, consult your intuition, and come up with a judgment. In fact, clinical judgment is the process that we have described simply as judgment in this book.

Now suppose that you performed the prediction task as a participant in an experiment. Monica and Nathalie were drawn from a database of several hundred managers who were hired some years ago, and who received ratings on five separate dimensions. You used these ratings to predict the managers' success on the job. Evaluations of their performance in their new roles are now available. How closely would these evaluations align with your clinical judgments of their potential?

This example is loosely based on an actual study of performance prediction. If you had been a participant in that study, you would probably not be pleased with its results. Doctoral-level psychologists, employed by an international consulting firm to make such predictions, achieved a correlation of .15 with performance evaluations (PC = 55%). In other words, when they rated one candidate as stronger than another — as you did with Monica and Nathalie — the probability that their favored candidate would end up with a higher performance rating was 55%, barely better than chance. To say the least, that is not an impressive result.

Perhaps you think that accuracy was poor because the ratings you were shown were useless for prediction. So we must ask, how much useful predictive information do the candidates' ratings actually contain? How can they be combined into a predictive score that will have the highest possible correlation with performance?

A standard statistical method answers these questions. In the present study, it yields an optimal correlation of .32 (PC = 60%), far from impressive but substantially higher than what clinical predictions achieved.

This technique, called *multiple regression,* produces a predictive score that is a weighted average of the predictors. It finds the optimal set of weights, chosen to maximize the correlation between the composite prediction and the target variable. The optimal weights minimize the MSE (mean squared error) of the predictions — a prime example of the dominant role of the least squares principle in statistics. As you might expect, the predictor that is most closely correlated with the target variable gets a large weight, and useless predictors get a weight of zero. Weights could also be negative: the candidate's number of unpaid traffic tickets would probably get a negative weight as a predictor of managerial success.

The use of multiple regression is an example of *mechanical prediction.* There are many kinds of mechanical prediction, ranging from simple rules ("hire anyone who completed high school") to sophisticated artificial intelligence models. But linear regression models are the most common (they have been called "the workhorse of judgment and decision-making research"). To minimize jargon, we will refer to linear models as *simple models.*

The study that we illustrated with Monica and Nathalie was one of many comparisons of clinical and mechanical predictions, which all share a simple structure:

❑ A set of *predictor variables* (in our example, the ratings of candidates) are used to predict a *target outcome* (the job evaluations of the same people);
❑ Human judges make *clinical predictions;*
❑ A rule (such as multiple regression) uses the same predictors to produce *mechanical predictions* of the same outcomes;
❑ The overall accuracy of clinical and mechanical predictions is compared.

Meehl: The Optimal Model Beats You

When people are introduced to clinical and mechanical prediction, they want to know how the two compare. How good is human judgment, relative to a formula?

The question had been asked before, but it attracted much attention only in 1954, when Paul Meehl, a professor of psychology at the University of Minnesota, published a book titled *Clinical Versus Statistical Prediction: A Theoretical Analysis and a Review of the Evidence.* Meehl reviewed twenty studies in which a clinical judgment was pitted against a mechanical prediction for such outcomes as academic success and psychiatric prognosis. He reached the strong conclusion that simple mechanical rules were generally superior to human judgment. Meehl discovered that clinicians and other professionals are distressingly weak in what they often see as their unique strength: the ability to integrate information.

To appreciate how surprising this finding is, and how it relates to noise, you have to understand how a simple mechanical prediction model works. Its defining characteristic is that the same rule is applied to all the cases. Each predictor has a weight, and that weight does not vary from one case to the next. You might think that this severe constraint puts models at a great disadvantage relative to human judges. In our example, perhaps you thought that Monica's combination of motivation and technical skills would be an important asset and would offset her limitations in other areas. And perhaps you also thought that Nathalie's weaknesses in these two areas would not be a serious issue, given her other strengths. Implicitly, you imagined different routes to success for the two women. These plausible clinical speculations effectively assign different weights to the same predictors in the two cases — a subtlety that is out of the reach of a simple model.

Another constraint of the simple model is that an increase of 1 unit in a predictor always produces the same effect (and half the effect of an increase of 2 units). Clinical intuition often violates this rule. If, for instance, you were impressed by Nathalie's perfect 10 on communication skills and decided this score was worth a boost in your prediction, you did something that a simple model will not do. In a weighted-average formula, the difference between a score of 10 and a score of 9 must be the same as the difference between a 7 and a 6. Clinical judgment does not obey that rule. Instead, it reflects the common intuition that the same difference can be inconsequential in one context and critical in another. You may want to check, but we suspect that no simple model could account exactly for your judgments about Monica and Nathalie.

The study we used for these cases was a clear example of Meehl's pattern. As we noted, clinical predictions achieved a .15 correlation (PC = 55%) with job performance, but mechanical prediction achieved a correlation of .32 (PC = 60%). Think about the confidence that you experienced in the relative merits of the cases of Monica and Nathalie. Meehl's results strongly suggest that any satisfaction you felt with the quality of your judgment was an illusion: the *illusion of validity.*

The illusion of validity is found wherever predictive judgments are made, because of a common failure to distinguish between two stages of the prediction task: evaluating cases on the evidence available and predicting actual outcomes. You can often be quite confident in your assessment of which of two candidates *looks* better, but guessing which of them will actually *be* better is an altogether different kettle of fish. It is safe to assert, for instance, that Nathalie looks like a stronger candidate than Monica, but it is not at all safe to assert that Nathalie will be a more successful executive than Monica. The reason is straightforward: you know most of what you need to know to assess the two cases, but gazing into the future is deeply uncertain.

Unfortunately, the difference gets blurred in our thinking. If you find yourself confused by the distinction between cases and predictions, you are in excellent company: Everybody finds that distinction confusing. If you are as confident in your predictions as you are in your evaluation of cases, however, you are a victim of the illusion of validity.

Clinicians are not immune to the illusion of validity. You can surely imagine the response of clinical psychologists to Meehl's finding that trivial formulas, consistently applied, outdo clinical judgment. The reaction combined shock, disbelief, and contempt for the shallow research that pretended to study the marvels of clinical intuition. The reaction is easy to understand: Meehl's pattern contradicts the subjective experience of judgment, and most of us will trust our experience over a scholar's claim.

Meehl himself was ambivalent about his findings. Because his name is associated with the superiority of statistics over clinical judgment, we might imagine him as a relentless critic of human insight, or as the godfather of quants, as we would say today. But that would be a caricature. Meehl, in addition to his academic career, was a practicing psychoanalyst. A picture of Freud hung in his office. He was a polymath who taught classes not just in psychology but also in philosophy and law and who wrote about metaphysics, religion, political science, and even parapsychology. (He insisted that "there is something to telepathy.") None of these characteristics fits the stereotype of a hard-nosed numbers guy. Meehl had no ill will toward clinicians — far from it. But as he put it, the evidence for the advantage of the mechanical approach to combining inputs was "massive and consistent."

"Massive and consistent" is a fair description. A 2000 review of 136 studies confirmed unambiguously that mechanical aggregation outperforms clinical judgment. The research surveyed in the article covered a wide variety of topics, including diagnosis of jaundice, fitness for military service, and marital satisfaction. Mechanical prediction was more accurate in 63 of the studies, a statistical tie was declared for another 65, and clinical prediction won the contest in 8 cases. These results understate the advantages of mechanical prediction, which is also faster and cheaper than clinical judgment. Moreover, human judges actually had an unfair advantage in many of these studies, because they had access to "private" information that was not supplied to the computer model. The findings support a blunt conclusion: *simple models beat humans.*

Goldberg: The Model of You Beats You

Meehl's finding raises important questions. Why, exactly, is the formula superior? What does the formula do better? In fact, a better question would be to ask what humans do worse. The answer is that people are inferior to statistical models in many ways. One of their critical weaknesses is that they are noisy.

To support this conclusion, we turn to a different stream of research on simple models, which began in the small city of Eugene, Oregon. Paul Hoffman was a wealthy and visionary psychologist who was impatient with academia. He founded a research institute where he collected under one roof a few extraordinarily effective researchers, who turned Eugene into a world-famous center for the study of human judgment.

One of these researchers was Lewis Goldberg, who is best known for his leading role in the development of the Big Five model of personality. In the late 1960s, following earlier work by Hoffman, Goldberg studied statistical models that describe the judgments of an individual.

It is just as easy to build such a model of a judge as it is to build a model of reality. The same predictors are used. In our initial example, the predictors are the five ratings of a manager's performance. And the same tool, multiple regression, is used. The only difference is the target variable. Instead of predicting a set of real outcomes, the formula is applied to predict a set of judgments — for instance, *your* judgments of Monica, Nathalie, and other managers.

The idea of modeling your judgments as a weighted average may seem altogether bizarre, because this is not how you form your opinions. When you thought clinically about Monica and Nathalie, you didn't apply the same rule to both cases. Indeed, you did not apply any rule at all. The model of the judge is not a realistic description of how a judge actually judges.

However, even if you do not actually compute a linear formula, you might still make your judgments *as if* you did. Expert billiard

117

players act as if they have solved the complex equations that describe the mechanics of a particular shot, even if they are doing nothing of the kind. Similarly, you could be generating predictions as if you used a simple formula — even if what you actually do is vastly more complex. An as-if model that predicts what people will do with reasonable accuracy is useful, even when it is obviously wrong as a description of the process. This is the case for simple models of judgment. A comprehensive review of studies of judgment found that, in 237 studies, the average correlation between the model of the judge and the judge's clinical judgments was .80 (PC = 79%). While far from perfect, this correlation is high enough to support an as-if theory.

The question that drove Goldberg's research was how well a simple model of the judge would predict real outcomes. Since the model is a crude approximation of the judge, we could sensibly assume that it cannot perform as well. How much accuracy is lost when the model replaces the judge?

The answer may surprise you. Predictions did not lose accuracy when the model generated predictions. They improved. In most cases, the model out-predicted the professional on which it was based. The ersatz was better than the original product.

This conclusion has been confirmed by studies in many fields. An early replication of Goldberg's work involved the forecasting of graduate school success. The researchers asked ninety-eight participants to predict the GPAs of ninety students from ten cues. On the basis of these predictions, the researchers built a linear model of each participant's judgments and compared how accurately the participants and the models of the participants predicted GPA. For every one of the ninety-eight participants, the model did better than the participant did! Decades later, a review of fifty years of research concluded that models of judges consistently outperformed the judges they modeled.

We do not know if the participants in these studies received personal feedback on their performance. But you can surely imagine your own dismay if someone told you that a crude model of your judgments — almost a caricature — was actually more accurate than you were. For most of us, the activity of judgment is complex, rich, and interesting precisely because it does not fit simple rules. We feel best about ourselves and about our ability to make judgments when we invent and apply complex rules or have an insight that makes an individual case different from others — in short, when we make judgments that are not reducible to a plain operation of weighted averaging. The model-of-the-judge studies reinforce Meehl's conclusion that the subtlety is largely wasted. Complexity and richness do not generally lead to more accurate predictions.

Why is that so? To understand Goldberg's finding, we need to understand what accounts for the differences between you and the model of you. What causes the discrepancies between your actual judgments and the output of a simple model that predicts them?

A statistical model of your judgments cannot possibly add anything to the information they contain. All the model can do is subtract and simplify. In particular, the simple model of your judgments will not represent any complex rules that you consistently follow. If you think that the difference between 10 and 9 on a rating of communications skill is more significant than the difference between 7 and 6, or that a well-rounded candidate who scores a solid 7 on all dimensions is preferable to one who achieves the same average with clear strengths and marked weaknesses, the model of you will not reproduce your complex rules — even if you apply them with flawless consistency.

Failing to reproduce your subtle rules will result in a loss of accuracy when your subtlety is valid. Suppose, for instance, that you must predict success at a difficult task from two inputs, skill and motivation. A weighted average is not a good formula, because no amount of motivation is sufficient to overcome a severe skill deficit, and vice versa. If you use a more complex combination of the two inputs, your predictive accuracy will be enhanced and will be higher than that achieved by a model that fails to capture this subtlety. On the other hand, complex rules will often give you only the illusion of validity and in fact harm the quality of your judgments. Some subtleties are valid, but many are not.

In addition, a simple model of you will not represent the pattern noise in your judgments. It cannot replicate the positive and negative errors that arise from arbitrary reactions you may have to a particular case. Neither will the model capture the influences of the momentary context and of your mental state when you make a particular judgment. Most likely, these noisy errors of judgment are not systematically correlated with anything, which means that for most purposes, they can be considered random.

The effect of removing noise from your judgments will always be an improvement of your predictive accuracy. For example, suppose that the correlation between your forecasts and an outcome is .50 (PC = 67%), but 50% of the variance of your judgments consists of noise. If your judgments could be made noise-free — as a model of you would be — their correlation with the same outcome would jump to .71 (PC = 75%). Reducing noise mechanically increases the validity of predictive judgment.

In short, replacing you with a model of you does two things: it eliminates your subtlety, and it eliminates your pattern noise. The robust finding that the model of the judge is more valid than the judge conveys an important message: the gains from subtle rules in human judgment — when they exist — are generally not sufficient to compensate for the detrimental effects of noise. You may believe that you are subtler, more insightful, and more nuanced than the linear caricature of your thinking. But in fact, you are mostly noisier.

Why do complex rules of prediction harm accuracy, despite the strong feeling we have that they draw on valid insights? For one thing, many of the complex rules that people invent are not likely to be generally true. But there is another problem: even when the complex rules are valid in principle, they inevitably apply under conditions that are rarely observed. For example, suppose you have concluded that exceptionally original candidates are worth hiring, even when their scores on other dimensions are mediocre. The problem is that exceptionally original candidates are, by definition, exceptionally rare. Since an evaluation of originality is likely to be unreliable, many high scores on that metric are flukes, and truly original talent often remains undetected. The performance evaluations that could confirm that "originals" end up as superstars are also imperfect. Errors of measurement at both ends inevitably attenuate the validity of predictions — and rare events are particularly likely to be missed. The advantages of true subtlety are quickly drowned in measurement error.

A study by Martin Yu and Nathan Kuncel reported a more radical version of Goldberg's demonstration. This study (which was the basis for the example of Monica and Nathalie) used data from an international consulting firm that employed experts to assess 847 candidates for executive positions, in three separate samples. The experts scored the results on seven distinct assessment dimensions and used their clinical judgment to assign an overall predictive score to each, with rather unimpressive results.

Yu and Kuncel decided to compare judges not to the best simple model of themselves but to a *random* linear model. They generated ten thousand sets of random weights for the seven predictors, and applied the ten thousand random formulas to predict job performance.

Their striking finding was that *any* linear model, when applied consistently to all cases, was likely to outdo human judges in predicting an outcome from the same information. In one of the three samples, 77% of the ten thousand randomly weighted linear models did better than the human experts. In the other two samples, 100% of the random models outperformed the humans. Or, to put it bluntly, it proved almost impossible in that study to generate a simple model that did worse than the experts did.

The conclusion from this research is stronger than the one we took away from Goldberg's work on the model of the judge — and indeed it is an extreme example. In this setting, human judges

NOISE IN PREDICTIVE JUDGMENTS

performed very poorly in absolute terms, which helps explain why even unimpressive linear models outdid them. Of course, we should not conclude that any model beats any human. Still, the fact that mechanical adherence to a simple rule (Yu and Kuncel call it "mindless consistency") could significantly improve judgment in a difficult problem illustrates the massive effect of noise on the validity of clinical predictions.

This quick tour has shown how noise impairs clinical judgment. In predictive judgments, human experts are easily outperformed by simple formulas — models of reality, models of a judge, or even randomly generated models. This finding argues in favor of using noise-free methods: rules and algorithms, which are the topic of the next chapter.

Speaking of Judgments and Models

"People believe they capture complexity and add subtlety when they make judgments. But the complexity and the subtlety are mostly wasted — usually they do not add to the accuracy of simple models."

"More than sixty years after the publication of Paul Meehl's book, the idea that mechanical prediction is superior to people is still shocking."

"There is so much noise in judgment that a noise-free model of a judge achieves more accurate predictions than the actual judge does."

CHAPTER 10

Noiseless Rules

In recent years, artificial intelligence (AI), particularly machine-learning techniques, has enabled machines to perform many tasks formerly regarded as quintessentially human. Machine-learning algorithms can recognize faces, translate languages, and read radiology images. They can solve computational problems, such as generating driving directions for thousands of drivers at once, with astonishing speed and accuracy. And they perform difficult prediction tasks: machine-learning algorithms forecast the decisions of the US Supreme Court, determine which defendants are more likely to jump bail, and assess which calls to child protective services most urgently require a case worker's visit.

Although nowadays these are the applications we have in mind when we hear the word *algorithm,* the term has a broader meaning. In one dictionary's definition, an algorithm is a "process or set of rules to be followed in calculations or other problem-solving operations, especially by a computer." By this definition, simple models and other forms of mechanical judgment we described in the previous chapter are algorithms, too.

In fact, many types of mechanical approaches, from almost

laughably simple rules to the most sophisticated and impenetrable machine algorithms, can outperform human judgment. And one key reason for this outperformance — albeit not the only one — is that all mechanical approaches are noise-free.

To examine different types of rule-based approaches and to learn how and under what conditions each approach can be valuable, we start our journey with the models of chapter 9: simple models based on multiple regression (i.e., linear regression models). From this starting point, we will travel in the two opposite directions on the spectrum of sophistication — first to seek extreme simplicity, then to add greater sophistication (figure 11).

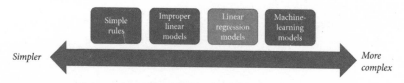

FIGURE 11: *Four types of rules and algorithms*

More Simplicity: Robust and Beautiful

Robyn Dawes was another member of the Eugene, Oregon, team of stars that studied judgment in the 1960s and 1970s. In 1974, Dawes achieved a breakthrough in the simplification of prediction tasks. His idea was surprising, almost heretical: instead of using multiple regression to determine the precise weight of each predictor, he proposed giving all the predictors equal weights.

Dawes labeled the equal-weight formula an *improper linear model*. His surprising discovery was that these equal-weight models are about as accurate as "proper" regression models, and far superior to clinical judgments.

Even the proponents of improper models admit that this claim is implausible and "contrary to statistical intuition." Indeed, Dawes and his assistant, Bernard Corrigan, initially struggled to publish their paper in scientific journals; editors simply did not believe them. If you think about the example of Monica and Nathalie in the previous chapter, you probably believe that some predictors matter more than others. Most people, for instance, would give leadership a higher weight than technical skills. How can a straight unweighted average predict someone's performance better than a carefully weighted average, or better than the judgment of an expert?

Today, many years after Dawes's breakthrough, the statistical phenomenon that so surprised his contemporaries is well understood. As explained earlier in this book, multiple regression computes "optimal" weights that minimize squared errors. But multiple regression minimizes error *in the original data*. The formula therefore adjusts itself to predict every random fluke in the data. If, for instance, the sample includes a few managers who have high technical skills and who also performed exceptionally well for unrelated reasons, the model will exaggerate the weight of technical skill.

The challenge is that when the formula is applied *out of sample*— that is, when it is used to predict outcomes in a different data set— the weights will no longer be optimal. Flukes in the original sample are no longer present, precisely because they were flukes; in the new sample, managers with high technical skills are not all superstars. And the new sample has different flukes, which the formula cannot predict. The correct measure of a model's predictive accuracy is its performance in a new sample, called its *cross-validated correlation*. In effect, a regression model is *too* successful in the original sample, and a cross-validated correlation is almost always lower than it was in the original data. Dawes and Corrigan compared equal-weight models to multiple regression models (cross-validated) in several situations. One of their examples involved predictions of the first-year GPA of ninety graduate students in psychology at the University of Illinois, using ten variables related to academic success: aptitude test scores, college grades, various peer ratings (e.g., extroversion), and various self-ratings (e.g., conscientiousness). The standard multiple regression model achieved a correlation of .69, which shrank to .57

(PC = 69%) in cross-validation. The correlation of the equal-weight model with first-year GPA was about the same: .60 (PC = 70%). Similar results have been obtained in many other studies.

The loss of accuracy in cross-validation is worst when the original sample is small, because flukes loom larger in small samples. The problem Dawes pointed out is that the samples used in social science research are generally so small that the advantage of so-called optimal weighting disappears. As statistician Howard Wainer memorably put it in the subtitle of a scholarly article on the estimation of proper weights, "It Don't Make No Nevermind." Or, in Dawes's words, "we do not need models more precise than our measurements." Equal-weight models do well because they are not susceptible to accidents of sampling.

The immediate implication of Dawes's work deserves to be widely known: you can make valid statistical predictions without prior data about the outcome that you are trying to predict. All you need is a collection of predictors that you can trust to be correlated with the outcome.

Suppose you must make predictions of the performance of executives who have been rated on a number of dimensions, as in the example in chapter 9. You trust that these scores measure important qualities, but you have no data about how well each score predicts performance. Nor do you have the luxury of waiting a few years to track the performance of a large sample of managers. You could nevertheless take the seven scores, do the statistical work required to weight them equally, and use the result as your prediction. How good would this equal-weight model be? Its correlation with the outcome would be .25 (PC = 58%), far superior to clinical predictions (r = .15, PC = 55%), and surely quite similar to a cross-validated regression model. And it does not require any data you don't have or any complicated calculations.

To use Dawes's phrase, which has become a meme among students of judgment, there is a "robust beauty" in equal weights. The final sentence of the seminal article that introduced the idea offered another pithy summary: "The whole trick is to decide what variables to look at and then to know how to add."

Even More Simplicity: Simple Rules

Another style of simplification is through *frugal models,* or *simple rules.* Frugal models are models of reality that look like ridiculously simplified, back-of-the-envelope calculations. But in some settings, they can produce surprisingly good predictions.

These models build on a feature of multiple regression that most people find surprising. Suppose you are using two predictors that are strongly predictive of the outcome — their correlations with the outcome are .60 (PC = 71%) and .55 (PC = 69%). Suppose also that the two predictors are correlated to each other, with a correlation of .50. How good would you guess your prediction is going to be when the two predictors are optimally combined? The answer is quite disappointing. The correlation is .67 (PC = 73%), higher than before, but not much higher.

The example illustrates a general rule: the combination of two or more correlated predictors is barely more predictive than the best of them on its own. Because, in real life, predictors are almost always correlated to one another, this statistical fact supports the use of frugal approaches to prediction, which use a small number of predictors. Simple rules that can be applied with little or no computation have produced impressively accurate predictions in some settings, compared with models that use many more predictors.

A team of researchers published in 2020 a large-scale effort to apply a frugal approach to a variety of prediction problems, including the choice that bail judges face when they decide whether to release or retain defendants pending trial. That decision is an implicit prediction of the defendant's behavior. If wrongly denied bail, that person will be detained needlessly, at a significant cost to the individual and to society. If bail is granted to the wrong defendant, the person may flee before trial or even commit another crime.

The model that the researchers built uses just two inputs known to be highly predictive of a defendant's likelihood to jump bail: the defendant's age (older people are lower flight risks) and the number of past court dates missed (people who have failed to appear before tend to recidivate). The model translates these two inputs into a number of points, which can be used as a risk score. The calculation of risk for a defendant does not require a computer—in fact, not even a calculator.

When tested against a real data set, this frugal model performed as well as statistical models that used a much larger number of variables. The frugal model did better than virtually all human bail judges did in predicting flight risk.

The same frugal approach, using up to five features weighted by small whole numbers (between –3 and +3), was applied to tasks as varied as determining the severity of a tumor from mammographic data, diagnosing heart disease, and predicting credit risk. In all these tasks, the frugal rule did as well as more complex regression models did (though generally not as well as machine learning did).

In another demonstration of the power of simple rules, a separate team of researchers studied a similar but distinct judicial problem: recidivism prediction. Using only two inputs, they were able to match the validity of an existing tool that uses 137 variables to assess a defendant's risk level. Not surprisingly, these two predictors (age and the number of previous convictions) are closely related to the two factors used in the bail model, and their association with criminal behavior is well documented.

The appeal of frugal rules is that they are transparent and easy to apply. Moreover, these advantages are obtained at relatively little cost in accuracy relative to more complex models.

More Complexity: Toward Machine Learning

For the second part of our journey, let us now travel in the opposite direction on the spectrum of sophistication. What if we could use many more predictors, gather much more data about each of them, spot relationship patterns that no human could detect, and model these patterns to achieve better prediction? This, in essence, is the promise of AI.

Very large data sets are essential for sophisticated analyses, and the increasing availability of such data sets is one of the main causes of the rapid progress of AI in recent years. For example, large data sets make it possible to deal mechanically with *broken-leg exceptions.* This somewhat cryptic phrase goes back to an example that Meehl imagined: Consider a model that was designed to predict the probability that people will go to the movies tonight. Regardless of your confidence in the model, if you happen to know that a particular person just broke a leg, you probably know better than the model what their evening will look like.

When using simple models, the broken-leg principle holds an important lesson for decision makers: it tells them when to override the model and when not to. If you have decisive information that the model could not take into consideration, there is a true broken leg, and you should override the model's recommendation. On the other hand, you will sometimes disagree with a model's recommendation even if you lack such private information. In those cases, your temptation to override the model reflects a personal pattern you are applying to the same predictors. Since this personal pattern is highly likely to be invalid, you should refrain from overriding the model; your intervention is likely to make the prediction less accurate.

One of the reasons for the success of machine-learning models in prediction tasks is that they are capable of discovering such broken legs — many more than humans can think of. Given a vast amount of data about a vast number of cases, a model tracking the behavior of moviegoers could actually learn, for example, that people who have visited the hospital on their regular movie day are unlikely to see a film that evening. Improving predictions of rare events in this way reduces the need for human supervision.

What AI does involves no magic and no understanding; it is mere pattern finding. While we must admire the power of machine learning, we should remember that it will probably take some time for an AI to understand *why* a person who has broken a leg will miss movie night.

An Example: Better Bail Decisions

At about the same time that the previously mentioned team of researchers applied simple rules to the problem of bail decisions, another team, led by Sendhil Mullainathan, trained sophisticated AI models to perform the same task. The AI team had access to a bigger set of data — 758,027 bail decisions. For each case, the team had access to information also available to the judge: the defendant's current offense, rap sheet, and prior failures to appear. Except for age, no other demographic information was used to train the algorithm. The researchers also knew, for each case, whether the defendant was released and, if so, whether the individual failed to appear in court or was rearrested. (Of the defendants, 74% were released, and of these, 15% failed to appear in court and 26% were rearrested.) With this data, the researchers trained a machine-learning algorithm and evaluated its performance. Since the model was built through machine learning, it was not restricted to linear combinations. If it detected a more complex regularity in the data, it could use this pattern to improve its predictions.

The model was designed to produce a prediction of flight risk quantified as a numerical score, rather than a bail/no-bail decision. This approach recognizes that the maximum acceptable risk threshold, that is, the level of risk above which a defendant should be denied bail, requires an evaluative judgment that a model cannot make. However, the researchers calculated that, no matter where the risk threshold is set, using their model's predictive score would result in improvements over the performance of human judges. If the risk threshold is set so that the number of people who are denied bail remains the same as when the judges decide, Mullainathan's team calculated, crime rates could be reduced by up to 24%, because the people behind bars would be the ones most likely to recidivate.

Conversely, if the risk threshold is set to reduce the number of people denied bail as much as possible without increasing crime, the researchers calculated that the number of people detained could be reduced by up to 42%. In other words, the machine-learning model performs much better than human judges do at predicting which defendants are high risks.

The model built by machine learning was also far more successful than linear models that used the same information. The reason is intriguing: "The machine-learning algorithm finds significant signal in combinations of variables that might otherwise be missed." The algorithm's ability to find patterns easily missed by other methods is especially pronounced for the defendants whom the algorithm classifies as highest risk. In other words, some patterns in the data, though rare, strongly predict high risk. This finding — that the algorithm picks up rare but decisive patterns — brings us back to the concept of broken legs.

The researchers also used the algorithm to build a model of each judge, analogous to the model of the judge we described in chapter 9 (but not restricted to simple linear combinations). Applying these models to the entire set of data enabled the team to simulate the decisions judges would have made if they had seen the same cases, and to compare the decisions. The results indicated considerable system noise in bail decisions. Some of it is level noise: when judges are sorted by leniency, the most lenient quintile (that is, the 20% of judges who have the highest release rates) released 83% of the defendants, whereas the least lenient quintile of judges released only 61%. Judges also have very different patterns of judgments about which defendants are higher flight risks. A defendant who is seen as a low flight risk by one judge can be considered a high flight risk by another judge, who is not stricter in general. These results offer clear evidence of pattern noise. A more detailed analysis revealed that differences between cases accounted for 67% of the variance, and system noise for 33%. System noise included some level noise, i.e., differences in average severity, but most of it (79%) was pattern noise.

Finally, and fortunately, the greater accuracy of the machine-learning program does not come at the expense of other identifiable goals that the judges might have pursued — notably, racial fairness. In theory, although the algorithm uses no racial data, the program might inadvertently aggravate racial disparities. These disparities could arise if the model used predictors that are highly correlated with race (such as zip code) or if the source of the data on which the algorithm is trained is biased. If, for instance, the number of past arrests is used as a predictor, and if past arrests are affected by racial discrimination, then the resulting algorithm will discriminate as well.

While this sort of discrimination is certainly a risk in principle, the decisions of this algorithm are in important respects less racially biased than those of the judges, not more. For instance, if the risk threshold is set to achieve the same crime rate as the judges' decisions did, then the algorithm jails 41% fewer people of color. Similar results are found in other scenarios: the gains in accuracy need not exacerbate racial disparities — and as the research team also showed, the algorithm can easily be instructed to reduce them.

Another study in a different domain illustrates how algorithms can simultaneously increase accuracy and reduce discrimination. Bo Cowgill, a professor at Columbia Business School, studied the recruitment of software engineers at a large tech company. Instead of using (human) résumé screeners to select who would get an interview, Cowgill developed a machine-learning algorithm to screen the résumés of candidates and trained it on more than three hundred thousand submissions that the company had received and evaluated. Candidates selected by the algorithm were 14% more likely than those selected by humans to receive a job offer after interviews. When the candidates received offers, the algorithm group was 18% more likely than the human-selected group to accept them. The algorithm also picked a more diverse group of candidates, in terms of race, gender, and other metrics; it was much more likely to select "nontraditional" candidates, such as those who did not graduate from an elite school, those who lacked prior work experience, and those who did not have a referral. Human beings tended to favor résumés that checked all the boxes of the "typical" profile for a software engineer, but the algorithm gave each relevant predictor its proper weight.

To be clear, these examples do not prove that algorithms are always fair, unbiased, or nondiscriminatory. A familiar example is an algorithm that is supposed to predict the success of job candidates, but is actually trained on a sample of past promotion decisions. Of course, such an algorithm will replicate all the human biases in past promotion decisions.

It is possible, and perhaps too easy, to build an algorithm that perpetuates racial or gender disparities, and there have been many reported cases of algorithms that did just that. The visibility of these cases explains the growing concern about bias in algorithmic decision making. Before drawing general conclusions about algorithms, however, we should remember that some algorithms are not only more accurate than human judges but also fairer.

Why Don't We Use Rules More Often?

To summarize this short tour of mechanical decision making, we review two reasons for the superiority of rules of all kinds over human judgment. First, as described in chapter 9, all mechanical prediction techniques, not just the most recent and more sophisticated ones, represent significant improvements on human judgment. The combination of personal patterns and occasion noise weighs so heavily on the quality of human judgment that simplicity and noiselessness are sizable advantages. Simple rules that are merely sensible typically do better than human judgment.

Second, the data is sometimes rich enough for sophisticated AI techniques to detect valid patterns and go well beyond the predictive power of a simple model. When AI succeeds in this way, the advantage of these models over human judgment is not just the absence of noise but also the ability to exploit much more information.

Given these advantages and the massive amount of evidence

supporting them, it is worth asking why algorithms are not used much more extensively for the types of professional judgments we discuss in this book. For all the spirited talk about algorithms and machine learning, and despite important exceptions in particular fields, their use remains limited. Many experts ignore the clinical-versus-mechanical debate, preferring to trust their judgment. They have faith in their intuitions and doubt that machines could do better. They regard the idea of algorithmic decision making as dehumanizing and as an abdication of their responsibility.

The use of algorithms in medical diagnosis, for instance, is not yet routine, notwithstanding impressive advances. Few organizations use algorithms in their hiring and promotion decisions. Hollywood studio executives green-light movies on the basis of their judgment and experience, not according to a formula. Book publishers do the same thing. And if the tale of the statistics-obsessed Oakland Athletics baseball team, as told in Michael Lewis's bestseller *Moneyball*, has made such an impression, it is precisely because algorithmic rigor had long been the exception, not the rule, in the decision-making process of sports teams. Even today, coaches, managers, and people who work with them often trust their gut and insist that statistical analysis cannot possibly replace good judgment.

In a 1996 article, Meehl and a coauthor listed (and rebutted) no fewer than seventeen types of objections that psychiatrists, physicians, judges, and other professionals had to mechanical judgment. The authors concluded that the resistance of clinicians can be explained by a combination of sociopsychological factors, including their "fear of technological unemployment," "poor education," and a "general dislike of computers."

Since then, researchers have identified additional factors that contribute to this resistance. We do not aim to offer a full review of that research here. Our goal in this book is to offer suggestions for the improvement of human judgment, not to argue for the "displacement of people by machines," as Judge Frankel would have put it.

But some findings about what drives human resistance to

mechanical prediction are relevant to our discussion of human judgment. One key insight has emerged from recent research: people are not systematically suspicious of algorithms. When given a choice between taking advice from a human and an algorithm, for instance, they often prefer the algorithm. Resistance to algorithms, or *algorithm aversion*, does not always manifest itself in a blanket refusal to adopt new decision support tools. More often, people are willing to give an algorithm a chance but stop trusting it as soon as they see that it makes mistakes.

On one level, this reaction seems sensible: why bother with an algorithm you can't trust? As humans, we are keenly aware that we make mistakes, but that is a privilege we are not prepared to share. We expect machines to be perfect. If this expectation is violated, we discard them.

Because of this intuitive expectation, however, people are likely to distrust algorithms and keep using their judgment, even when this choice produces demonstrably inferior results. This attitude is deeply rooted and unlikely to change until near-perfect predictive accuracy can be achieved.

Fortunately, much of what makes rules and algorithms better can be replicated in human judgment. We cannot hope to use information as efficiently as an AI model does, but we can strive to emulate the simplicity and noiselessness of simple models. To the extent that we can adopt methods that reduce system noise, we should see improvements in the quality of predictive judgments. How to improve our judgments is the main theme of part 5.

Speaking of Rules and Algorithms

"When there is a lot of data, machine-learning algorithms will do better than humans and better than simple models. But even the simplest rules and algorithms have big advantages over human judges: they are free of noise, and they do not attempt to apply complex, usually invalid insights about the predictors."

"Since we lack data about the outcome we must predict, why don't we use an equal-weight model? It will do almost as well as a proper model, and will surely do better than case-by-case human judgment."

"You disagree with the model's forecast. I get it. But is there a broken leg here, or do you just dislike the prediction?"

"The algorithm makes mistakes, of course. But if human judges make even more mistakes, whom should we trust?"

CHAPTER 11

Objective Ignorance

We have often had the experience of sharing with audiences of executives the material of the last two chapters, with its sobering findings about the limited achievements of human judgment. The message we aim to convey has been around for more than half a century, and we suspect that few decision makers have avoided exposure to it. But they are certainly able to resist it.

Some of the executives in our audiences tell us proudly that they trust their gut more than any amount of analysis. Many others are less blunt but share the same view. Research in managerial decision making has shown that executives, especially the more senior and experienced ones, resort extensively to something variously called *intuition, gut feel,* or, simply, *judgment* (used in a different sense from the one we use in this book).

In short, decision makers like to listen to their gut, and most seem happy with what they hear. Which raises a question: what, exactly, do these people, who are blessed with the combination of authority and great self-confidence, hear from their gut?

One review of intuition in managerial decision making defines it as "a judgment for a given course of action that comes to mind with an aura or conviction of rightness or plausibility, but without clearly articulated reasons or justifications — essentially 'knowing' but without knowing why." We propose that this sense of knowing without knowing why is actually the *internal signal* of judgment completion that we mentioned in chapter 4.

The internal signal is a self-administered reward, one people work hard (or sometimes not so hard) to achieve when they reach closure on a judgment. It is a satisfying emotional experience, a pleasing sense of coherence, in which the evidence considered and the judgment reached feel right. All the pieces of the jigsaw puzzle seem to fit. (We will see later that this sense of coherence is often bolstered by hiding or ignoring pieces of evidence that don't fit.)

What makes the internal signal important — and misleading — is that it is construed not as a feeling but as a belief. This emotional experience ("the evidence feels right") masquerades as rational confidence in the validity of one's judgment ("I know, even if I don't know why").

Confidence is no guarantee of accuracy, however, and many confident predictions turn out to be wrong. While both bias and noise contribute to prediction errors, the largest source of such errors is not the limit on how good predictive judgments *are*. It is the limit on how good they *could be*. This limit, which we call *objective ignorance*, is the focus of this chapter.

Objective Ignorance

Here is a question you can ask yourself if you find yourself making repeated predictive judgments. The question could apply to any task — picking stocks, for instance, or predicting the performance of professional athletes. But for simplicity, we'll choose the same example we used in chapter 9: the selection of job candidates. Imagine you have evaluated a hundred candidates over the years. You now have a chance to assess how good your decisions were, by comparing the evaluations you had made with the candidates' objectively assessed performance since then. If you pick a pair of candidates at random, how often would your ex ante judgment and the ex post evaluations agree? In other words, when comparing any two candidates, what is the probability that the one you thought had more potential did in fact turn out to be the higher performer?

We often informally poll groups of executives on this question. The most frequent answers are in the 75–85% range, and we suspect that these responses are constrained by modesty and by a wish not to appear boastful. Private, one-on-one conversations suggest that the true sense of confidence is often even higher.

Since you are now familiar with the percent concordant statistic, you can easily see the problem this evaluation raises. A PC of 80% roughly corresponds to a correlation of .80. This level of predictive power is rarely achieved in the real world. In the field of personnel selection, a recent review found that the performance of human judges does not come close to this number. On average, they achieve a predictive correlation of .28 (PC = 59%).

If you consider the challenge of personnel selection, the disappointing results are not that surprising. A person who starts a new job today will encounter many challenges and opportunities, and chance will intervene to change the direction of her life in many ways. She may encounter a supervisor who believes in her, creates opportunities, promotes her work, and builds her self-confidence and motivation. She may also be less lucky and, through no fault of her own, start her career with a demoralizing failure. In her personal life, too, there may be events that affect her job performance. None of these events and circumstances can be predicted today — not by you, not by anyone else, and not by the best predictive model in the world. This intractable uncertainty includes everything that cannot be known at this time about the outcome that you are trying to predict.

Furthermore, much about the candidates is in principle knowable but is not known when you make your judgment. For our purposes, it does not matter whether these gaps in knowledge come from the lack of sufficiently predictive tests, from your decision that the cost of acquiring more information was not justified, or from your own negligence in fact-finding. One way or the other, you are in a state of less-than-perfect information.

Both intractable uncertainty (what cannot possibly be known) and imperfect information (what could be known but isn't) make perfect prediction impossible. These unknowns are not problems of bias or noise in your judgment; they are objective characteristics of the task. This objective ignorance of important unknowns severely limits achievable accuracy. We take a terminological liberty here, replacing the commonly used *uncertainty* with *ignorance*. This term helps limit the risk of confusion between uncertainty, which is about the world and the future, and noise, which is variability in judgments that should be identical.

There is more information (and less objective ignorance) in some situations than in others. Most professional judgments are pretty good. With respect to many illnesses, doctors' predictions are excellent, and for many legal disputes, lawyers can tell you, with great accuracy, how judges are likely to rule.

In general, however, you can safely expect that people who engage in predictive tasks will underestimate their objective ignorance. Overconfidence is one of the best-documented cognitive biases. In particular, judgments of one's ability to make precise predictions, even from limited information, are notoriously overconfident. What we said of noise in predictive judgments can also be said of objective ignorance: wherever there is prediction, there is ignorance, and more of it than you think.

Overconfident Pundits

A good friend of ours, the psychologist Philip Tetlock, is armed with a fierce commitment to truth and a mischievous sense of humor. In 2005, he published a book titled *Expert Political Judgment*. Despite that neutral-sounding title, the book amounted to a devastating attack on the ability of experts to make accurate predictions about political events.

Tetlock studied the predictions of almost three hundred experts: prominent journalists, respected academics, and high-level advisers to national leaders. He asked whether their political, economic, and social forecasts came true. The research spanned two decades; to find out whether long-term predictions are right, you need patience.

Tetlock's key finding was that in their predictions about major political events, the supposed experts are stunningly unimpressive. The book became famous for its arresting punch line: "The average expert was roughly as accurate as a dart-throwing chimpanzee." A more precise statement of the book's message was that experts who make a living "commenting or offering advice on political and economic trends" were not "better than journalists or attentive readers of the *New York Times* in 'reading' emerging situations." For sure, the experts told great stories. They could analyze a situation, paint a compelling picture of how it would evolve, and refute, with great confidence, the objections of those who disagreed with them in television studios. But did they actually know what would happen? Hardly.

Tetlock reached this conclusion by cutting through the storytelling. For each issue, he asked the experts to assign probabilities to three possible outcomes: status quo, more of something, or less of it. A dart-throwing chimp would "choose" each of these outcomes with the same probability — one-third — regardless of reality. Tetlock's experts barely exceeded this very low standard. On average, they assigned slightly higher probabilities to events that occurred than to those that did not, but the most salient feature of their performance was their excessive confidence in their predictions. Pundits blessed with clear theories about how the world works were the most confident and the least accurate.

Tetlock's findings suggest that detailed long-term predictions about specific events are simply impossible. The world is a messy place, where minor events can have large consequences. For example, consider the fact that at the instant of conception, there was an even chance that every significant figure in history (and also the insignificant ones) would be born with a different gender. Unforeseeable events are bound to occur, and the consequences of these unforeseeable events are also unforeseeable. As a result, objective ignorance accumulates steadily the further you look into the future. The limit on expert political judgment is set not by the cognitive limitation of forecasters but by their intractable objective ignorance of the future.

Our conclusion, then, is that pundits should not be blamed for the failures of their distant predictions. They do, however, deserve some criticism for attempting an impossible task and for believing they can succeed in it.

Some years after his shocking discovery of the futility of much long-term forecasting, Tetlock teamed up with his spouse, Barbara Mellers, to study how well people do when asked to forecast world events in the relatively short term — usually less than a year. The team discovered that short-term forecasting is difficult but not impossible, and that some people, whom Tetlock and Mellers called *superforecasters*, are consistently better at it than most others, including professionals in the intelligence community. In the terms we use here, their new findings are compatible with the notion that objective ignorance increases as we look further into the future. We return to superforecasters in chapter 21.

Poor Judges and Barely Better Models

Tetlock's early research demonstrated people's general inability to do well in long-term political forecasting. Finding even one person with a clear crystal ball would have changed the conclusions completely. A task can be deemed impossible only after many credible actors have tried their hand and failed. As we have shown that mechanical aggregation of information is often superior to human judgment, the predictive accuracy of rules and algorithms provides a better test of how intrinsically predictable, or unpredictable, outcomes are.

The previous chapters may have given you the impression that algorithms are crushingly superior to predictive judgments. That impression, however, would be misleading. Models are consistently better than people, but not much better. There is essentially no evidence of situations in which people do very poorly and models do very well with the same information.

In chapter 9, we mentioned a review of 136 studies that demonstrated the superiority of mechanical aggregation over clinical judgment. While the evidence of that superiority is indeed "massive and consistent," the performance gap is not large. Ninety-three of the studies in the review focused on binary decisions and measured the "hit rate" of clinicians and formulas. In the median study, clinicians were right 68% of the time, formulas 73% of the time. A smaller subset of 35 studies used the correlation coefficient as a measure of accuracy. In these studies, clinicians achieved a median correlation with the outcome of .32 (PC = 60%), while formulas achieved .56 (PC = 69%). On both metrics, formulas are consistently better than clinicians, but the limited validity of the mechanical predictions remains striking. The performance of models does not change the picture of a fairly low ceiling of predictability.

What about artificial intelligence? As we noted, AI often performs better than simpler models do. In most applications, however, its performance remains far from perfect. Consider, for instance, the bail-prediction algorithm we discussed in chapter 10. We noted that, keeping constant the number of people who are denied bail, the algorithm could reduce crime rates by up to 24%. This is an impressive improvement on the predictions of human bail judges, but if the algorithm could predict with perfect accuracy which defendants will reoffend, it could reduce the crime rate much more. The supernatural predictions of future crimes in *Minority Report* are science fiction for a reason: there is a large amount of objective ignorance in the prediction of human behavior.

Another study, led by Sendhil Mullainathan and Ziad Obermeyer, modeled the diagnosis of heart attacks. When patients present signs of a possible heart attack, emergency room physicians must decide whether to prescribe additional tests. In principle, patients should be tested only when the risk of a heart attack is high enough: because testing is not just costly but also invasive and risky, it is undesirable for low-risk patients. Thus a physician's decision to prescribe tests requires an assessment of heart attack risk. The researchers built an AI model to make this assessment. The model uses more than twenty-four hundred variables and is based on a large sample of cases (4.4 million Medicare visits by 1.6 million patients). With this amount of data, the model probably approaches the limits of objective ignorance.

Not surprisingly, the AI model's accuracy is distinctly superior to that of physicians. To evaluate the performance of the model, consider the patients whom the model placed in the highest decile of risk. When these patients were tested, 30% of them turned out to have had a heart attack, whereas 9.3% of the patients in the middle of the risk distribution had experienced one. This level of discrimination is impressive, but it is also far from perfect. We can reasonably conclude that the performance of the physicians is limited at least as much by the constraints of objective ignorance as by the imperfections of their judgments.

The Denial of Ignorance

By insisting on the impossibility of perfect prediction, we might seem to be stating the obvious. Admittedly, asserting that the future is unpredictable is hardly a conceptual breakthrough. However, the obviousness of this fact is matched only by the regularity with which it is ignored, as the consistent findings about predictive overconfidence demonstrate.

The prevalence of overconfidence sheds new light on our informal poll of gut-trusting decision makers. We have noted that people often mistake their subjective sense of confidence for an indication of predictive validity. After you reviewed the evidence in chapter 9 about Nathalie and Monica, for instance, the internal signal you felt when you reached a coherent judgment gave you confidence that Nathalie was the stronger candidate. If you were confident in that prediction, however, you fell for the illusion of validity: the accuracy you can achieve with the information you were given is quite low.

People who believe themselves capable of an impossibly high level of predictive accuracy are not just overconfident. They don't merely deny the risk of noise and bias in their judgments. Nor do they simply deem themselves superior to other mortals. They also believe in the predictability of events that are in fact unpredictable, implicitly denying the reality of uncertainty. In the terms we have used here, this attitude amounts to a *denial of ignorance*.

The denial of ignorance adds an answer to the puzzle that baffled Meehl and his followers: why his message has remained largely unheeded, and why decision makers continue to rely on their intuition. When they listen to their gut, decision makers hear the internal signal and feel the emotional reward it brings. This internal signal that a good judgment has been reached is the voice of confidence, of "knowing without knowing why." But an objective assessment of the evidence's true predictive power will rarely justify that level of confidence.

Giving up the emotional reward of intuitive certainty is not easy. Tellingly, leaders say they are especially likely to resort to intuitive decision making in situations that they perceive as highly uncertain. When the facts deny them the sense of understanding and confidence they crave, they turn to their intuition to provide it. The denial of ignorance is all the more tempting when ignorance is vast.

The denial of ignorance also explains another puzzle. When faced with the evidence we have presented here, many leaders draw a seemingly paradoxical conclusion. Their gut-based decisions may not be perfect, they argue, but if the more systematic alternatives are also far from perfect, they are not worth adopting. Recall, for instance, that the average correlation between the ratings of human judges and employee performance is .28 (PC = 59%). According to the same study, and consistent with the evidence we reviewed, mechanical prediction might do better, but not by much: its predictive accuracy is .44 (PC = 65%). An executive might ask: why bother?

The answer is that in something as important as decisions about whom to hire, this increase in validity has a great deal of value. The same executives routinely make significant changes in their ways of working to capture gains that are not nearly as large. Rationally, they understand that success can never be guaranteed and that a higher chance of success is what they are striving for in their decisions. They also understand probability. None of them would buy a lottery ticket that had a 59% chance of winning if they could buy, for the same price, one with a 65% chance.

The challenge is that the "price" in this situation is not the same. Intuitive judgment comes with its reward, the internal signal. People are prepared to trust an algorithm that achieves a very high level of accuracy because it gives them a sense of certainty that matches or exceeds that provided by the internal signal. But giving up the emotional reward of the internal signal is a high price to pay when the alternative is some sort of mechanical process that does not even claim high validity.

This observation has an important implication for the improvement of judgment. Despite all the evidence in favor of mechanical and algorithmic prediction methods, and despite the rational calculus that clearly shows the value of incremental improvements in predictive accuracy, many decision makers will reject decision-making approaches that deprive them of the ability to exercise their intuition. As long as algorithms are not nearly perfect — and, in many domains, objective ignorance dictates that they will never be — human judgment will not be replaced. That is why it must be improved.

Speaking of Objective Ignorance

"Wherever there is prediction, there is ignorance, and probably more of it than we think. Have we checked whether the experts we trust are more accurate than dart-throwing chimpanzees?"

"When you trust your gut because of an internal signal, not because of anything you really know, you are in denial of your objective ignorance."

"Models do better than people, but not by much. Mostly, we find mediocre human judgments and slightly better models. Still, better is good, and models are better."

"We may never be comfortable using a model to make these decisions — we just need the internal signal to have enough confidence. So let's make sure we have the best possible decision process."

CHAPTER 12

The Valley of the Normal

We now turn to a broader question: how do we achieve comfort in a world in which many problems are easy but many others are dominated by objective ignorance? After all, where objective ignorance is severe, we should, after a while, become aware of the futility of crystal balls in human affairs. But that is not our usual experience of the world. Instead, as the previous chapter suggested, we maintain an unchastened willingness to make bold predictions about the future from little useful information. In this chapter, we address the prevalent and misguided sense that events that could not have been predicted can nevertheless be understood.

What does this belief really mean? We raise that question in two contexts: the conduct of social science and the experience of the events of daily life.

Predicting Life Trajectories

In 2020, a group of 112 researchers, led by Sara McLanahan and Matthew Salganik, both professors of sociology at Princeton University, published an unusual article in the *Proceedings of the National*

Academy of Sciences. The researchers aimed to figure out how much social scientists actually understand about what will happen in the life trajectories of socially fragile families. Knowing what they know, how well can social scientists predict events in a family's life? Specifically, what level of accuracy can experts achieve when predicting life events, using the information that sociologists normally collect and apply in their research? In our terms, the aim of the study was to measure the level of objective ignorance that remains in these life events after sociologists have done their work.

The authors drew material from the Fragile Families and Child Wellbeing Study, a large-scale longitudinal investigation of children who were followed from birth to fifteen years of age. The huge database contains several thousand items of information about the families of almost five thousand children, most of them born to unmarried parents in large US cities. The data covers topics such as the education and employment of the child's grandparents, details about the health of all family members, indices of economic and social status, answers to multiple questionnaires, and tests of cognitive aptitude and personality. This is an extraordinary wealth of information, and social scientists have made good use of it: more than 750 scientific articles have been written based on data from the Fragile Families study. Many of these papers used the background data about children and their families to explain life outcomes such as high school grades and criminal record.

The study led by the Princeton team focused on the predictability of six outcomes observed when the child was fifteen years old, including the occurrence of a recent eviction, the child's GPA, and a general measure of the household's material circumstances. The organizers used what they called the "common task method." They invited teams of researchers to compete in generating accurate predictions of the six chosen outcomes, using the mass of data available about each family in the Fragile Families study. This type of challenge is novel in the social sciences but common in computer science, where teams are often invited to compete in tasks such as machine translation of a standard set of texts or detection of an animal in a large set of photographs. The achievement of the winning team in these competitions defines the state of the art at a point in time, which is always exceeded in the next competition. In a social science prediction task, where rapid improvement is not expected, it is reasonable to use the most accurate prediction achieved in the competition as a measure of the predictability of the outcome from these data — in other words, the residual level of objective ignorance.

The challenge evoked considerable interest among researchers. The final report presented results from 160 highly qualified teams drawn from a much larger international pool of applicants. Most of the selected competitors described themselves as data scientists and used machine learning.

In the first stage of the competition, the participating teams had access to all the data for half of the total sample; the data included the six outcomes. They used this "training data" to train a predictive algorithm. Their algorithms were then applied to a holdout sample of families that had not been used to train the algorithm. The researchers measured accuracy using MSE: the prediction error for each case was the square of the difference between the real outcome and the algorithm's prediction.

How good were the winning models? The sophisticated machine-learning algorithms trained on a large data set did, of course, outperform the predictions of simple linear models (and would, by extension, out-predict human judges). But the improvement the AI models delivered over a very simple model was slight, and their predictive accuracy remained disappointingly low. When predicting evictions, the best model achieved a correlation of .22 (PC = 57%). Similar results were found for other single-event outcomes, such as whether the primary caregiver had been laid off or had been in job training and how the child would score on a self-reported measure of "grit," a personality trait that combines perseverance and passion for a particular goal. For these, the correlations fell between .17 and .24 (PC = 55 – 58%).

Two of the six target outcomes were aggregates, which were much more predictable. The predictive correlations were .44 (PC = 65%) with the child's GPA, and .48 (PC = 66%) with a summary measure of material hardship during the preceding twelve months. This measure was based on eleven questions, including "Were you ever hungry?" and "Was your telephone service canceled?" Aggregate measures are widely known to be both more predictive and more predictable than are measures of single outcomes. The main conclusion of the challenge is that a large mass of predictive information does not suffice for the prediction of single events in people's lives — and even the prediction of aggregates is quite limited.

The results observed in this research are typical, and many correlations that social scientists report fall in this range. An extensive review of research in social psychology, covering 25,000 studies and involving 8 million subjects over one hundred years, concluded that "social psychological effects typically yield a value of r [correlation coefficient] equal to .21." Much higher correlations, like the .60 we mentioned earlier between adult height and foot size, are common for physical measurements but are very rare in the social sciences. A review of 708 studies in the behavioral and cognitive sciences found that only 3% of reported correlations were .50 or more.

Such low correlation coefficients may come as a surprise if you are used to reading about findings that are presented as "statistically significant" or even "highly significant." Statistical terms are often misleading to the lay reader, and "significant" may be the worst example of this. When a finding is described as "significant," we should not conclude that the effect it describes is a strong one. It simply means that the finding is unlikely to be the product of chance alone. With a sufficiently large sample, a correlation can be at once very "significant" and too small to be worth discussing.

The limited predictability of single outcomes in the challenge study carries a troubling message about the difference between understanding and prediction. The Fragile Families study is considered a treasure trove of social science, and as we have seen, its data has been used in a vast body of research. The scholars who produced that research surely felt that their work advanced the understanding of the lives of fragile families. Unfortunately, this sense of progress was not matched by an ability to make granular predictions about individual events in individual lives. The introductory abstract of the multiauthored report on the Fragile Families challenge contained a stark admonition: "Researchers must reconcile the idea that they understand life trajectories with the fact that none of the predictions were very accurate."

Understanding and Prediction

The logic behind this pessimistic conclusion requires some elaboration. When the authors of the Fragile Families challenge equate understanding with prediction (or the absence of one with the absence of the other), they use the term *understanding* in a specific sense. There are other meanings of the word: if you say you understand a mathematical concept or you understand what love is, you are probably not suggesting an ability to make any specific predictions.

However, in the discourse of social science, and in most everyday conversations, a claim to understand something is a claim to understand what *causes* that thing. The sociologists who collected and studied the thousands of variables in the Fragile Families study were looking for the causes of the outcomes they observed. Physicians who understand what ails a patient are claiming that the pathology they have diagnosed is the cause of the symptoms they have observed. To understand is to describe a causal chain. The ability to make a prediction is a measure of whether such a causal chain has indeed been identified. And correlation, the measure of predictive accuracy, is a measure of how much causation we can explain.

This last statement may surprise you if you have been exposed to elementary statistics and remember the often-repeated warning that "correlation does not imply causation." Consider, for instance, the correlation between shoe size and mathematical ability in children: obviously, one variable does not cause the other. The correlation arises from the fact that both shoe size and math knowledge increase with a child's age. The correlation is real and supports a prediction: if you know that a child has large feet, you should predict a higher math level than you would if you know that the child has small feet. But you should not infer a causal link from this correlation.

We must, however, remember that while correlation does not imply causation, causation *does* imply correlation. Where there is a causal link, we should find a correlation. If you find no correlation between age and shoe size among adults, then you can safely conclude that after the end of adolescence, age does not make feet grow larger and that you have to look elsewhere for the causes of differences in shoe size.

In short, wherever there is causality, there is correlation. It follows that where there is causality, we should be able to predict — and correlation, the accuracy of this prediction, is a measure of how much causality we understand. Hence the conclusion of the Princeton researchers is this: the extent to which sociologists can predict events like evictions, as measured by a correlation of .22, is an indication of how much — or how little — they understand about the life trajectories of these families. Objective ignorance sets a ceiling not only on our predictions but also on our understanding.

What, then, do most professionals mean when they confidently claim to understand their field? How can they make pronouncements about what causes the phenomena they are observing and offer confident predictions about them? In short, why do professionals — and why do we all — seem to underestimate our objective ignorance of the world?

Causal Thinking

If, as you read the first part of this chapter, you asked yourself what drives evictions and other life outcomes among fragile families, you engaged in the same sort of thinking as that of the researchers whose efforts we described. You applied *statistical thinking:* you were concerned with ensembles, such as the population of fragile families, and with the statistics that describe them, including averages, variances, correlations, and so on. You were not focused on individual cases.

A different mode of thinking, which comes more naturally to our minds, will be called here *causal thinking*. Causal thinking creates stories in which specific events, people, and objects affect one another. To experience causal thinking, picture yourself as a social worker who follows the cases of many underprivileged families. You have just heard that one of these families, the Joneses, has been evicted. Your reaction to this event is informed by what you know about the Joneses. As it happens, Jessica Jones, the family's breadwinner, was laid off a few months ago. She could not find another job, and since then, she has been unable to pay the rent in full. She made partial payments, pleaded with the building manager several times, and even asked you to intervene (you did, but he remained unmoved). Given this context, the Joneses' eviction is sad but not surprising. It feels, in fact, like the logical end of a chain of events, the inevitable denouement of a foreordained tragedy.

When we give in to this feeling of inevitability, we lose sight of how easily things could have been different — how, at each fork in the road, fate could have taken a different path. Jessica could have kept her job. She could have quickly found another one. A relative could have come to her aid. You, the social worker, could have been a more effective advocate. The building manager could have been more understanding and allowed the family a few weeks of respite, making it possible for Jessica to find a job and catch up with the rent.

These alternate narratives are as unsurprising as the main one — if the end is known. Whatever the outcome (eviction or not), once it has happened, causal thinking makes it feel entirely explainable, indeed predictable.

Understanding in the Valley of the Normal

There is a psychological explanation for this observation. Some events are surprising: a deadly pandemic, an attack on the Twin

Towers, a star hedge fund that turns out to be a Ponzi scheme. In our personal lives as well, there are occasional shocks: falling in love with a stranger, the sudden death of a young sibling, an unexpected inheritance. Other events are actively expected, like a second-grader's return from school at the appointed time.

But most human experience falls between these two extremes. We are sometimes in a state in which we actively expect a specific event, and we are sometimes surprised. But most things take place in the broad valley of the normal, where events are neither entirely expected nor especially surprising. At this moment, for example, you have no specific expectation of what is coming in the next paragraph. You would be surprised to find we suddenly switched to Turkish, but there is a wide range of things we could say without shocking you.

In the valley of the normal, events unfold just like the Joneses' eviction: they appear normal in hindsight, although they were not expected, and although we could not have predicted them. This is because the process of understanding reality is backward-looking. An occurrence that was not actively anticipated (the eviction of the Jones family) triggers a search of memory for a candidate cause (the tough job market, the inflexible manager). The search stops when a good narrative is found. Given the opposite outcome, the search would have produced equally compelling causes (Jessica Jones's tenacity, the understanding manager).

As these examples illustrate, many events in a normal story are literally self-explanatory. You may have noted that the building manager in the two versions of the eviction story was not really the same person: the first one was unsympathetic, the second was kind. But your only clue to the manager's character was the behavior that his character exhibits. Given what we now know about him, his behavior appears coherent. It is the occurrence of the event that tells you its cause.

When you explain an unexpected but unsurprising outcome in this way, the destination that is eventually reached always makes sense. This is what we mean by *understanding* a story, and this is what makes reality appear predictable — in hindsight. Because the event explains itself as it occurs, we are under the illusion that it could have been anticipated.

More broadly, our sense of understanding the world depends on our extraordinary ability to construct narratives that explain the events we observe. The search for causes is almost always successful because causes can be drawn from an unlimited reservoir of facts and beliefs about the world. As anyone who listens to the evening news knows, for example, few large movements of the stock market remain unexplained. The same news flow can "explain" either a fall of the indices (nervous investors are worried about the news!) or a rise (sanguine investors remain optimistic!).

When the search for an obvious cause fails, our first resort is to produce an explanation by filling a blank in our model of the world. This is how we infer a fact we had not known before (for instance, that the manager was an unusually kind person). Only when our model of the world cannot be tweaked to generate the outcome do we tag this outcome as surprising and start to search for a more elaborate account of it. Genuine surprise occurs only when routine hindsight fails.

This continuous causal interpretation of reality is how we "understand" the world. Our sense of understanding life as it unfolds consists of the steady flow of hindsight in the valley of the normal. This sense is fundamentally causal: new events, once known, eliminate alternatives, and the narrative leaves little room for uncertainty. As we know from classic research on hindsight, even when subjective uncertainty does exist for a while, memories of it are largely erased when the uncertainty is resolved.

Inside and Outside

We have contrasted two ways of thinking about events: statistical and causal. The causal mode saves us much effortful thinking by categorizing events in real time as normal or abnormal. Abnormal events quickly mobilize costly effort in a search for relevant information, both in the environment and in memory. Active expectation — attentively waiting for something to happen — also demands effort. In contrast, the flow of events in the valley of the normal requires little mental work. Your neighbor may smile as your paths cross or may appear preoccupied and just nod — neither of these events will attract much attention if both have been reasonably frequent in the past. If the smile is unusually wide or the nod unusually perfunctory, you may well find yourself searching your memory for a possible cause. Causal thinking avoids unnecessary effort while retaining the vigilance needed to detect abnormal events.

In contrast, statistical thinking is effortful. It requires the attention resources that only System 2, the mode of thinking associated with slow, deliberate thought, can bring to bear. Beyond an elementary level, statistical thinking also demands specialized training. This type of thinking begins with ensembles and considers individual cases as instances of broader categories. The eviction of the Joneses is not seen as resulting from a chain of specific events but is viewed as a statistically likely (or unlikely) outcome, given prior observations of cases that share predictive characteristics with the Joneses.

The distinction between these two views is a recurring theme of this book. Relying on causal thinking about a single case is a source of predictable errors. Taking the statistical view, which we will also call the *outside view,* is a way to avoid these errors.

At this point, all we need to emphasize is that the causal mode comes much more naturally to us. Even explanations that should properly be treated as statistical are easily turned into causal narratives. Consider assertions such as "they failed because they lacked experience" or "they succeeded because they had a brilliant leader." It would be easy for you to think of counterexamples, in which inexperienced teams succeeded and brilliant leaders failed. The correlations of experience and brilliance with success are at best moderate and probably low. Yet a causal attribution is readily made. Where causality is plausible, our mind easily turns a correlation, however low, into a causal and explanatory force. Brilliant leadership is accepted as a satisfactory explanation of success, and inexperience as an explanation of failure.

The reliance on flawed explanations is perhaps inevitable, if the alternative is to give up on understanding our world. However, causal thinking and the illusion of understanding the past contribute to overconfident predictions of the future. As we will see, the preference for causal thinking also contributes to the neglect of noise as a source of error, because noise is a fundamentally statistical notion.

Causal thinking helps us make sense of a world that is far less predictable than we think. It also explains why we view the world as far more predictable than it really is. In the valley of the normal, there are no surprises and no inconsistencies. The future seems as predictable as the past. And noise is neither heard nor seen.

Speaking of the Limits of Understanding

"Correlations of about .20 (PC = 56%) are quite common in human affairs."

"Correlation does not imply causation, but causation does imply correlation."

"Most normal events are neither expected nor surprising, and they require no explanation."

"In the valley of the normal, events are neither expected nor surprising — they just explain themselves."

"We think we understand what is going on here, but could we have predicted it?"

PART IV

How Noise Happens

What is the origin of noise — and of bias? What mental mechanisms give rise to the variability of our judgments and to the shared errors that affect them? In short, what do we know about the psychology of noise? These are the questions to which we now turn.

First, we describe how some of the operations of fast, *System 1* thinking are responsible for many judgment errors. In chapter 13, we present three important judgment heuristics on which System 1 extensively relies. We show how these heuristics cause predictable, directional errors (statistical bias) as well as noise.

Chapter 14 focuses on matching — a particular operation of System 1 — and discusses the errors it can produce.

In chapter 15, we turn to an indispensable accessory in all judgments: the scale on which the judgments are made. We show that the choice of an appropriate scale is a prerequisite for good judgment and that ill-defined or inadequate scales are an important source of noise.

Chapter 16 explores the psychological source of what may be the most intriguing type of noise: the patterns of responses that different people have to different cases. Like individual personalities, these patterns are not random and are mostly stable over time, but their effects are not easily predictable.

Finally, in chapter 17, we summarize what we have learned about noise and its components. This exploration leads us to propose an answer to the puzzle we raised earlier: why is noise, despite its ubiquity, rarely considered an important problem?

CHAPTER 13

Heuristics, Biases, and Noise

This book extends half a century of research on intuitive human judgment, the so-called heuristics and biases program. The first four decades of this research program were reviewed in *Thinking, Fast and Slow*, which explored the psychological mechanisms that explain both the marvels and the flaws of intuitive thinking. The central idea of the program was that people who are asked a difficult question use simplifying operations, called *heuristics*. In general, heuristics, which are produced by fast, intuitive thinking, also known as *System 1 thinking*, are quite useful and yield adequate answers. But sometimes they lead to biases, which we have described as systematic, predictable errors of judgment.

The heuristics and biases program focused on what people have in common, not on how they differ. It showed that the processes that cause judgment errors are widely shared. Partly because of this history, people who are familiar with the notion of psychological bias often assume that it always produces *statistical bias*, a term we use in this book to mean measurements or judgments that mostly deviate from the truth in the same direction. Indeed, psychological biases create statistical bias when they are broadly shared. However, psychological biases create system noise when judges are biased in different ways, or to a different extent. Whether they cause statistical bias or noise, of course, psychological biases always create error.

Diagnosing Biases

Judgment biases are often identified by reference to a true value. There is bias in predictive judgments if errors are mostly in one direction rather than the other. For instance, when people forecast how long it will take them to complete a project, the mean of their estimates is usually much lower than the time they will actually need. This familiar psychological bias is known as the *planning fallacy.*

Often, though, there is no true value to which judgments can be compared. Given how much we stressed that statistical bias can be detected only when the true value is known, you may wonder how psychological biases can be studied when the truth is unknown. The answer is that researchers confirm a psychological bias either by observing that a factor that should not affect judgment does have a statistical effect on it, or that a factor that should affect judgment does not.

To illustrate this method, let us return to the shooting range analogy. Imagine that Teams A and B have taken their shots, and we are looking at the back of the target (figure 12). In this example, you don't know where the bull's-eye is (the true value is unknown). Therefore, you don't know how biased the two teams are relative to the center of the target. However, you are told that, in panel 1, the two teams were aiming at the same bull's-eye, and that, in panel 2, Team A was aiming at one bull's-eye and Team B at a different one.

In spite of the absence of a target, both panels provide evidence of systematic bias. In panel 1, the shots of the two teams differ, although they should be identical. This pattern resembles what you would see in an experiment in which two groups of investors read business plans that are substantively identical but printed in a different font and on a different paper. If these irrelevant details make a difference

Panel 1
Aiming at *the same* bull's-eye,
but hitting different spots

Panel 2
Aiming at *different* bull's-eyes,
but hitting the same area

FIGURE 12: *A look at the back of the target in an experiment to test for bias*

in the investors' judgment, there is psychological bias. We don't know if the investors who were impressed by the sleek font and glossy paper are too positive or if those who read the rougher version are too negative. But we know their judgments are different, although they should not be.

Panel 2 illustrates the opposite phenomenon. Since the teams were aiming at different targets, the clusters of shots should be distinct, but they are centered on the same spot. For example, imagine that two groups of people are asked the same question you were asked in chapter 4 about Michael Gambardi, but with a twist. One group is asked, as you were, to estimate the probability that Gambardi will still be in his job in two years; the other is asked to estimate the probability that he will still be in his job in three years. The two groups should reach different conclusions, because there are obviously more ways to lose your job in three years than in two. However, the evidence suggests that the probability estimates of the two groups will differ little, if at all. The answers should be clearly different, but they are not, suggesting that a factor that should influence judgments is ignored. (This psychological bias is called *scope insensitivity*.)

Systematic errors of judgment have been demonstrated in many fields, and the term *bias* is now used in many domains, including business, politics, policymaking, and law. As the word is commonly used, its meaning is broad. In addition to the cognitive definition we use here (referring to a psychological mechanism and to the error that this mechanism typically produces), the word is frequently used to suggest that someone is biased against a certain group (e.g., gender biases or racial biases). It can also mean that someone favors a particular conclusion, as when we read that someone is biased by a conflict of interest or by a political opinion. We include these types of bias in our discussion of the psychology of judgment errors because all psychological biases cause both statistical bias and noise.

There is one usage to which we strongly object. In this usage, costly failures are attributed to unspecified "bias," and acknowledgments of error are accompanied by promises to "work hard to eliminate biases in our decision making." These statements mean nothing more than "mistakes were made" and "we will try hard to do better." To be sure, some failures truly are caused by predictable errors associated with specific psychological biases, and we believe in the feasibility of interventions to reduce bias (and noise) in judgments and decisions. But blaming every undesirable outcome on biases is a worthless explanation. We recommend reserving the word *bias* for specific and identifiable errors and the mechanisms that produce them.

Substitution

To experience the heuristic process, please try your hand at answering the following question, which illustrates several essential themes of the heuristics and biases approach. As usual, you will get more from the example if you produce your own answers.

> *Bill is thirty-three years old. He is intelligent but unimaginative, compulsive, and generally lifeless. In school, he was strong in mathematics but weak in social studies and humanities.*
>
> *The following is a list of eight possibilities for Bill's current situation.*
>
> *Please go over the list and select the two that you consider* most probable.

❑ *Bill is a physician who plays poker as a hobby.*
❑ *Bill is an architect.*
❑ *Bill is an accountant.*
❑ *Bill plays jazz as a hobby.*
❑ *Bill surfs as a hobby.*
❑ *Bill is a reporter.*
❑ *Bill is an accountant who plays jazz as a hobby.*
❑ *Bill climbs mountains as a hobby.*
Now, go back over the list and select the two categories where Bill most resembles a typical person in that category. You may pick the same or different categories as before.

We are almost certain that you picked the same categories as highest in probability and in resemblance. The reason for our confidence is that multiple experiments have shown that people give identical answers to the two questions. But similarity and probability are actually quite different. For example, ask yourself, which of the following statements makes more sense?

❑ *Bill fits my idea of a person who plays jazz as a hobby.*
❑ *Bill fits my idea of an accountant who plays jazz as a hobby.*

Neither of these statements is a good fit, but one of them is clearly less awful than the other. Bill has more in common with an accountant who plays jazz as a hobby than with a person who plays jazz as a hobby. Now consider this: which of the following is more probable?

❑ *Bill plays jazz as a hobby.*
❑ *Bill is an accountant who plays jazz as a hobby.*

You may be tempted to pick the second answer, but logic won't allow it. The probability that Bill plays jazz as a hobby *must be* higher than the probability of his being a jazz-playing accountant.

Remember your Venn diagrams! If Bill is a jazz player and an accountant, he is certainly a jazz player. Adding detail to a description can only make it less probable, although it can make it more representative, and thus a better "fit," as in the present case.

The theory of judgment heuristics proposes that people will sometimes use the answer to an easier question in responding to the harder one. So, which question is more easily answered: "How similar is Bill to a typical amateur jazz player?" or "How probable is it that Bill is an amateur jazz player?" By acclamation, the similarity question is easier, which makes it likely that it was the one that people answer when asked to assess probability.

You have now experienced the essential idea of the heuristics and biases program: a heuristic for answering a difficult question is to find the answer to an easier one. The substitution of one question for the other causes predictable errors, called psychological biases.

This sort of bias is manifest in the Bill example. Errors are bound to occur when a judgment of similarity is substituted for a judgment of probability, because probability is constrained by a special logic. In particular, Venn diagrams apply only to probability, not to similarity. Hence the predictable logical error that many people make.

For another example of a neglected statistical property, recall how you thought about the Gambardi question in chapter 4. If you are like most people, your assessment of Michael Gambardi's chances of success was based entirely on what the case told you about him. You then attempted to match his description to the image of a successful CEO.

Did it occur to you to consider the probability that a randomly chosen CEO will still hold the same job two years later? Probably not. You can think of this *base-rate information* as a measure of the difficulty of surviving as a CEO. If this approach seems odd, consider how you would estimate the probability that a particular student would pass a test. Surely, the proportion of students who fail the test is relevant, as it gives you an indication of how difficult the test is. In the same manner, the base rate of CEO survival is relevant to the Gambardi problem. Both questions are examples of taking what we have called the outside view: when you take this view, you think of the student, or of Gambardi, as a member of a class of similar cases. You think statistically about the class, instead of thinking causally about the focal case.

Taking the outside view can make a large difference and prevent significant errors. A few minutes of research would reveal that estimates of CEO turnover in US companies hover around 15% annually. This statistic suggests that the average incoming CEO has a roughly 72% probability of still being around after two years. Of course, this number is only a starting point, and the specifics of Gambardi's case will affect your final estimate. But if you focused solely on what you were told about Gambardi, you neglected a key piece of information. (Full disclosure: We wrote the Gambardi case to illustrate noisy judgment; it took us weeks before we realized that it was also a prime example of the bias we describe here, which is called *base-rate neglect*. Thinking of base rates is no more automatic for the authors of this book than for anyone else.)

Substitution of one question for another is not restricted to similarity and probability. Another example is the replacement of a judgment of frequency by an impression of the ease with which instances come to mind. For example, the perception of the risk of airplane crashes or hurricanes rises briefly after well-publicized instances of such events. In theory, a judgment of risk should be based on a long-term average. In reality, recent incidents are given more weight because they come more easily to mind. Substituting a judgment of how easily examples come to mind for an assessment of frequency is known as the *availability heuristic*.

The substitution of an easy judgment for a hard one is not limited to these examples. In fact, it is very common. Answering an easier question can be thought of as a general-purpose procedure for answering a question that could stump you. Consider how we tend to answer each of the following questions by using its easier substitute:

Do I believe in climate change?
   Do I trust the people who say it exists?

Do I think this surgeon is competent?
   Does this individual speak with confidence and authority?

Will the project be completed on schedule?
   Is it on schedule now?

Is nuclear energy necessary?
   Do I recoil at the word **nuclear**?

Am I satisfied with my life as a whole?
   What is my mood right now?

Regardless of the question, substituting one question for another will lead to an answer that does not give different aspects of the evidence their appropriate weights, and incorrect weighting of the evidence inevitably results in error. For example, a full answer to a question about life satisfaction clearly requires consulting more than your current mood, but evidence suggests that mood is in fact overly weighted.

In the same manner, substituting similarity for probability leads to neglect of base rates, which are quite properly irrelevant when judging similarity. And factors such as irrelevant variations in the aesthetics of the document that presents a business plan should be given little or no weight in assessing the value of a company. Any impact they have on the judgment is likely to reflect a misweighting of the evidence and will produce error.

Conclusion Biases

At a key moment in the development of the screenplay for *Return of the Jedi*, the third Star Wars film, George Lucas, the mastermind behind the series, had a heated debate with his great collaborator Lawrence Kasdan. Kasdan strongly advised Lucas, "I think you should kill Luke and have Leia take over." Lucas promptly rejected the idea. Kasdan suggested that if Luke lived, another major character should die. Lucas again disagreed, adding, "You don't go around killing people." Kasdan responded with a heartfelt claim about the nature of cinema. He explained to Lucas that "the movie has more emotional weight if someone you love is lost along the way; the journey has more impact."

Lucas's response was quick and unequivocal: "I don't like that and I don't believe that."

The thought process here looks quite different from the one you experienced when you thought about Bill, the jazz-playing accountant. Read Lucas's answer again: "Not liking" precedes "Not believing." Lucas had an automatic response to Kasdan's suggestion. That response helped motivate his judgment (even if it turned out to be right).

This example illustrates a different type of bias, which we call *conclusion bias*, or *prejudgment*. Like Lucas, we often start the process of judgment with an inclination to reach a particular conclusion. When we do that, we let our fast, intuitive System 1 thinking suggest a conclusion. Either we jump to that conclusion and simply bypass the process of gathering and integrating information, or we mobilize System 2 thinking — engaging in deliberate thought — to come up with arguments that support our prejudgment. In that case, the evidence will be selective and distorted: because of *confirmation bias* and *desirability bias*, we will tend to collect and interpret evidence selectively to favor a judgment that, respectively, we already believe or wish to be true.

People often come up with plausible rationalizations for their judgments and will actually think that they are the cause of their beliefs. A good test of the role of prejudgment is to imagine that the arguments seemingly supporting our belief are suddenly proven invalid. Kasdan, for instance, might well have pointed out to Lucas that "You don't go around killing people" is hardly a compelling argument. The author of *Romeo and Juliet* would not have agreed with Lucas, and if the writers of *The Sopranos* and *Game of Thrones* had decided against killings, both shows would probably have been canceled in their first season. But we can bet that a strong counterargument wouldn't have changed Lucas's mind. Instead, he would have come up with other arguments to support his judgment. (For example, "Star Wars is different.")

Prejudgments are evident wherever we look. Like Lucas's reaction, they often have an emotional component. The psychologist Paul Slovic terms this the *affect heuristic:* people determine what they think by consulting their feelings. We like most things about politicians we favor, and we dislike even the looks and the voices of politicians we dislike. That is one reason that smart companies work so hard to attach a positive affect to their brand. Professors often notice that in a year when they get high marks for teaching, students also give the course material a high rating. In a year when students don't like the professor so much, they give a low rating to the identical assigned readings. The same mechanism is at work even when emotion is not involved: regardless of the true reasons for your belief, you will be inclined to accept any argument that appears to support it, even when the reasoning is wrong.

A subtler example of a conclusion bias is the *anchoring effect*, which is the effect that an arbitrary number has on people who must make a quantitative judgment. In a typical demonstration, you might be presented with a number of items whose price is not easy to guess, such as an unfamiliar bottle of wine. You are asked to jot down the last two digits of your Social Security number and indicate whether you would pay that amount for the bottle. Finally, you are asked to state the maximum amount you would be willing to pay for it. The results show that anchoring on your Social Security number will affect your final buying price. In one study, people whose Social Security numbers generated a high anchor (more than eighty dollars) stated that they were willing to pay about three times more than those with a low anchor (less than twenty dollars).

Clearly, your Social Security number should not have a large effect on your judgment about how much a bottle of wine is worth, but it does. Anchoring is an extremely robust effect and is often deliberately used in negotiations. Whether you're haggling in a bazaar or sitting down for a complex business transaction, you probably have an advantage in going first, because the recipient of the anchor is involuntarily drawn to think of ways your offer could be reasonable. People always attempt to make sense of what they hear; when they encounter an implausible number, they automatically bring to mind considerations that would reduce its implausibility.

Excessive Coherence

Here is another experiment that will help you experience a third type of bias. You will read a description of a candidate for an executive position. The description consists of four adjectives, each written on a card. The deck of cards has just been shuffled. The first two cards have these two descriptors:

    Intelligent, Persistent.

It would be reasonable to suspend judgment until the information is complete, but this is not what has happened: you already have an evaluation of the candidate, and it is positive. This judgment simply happened. You had no control over the process, and suspending judgment was not an option.

Next, you draw the last two cards. Here is the full description now:

    Intelligent, Persistent, Cunning, Unprincipled.

Your evaluation is no longer favorable, but it did not change enough. For comparison, consider the following description, which another shuffling of the deck could have produced:

    Unprincipled, Cunning, Persistent, Intelligent.

This second description consists of the same adjectives, and yet — because of the order in which they are introduced — it is clearly much less appealing than the first. The word *Cunning* was only mildly negative when it followed *Intelligent* and *Persistent,* because we still believed (without reason) that the executive's intentions were good. Yet when it follows *Unprincipled,* the word *Cunning* is awful. In this context, persistence and intelligence are not positives anymore: they make a bad person even more dangerous.

This experiment illustrates *excessive coherence:* we form coherent impressions quickly and are slow to change them. In this example, we immediately developed a positive attitude toward the candidate, in light of little evidence. Confirmation bias — the same tendency that leads us, when we have a prejudgment, to disregard conflicting evidence altogether — made us assign less importance than we should to subsequent data. (Another term to describe this phenomenon is the *halo effect,* because the candidate was evaluated in the positive "halo" of the first impression. We will see in chapter 24 that the halo effect is a serious problem in hiring decisions.)

Here is another example. In the United States, public officials have required chain restaurants to include calorie labels to ensure that consumers see the calories associated with, for example, cheeseburgers, hamburgers, and salads. After seeing those labels, do consumers change their choices? The evidence is disputed and mixed. But in a revealing study, consumers were found to be more likely to be affected by calorie labels if they were placed to the left of the food item rather than the right. When calories are on the left, consumers receive that information first and evidently think "a lot of calories!" or "not so many calories!" before they see the item. Their initial positive or negative reaction greatly affects their choices. By contrast, when people see the food item first, they apparently think "delicious!" or "not so great!" before they see the calorie label. Here again, their initial reaction greatly affects their choices. This hypothesis is supported by the authors' finding that for Hebrew speakers, who read right to left, the calorie label has a significantly larger impact if it is on the right rather than the left.

In general, we jump to conclusions, then stick to them. We think we base our opinions on evidence, but the evidence we consider and our interpretation of it are likely to be distorted, at least to some extent, to fit our initial snap judgment. As a result, we maintain the coherence of the overall story that has emerged in our mind. This process is fine, of course, if the conclusions are correct. When the initial evaluation is erroneous, however, the tendency to stick to it in the face of contradictory evidence is likely to amplify errors. And this effect is difficult to control, because information that we have heard or seen is impossible to ignore and often difficult to forget. In court, judges sometimes instruct jurors to disregard an inadmissible piece of evidence they have heard, but this is not a realistic instruction (although it may be helpful in jury deliberation, where arguments explicitly based on this evidence can be rejected).

Psychological Biases Cause Noise

We have briefly presented three types of biases that operate in different ways: substitution biases, which lead to a misweighting of the evidence; conclusion biases, which lead us either to bypass the evidence or to consider it in a distorted way; and excessive coherence, which magnifies the effect of initial impressions and reduces the impact of contradictory information. All three types of biases can, of course, produce statistical bias. They can also produce noise.

Let's start with substitution. Most people judge the probability that Bill is an accountant by the similarity of his profile to a stereotype: the result, in this experiment, is a shared bias. If every respondent makes the same mistake, there is no noise. But substitution does not always produce such unanimity. When the question "Is there climate change?" is replaced with "Do I trust the people who say it is real?," it is easy to see that the answer will vary from one person to the next, depending on that person's social circles, preferred sources of information, political affiliation, and so on. The same psychological bias creates variable judgments and between-person noise.

Substitution can also be a source of occasion noise. If a question on life satisfaction is answered by consulting one's immediate mood, the answer will inevitably vary for the same person from one moment to the next. A happy morning can be followed by a distressing afternoon, and changing moods over time can lead to very different reports of life satisfaction depending on when the interviewer happens to call. In chapter 7, we reviewed examples of occasion noise that can be traced to psychological biases.

Prejudgments also produce both bias and noise. Return to an example we mentioned in the introduction: the shocking disparities in the percentage of asylum seekers that judges admit. When one judge admits 5% of applicants and another in the same courthouse admits 88%, we can be quite certain that they are biased in different directions. From a broader perspective, individual differences in biases can cause massive system noise. Of course, the system can also be biased to the extent that most or all judges are biased similarly.

Finally, excessive coherence can produce either bias or noise, depending on whether the sequence of information and the meaning assigned to it are identical for all (or most) judges. Consider, for instance, a physically attractive candidate whose good looks create an early positive impression in most recruiters. If physical appearance is irrelevant to the position for which the candidate is considered, this positive halo will result in a shared error: a bias.

On the other hand, many complex decisions require compiling information that arrives in an essentially random order. Consider the claims adjusters of chapter 2. The order in which data about a claim becomes available varies haphazardly from one adjuster to the next and from one case to the next, causing random variation in initial impressions. Excessive coherence means that these random variations will produce random distortions in the final judgments. The effect will be system noise.

———

In short, psychological biases, as a mechanism, are universal, and they often produce shared errors. But when there are large individual differences in biases (different prejudgments) or when the effect of biases depends on context (different triggers), there will be noise.

Both bias and noise create error, which suggests that anything that reduces psychological biases will improve judgment. We will return to the topic of debiasing, or removing bias, in part 5. But for now, we continue our exploration of the process of judgment.

Speaking of Heuristics, Biases, and Noise

"We know we have psychological biases, but we should resist the urge to blame every error on unspecified 'biases.'"

"When we substitute an easier question for the one we should be answering, errors are bound to occur. For instance, we will ignore the base rate when we judge probability by similarity."

"Prejudgments and other conclusion biases lead people to distort evidence in favor of their initial position."

"We form impressions quickly and hold on to them even when contradictory information comes in. This tendency is called excessive coherence."

"Psychological biases cause statistical bias if many people share the same biases. In many cases, however, people differ in their biases. In those cases, psychological biases create system noise."

CHAPTER 14

The Matching Operation

L ook at the sky. How likely is it to rain in two hours?
You probably had no difficulty answering this question. The
judgment you made — for example, that it is "very likely" to rain
soon — was produced effortlessly. Somehow, your evaluation of the
sky's darkness was converted into a probability judgment.

What you just performed is an elementary example of *matching*.
We have described judgment as an operation that assigns a value on a
scale to a subjective impression (or to an aspect of an impression).
Matching is an essential part of that operation. When you answer the
question "On a scale of 1 to 10, how good is your mood?" or "Please
give one to five stars to your shopping experience this morning," you
are matching: your task is to find a value on the judgment scale that
matches your mood or experience.

Matching and Coherence

You met Bill in the previous chapter, and here he is again: "Bill is
thirty-three years old. He is intelligent but unimaginative, compul-
sive and generally lifeless. In school, he was strong in mathematics

but weak in social studies and humanities." We asked you to estimate the probability that Bill had various occupations and hobbies, and we saw that you answered this question by substituting a judgment of similarity for one of probability. You did not really ask how likely Bill was to be an accountant, but how similar he was to the stereotype of that profession. We now turn to a question we left unanswered: how you made that judgment.

It is not difficult to assess the degree to which Bill's description matches the stereotypes of professions and hobbies. Bill is clearly less similar to a typical jazz player than to an accountant, and he is even less similar to a surfer. The example illustrates the extraordinary versatility of matching, which is particularly obvious in judgments about people. There is hardly a limit to the questions you could have answered about Bill. For example, how would you feel about being stranded on a desert island with him? You probably had an immediate intuitive answer to this question on the basis of the scant information provided. Yet, we have news for you: Bill, as we know him, happens to be a hardened explorer with extraordinary survival skills. If this surprises you (and it probably does), you just experienced a failure to achieve coherence.

The surprise is intense because the new information is incompatible with the image of Bill that you had constructed earlier. Now imagine that Bill's prowess and survival skills had been included in the original description. You would have ended up with a different overall image of the man, perhaps as a person who comes alive only in the great outdoors. The overall impression of Bill would have been less coherent, and therefore more difficult to match to categories of professions or hobbies, but you would have experienced far less dissonance than you just did.

Conflicting cues make it more difficult to achieve a sense of coherence and to find a judgment that is a satisfactory match. The presence of conflicting cues characterizes complex judgments, in which we expect to find a lot of noise. The Gambardi problem, where some of the indications were positive and others negative, was such a judgment. We return to complex judgments in chapter 16. In the remainder of this chapter we focus on relatively simple judgments — especially those made on *intensity scales.*

Matching Intensities

Some of the scales on which we express judgments are qualitative: professions, hobbies, and medical diagnoses are examples. They are identified by the fact that the values of the scale are not ordered: red is neither more nor less than blue.

Many judgments, however, are made on quantitative intensity scales. Physical measurements of size, weight, brightness, temperature, or loudness; measures of cost or value; judgments of probability or frequency — all these are quantitative. So are judgments on more abstract scales, like confidence, strength, attractiveness, anger, fear, immorality, or the severity of punishments.

The distinctive feature shared by these quantitative dimensions is that the question "Which is more?" can be answered about any pair of values on the same dimension. You can tell that a flogging is a more severe punishment than a slap on the wrist or that you like *Hamlet* more than you liked *Waiting for Godot,* just as you can tell that the sun is brighter than the moon, that an elephant weighs more than a hamster, and that the average temperature in Miami is higher than in Toronto.

People have a remarkable intuitive ability to match intensities across unrelated dimensions, by mapping one intensity scale onto another. You can match the intensity of your affection for different singers to the height of buildings in your city. (If you think that Bob Dylan is especially great, for example, you might match your level of enthusiasm for him to the tallest building in your city.) You could match the current level of political discord in your country to a summer temperature in a city you know well. (If there is remarkable political harmony, you might match it to a breezy seventy-degree summer day in New York.) And if you were asked to express your appreciation of a restaurant by comparing it to the length of a novel instead of the usual 1-to-5-star rating scale, this request would strike you as quite bizarre but not at all infeasible. (Your favorite restaurant might be like *War and Peace*.) In each case, it is — oddly — quite clear what you mean.

In ordinary conversation, the range of values for a scale is a function of the context. The comment "She has been saving a lot of money" has a different meaning when you are toasting the retirement of a successful investment banker than it has when you are congratulating a teenager who has been babysitting. And the meaning of words like *large* and *small* depends entirely on a frame of reference. We can, for example, make sense of a statement like "The large mouse ran up the trunk of the small elephant."

The Bias of Matching Predictions

The following puzzle illustrates both the power of matching and a systematic judgment error that is associated with it.

> *Julie is a graduating student at a university. Read the following piece of information about her, then guess her GPA (on the standard scale of 0.0 to 4.0):*
> *Julie read fluently when she was four years old.*
> *What is her GPA?*

If you are familiar with the grade point average system in the United States, a number came to your mind quite quickly, and it was probably close to 3.7 or 3.8. How a guess about Julie's GPA instantly came to your mind illustrates the matching process we just described.

First, you evaluated how precocious a reader Julie was. The evaluation was easy because Julie read unusually early, and that precociousness placed Julie in a category on some scale. If you had to describe the scale you used, you would probably say its highest category is something like "extraordinarily precocious," and you would note that Julie does not quite belong in that category (some children read before they are two). Julie probably belongs in the next one, the band of "unusually but not extraordinarily precocious" children.

In the second step, you matched a judgment of GPA to your evaluation of Julie. Although you were unaware of doing so, you must have been looking for a value of GPA that would also fit the label "unusual but not extraordinary." A *matching prediction* came to your mind, seemingly out of nowhere, when you heard Julie's story.

Deliberately carrying out the calculations required to perform these tasks of evaluation and matching would take quite a while, but in fast, System 1 thinking, the judgment is achieved quickly and effortlessly. The story we tell here about guessing Julie's GPA involves a complex, multistage sequence of mental events that cannot be directly observed. The specificity of the mental mechanism of matching is unusual in psychology — but the evidence for it is unusually conclusive. We can be certain from many similar experiments that the following two questions, when posed to different groups of people, will elicit exactly the same numbers:

- ❑ *What percentage of Julie's class read at an earlier age than she did?*
- ❑ *What percentage of Julie's class has a higher GPA than she does?*

The first question is manageable on its own: it simply asks you to evaluate the evidence you were given about Julie. The second question, which requires a distant prediction, is certainly harder — but it is intuitively tempting to answer it by answering the first.

The two questions we ask about Julie are analogous to two questions that we described as universally confusing in an earlier discussion of the illusion of validity. The first question about Julie requires you to evaluate the "intensity" of the information you have about her case. The second question asks about the intensity of a prediction. And we suspect that they are still difficult to tell apart.

The intuitive prediction of Julie's GPA is a case of the psychological mechanism that we described in chapter 13: the substitution of an easy question for a difficult one. Your System 1 simplifies a difficult prediction question by answering a much easier one: how impressive was Julie's achievement as a four-year-old reader? An extra step of matching is required to move directly from reading age, measured in years, to GPA, measured in points.

The substitution happens, of course, only if the available information is relevant. If all you knew about Julie was that she was a fast runner or a mediocre dancer, you would have no information at all. But any fact that can be interpreted as a plausible indication of intelligence is likely to be an acceptable substitute.

Substituting one question for another inevitably causes errors when the true answers to the two questions are different. Substituting reading age for GPA, though seemingly plausible, is manifestly absurd. To see why, think of events that could have happened since Julie was four years old. She could have been in a terrible accident. Her parents could have had a traumatic divorce. She could have encountered an inspiring teacher who influenced her greatly. She could have become pregnant. Any of these events and many more could have affected her work in college.

The matching prediction can be justified only if reading precocity and college GPA are perfectly correlated, which is clearly not the case. On the other hand, completely ignoring the information about Julie's reading age would also be a mistake, because her reading age does provide some relevant information. The optimal prediction must lie between these two extremes of perfect knowledge and zero knowledge.

What do you know about a case when you know nothing specific about it — only the category to which it belongs? The answer to that question is what we have called the outside view of the case. If we were asked to predict Julie's GPA but given no information about her, we would surely predict the average — perhaps 3.2. This is the outside-view prediction. The best estimate of Julie's GPA must therefore be higher than 3.2 and lower than 3.8. The precise location of the estimate depends on the predictive value of the information: the more you trust reading age as a predictor of GPA, the higher the estimate. In Julie's case, the information is certainly quite weak, and the most reasonable prediction will accordingly be closer to the average GPA. There is a technical but fairly easy way to correct the error of matching predictions; we detail it in appendix C.

Although they lead to statistically absurd predictions, predictions that match the evidence are hard to resist. Sales managers often assume that the salesperson who was more successful than the rest of the sales team last year will continue to overperform. Senior executives sometimes meet an exceptionally talented candidate and imagine how the new hire will rise to the top of the organization. Producers routinely anticipate that the next movie of a director whose previous movie was a hit will be just as successful.

These examples of matching predictions are more likely than not to end in disappointment. On the other hand, matching predictions that are made when things are at their worst are more likely than not to be overly negative. Intuitive predictions that match the evidence are too extreme, both when they are optimistic and when they are pessimistic. (The technical term for such prediction errors is that they are *nonregressive*, because they fail to take into account a statistical phenomenon called *regression to the mean*.)

It should be noted, however, that substitution and matching do not always govern predictions. In the language of two systems, the intuitive System 1 proposes quick associative solutions to problems as they arise, but these intuitions must be endorsed by the more reflective System 2 before they become beliefs. Matching predictions are sometimes rejected in favor of more complex responses. For example, people are more reluctant to match predictions to unfavorable than to favorable evidence. We suspect that you would hesitate to make a matching prediction of inferior college performance if Julie had been a late reader. The asymmetry between favorable and unfavorable predictions disappears when more information is available.

We offer the outside view as a corrective for intuitive predictions of all kinds. In an earlier discussion of Michael Gambardi's future prospects, for example, we recommended anchoring your judgment about Michael's probability of success on the relevant base rate (the two-year success rate for incoming CEOs). In the case of quantitative predictions such as Julie's GPA, taking the outside view means anchoring your prediction on the average outcome. The outside view can be neglected only in very easy problems, when the information available supports a prediction that can be made with complete confidence. When serious judgment is necessary, the outside view must be part of the solution.

Noise in Matching: Limitations of Absolute Judgment

Our limited ability to distinguish categories on intensity scales constrains the accuracy of the matching operation. Words such as *large* or *rich* assign the same label to a range of values on the dimension of size or wealth. This is a potentially important source of noise.

The retiring investment banker surely deserves the label *rich*, but how rich is she? We have many adjectives to choose from: *well-off, affluent, comfortable, wealthy, super-rich,* and others. If you were given detailed descriptions of the wealth of some individuals and had to attach an adjective to each, how many distinct categories could you form — without resorting to detailed comparisons across cases?

The number of categories that we can distinguish on an intensity scale is given in the title of an all-time classic article in psychology, published in 1956: "The Magical Number Seven, Plus or Minus Two." Beyond this limit, people tend to start to make errors — for instance, to assign A to a higher category than B when they would in fact rate B higher than A in a head-to-head comparison.

Imagine a set of lines of four different lengths of between 2 and 4 inches, each line the same amount longer than the next one. You are shown one line at a time and have to call out a number between 1 and 4, where 1 goes with the shortest line and 4 with the longest. The task is easy. Now suppose you are shown lines of five different lengths and have to repeat the task calling out numbers 1 through 5. Still easy. When will you start making errors? Around the magical number of seven lines. Surprisingly, this number depends very little on the range of line lengths: if the lines were spaced between 2 and 6 inches, rather than between 2 and 4, you would still start making mistakes beyond seven lines. Much the same result is obtained when you are presented with tones that vary in loudness, or with lights of different brightness. There is a genuine limit on people's ability to assign distinct labels to stimuli on a dimension, and that limit is around seven labels.

This limit of our discriminating power matters, because our ability to match values across intensity dimensions cannot be better than our ability to assign values on these dimensions. The matching operation is a versatile tool of fast, System 1 thinking and the core of many intuitive judgments, but it is crude.

The magical number is not an absolute constraint. People can be trained to make finer distinctions by hierarchical categorization. For example, we can certainly discriminate several categories of wealth among multimillionaires, and judges can discriminate degrees of severity in multiple categories of crimes, themselves ordered in severity. For this refinement process to work, however, the categories must exist in advance and their boundaries must be clear. When assigning labels to a set of lines, you cannot decide to separate the longer lines from the shorter ones and treat them as two separate categories. Categorization is not under voluntary control when you are in the fast-thinking mode.

There is a way to overcome the limited resolution of adjective scales: instead of using labels, use comparisons. Our ability to compare cases is much better than our ability to place them on a scale.

Consider what you would do if instructed to use a twenty-point scale of quality to evaluate a large set of restaurants, or singers. A five-star scale would be easily manageable, but you could not possibly maintain perfect reliability with a twenty-point scale. (Joe's Pizza is worth three stars, but is it an eleven or a twelve?) The solution to this problem is simple, if time-consuming. You would first rate the restaurants, or singers, using the five-point rating scale to sort them into five categories. You would then rank the cases within each category, which you will usually be able to do with only a few ties: you probably know whether you prefer Joe's Pizza to Fred's Burgers, or Taylor Swift to Bob Dylan, even if you assigned them to the same category. To keep things simple, you could now distinguish four levels within each of the five categories. You can probably discriminate levels of contempt even among the singers you most dislike.

The psychology of this exercise is straightforward. Explicit comparisons between objects of judgment support much finer discriminations than do ratings of objects evaluated one at a time. Judgments of line length tell a similar story: your ability to compare the length of lines that are shown in immediate succession is much better than your ability to label lengths, and you will be even more accurate when comparing lines that are in view at the same time.

The advantage of comparative judgments applies to many domains. If you have a rough idea of people's wealth, you will do better comparing individuals in the same range than you would by labeling their wealth individually. If you grade essays, you will be more precise when you rank them from best to worst than you are when you read and grade essays one by one. Comparative or relative judgments are more sensitive than categorical or absolute ones. As these examples suggest, they are also more effortful and time-consuming.

Rating objects individually on scales that are explicitly comparative retains some of the benefits of comparative judgment. In some contexts, notably in education, recommendations of candidates for acceptance or promotion often require the recommender to locate the candidate in the "top 5%" or "top 20%" of some designated population, such as "students that you have taught" or "programmers with the same level of experience." These ratings rarely deserve to be taken at face value because there is no way to keep the recommenders accountable for using the scale properly. Accountability is possible in some contexts: when managers rate employees or when analysts assess investments, a person who assigns 90% of cases to the "top 20%" category can be identified and corrected. The use of comparative judgments is one of the remedies for noise that we will discuss in part 5.

Many tasks of judgment require matching individual cases to a category on a scale (for instance, a seven-point agreement scale) or using an ordered set of adjectives (for example, "unlikely" or "extremely unlikely" in rating the probabilities of events). This type of matching is noisy because it is crude. Individuals may differ in the interpretation of labels even when they agree on the substance of the judgment. A procedure that compels explicitly comparative judgments is likely to reduce noise. In the next chapter, we further explore how using the wrong scales can add to noise.

Speaking of Matching

"Both of us say this movie is very good, but you seem to have enjoyed it a lot less than I did. We're using the same words, but are we using the same scale?"

"We thought Season 2 of this series would be just as spectacular as Season 1. We made a matching prediction, and it was wrong."

"It is hard to remain consistent when grading these essays. Should you try ranking them instead?"

CHAPTER 15

Scales

I magine yourself a juror in a civil trial. You have heard the evidence summarized below, and you will be required to make some judgments about it.

Joan Glover v. General Assistance

Joan Glover, a six-year-old child, ingested a large num-ber of pills of Allerfree, a nonprescription allergy medicine, and required an extensive hospital stay. Because the over-dose weakened her respiratory system, she will be more sus-ceptible to breathing-related diseases such as asthma and emphysema for the rest of her life. The Allerfree bottle used an inadequately designed childproof safety cap.

The manufacturer of Allerfree is General Assistance, a large company (with annual profits of $100 million to $200 million) that produces a variety of nonprescription medi-cines. A federal regulation requires childproof safety caps on all medicine bottles. General Assistance has systemati-cally ignored the intent of this regulation by using a child-proof safety cap that had a much higher failure rate than that of others in the industry. An internal company *document says that "this stupid, unnecessary federal regulation is a waste of our money" and states that the risk of being punished is low. The document adds that, in any case, "the punishments for violating the regulation are extremely mild; basically we'd be asked to improve the safety caps in the future." Although it was warned about its safety cap by an official of the US Food and Drug Administration, the company decided to take no corrective action.*

Next we ask you to make three judgments. Please slow down enough to choose your answers.

Outrage:

Which of the following best expresses your opinion of the defendant's actions? (Please circle your answer.)

Completely acceptable		Objectionable		Shocking		Absolutely outrageous
0	1	2	3	4	5	6

Punitive intent:

In addition to paying compensatory damages, how much should the defendant be punished? (Please circle the number that best expresses your opinion of the appropriate level of punishment.)

No punishment		Mild punishment		Severe punishment		Extremely severe punishment
0	1	2	3	4	5	6

Damages: In addition to paying compensatory damages, what amount of *punitive* damages (if any) should the defendant be required to pay as punishment and to deter the defendant and others from similar actions in the future? (Please write your answer in the blank below.)

$ ....

The story of Joan Glover is a slightly abbreviated version of a case used in a study that two of us (Kahneman and Sunstein, along with our friend and collaborator David Schkade) reported in 1998. We describe this study in some detail in this chapter, and we wanted you to experience one of the tasks the study includes, because we now see it as an instructive example of a noise audit, which reprises many of the themes of this book.

This chapter focuses on the role of the *response scale* as a pervasive source of noise. People may differ in their judgments, not because they disagree on the substance but because they use the scale in different ways. If you were rating the performance of an employee, you might say that on a scale of 0 to 6, the performance was a 4 — which, in your view, is pretty good. Someone else might say that on the same scale, the employee's performance was a 3 — which, in his view, is also pretty good. Ambiguity in the wording of scales is a general problem. Much research has been conducted on the difficulties of communication that arise from vague expressions such as "beyond a reasonable doubt," "clear and convincing evidence," "outstanding performance," and "unlikely to happen." Judgments that are expressed in such phrases are inevitably noisy because they are interpreted differently by both speakers and listeners.

In the study for which the Joan Glover case was written, we observed the effects of an ambiguous scale in a situation in which it has serious consequences. The topic of the study was noise in jury-awarded punitive damages. As you could infer from the third question about Joan Glover's case, the law in the United States (and in some other countries) allows juries in civil cases to impose punitive damages on a defendant whose actions were particularly egregious. Punitive damages are supplemental to compensatory awards, which are designed to make injured people whole. When, as in the Glover example, a product has caused injuries and plaintiffs have successfully sued the company, they will be awarded money to pay their medical bills and any lost wages. But they could also receive a punitive award, intended to send the defendant and similar companies a warning. The behavior of General Assistance in this case was obviously reprehensible; it falls in the range of actions for which a jury could reasonably impose punitive damages.

A major concern about the institution of punitive damages has been their unpredictability. The same wrongdoing may be punished by damages that range from very modest to massive. Using the terminology of this book, we would say the system is noisy. Requests for punitive damages are often denied, and even when they are granted, the awards frequently do not add much to compensatory damage. There are striking exceptions, however, and the very large amounts that juries sometimes award appear surprising and arbitrary. An often-mentioned example is a punitive award of $4 million imposed on a car dealership for nondisclosure of the fact that the plaintiff's new BMW had been repainted.

In our study of punitive damages, 899 participants were asked to evaluate Joan Glover's case and nine other similar cases — all of them involving plaintiffs who had suffered some harm and sued the company that was allegedly responsible. Unlike you, the participants answered only one of the three questions (outrage, punitive intent, or dollar amount) for all ten cases. The participants were further divided into smaller groups, each assigned to one version of each case. The different versions varied the harm suffered by the plaintiff and the revenue of the defendant company. There were a total of twenty-eight scenarios. Our goals were to test a theory about the psychology of punitive damages and to investigate the role of the monetary scale (here dollars) as a main source of noise in this legal institution.

The Outrage Hypothesis

How to determine a just punishment has been debated by philosophers and legal scholars for centuries. Our hypothesis, however, was that the question that philosophers find difficult is quite easy for ordinary people, who simplify the task by substituting an easy question for the hard one. The easy question, which is answered immediately when you are asked how much General Assistance should be punished is, "How angry am I?" The intensity of the intended punishment will then be matched to the intensity of the outrage.

To test this outrage hypothesis, we asked different groups of participants to answer either the punitive intent question or the outrage question. We then compared the average ratings obtained on the two questions for the twenty-eight scenarios used in the study. As expected from the substitution idea, the correlation between the mean ratings of outrage and of punitive intent was a close-to-perfect 0.98 (PC = 94%). This correlation supports the outrage hypothesis: the emotion of outrage is the primary determinant of punitive intent.

Outrage is the main driver of punitive intent but not the only one. Did you notice anything in Joan's story that attracted more attention when you rated punitive intent than when you rated outrage? If you did, we suspect it was the harm she suffered. You can tell whether a behavior is outrageous without knowing its consequences; in this instance, the behavior of General Assistance was surely outrageous. In contrast, intuitions about punitive intent have a retributive aspect, which is crudely expressed in the eye-for-an-eye principle. The urge for retribution explains why attempted murder and murder are treated differently by the law and by juries; a would-be murderer who is lucky enough to miss his target will be punished less severely.

To find out whether harm does indeed make a difference in punitive intent but not in outrage, we showed different groups of respondents "severe-harm" and "mild-harm" versions of the Joan Glover case and of several others. The severe-harm version is the one you saw. In the mild-harm version, Joan "had to spend several days in a hospital and is now deeply traumatized by pills of any kind. When her parents try to get her to take even beneficial medications such as vitamins, aspirin, or cold remedies, she cries uncontrollably and says that she is afraid." This version describes a traumatic experience for the child, but a much lower level of harm than the long-term medical damage described in the first version you read. As expected, the average ratings of outrage were almost identical for the severe-harm version (4.24) and the mild-harm version (4.19). Only the defendant's behavior matters to outrage; its consequences do not. In contrast, the ratings of punitive intent averaged 4.93 for severe harm and 4.65 for mild harm, a small but statistically reliable difference. The median monetary awards were two million dollars for the severe-harm version and one million for the milder version. Similar results were obtained for several other cases.

These findings highlight a key feature of the process of judgment: the subtle effect of the judgment task on the weighting of different aspects of the evidence. The participants who rated punitive intent and outrage were not aware that they were taking a stand on the philosophical issue of whether justice should be retributive. They were not even aware of assigning weights to the various features of the case. Nevertheless, they assigned a near-zero weight to harm when rating outrage and a significant weight to the same factor when determining punishment. Recall that the participants saw only one version of the story; their assignment of a higher punishment to the worse harm was not an explicit comparison. It was the outcome of an automatic operation of matching in the two conditions. The responses of participants relied more on fast than on slow thinking.

Noisy Scales

The second goal of the study was to find out why punitive damages are noisy. Our hypothesis was that jurors generally agree on how severely they wish the defendant to be punished but differ widely in how they translate their punitive intent onto the scale of dollars.

The design of the study allows us to compare the amount of noise in judgments of the same cases on three scales: outrage, punitive intent, and damage awards in dollars. To measure noise, we apply the method that was used to analyze the results of the noise audit of federal judges in chapter 6. We assume, as we did in that analysis, that the average of individual judgments of a case can be treated as an unbiased, just value. (This is an assumption for purposes of analysis; we emphasize that it might be wrong.) In an ideal world, all jurors who use a particular scale would agree in their judgments of every case. Any deviation from the average judgment counts as an error, and these errors are the source of system noise.

As we also noted in chapter 6, system noise can be broken down into level noise and pattern noise. Here, level noise is the variability among jurors in how severe they are in general. Pattern noise is the variability in how a given juror responds to particular cases, relative to this juror's own average. We can therefore break down the overall variance of judgments into three elements:

Variance of Judgments =
Variance of Just Punishments + (Level Noise)^2 + (Pattern Noise)^2

This analysis, decomposing the variance of judgments into three terms, was conducted separately for the three judgments of outrage, punitive intent, and dollar award.

Figure 13 shows the results. The least noisy scale is punitive intent, where system noise accounts for 51% of the variance — there is about as much noise as there is justice. The outrage scale is distinctly noisier: 71% noise. And the dollar scale is by far the worst: fully 94% of the variance in judgments is noise!

The differences are striking because the three scales are, in terms of their content, almost identical. We saw earlier that the just values of outrage and punitive intent were almost perfectly correlated, as implied by the outrage hypothesis. The ratings of punitive intent and the dollar awards answer precisely the same question — how severely General Assistance should be punished — in different units. How can we explain the large differences seen in figure 13?

We can probably agree that outrage is not a very precise scale. True, there is such a thing as "completely acceptable" behavior, but if there is a limit to how angry you can get at General Assistance or at the other defendants, that limit is rather vague. What does it mean for a behavior to be "absolutely outrageous"? The lack of clarity on the upper end of the scale makes some noise inevitable.

Punitive intent is more specific. "Severe punishment" is more

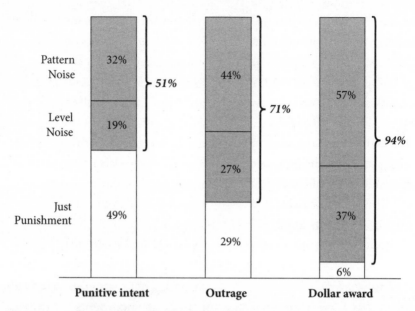

FIGURE 13: *Components of judgment variance*

precise than "absolutely outrageous," because an "extremely severe punishment" is bounded by the maximum prescribed by the law. You may wish to "throw the book" at the culprit, but you may not, for instance, recommend putting the CEO of General Assistance and its entire executive team to death. (We hope.) The punitive-intent scale is less ambiguous because its upper bound is more clearly specified. As we might expect, it is also less noisy.

Outrage and punitive intent were both measured on similar rating scales, defined more or less clearly by verbal labels. The dollar scale belongs to a different family, which is far more problematic.

Dollars and Anchors

The title of our academic paper expresses its central message: "Shared Outrage and Erratic Awards: The Psychology of Punitive Damages." There was a fair amount of agreement among our experimental jurors in their ratings of punitive intent; the ratings were mostly explained by outrage. However, the dollar measure most closely simulated the courtroom situation, and it was unacceptably noisy.

The reason is not mysterious. If you actually generated a specific dollar amount of damages in the Joan Glover case, you surely experienced the feeling that your choice of a number was essentially arbitrary. The feeling of arbitrariness conveys important information: it tells you that other people will make widely different arbitrary decisions and that the judgments will be very noisy. This turns out to be a characteristic of the family of scales to which dollar awards belong.

The legendary Harvard psychologist S. S. Stevens discovered the surprising fact that people share strong intuitions about the *ratios* of intensity of many subjective experiences and attitudes. They can adjust a light so that it appears "twice as bright" as another, and they agree that the emotional significance of a ten-month prison sentence is not nearly ten times as bad as that of a sentence of one month. Stevens called scales that draw on such intuitions *ratio scales.*

You can tell that our intuitions about money are expressed in ratios from the ease with which we understand such expressions as "Sara got a 60% raise!" or "Our rich neighbor lost half his wealth overnight." The dollar scale of punitive damages is a ratio scale for the measurement of the intention to punish. Like other ratio scales, it has a meaningful zero (zero dollars) and is unbounded at the top.

Stevens discovered that a ratio scale (like the dollar scale) can be tied down by a single intermediate anchor (the jargon term is *modulus*). In his laboratory, he would expose observers to a light of a certain brightness, with the instruction to "call the brightness of that light 10 (or 50, or 200) and assign numbers to other brightnesses accordingly." As expected, the numbers that observers assigned to lights of different brightness were proportional to the arbitrary anchor they were instructed to adopt. An observer who was anchored on the number 200 would make judgments that were 20 times higher than if the anchor had been 10; the standard deviation of the observer's judgments would also be proportional to the anchor.

In chapter 13, we described an amusing example of anchoring, in which people's willingness to pay for an object was strongly influenced by asking them first if they would pay (in dollars) the last two digits of their Social Security number. A more striking result was that the initial anchor also affected their willingness to pay for a whole list of other objects. Participants who were induced to agree to pay a large amount for a cordless trackball agreed to pay a correspondingly larger amount for a cordless keyboard. It appears that people are much more sensitive to the *relative* value of comparable goods than to their absolute value. The authors of the study named the persistent effect of a single anchor "coherent arbitrariness."

To appreciate the effect of an arbitrary anchor in the Joan Glover case, suppose that the text at the beginning of this chapter included the following information:

> *In a similar case involving another pharmaceutical company, a little girl who was the victim suffered moderate psychological trauma (as in the mild-harm version you read earlier). The punitive damages were set at $1.5 million.*

Notice that the problem of setting a punishment for General Assistance has suddenly become much easier. Indeed, an amount may have come to your mind already. There is a multiplier (or ratio) of the dollar awards that corresponds to the contrast between the severe harm that was done to Joan and the mild harm suffered by the other little girl. Furthermore, the single anchor you read ($1.5 million) is sufficient to tie down the entire dollar scale of punishment. It is now easy for you to set damages for cases both more severe and milder than the two considered so far.

If anchors are required to make judgments on a ratio scale, what happens when people are not given an anchor? Stevens reported the answer. In the absence of guidance from the experimenter, people are forced to make an arbitrary choice when they use the scale for the first time. From that point, they make their judgments consistently, using their first answer as an anchor.

You may recognize the task you faced in setting damages for the

Joan Glover case as an instance of scaling without an anchor. Like the anchorless observers in Stevens's lab, you made an arbitrary decision about the correct punishment for General Assistance. The participants in our study of punitive damages faced the same problem: they were also compelled to make an initial arbitrary decision about the first case they saw. Unlike you, however, they did not just make one arbitrary decision: they went on to set punitive damages for nine other cases. These nine judgments were not arbitrary because they could be made consistent with the initial anchoring judgment, and therefore with one another.

The findings of Stevens's laboratory suggest that the anchor that individuals produce should have a large effect on the absolute values of their subsequent dollar judgments but no effect whatsoever on the relative positions of the ten cases. A large initial judgment causes all the other judgments to be proportionately large without affecting their relative size. This reasoning leads to a surprising conclusion: although they appear hopelessly noisy, dollar judgments actually reflect the judges' punitive intentions. To discover these intentions, we need only replace the absolute dollar values with relative scores.

To test this idea, we repeated the analysis of noise after replacing each dollar award by its rank among an individual's ten judgments. The highest dollar award was scored 1, the next highest was scored 2, and so forth. This transformation of dollar awards to ranks eliminates all juror-level errors, because the 1 to 10 distribution of ranks is the same for everyone, except for occasional ties. (In case you wondered, there were multiple versions of the questionnaire because each individual judged ten of the twenty-eight scenarios. We conducted the analysis separately for each group of participants who had responded to the same ten scenarios, and we report an average.)

The results were striking: the proportion of noise in the judgments dropped from 94% to 49% (figure 14). Transforming the dollar awards into rankings revealed that jurors were actually in substantial agreement about the appropriate punishment in different cases. Indeed, the rankings of dollar awards were, if anything, slightly *less* noisy than the original ratings of punitive intent.

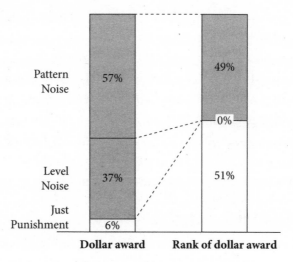

FIGURE 14: *Noise in value vs. noise in ranking*

An Unfortunate Conclusion

The results are consistent with the theory we have outlined: dollar awards for all cases were anchored on the arbitrary number that each juror picked for the first case they saw. The relative ranking of cases reflects attitudes with fair accuracy and is thus not very noisy, but the absolute values of the dollar awards are essentially meaningless because they depend on the arbitrary number chosen in the first case.

Ironically, the case that jurors assess in real trials is the first and only one they see. American legal practice requires civil juries to set a dollar award for one case, without the benefit of any guiding anchor. The law explicitly prohibits any communication to the jury of the size of punitive awards in other cases. The assumption implicit in the law is that jurors' sense of justice will lead them directly from a consideration of an offense to the correct punishment. This assumption is psychological nonsense — it assumes an ability that humans do not have. The institutions of justice should acknowledge the limitations of the people who administer it.

The example of punitive damages is extreme; professional

judgments are rarely expressed on scales that are so hopelessly ambiguous. Nonetheless, ambiguous scales are common, which means that the punitive-damages study holds two general lessons, applicable in business, education, sports, government, and elsewhere. First, the choice of a scale can make a large difference in the amount of noise in judgments, because ambiguous scales are noisy. Second, replacing absolute judgments with relative ones, when feasible, is likely to reduce noise.

Speaking of Scales

"There is a lot of noise in our judgments. Could this be because we understand the scale differently?"

"Can we agree on an anchor case that will serve as a reference point on the scale?"

"To reduce noise, maybe we should replace our judgments with a ranking?"

CHAPTER 16

Patterns

Remember Julie, the precocious child whose college GPA you tried to guess in chapter 14? Here is a fuller description.

Julie was an only child. Her father was a successful lawyer, her mother an architect. When Julie was about three years old, her father contracted an autoimmune disease that forced him to work at home. He spent a lot of time with Julie and patiently taught her to read. She was reading fluently when she was four years old. Her dad also tried to teach her arithmetic, but she found that topic difficult. Julie was a good pupil in elementary school, but she was emotionally needy and rather unpopular. She spent much time alone and became a passionate bird-watcher after being inspired by watching birds with her favorite uncle.

Her parents divorced when she was eleven, and Julie took the divorce hard. Her grades plummeted, and she had frequent outbursts at school. In high school, she did very well in some subjects, including biology and creative writing. She surprised everyone by excelling in physics. But she

*neglected most of her other subjects, and she graduated
from high school a B student.*

*Not admitted to the prestigious schools to which she
applied, Julie eventually attended a good state school,
where she majored in environmental studies. During her
first two years in college, she continued a pattern of frequent emotional entanglements and smoked pot fairly reg-
ularly. In her fourth semester, however, she developed a
strong wish to go to medical school and began to take her
work much more seriously.*

What is your best guess about Julie's graduating GPA?

Problems: Hard and Easy

Obviously, this problem (let's call it Julie 2.0) has become much more
difficult. All you knew about Julie 1.0 was that she could read when
she was four. With only one cue, the power of matching did the work,
and an intuitive estimate of her GPA came quickly to mind.

Matching would still be available if you had several cues that
pointed in the same general direction. For instance, when you read a
description of Bill, the jazz-playing accountant, all the information
you had ("unimaginative," "strong in mathematics," "weak in social
studies") painted a coherent, stereotypical picture. Similarly, if most
of the events in the life of Julie 2.0 were consistent with a story of
precociousness and superior achievement (with perhaps a few data
points suggesting merely "average" performance), you would not find
the task so difficult. When the evidence available paints a coherent
picture, our fast, System 1 thinking has no difficulty making sense of
it. Simple judgment problems like these are easily resolved, and most
people agree on their solution.

Not so with Julie 2.0. What makes this problem difficult is the
presence of multiple, conflicting cues. There are indications of ability
and motivation but also of character weaknesses and mediocre

achievement. The story seems to be all over the place. It does not easily make sense, because the elements cannot be fit in a coherent interpretation. Of course, the incoherence does not make the story unrealistic or even implausible. Life is often more complex than the stories we like to tell about it.

Multiple, conflicting cues create the ambiguity that defines difficult judgment problems. Ambiguity also explains why complex problems are noisier than simple ones. The rule is simple: if there is more than one way to see anything, people will vary in how they see it. People can pick different pieces of evidence to form the core of their narrative, so there are many possible conclusions. If you found it difficult to construct a story that makes sense of Julie 2.0, you can be quite certain that other readers will construct different stories that justify judgments other than yours. This is the variability that produces pattern noise.

When do you feel confident in a judgment? Two conditions must be satisfied: the story you believe must be comprehensively coherent, and there must be no attractive alternatives. Comprehensive coherence is achieved when all the details of the chosen interpretation fit with the story and reinforce each other. Of course, you can also achieve coherence, albeit less elegantly, by ignoring or explaining away whatever does not fit. It is the same with alternative interpretations. The true expert who has "solved" a judgment problem knows not only why her explanatory story is correct; she is equally fluent in explaining why other stories are wrong. Here again, a person can gain confidence of equal strength but poorer quality by failing to consider alternatives or by actively suppressing them.

The main implication of this view of confidence is that subjective confidence in one's judgment by no means guarantees accuracy. Moreover, the suppression of alternative interpretations — a well-documented process in perception — could induce what we have called the *illusion of agreement* (see chapter 2). If people cannot imagine possible alternatives to their conclusions, they will naturally assume that other observers must reach the same conclusion, too. Of course, few of us have the good fortune of being highly confident about all our judgments, and all of us have had the experience of uncertainty, perhaps as recently as your reading about Julie 2.0. We are not all highly confident all the time, but most of the time we are more confident than we should be.

Pattern Noise: Stable or Transient

We have defined a pattern error as an error in an individual's judgment of a case that cannot be explained by the sum of the separate effects of the case and the judge. An extreme example may be the normally lenient judge who is unusually severe in sentencing a particular kind of defendant (say, people who have committed traffic offenses). Or, say, the normally cautious investor who drops his usual caution when shown the plan of an exciting start-up. Of course, most pattern errors are not extreme: we observe a moderate pattern error in the lenient judge who is less lenient than usual when dealing with recidivists, or even more lenient than usual when sentencing young women.

Pattern errors arise from a combination of transient and permanent factors. The transient factors include those we have described as sources of occasion noise, such as a judge's good mood at the relevant moment or some unfortunate recent occurrence that is currently on the judge's mind. Other factors are more permanent — for example, an employer's unusual enthusiasm for people who attended certain universities or a doctor's unusual propensity to recommend hospitalization for people with pneumonia. We can write a simple equation that describes an error in a single judgment:

Pattern Error = Stable Pattern Error + Transient (Occasion) Error

Because stable pattern error and transient (occasion) error are independent and uncorrelated, we can extend the equation above to analyze their variances:

$$\text{(Pattern Noise)}^2 = \text{(Stable Pattern Noise)}^2 + \text{(Occasion Noise)}^2$$

As we did for other components of error and noise, we can represent this equation graphically as a sum of squares on the sides of a right triangle (Figure 15):

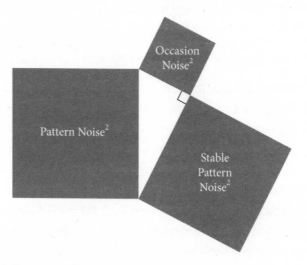

FIGURE 15: *Decomposing pattern noise*

For a simple case of stable pattern noise, consider recruiters who predict the future performance of executives on the basis of a set of ratings. In chapter 9 we spoke of a "model of the judge." The model of an individual recruiter assigns a weight to each rating, which corresponds to its importance in that recruiter's judgments. The weights vary among recruiters: leadership may count more for one recruiter, communication skills for another. Such differences produce variability in the recruiters' ranking of candidates — an instance of what we call stable pattern noise.

Personal reactions to individual cases can also produce patterns that are stable but highly specific. Consider what led you to pay more attention to some aspects of Julie's story than to others. Some details of the case may resonate with your life experience. Perhaps something about Julie reminds you of a close relative who kept almost succeeding but ultimately failing, because of what you believe are deep character flaws that were evident since that relative's teenage years.

Conversely, Julie's story may evoke memories of a close friend who, after a troubled adolescence, did make it to medical school and is now a successful specialist. The associations that Julie evokes in different people are idiosyncratic and unpredictable, but they are likely to be stable: if you had read Julie's story last week, you would have been reminded of the same people and would have seen her story in the same distinctively personal light.

Individual differences in the quality of judgments are another source of pattern noise. Imagine a single forecaster with crystal-ball powers that no one knows about (including herself). Her accuracy would make her deviate in many cases from the average forecast. In the absence of outcome data, these deviations would be regarded as pattern errors. When judgments are unverifiable, superior accuracy will look like pattern noise.

Pattern noise also arises from systematic differences in the ability to make valid judgments about different dimensions of a case. Consider the process of selection for professional sports teams. Coaches may focus on skills in various aspects of the game, physicians on susceptibility to injuries, and psychologists on motivation and resilience. When these different specialists evaluate the same players, we can expect a considerable amount of pattern noise. Similarly, professionals in the same generalist role may be more skilled at some aspects of the judgment task than at others. In such cases, pattern noise is better described as variability in what people know than as error.

When professionals make decisions on their own, variability in skills is simply noise. However, when management has the opportunity to construct teams that will reach judgments together, diversity of skills becomes a potential asset, because different professionals will cover different aspects of the judgment and complement one another. We discuss this opportunity — and what is required to capture it — in chapter 21.

In earlier chapters, we spoke of the two lotteries that face the client of an insurance company or the defendant who is assigned the judge who will try him. We can now see that the first lottery, which picks a professional from a group of colleagues, selects much more than the average level of that professional's judgments (the level error). The lottery also selects a kaleidoscopic assemblage of values, preferences, beliefs, memories, experiences, and associations that are unique to this particular professional. Whenever you make a judgment, you carry your own baggage, too. You come with the habits of mind you formed on the job and the wisdom you gained from your mentors. You bring along the successes that built your confidence and the mistakes that you are careful not to repeat. And somewhere in your brain are the formal rules you remember, those you forgot, and those you learned that it is okay to ignore. No one is exactly like you in all these respects; your stable pattern errors are unique to you.

The second lottery is the one that picks the moment when you make your judgment, the mood you are in, and other extraneous circumstances that should not affect your judgment but do. This lottery creates occasion noise. Imagine, for instance, that shortly before you read Julie's case, you read a newspaper article about drug use on college campuses. The piece featured the story of a gifted student who was determined to go to law school and worked hard — but was unable to make up for the deficit he had accumulated while using drugs in his early years of college. Because it is fresh in your mind, this story will lead you to pay more attention to Julie's pot-smoking habit in your assessment of her overall chances. However, you probably would not remember the article if you encountered the question about Julie in a couple of weeks (and you would obviously not have known about it if you had read the case yesterday). The effect of reading the newspaper article is transient; it is occasion noise.

As this example illustrates, there is no sharp discontinuity between stable pattern noise and the unstable variant that we call occasion noise. The main difference is whether a person's unique sensitivity to some aspects of the case is itself permanent or transient. When the triggers of pattern noise are rooted in our personal experiences and values, we can expect the pattern to be stable, a reflection of our uniqueness.

The Personality Analogy

The idea of uniqueness in the responses of particular people to certain features or combinations of features is not immediately intuitive. To understand it, we might consider another complex combination of features that we all know well: the personalities of people around us. In fact, the event of a judge making a judgment about a case should be seen as a special case of a broader topic that is the domain of personality research: how a person acts in a situation. There is something to be learned about judgment from the decades of intensive study of the broader topic.

Psychologists have long sought to understand and measure individual differences in personality. People differ from one another in many ways; an early attempt to scan the dictionary for terms that may describe a person identified eighteen thousand words. Today, the dominant model of personality, the Big Five model, combines traits into five groupings (extraversion, agreeableness, conscientiousness, openness to experience, neuroticism), with each of the Big Five covering a range of distinguishable traits. A personality trait is understood as a predictor of actual behaviors. If someone is described as conscientious, we expect to observe some corresponding behaviors (arriving on time, keeping commitments, and so on). And if Andrew scores higher than Brad on a measure of aggressiveness, we should observe that, in most situations, Andrew behaves more aggressively than Brad does. In fact, however, the validity of broad traits for predicting specific behaviors is quite limited; a correlation of .30 (PC = 60%) would be considered high.

Common sense suggests that while behavior may be driven by personality, it is also strongly affected by *situations*. In some situations no one is aggressive, and in other situations everyone is. When consoling a bereaved friend, neither Andrew nor Brad will act aggressively; at a football game, however, both will display some aggression. In short — and unsurprisingly — behaviors are a function of personalities *and* of situations.

What makes people unique and endlessly interesting is that this joining of personality and situation is not a mechanical, additive function. For example, the situations that trigger more or less aggression are not the same for all people. Even if Andrew and Brad are equally aggressive on average, they do not necessarily display equal aggressiveness in every context. Perhaps Andrew is aggressive toward his peers but docile with superiors, whereas Brad's level of aggressiveness is not sensitive to hierarchical level. Perhaps Brad is particularly prone to aggression when criticized and unusually restrained when physically threatened.

These signature patterns of response to situations are likely to be fairly stable over time. They constitute much of what we consider someone's *personality*, although they do not lend themselves to a description by a broad trait. Andrew and Brad may share the same score on a test of aggression, but they are unique in their pattern of response to aggression triggers and contexts. Two people who share a trait level — if, for example, they are equally obstinate or equally generous — should be described by two distributions of behaviors that have the same average but not necessarily the same pattern of responses to different situations.

You can now see the parallel between this discussion of personality and the model of judgment we have presented. Level differences between judges correspond to the differences among scores on personality traits, which represent an average of behaviors in multiple situations. Cases are analogous to situations. A person's judgment of a particular problem is only moderately predictable from that person's average level, just as specific behaviors are only moderately predictable from personality traits. The ranking of individuals by their judgment varies substantially from one case to another because people differ in their reaction to the features and combinations of features that they find in each case. The signature of an individual who makes judgments and decisions is a unique pattern of sensitivity to features and a correspondingly unique pattern in the judgment of cases.

The uniqueness of personality is normally a cause for celebration, but this book is concerned with professional judgments, where variation is problematic and noise is error. The point of the analogy is that pattern noise in judgment is not random — even if we have little hope of explaining it and even if the individuals who make distinctive judgments could not explain them.

Speaking of Pattern Noise

"You seem confident in your conclusion, but this is not an easy problem: there are cues pointing in different directions. Have you overlooked alternative interpretations of the evidence?"

"You and I have interviewed the same candidate, and usually we are equally demanding interviewers. Yet we have completely different judgments. Where does this pattern noise come from?"

"The uniqueness of people's personalities is what makes them capable of innovation and creativity, and simply interesting and exciting to be around. When it comes to judgment, however, that uniqueness is not an asset."

CHAPTER 17

The Sources of Noise

W e hope that by now, you agree that wherever there is judgment, there is noise. We also hope that for you, there is no
longer more of it than you think. This mantra about noise motivated
us when we started our project, but our thinking about the topic has
evolved over the years of working on it. We now review the main lessons we have learned about the components of noise, about their
respective importance in the general picture of noise, and about the
place of noise in the study of judgment.

The Components of Noise

Figure 16 offers a combined graphical representation of the three
equations we introduced in chapters 5, 6, and 16. The figure illustrates three successive breakdowns of error:

- error into bias and system noise,

- system noise into level noise and pattern noise,

- pattern noise into stable pattern noise and occasion noise.

You can now see how MSE breaks down into the squares of bias and of the three components of noise we have discussed.

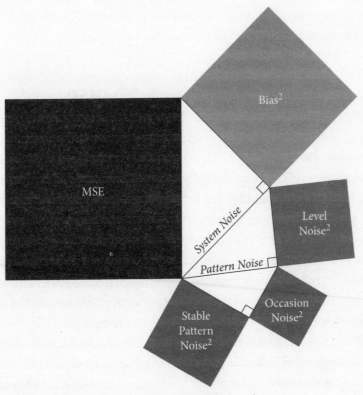

FIGURE 16: *Error, bias, and the components of noise*

When we began our research, we were focusing on the relative weights of bias and noise in total error. We soon concluded that noise is often a larger component of error than bias is, and certainly well worth exploring in more detail.

Our early thinking on the constituents of noise was guided by the structure of complex noise audits, in which multiple people make individual judgments about multiple cases. The study of federal judges was an example, and the study of punitive damages another. Data from these studies provided solid estimates of level noise. On the other hand, because every participant judges every case but does so only once, there is no way of telling whether the residual error, which we have called pattern error, is transient or stable. In the conservative spirit of statistical analysis, the residual error is commonly labeled an error term and is treated as random. In other words, the default interpretation of pattern noise is that it consists entirely of occasion noise.

This conventional interpretation of pattern noise as random error constrained our thinking for a long time. It seemed natural to focus on level noise — the consistent differences between harsh and lenient judges or between optimistic and pessimistic forecasters. We were also intrigued by evidence of the influence on judgments of the irrelevant and transient circumstances that create occasion noise.

The evidence gradually led us to realize that the noisy judgments that different people make are largely determined by something that is neither a general bias of the individual nor transient and random: the persistent personal reactions of particular individuals to a multitude of features, which determine their reactions to specific cases. We eventually concluded that our default assumption about the transient nature of pattern noise should be abandoned.

Though we want to be careful not to overgeneralize from what remains a limited selection of examples, the studies we have assembled, taken together, suggest that stable pattern noise is actually more significant than the other components of system noise. Because we rarely have a full picture of the components of error in the same study, it requires some triangulation to formulate this tentative conclusion. In short, here is what we know — and what we don't.

Sizing the Components

First, we have several estimates of the relative weights of level noise and pattern noise. Overall, it appears that pattern noise contributes more than level noise. In the insurance company of chapter 2, for instance, differences between underwriters in the average of the premiums they set accounted for only 20% of total system noise; the remaining 80% was pattern noise. Among the federal judges of chapter 6, level noise (differences in average severity) represented slightly less than half of total system noise; pattern noise was the larger component. In the punitive damages experiment, the total amount of system noise varied widely depending on the scale used (punitive intent, outrage, or damages in dollars), but the share of pattern noise in that total was roughly constant: it accounted for 63%, 62%, and 61% of total system noise for the three scales used in the study. Other studies we will review in part 5, notably on personnel decisions, are consistent with this tentative conclusion.

The fact that in these studies level noise is generally not the larger component of system noise is already an important message, because level noise is the only form of noise that organizations can (sometimes) monitor without conducting noise audits. When cases are assigned more or less randomly to individual professionals, the differences in the average level of their decisions provide evidence of level noise. For example, studies of patent offices observed large differences in the average propensity of examiners to grant patents, with subsequent effects on the incidence of litigation about these patents. Similarly, case officers in child protection services vary in their propensity to place children in foster care, with long-term consequences for the children's welfare. These observations are based solely on an estimation of level noise. If there is more pattern noise than level noise, then these already-shocking findings understate the magnitude of the noise problem by at least a factor of two. (There are exceptions to this tentative rule. The scandalous variability in the decisions of asylum judges is almost certainly due more to level noise than to pattern noise, which we suspect is large as well.)

The next step is to analyze pattern noise by separating its two components. There are good reasons to assume that stable pattern noise, rather than occasion noise, is the dominant component. The audit of the sentences of federal judges illustrates our reasoning. Start with the extreme possibility that all pattern noise is transient. On that assumption, sentencing would be unstable and inconsistent over time, to an extent that we find implausible: we would have to expect that the average difference between judgments of *the same case by the same judge* on different occasions is about 2.8 years. The variability of average sentencing among judges is already shocking. The same variability in the sentences of an individual judge over occasions would be grotesque. It seems more reasonable to conclude that judges differ in their reactions to different defendants and different crimes and that these differences are highly personal but stable.

To quantify more precisely how much of pattern noise is stable and how much is occasion noise, we need studies in which the same judges make two independent assessments of each case. As we have noted, obtaining two independent judgments is generally impossible in studies of judgment, because it is difficult to guarantee that the second judgment of a case is truly independent of the first. Especially when the judgment is complex, there is a high probability that the individual will recognize the problem and repeat the original judgment.

A group of researchers at Princeton, led by Alexander Todorov, has designed clever experimental techniques to overcome this problem. They recruited participants from Amazon Mechanical Turk, a site where individuals provide short-term services, such as answering questionnaires, and are paid for their time. In one experiment, participants viewed pictures of faces (generated by a computer program, but perfectly indistinguishable from the faces of real people) and rated them on various attributes, such as likability and trustworthiness. The experiment was repeated, with the same faces and the same respondents, one week later.

It is fair to expect less consensus in this experiment than in professional judgments such as those of sentencing judges. Everyone might agree that some people are extremely attractive and that others are extremely unattractive, but across a significant range, we expect reactions to faces to be largely idiosyncratic. Indeed, there was little agreement among observers: on the ratings of trustworthiness, for instance, differences among pictures accounted for only 18% of the variance of judgments. The remaining 82% of the variance was noise.

It is also fair to expect less stability in these judgments, because the quality of judgments made by participants who are paid to answer questions online is often substantially lower than in professional settings. Nevertheless, the largest component of noise was stable pattern noise. The second largest component of noise was level noise — that is, differences among observers in their average ratings of trustworthiness. Occasion noise, though still substantial, was the smallest component.

The researchers reached the same conclusions when they asked participants to make other judgments — about preferences among cars or foods, for example, or on questions that are closer to what we call professional judgments. For instance, in a replication of the study of punitive damages discussed in chapter 15, participants rated their punitive intent in ten cases of personal injury, on two separate occasions separated by a week. Here again, stable pattern noise was the largest component. In all these studies, individuals generally did not agree with one another, but they remained quite stable in their judgments. This "consistency without consensus," in the researchers' words, provides clear evidence of stable pattern noise.

The strongest evidence for the role of stable patterns comes from the large study of bail judges we mentioned in chapter 10. In one part of this exceptional study, the authors created a statistical model that simulated how each judge used the available cues to decide whether to grant bail. They built custom-made models of 173 judges. Then they applied the simulated judges to make decisions about 141,833 cases, yielding 173 decisions for each case — a total of more than 24 million decisions. At our request, the authors generously carried a special analysis in which they separated the variance judgments into three components: the "true" variance of the average decisions for each of the cases, the level noise created by differences among judges in their propensity to grant bail, and the remaining pattern noise.

This analysis is relevant to our argument because pattern noise, as measured in this study, is entirely stable. The random variability of occasion noise is not represented, because this is an analysis of *models* that predict a judge's decision. Only the verifiably stable individual rules of prediction are included.

The conclusion was unequivocal: this stable pattern noise was almost four times larger than level noise (stable pattern noise accounted for 26%, and level noise 7%, of total variance). The stable, idiosyncratic individual patterns of judgment that could be identified were much larger than the differences in across-the-board severity.

All this evidence is consistent with the research on occasion noise that we reviewed in chapter 7: while the existence of occasion noise is surprising and even disturbing, there is no indication that within-person variability is larger than between-person differences. The most important component of system noise is the one we had initially neglected: stable pattern noise, the variability among judges in their judgments of particular cases.

Given the relative scarcity of relevant research, our conclusions are tentative, but they do reflect a change in how we think about noise — and about how to tackle it. In principle at least, level noise — or simple, across-the-board differences between judges — should be a relatively easy problem to measure and address. If there are abnormally "tough" graders, "cautious" child custody officers, or "risk-averse" loan officers, the organizations that employ them could aim to equalize the average level of their judgments. Universities, for instance, address this problem when they require professors to abide by a predetermined distribution of grades within each class.

Unfortunately, as we now realize, focusing on level noise misses a large part of what individual differences are about. Noise is mostly a product not of level differences but of interactions: how different judges deal with particular defendants, how different teachers deal with particular students, how different social workers deal with particular families, how different leaders deal with particular visions of the future. Noise is mostly a by-product of our uniqueness, of our "judgment personality." Reducing level noise is still a worthwhile objective, but attaining only this objective would leave most of the problem of system noise without a solution.

Explaining Error

We found a lot to say about noise, but the topic is almost entirely absent from public awareness and from discussions of judgment and error. Despite the evidence of its presence and the multiple mechanisms that produce it, noise is rarely mentioned as a major factor in judgment. How is this possible? Why do we never invoke noise to explain bad judgments, whereas we routinely blame biases? Why is it so unusual to give much thought to noise as a source of error, despite its ubiquity?

The key to this puzzle is that although the average of errors (the bias) and the variability of errors (the noise) play equivalent roles in the error equation, we think about them in profoundly different ways. And our ordinary way of making sense of the world around us makes it all but impossible to recognize the role of noise.

Earlier in this book, we noted that we easily make sense of events in hindsight, although we could not have predicted them before they happened. In the valley of the normal, events are unsurprising and easily explained.

The same can be said of judgments. Like other events, judgments and decisions mostly happen in the valley of the normal; they usually do not surprise us. For one thing, judgments that produce satisfactory outcomes are normal, and seldom questioned. When the shooter who is picked for the free kick scores the goal, when the heart surgery is successful, or when a start-up prospers, we assume that the reasons the decision makers had for their choices must have been the right ones. After all, they have been proven right. Like any other unsurprising story, a success story explains itself once the outcome is known.

We do, however, feel a need to explain abnormal outcomes: the bad ones and, occasionally, the surprisingly good ones — such as the shocking business gamble that pays off. Explanations that appeal to error or to special flair are far more popular than they deserve to be, because important gambles of the past easily become acts of genius or folly when their outcome is known. A well-documented psychological bias called the *fundamental attribution error* is a strong tendency to assign blame or credit to agents for actions and outcomes that are better explained by luck or by objective circumstances. Another bias, hindsight, distorts judgments so that outcomes that could not have been anticipated appear easily foreseeable in retrospect.

Explanations for errors of judgment are not hard to come by; finding reasons for judgments is, if anything, easier than finding causes for events. We can always invoke the motives of the people making the judgments. If that is not sufficient, we can blame their incompetence. And another explanation for poor judgments has become common in recent decades: psychological bias.

A substantial body of research in psychology and behavioral economics has documented a long list of psychological biases: the planning fallacy, overconfidence, loss aversion, the endowment effect, the status quo bias, excessive discounting of the future ("present bias"), and many others — including, of course, biases for or against various categories of people. Much is known about the conditions under which each of these biases is likely to influence judgments and decisions, and a fair amount is known that would allow an observer of decision making to recognize biased thinking in real time.

A psychological bias is a legitimate causal explanation of a judgment error if the bias could have been predicted in advance or detected in real time. A psychological bias that is identified only after the fact can still provide a useful, if tentative, explanation if it also offers a prediction about the future. For example, the surprising rejection of a strong woman candidate for a position may suggest a more general hypothesis of gender bias that future appointments by the same committee will confirm or refute. Consider, in contrast, a causal explanation that applies only to one event: "In that case they failed, so they must have been overconfident." The statement is completely vacuous, but it provides an illusion of understanding that can be quite satisfying. Business school professor Phil Rosenzweig has convincingly argued that empty explanations in terms of biases are common in discussions of business outcomes. Their popularity attests to the prevalent need for causal stories that make sense of experience.

Noise Is Statistical

As we noted in chapter 12, our normal way of thinking is causal. We naturally attend to the particular, following and creating causally coherent stories about individual cases, in which failures are often attributed to errors, and errors to biases. The ease with which bad judgments can be explained leaves no space for noise in our accounts of errors.

The invisibility of noise is a direct consequence of causal thinking. Noise is inherently statistical: it becomes visible only when we think statistically about an ensemble of similar judgments. Indeed, it then becomes hard to miss: it is the variability in the backward-looking statistics about sentencing decisions and underwriting premiums. It is the range of possibilities when you and others consider how to predict a future outcome. It is the scatter of the hits on the target. Causally, noise is nowhere; statistically, it is everywhere.

Unfortunately, taking the statistical view is not easy. We effortlessly invoke causes for the events we observe, but thinking statistically about them must be learned and remains effortful. Causes are natural; statistics are difficult.

The result is a marked imbalance in how we view bias and noise as sources of error. If you have been exposed to any introductory psychology, you probably remember the illustrations in which a salient and richly detailed figure stands out from an indistinct background. Our attention is firmly fixed on the figure even when it is small against the background. The figure/ground demonstrations are an apt metaphor for our intuitions about bias and noise: bias is a compelling figure, while noise is the background to which we pay no attention. That is how we remain largely unaware of a large flaw in our judgment.

Speaking of the Sources of Noise

"We easily see differences in the average level of judgments, but how large is the pattern noise we do not see?"

"You say this judgment was caused by biases, but would you say the same thing if the outcome had been different? And can you tell if there was noise?"

"We are rightly focused on reducing biases. Let's also worry about reducing noise."

PART V

Improving Judgments

How can an organization improve the judgments its professionals make? In particular, how can an organization reduce judgment noise? If you were in charge of answering these questions, how would you go about it?

A necessary first step is to get the organization to recognize that noise in professional judgments is an issue that deserves attention. To get to that point, we recommend a noise audit (see appendix A for a detailed description). In a noise audit, multiple individuals judge the same problems. Noise is the variability of these judgments. There will be cases in which this variability can be attributed to incompetence: some judges know what they are talking about, others do not. When there is such a skill gap (either in general, or on certain types of cases), the priority should of course be to improve the deficient skills. But, as we have seen, there can be a large amount of noise even in the judgments of competent and well-trained professionals.

If the amount of system noise is worth addressing, replacing judgment with rules or algorithms is an option that you should consider, as it will eliminate noise entirely. But rules have their own problems (as we will see in part 6), and even the most enthusiastic proponents of AI agree that algorithms are not, and will not soon be, a universal substitute for human judgment. The task of improving judgment is as urgent as ever, and it is the topic of this part of the book.

A sensible way to improve judgments is, of course, to select the best possible human judges. At the shooting range, some shooters have an especially good aim. The same is true of any professional judgment task: the most highly skilled will be both less noisy and less biased. How to find the best judges is sometimes obvious; if you want to solve a chess problem, ask a grandmaster, not the authors of this book. But in most problems, the characteristics of superior judges are harder to discern. These characteristics are the subject of chapter 18.

Next, we discuss approaches to the reduction of judgment errors. Psychological biases are implicated in both statistical bias and noise. As we see in chapter 19, there have been many attempts to counteract psychological biases, with some clear failures and some clear successes. We briefly review debiasing strategies and suggest a promising approach that, to our knowledge, has not been systematically explored: asking a designated *decision observer* to search for diagnostic signs that could indicate, in real time, that a group's work is being affected by one or several familiar biases. Appendix B provides an example of a bias checklist that a decision observer could use.

We then proceed to our main focus in this part of the book: the fight against noise. We introduce the theme of *decision hygiene,* the approach we recommend to reduce noise in human judgments. We present case studies in five different domains. In each domain, we examine the prevalence of noise and some of the horror stories it generates. We also review the success — or the lack of success — of efforts to reduce noise. In each domain, of course, multiple approaches have been used, but for ease of exposition, each chapter emphasizes a single decision hygiene strategy.

We start in chapter 20 with the case of forensic science, which illustrates the importance of *sequencing information.* The search for coherence leads people to form early impressions based on the limited evidence available and then to confirm their emerging prejudgment. This makes it important not to be exposed to irrelevant information early in the judgment process.

In chapter 21, we turn to the case of forecasting, which illustrates the value of one of the most important noise-reduction strategies: *aggregating multiple independent judgments.* The "wisdom of crowds" principle is based on the averaging of multiple independent judgments, which is guaranteed to reduce noise. Beyond straight averaging, there are other methods for aggregating judgments, also illustrated by the example of forecasting.

Chapter 22 offers a review of noise in medicine and efforts to reduce it. It points to the importance and general applicability of a noise-reduction strategy we already introduced with the example of criminal sentencing: *judgment guidelines.* Guidelines can be a powerful noise-reduction mechanism because they directly reduce between-judge variability in final judgments.

In chapter 23, we turn to a familiar challenge in business life: performance evaluations. Efforts to reduce noise there demonstrate the critical importance of using a *shared scale grounded in an outside view.* This is an important decision hygiene strategy for a simple reason: judgment entails the translation of an impression onto a scale, and if different judges use different scales, there will be noise.

Chapter 24 explores the related but distinct topic of personnel selection, which has been extensively researched over the past hundred years. It illustrates the value of an essential decision hygiene strategy: *structuring complex judgments.* By *structuring,* we mean decomposing a judgment into its component parts, managing the process of data collection to ensure the inputs are independent of one another, and delaying the holistic discussion and the final judgment until all these inputs have been collected.

We build on the lessons learned from the field of personnel selection to propose, in chapter 25, a general approach to option evaluation called the *mediating assessments protocol,* or MAP for short. MAP starts from the premise that "options are like candidates" and describes schematically how structured decision making, along with the other decision hygiene strategies mentioned above, can be introduced in a typical decision process for both recurring and singular decisions.

A general point before we embark: it would be valuable to be able to specify, and even to quantify, the likely benefits of each decision hygiene strategy in various contexts. It would also be valuable to know which of the strategies is most beneficial and how to compare them. When the information flow is controlled, to what extent is noise reduced? If the goal is to reduce noise, in practice, how many judgments should be aggregated? Structuring judgments can be valuable, but exactly how valuable is it in different contexts?

Because the topic of noise has attracted little attention, these remain open questions, which research could eventually address. For practical purposes, the benefits of one or another strategy will depend on the particular setting in which it is being used. Consider the adoption of guidelines: they will sometimes produce massive benefits (as we will see in some medical diagnoses). In other settings, however, the benefits of adopting guidelines might be modest — perhaps because there is not a lot of noise to begin with or perhaps because even the best possible guidelines do not reduce error much. In any given context, a decision maker should aspire to achieve a more precise understanding of the likely gains from each decision hygiene strategy — and of the corresponding costs, which we discuss in part 6.

CHAPTER 18

Better Judges for Better Judgments

Thus far, we have mostly spoken of human judges without distinguishing among them. Yet it is obvious that in any task that requires judgment, some people will perform better than others will. Even a wisdom-of-crowds aggregate of judgments is likely to be better if the crowd is composed of more able people. An important question, then, is how to identify these better judges.

Three things matter. Judgments are both less noisy and less biased when those who make them are well trained, are more intelligent, and have the right cognitive style. In other words: good judgments depend on what you know, how well you think, and *how* you think. Good judges tend to be experienced and smart, but they also tend to be actively open-minded and willing to learn from new information.

Experts and Respect-Experts

It is almost tautological to say that the skill of judges affects the quality of their judgments. For instance, radiologists who are skilled are more likely to diagnose pneumonia correctly, and in forecasting world events there are "superforecasters" who reliably out-predict their less-than-super peers. If you assemble a group of lawyers who are true specialists in some area of law, they are likely to make similar, and good, predictions about the outcome of common legal disputes in court. Highly skilled people are less noisy, and they also show less bias.

These people are true experts at the tasks in question. Their superiority over others is verifiable, thanks to the availability of outcome data. In principle at least, we can choose a doctor, forecaster, or lawyer according to how often they have been right in the past. (For obvious reasons, this approach may be difficult in practice; we don't recommend that you attempt to subject your family practitioner to a proficiency exam.)

As we have also noted, many judgments are not verifiable. Within certain boundaries, we cannot easily know or uncontroversially define the true value at which judgments are aiming. Underwriting and criminal sentencing fall in this category, as do wine tasting, essay grading, book and movie reviewing, and innumerable other judgments. Yet some professionals in these domains come to be called experts. The confidence we have in these experts' judgment is entirely based on the respect they enjoy from their peers. We call them *respect-experts*.

The term *respect-expert* is not meant to be disrespectful. The fact that some experts are not subject to an evaluation of the accuracy of their judgments is not a criticism; it is a fact of life in many domains. Many professors, scholars, and management consultants are respect-experts. Their credibility depends on the respect of their students, peers, or clients. In all these fields, and many more, the judgments of one professional can be compared only with those of her peers.

In the absence of true values to determine who is right or wrong, we often value the opinion of respect-experts even when they disagree with one another. Picture, for instance, a panel on which several political analysts have sharply different perspectives on what caused a diplomatic crisis and how it will unfold. (This disagreement is not unusual; it would not be a very interesting panel if they all agreed.) All the analysts believe that there is a correct view and that their own view is the one closest to it. As you listen, you may find several of the analysts equally impressive and their arguments equally convincing. You cannot know then which of them is correct (and you may not even know later, if their analyses are not formulated as clearly verifiable predictions). You know that at least some of the analysts are wrong, because they are in disagreement. Yet you respect their expertise.

Or consider a different set of experts, not making predictions at all. Three moral philosophers, all of them well trained, are gathered in a room. One of them follows Immanuel Kant; another, Jeremy Bentham; and a third, Aristotle. With respect to what morality requires, they disagree intensely. The issue might involve whether and when it is legitimate to lie, or the rights of animals, or the goal of criminal punishment. You listen closely. You might admire the clarity and precision of their thinking. You tend to agree with one philosopher, but you respect them all.

Why do you do that? More generally, how do people who are themselves respected for the quality of their judgment decide to trust someone as an expert when there is no data to establish expertise objectively? What makes a respect-expert?

Part of the answer is the existence of shared norms, or professional doctrine. Experts often obtain professional qualifications from professional communities and receive training and supervision in their organizations. Doctors who complete their residency and young lawyers who learn from a senior partner do not just learn the technical tools of their trade; they are trained to use certain methods and follow certain norms.

Shared norms give professionals a sense of which inputs should be taken into account and how to make and justify their final judgments. In the insurance company, for instance, claims adjusters had no difficulty agreeing on and describing the relevant considerations that should be included in a checklist to assess a claim.

This agreement, of course, did not stop the claims adjusters from varying widely in their claims assessments, because doctrine does not fully specify how to proceed. It is not a recipe that can be mechanically followed. Instead, doctrine leaves room for interpretation. Experts still produce judgments, not computations. That is why noise inevitably occurs. Even identically trained professionals who agree on the doctrine they are applying will drift away from one another in their application of it.

Beyond a knowledge of shared norms, experience is necessary, too. You can be a young prodigy if your specialty is chess, concert piano, or throwing the javelin, because results validate your level of performance. But underwriters, fingerprint examiners, or judges usually need some years of experience for credibility. There are no young prodigies in underwriting.

Another characteristic of respect-experts is their ability to make and explain their judgments with confidence. We tend to put more trust in people who trust themselves than we do in those who show their doubts. The confidence heuristic points to the fact that in a group, confident people have more weight than others, even if they have no reason to be confident. Respect-experts excel at constructing coherent stories. Their experience enables them to recognize patterns, to reason by analogy with previous cases, and to form and confirm hypotheses quickly. They easily fit the facts they see into a coherent story that inspires confidence.

Intelligence

Training, experience, and confidence enable respect-experts to command trust. But these attributes do not guarantee the quality of their judgments. How can we know which experts are likely to make good judgments?

There is good reason to believe that general intelligence is likely to be associated with better judgment. Intelligence is correlated with good performance in virtually all domains. All other things being

BETTER JUDGES FOR BETTER JUDGMENTS

equal, it is associated not only with higher academic achievement but also with higher job performance.

Many debates and misunderstandings arise in discussions of measures of intelligence or of general mental ability (GMA, the term now used in preference to intelligence quotient, or IQ). There are lingering misconceptions about the innate nature of intelligence; in fact, tests measure developed abilities, which are partly a function of heritable traits and partly influenced by the environment, including educational opportunities. Many people also have concerns about the adverse impact of GMA-based selection on identifiable social groups and the legitimacy of using GMA tests for selection purposes.

We need to separate these concerns about the use of tests from the reality of their predictive value. Since the US Army started using tests of mental ability more than a century ago, thousands of studies have measured the link between cognitive test scores and subsequent performance. The message that emerges from this mass of research is unambiguous. As one review put it, "GMA predicts both occupational level attained and performance within one's chosen occupation and does so better than any other ability, trait, or disposition and better than job experience." Of course, other cognitive abilities matter too (more on this later). So do many personality traits — including conscientiousness and *grit*, defined as perseverance and passion in the pursuit of long-term goals. And yes, there are various forms of intelligence that GMA tests do not measure, such as practical intelligence and creativity. Psychologists and neuroscientists distinguish between crystallized intelligence, the ability to solve problems by relying on a store of knowledge about the world (including arithmetical operations), and fluid intelligence, the ability to solve novel problems.

Yet for all its crudeness and limitations, GMA, as measured by standardized tests containing questions on verbal, quantitative, and spatial problems, remains by far the best single predictor of important outcomes. As the previously mentioned review adds, the predictive power of GMA is "larger than most found in psychological research." The strength of the association between general mental ability and job success increases, quite logically, with the complexity of the job in question: intelligence matters more for rocket scientists than it does for those with simpler tasks. For jobs of high complexity, the correlations that can be observed between standardized test scores and job performance are in the .50 range (PC = 67%). As we have noted, a correlation of .50 indicates a very strong predictive value by social-science standards.

Especially in discussions of skilled professional judgments, an important and frequent objection to the relevance of intelligence measures is that all those who make such judgments are likely to be high-GMA individuals. Doctors, judges, or senior underwriters are much more educated than the general population and highly likely to score much higher on any measure of cognitive ability. You might reasonably believe that high GMA makes little difference among them — that it is merely the entry ticket into the pool of high achievers, not the source of achievement differences within that pool.

This belief, although widespread, is incorrect. No doubt the range of GMAs found in a given occupation is wider at the bottom of the range of occupations than at the top: there are high-GMA individuals in lower-level occupations but almost no people with below-average GMA among lawyers, chemists, or engineers. From that perspective, therefore, high mental ability is apparently a necessary condition for gaining access to high-status professions.

However, this measure fails to capture differences in achievement *within* these groups. Even among the top 1% of people as measured by cognitive ability (evaluated at age thirteen), exceptional outcomes are strongly correlated with GMA. Compared with those who are in the bottom quartile of this top 1%, those who are in the top quartile are two to three times more likely to earn a doctoral-level degree, publish a book, or be granted a patent. In other words, not only does the difference in GMA matter between the 99th percentile and the 80th or 50th, but it still matters — a lot! — between the 99.88th percentile and the 99.13th.

In another striking illustration of the link between ability and outcomes, a 2013 study focused on the CEOs of Fortune 500 companies and the 424 American billionaires (the top 0.0001% of Americans by wealth). It found, predictably, that these hyper-elite groups are composed of people drawn from the most intellectually able. But the study also found that *within* these groups, higher education and ability levels are related to higher compensation (for CEOs) and net worth (for billionaires). Incidentally, famous college dropouts who become billionaires, such as Steve Jobs, Bill Gates, and Mark Zuckerberg, are the trees that hide the forest: whereas about one-third of American adults have earned a college degree, 88% of billionaires did so.

The conclusion is clear. GMA contributes significantly to the quality of performance in occupations that require judgment, even within a pool of high-ability individuals. The notion that there is a threshold beyond which GMA ceases to make a difference is not supported by the evidence. This conclusion in turn strongly suggests that if professional judgments are unverifiable but assumed to reach for an invisible bull's-eye, then the judgments of high-ability people are more likely to be close. If you must pick people to make judgments, picking those with the highest mental ability makes a lot of sense.

But this line of reasoning has an important limitation. Since you cannot give standardized tests to everyone, you will have to guess who the higher-GMA people are. And high GMA improves performance on many fronts, including the ability to convince others that you're right. People of high mental ability are more likely than others to make better judgments and to be true experts, but they are also more likely to impress their peers, earn others' trust, and become respect-experts in the absence of any reality feedback. Medieval astrologers must have been among the highest-GMA people of their time.

It can be sensible to place your trust in people who look and sound intelligent and who can articulate a compelling rationale for their judgments, but this strategy is insufficient and may even backfire. Are there, then, other ways to identify real experts? Do people with the best judgment have other recognizable traits?

Cognitive Style

Regardless of mental ability, people differ in their *cognitive style,* or their approach to judgment tasks. Many instruments have been developed to capture cognitive styles. Most of these measures correlate with GMA (and with one another), but they measure different things.

One such measure is the *cognitive reflection test* (CRT), made famous by the now-ubiquitous question about the ball and the bat: "A bat and a ball cost $1.10 in total. The bat costs $1.00 more than the ball. How much does the ball cost?" Other questions that have been proposed to measure cognitive reflection include this one: "If you're running a race and you pass the person in second place, what place are you in?" CRT questions attempt to measure how likely people are to override the first (and wrong) answer that comes to mind ("ten cents" for the ball-and-bat question, and "first" for the race example). Lower CRT scores are associated with many real-world judgments and beliefs, including belief in ghosts, astrology, and extrasensory perception. The scores predict whether people will fall for blatantly inaccurate "fake news." They are even associated with how much people will use their smartphones.

The CRT is seen by many as one instrument to measure a broader concept: the propensity to use reflective versus impulsive thought processes. Simply put, some people like to engage in careful thought, whereas others, faced with the same problem, tend to trust their first impulses. In our terminology, the CRT can be seen as a measure of people's propensity to rely on slow, System 2 thinking rather than on fast, System 1 thinking.

Other self-assessments have been developed to measure this propensity (and all these tests are, of course, intercorrelated). The need-for-cognition scale, for instance, asks people how much they like to think hard about problems. To score high on the scale, you would have to agree that "I tend to set goals that can be accomplished only by expending considerable mental effort" and disagree with "Thinking is not my idea of fun." People with a high need for cognition tend to be less susceptible to known cognitive biases. Some more bizarre associations have been reported, too: if you avoid movie reviews with a spoiler alert, you probably have a high need for cognition; those who are low on the need-for-cognition scale prefer spoiled stories.

Because that scale is a self-assessment and because the socially desirable answer is fairly obvious, the scale raises fair questions. Someone who is trying to impress is hardly likely to endorse the statement "Thinking is not my idea of fun." For that reason, other tests try to measure skills instead of using self-descriptions.

One example is the Adult Decision Making Competence scale, which measures how prone people are to make typical errors in judgment like overconfidence or inconsistency in risk perceptions. Another is the Halpern Critical Thinking Assessment, which focuses on critical thinking skills, including both a disposition toward rational thinking and a set of learnable skills. Taking this assessment, you would be asked questions like this: "Imagine that a friend asks you for advice about which of two weight-loss programs to choose. Whereas one program reports that clients lose an average of twenty-five pounds, the other program reports that they lose an average of thirty pounds. What questions would you like to have answered before choosing one of the programs?" If you answered, for instance, that you would want to know how many people lost this much weight and whether they maintained that weight loss for a year or more, you would score points for applying critical thinking. People who score well on the Adult Decision Making Competence scale or on the Halpern assessment seem to make better judgments in life: they experience fewer adverse life events driven by bad choices, such as needing to pay late fees for a movie rental and experiencing an unwanted pregnancy.

It seems sensible to assume that all these measures of cognitive style and skill — and many others — generally predict judgment. Their relevance seems, however, to vary with the task. When Uriel Haran, Ilana Ritov, and Barbara Mellers looked for the cognitive styles that might predict forecasting ability, they found that the need for cognition did not predict who would work harder to seek additional information. They also did not find that the need for cognition was reliably associated with higher performance.

The only measure of cognitive style or personality that they found to predict forecasting performance was another scale, developed by psychology professor Jonathan Baron to measure "actively open-minded thinking." To be actively open-minded is to actively search for information that contradicts your preexisting hypotheses. Such information includes the dissenting opinions of others and the careful weighing of new evidence against old beliefs. Actively open-minded people agree with statements like this: "Allowing oneself to be convinced by an opposing argument is a sign of good character." They disagree with the proposition that "changing your mind is a sign of weakness" or that "intuition is the best guide in making decisions."

In other words, while the cognitive reflection and need for cognition scores measure the propensity to engage in slow and careful thinking, actively open-minded thinking goes beyond that. It is the humility of those who are constantly aware that their judgment is a work in progress and who yearn to be corrected. We will see in chapter 21 that this thinking style characterizes the very best forecasters, who constantly change their minds and revise their beliefs in response to new information. Interestingly, there is some evidence that actively open-minded thinking is a teachable skill.

We do not aim here to draw hard-and-fast conclusions about how to pick individuals who will make good judgments in a given domain. But two general principles emerge from this brief review. First, it is wise to recognize the difference between domains in which expertise can be confirmed by comparison with true values (such as weather forecasting) and domains that are the province of respect-experts. A political analyst may sound articulate and convincing, and a chess grandmaster may sound timid and unable to explain the reasoning behind some of his moves. Yet we probably should treat the professional judgment of the former with more skepticism than that of the latter.

Second, some judges are going to be better than their equally qualified and experienced peers. If they are better, they are less likely to be biased or noisy. Among many things that explain these differences, intelligence and cognitive style matter. Although no single measure or scale unambiguously predicts judgment quality, you may want to look for the sort of people who actively search for new information that could contradict their prior beliefs, who are methodical in integrating that information into their current perspective, and who are willing, even eager, to change their minds as a result.

The personality of people with excellent judgment may not fit the generally accepted stereotype of a decisive leader. People often tend to trust and like leaders who are firm and clear and who seem to know, immediately and deep in their bones, what is right. Such leaders inspire confidence. But the evidence suggests that if the goal is to reduce error, it is better for leaders (and others) to remain open to counterarguments and to know that they might be wrong. If they end up being decisive, it is at the end of a process, not at the start.

Speaking of Better Judges

"You are an expert. But are your judgments verifiable, or are you a respect-expert?"

"We have to choose between two opinions, and we know nothing about these individuals' expertise and track record. Let's follow the advice of the more intelligent one."

"Intelligence is only part of the story, however. *How* people think is also important. Perhaps we should pick the most thoughtful, open-minded person, rather than the smartest one."

CHAPTER 19

Debiasing and Decision Hygiene

M any researchers and organizations have pursued the goal of debiasing judgments. This chapter examines their central findings. We will distinguish between different types of debiasing interventions and discuss one such intervention that deserves further investigation. We will then turn to the reduction of noise and introduce the idea of decision hygiene.

Ex Post and Ex Ante Debiasing

A good way to characterize the two main approaches to debiasing is to return to the measurement analogy. Suppose that you know that your bathroom scale adds, on average, half a pound to your weight. Your scale is biased. But this does not make it useless. You can address its bias in one of two possible ways. You can correct every reading from your unkindly scale by subtracting half a pound. To be sure, that might get a bit tiresome (and you might forget to do it). An alternative might be to adjust the dial and improve the instrument's accuracy, once and for all.

These two approaches to debiasing measurements have direct

analogues in interventions to debias judgments. They work either ex post, by correcting judgments after they have been made, or ex ante, by intervening before a judgment or decision.

Ex post, or corrective, debiasing is often carried out intuitively. Suppose that you are supervising a team in charge of a project and that the team estimates that it can complete its project in three months. You might want to add a buffer to the members' judgment and plan for four months, or more, thus correcting a bias (the planning fallacy) you assume is present.

This kind of bias correction is sometimes undertaken more systematically. In the United Kingdom, HM Treasury has published *The Green Book*, a guide on how to evaluate programs and projects. The book urges planners to address optimistic biases by applying percentage adjustments to estimates of the cost and duration of a project. These adjustments should ideally be based on an organization's historic levels of optimism bias. If no such historical data is available, *The Green Book* recommends applying generic adjustment percentages for each type of project.

Ex ante or preventive debiasing interventions fall in turn into two broad categories. Some of the most promising are designed to modify the environment in which the judgment or decision takes place. Such modifications, or *nudges*, as they are known, aim to reduce the effect of biases or even to enlist biases to produce a better decision. A simple example is automatic enrollment in pension plans. Designed to overcome inertia, procrastination, and optimistic bias, automatic enrollment ensures that employees will be saving for retirement unless they deliberately opt out. Automatic enrollment has proved to be extremely effective in increasing participation rates. The program is sometimes accompanied by Save More Tomorrow plans, by which employees can agree to earmark a certain percentage of their future wage increases for savings. Automatic enrollment can be used in many places — for example, automatic enrollment in green energy, in free school meal plans for poor children, or in various other benefits programs.

Other nudges work on different aspects of choice architecture. They might make the right decision the easy decision — for example, by reducing administrative burdens for getting access to care for mental health problems. Or they might make certain characteristics of a product or an activity salient — for example, by making once-hidden fees explicit and clear. Grocery stores and websites can easily be designed to nudge people in a way that overcomes their biases. If healthy foods are put in prominent places, more people are likely to buy them.

A different type of ex ante debiasing involves training decision makers to recognize their biases and to overcome them. Some of these interventions have been called *boosting;* they aim to improve people's capacities — for example, by teaching them statistical literacy.

Educating people to overcome their biases is an honorable enterprise, but it is more challenging than it seems. Of course, education is useful. For instance, people who have taken years of advanced statistics classes are less likely to make errors in statistical reasoning. But teaching people to avoid biases is hard. Decades of research have shown that professionals who have learned to avoid biases in their area of expertise often struggle to apply what they have learned to different fields. Weather forecasters, for instance, have learned to avoid overconfidence in their forecasts. When they announce a 70% chance of rain, it rains, by and large, 70% of the time. Yet they can be just as overconfident as other people when asked general-knowledge questions. The challenge of learning to overcome a bias is to recognize that a new problem is similar to one we have seen elsewhere and that a bias that we have seen in one place is likely to materialize in other places.

Researchers and educators have had some success using nontraditional teaching methods to facilitate this recognition. In one study, Carey Morewedge of Boston University and his colleagues used instructional videos and "serious games." Participants learned to recognize errors caused by confirmation bias, anchoring, and other psychological biases. After each game, they received feedback on the errors they had made and learned how to avoid making them again. The games (and, to a lesser extent, the videos) reduced the number of errors that participants made on a test immediately afterward and again eight weeks later, when they were asked similar questions. In a separate study, Anne-Laure Sellier and her colleagues found that MBA students who had played an instructional video game in which they learned to overcome confirmation bias applied this learning when solving a business case in another class. They did so even though they were not told that there was any connection between the two exercises.

A Limitation of Debiasing

Whether they correct biases ex post or prevent their effects through nudging or boosting, most debiasing approaches have one thing in common: they target a specific bias, which they assume is present. This often-reasonable assumption is sometimes wrong.

Consider again the example of project planning. You can reasonably assume that overconfidence affects project teams in general, but you cannot be sure that it is the only bias (or even the main one) affecting a particular project team. Maybe the team leader has had a bad experience with a similar project and so has learned to be especially conservative when making estimates. The team thus exhibits the opposite error from the one you thought you should correct. Or perhaps the team developed its forecast by analogy with another similar project and was anchored on the time it took to complete that project. Or maybe the project team, anticipating that you would add a buffer to its estimate, has preempted your adjustment by making its recommendation even more bullish than its true belief.

Or consider an investment decision. Overconfidence about the investment's prospects may certainly be at work, but another powerful bias, loss aversion, has the opposite effect, making decision makers loath to risk losing their initial outlay. Or consider a company allocating resources across multiple projects. Decision makers may be both bullish about the effect of new initiatives (overconfidence again) and too timid in diverting resources from existing units (a problem caused by *status quo bias,* which, as the name indicates, is our preference for leaving things as they are).

As these examples illustrate, it is difficult to know exactly which psychological biases are affecting a judgment. In any situation of some complexity, multiple psychological biases may be at work, conspiring to add error in the same direction or offsetting one another, with unpredictable consequences.

The upshot is that ex post or ex ante debiasing — which, respectively, correct or prevent specific psychological biases — are useful in some situations. These approaches work where the general direction of error is known and manifests itself as a clear statistical bias. Types of decisions that are expected to be strongly biased are likely to benefit from debiasing interventions. For instance, the planning fallacy is a sufficiently robust finding to warrant debiasing interventions against overconfident planning.

The problem is that in many situations, the likely direction of error is not known in advance. Such situations include all those in which the effect of psychological biases is variable among judges and essentially unpredictable — resulting in system noise. To reduce error under circumstances like these, we need to cast a broader net to try to detect more than one psychological bias at a time.

The Decision Observer

We suggest undertaking this search for biases neither before nor after the decision is made, but in real time. Of course, people are rarely aware of their own biases when they are being misled by them. This lack of awareness is itself a known bias, the *bias blind spot.* People often recognize biases more easily in others than they do in themselves. We suggest that observers can be trained to spot, in real time, the diagnostic signs that one or several familiar biases are affecting someone else's decisions or recommendations.

To illustrate how the process might work, imagine a group that attempts to make a complex and consequential judgment. The judgment could be of any type: a government deciding on possible responses to a pandemic or other crisis, a case conference in which physicians are exploring the best treatment for a patient with complex symptoms, a corporate board deciding on a major strategic move. Now imagine a *decision observer*, someone who watches this group and uses a checklist to diagnose whether any biases may be pushing the group away from the best possible judgment.

A decision observer is not an easy role to play, and no doubt, in some organizations it is not realistic. Detecting biases is useless if the ultimate decision makers are not committed to fighting them. Indeed, the decision makers must be the ones who initiate the process of decision observation and who support the role of the decision observer. We certainly do not recommend that you make yourself a self-appointed decision observer. You will neither win friends nor influence people.

Informal experiments suggest, however, that real progress can be made with this approach. At least, the approach is helpful under the right conditions, especially when the leaders of an organization or team are truly committed to the effort, and when the decision observers are well chosen — and not susceptible to serious biases of their own.

Decision observers in these cases fall in three categories. In some organizations, the role can be played by a supervisor. Instead of monitoring only the substance of the proposals that are submitted by a project team, the supervisor might also pay close attention to the *process* by which they are developed and to the team's dynamics. This makes the observer alert to biases that may have affected the proposal's development. Other organizations might assign a member of each working team to be the team's "bias buster"; this guardian of the decision process reminds teammates in real time of the biases that may mislead them. The downside of this approach is that the decision observer is placed in the position of a devil's advocate inside the team and may quickly run out of political capital. Finally, other organizations might rely on an outside facilitator, who has the advantage of a neutral perspective (and the attending disadvantages in terms of inside knowledge and costs).

To be effective, decision observers need some training and tools. One such tool is a checklist of the biases they are attempting to detect. The case for relying on a checklist is clear: checklists have a long history of improving decisions in high-stakes contexts and are particularly well suited to preventing the repetition of past errors.

Here is an example. In the United States, federal agencies must compile a formal regulatory impact analysis before they issue expensive regulations designed to clean the air or water, reduce deaths in the workplace, increase food safety, respond to public health crises, reduce greenhouse gas emissions, or increase homeland security. A dense, technical document with an unlovely name (OMB Circular A-4) and spanning nearly fifty pages sets out the requirements of the analysis. The requirements are clearly designed to counteract bias. Agencies must explain why the regulation is needed, consider both more and less stringent alternatives, consider both costs and benefits, present the information in an unbiased manner, and discount the future appropriately. But in many agencies, government officials have not complied with the requirements of that dense, technical document. (They might not even have read it.) In response, federal officials produced a simple checklist, consisting of just one and one-half pages, to reduce the risk that agencies will ignore, or fail to attend to, any of the major requirements.

To illustrate what a bias checklist might look like, we have included one as appendix B. This generic checklist is merely an example; any decision observer will certainly want to develop one that is customized to the needs of the organization, both to enhance its relevance and facilitate its adoption. Importantly, a checklist is not an exhaustive list of all the biases that can affect a decision; it aims to focus on the most frequent and most consequential ones.

Decision observation with appropriate bias checklists can help limit the effect of biases. Although we have seen some encouraging results in informal, small-scale efforts, we are not aware of any systematic exploration of the effects of this approach or of the pros and cons of the various possible ways to deploy it. We hope to inspire more experimentation, both by practitioners and by researchers, of the practice of real-time debiasing by decision observers.

Noise Reduction: Decision Hygiene

Bias is error we can often see and even explain. It is directional: that is why a nudge can limit the detrimental effects of a bias, or why an effort to boost judgment can combat specific biases. It is also often visible: that is why an observer can hope to diagnose biases in real time as a decision is being made.

Noise, on the other hand, is unpredictable error that we cannot easily see or explain. That is why we so often neglect it — even when it causes grave damage. For this reason, strategies for noise reduction are to debiasing what preventive hygiene measures are to medical treatment: the goal is to prevent an unspecified range of potential errors before they occur.

We call this approach to noise reduction *decision hygiene*. When you wash your hands, you may not know precisely which germ you are avoiding — you just know that handwashing is good prevention for a variety of germs (especially but not only during a pandemic). Similarly, following the principles of decision hygiene means that you adopt techniques that reduce noise without ever knowing which underlying errors you are helping to avoid.

The analogy with handwashing is intentional. Hygiene measures can be tedious. Their benefits are not directly visible; you might never know what problem they prevented from occurring. Conversely, when problems do arise, they may not be traceable to a specific breakdown in hygiene observance. For these reasons, handwashing compliance is difficult to enforce, even among health-care professionals, who are well aware of its importance.

Just like handwashing and other forms of prevention, decision hygiene is invaluable but thankless. Correcting a well-identified bias may at least give you a tangible sense of achieving something. But the procedures that reduce noise will not. They will, statistically, prevent many errors. Yet you will never know *which* errors. Noise is an invisible enemy, and preventing the assault of an invisible enemy can yield only an invisible victory.

Given how much damage noise can cause, that invisible victory is nonetheless worth the battle. The following chapters introduce several decision hygiene strategies used in multiple domains, including forensic science, forecasting, medicine, and human resources. In chapter 25, we will review these strategies and show how they can be combined in an integrated approach to noise reduction.

Speaking of Debiasing and Decision Hygiene

"Do you know what specific bias you're fighting and in what direction it affects the outcome? If not, there are probably several biases at work, and it is hard to predict which one will dominate."

"Before we start discussing this decision, let's designate a decision observer."

"We have kept good decision hygiene in this decision process; chances are the decision is as good as it can be."

CHAPTER 20

Sequencing Information in Forensic Science

I n March 2004, a series of bombs placed in commuter trains killed 192 people and injured more than 2,000 in Madrid. A fingerprint found on a plastic bag at the crime scene was transmitted via Interpol to law enforcement agencies worldwide. Days later, the US Federal Bureau of Investigation (FBI) crime lab conclusively identified the fingerprint as belonging to Brandon Mayfield, an American citizen living in Oregon.

Mayfield looked like a plausible suspect. A former officer in the US Army, he had married an Egyptian woman and converted to Islam. As a lawyer, he had represented men charged with (and later convicted of) attempting to travel to Afghanistan to join the Taliban. He was on the FBI's watch list.

Mayfield was placed under surveillance, his house bugged and searched, his phones wiretapped. When this scrutiny failed to yield any material information, the FBI arrested him. But he was never formally charged. Mayfield had not left the country in a decade. While he was in custody, the Spanish investigators, who had already informed the FBI that they considered Mayfield a negative match for the fingerprint on the plastic bag, matched that print to another suspect.

Mayfield was released after two weeks. Eventually, the US

government apologized to him, paid him a $2 million settlement, and ordered an extensive investigation into the causes of the mistake. Its key finding: "The error was a human error and not a methodology or technology failure."

Fortunately, such human errors are rare. They are nonetheless instructive. How could the best fingerprint experts in the United States mistakenly identify a fingerprint as belonging to a man who had never come close to the crime scene? To find out, we first need to understand how fingerprint examination works and how it relates to other examples of professional judgment. We will learn that forensic fingerprinting, which we tend to think of as an exact science, is in fact subject to the psychological biases of examiners. These biases can create more noise, and thus more error, than we would imagine. And we will see how the forensic science community is taking steps to tackle this problem by implementing a decision hygiene strategy that can apply to all environments: a tight control over the flow of information used to make judgments.

Fingerprints

Fingermarks are the impressions left by the friction ridges of our fingers on the surfaces we touch. Although there are examples of fingerprints being used as apparent identification marks in ancient times, modern fingerprinting dates back to the late nineteenth century, when Henry Faulds, a Scottish physician, published the first scientific paper suggesting the use of fingerprints as an identification technique.

In subsequent decades, fingerprints gained traction as identification marks in criminal records, gradually replacing the anthropometric measurement techniques developed by Alphonse Bertillon, a French police officer. Bertillon himself codified, in 1912, a formal system for the comparison of fingerprints. Sir Francis Galton, whom we previously encountered as the discoverer of the wisdom of crowds, had developed a similar system in England. (Still, it is no wonder that these founding fathers are rarely celebrated. Galton believed that fingerprints would be a useful tool for classifying individuals according to their race, and Bertillon, probably because of anti-Semitic prejudice, contributed decisive — and flawed — expert testimony during the 1894 and 1899 trials of Alfred Dreyfus.)

Police officers soon discovered that fingerprints could do more than serve as identification marks for repeat offenders. In 1892, Juan Vucetich, a police officer in Argentina, was the first to compare a latent fingerprint left at a crime scene with a suspect's thumb. Since then, the practice of collecting *latent prints* (those left by their owner at the scene of a crime) and comparing them with *exemplar prints* (those collected in controlled conditions from known individuals) has been the most decisive application of fingerprinting and has provided the most widely used form of forensic evidence.

If you have ever come across an electronic fingerprint reader (like those used by immigration services in many countries), you probably think of fingerprint comparison as a straightforward, mechanical, and easily automated task. But comparing a latent print collected from a crime scene with an exemplar print is a much more delicate exercise than matching two clean prints. When you press your fingers firmly on a reader purposely built to record a fingerprint impression, you produce a neat, standardized image. By contrast, latent prints are often partial, unclear, smudged, or otherwise distorted; they do not provide the same quantity and quality of information as does a print collected in a controlled and dedicated environment. Latent prints often overlap with other prints, either by the same person or by someone else, and include dirt and other artifacts present on the surface. Deciding whether they match a suspect's exemplar prints requires expert judgment. It is the job of human fingerprint examiners.

When provided with a latent print, examiners routinely follow a process called ACE-V, which stands for analysis, comparison, evaluation, and verification. First, they must analyze the latent print to determine whether it is of sufficient value for comparison. If it is, they compare it to an exemplar print. The comparison leads to an evaluation, which can produce an *identification* (the prints originated from the same person), an *exclusion* (the prints do not originate from the same person), or an inconclusive decision. An identification decision triggers the fourth step: verification by another examiner.

For decades, the reliability of this procedure remained unquestioned. Although eyewitness testimonies have been shown to be dangerously unreliable and even confessions can be false, fingerprints were accepted — at least until the advent of DNA analysis — as the most credible form of evidence. Until 2002, fingerprint evidence had never been successfully challenged in an American courtroom. The FBI website at the time, for example, was adamant: "Fingerprints offer an *infallible* means of personal identification." In the very rare cases when errors did happen, they were blamed on incompetence or fraud.

Fingerprint evidence remained unchallenged for so long in part because of the difficulty in proving it wrong. The true value of a set of fingerprints, that is, the ground truth of who actually committed the crime, is often unknown. For Mayfield and a handful of similar cases, the mistake was especially egregious. But in general, if a suspect disputes the examiner's conclusions, the fingerprint evidence will, of course, be considered more reliable.

We have noted that not knowing the true value is neither unusual nor an impediment to measuring noise. How much noise is there in fingerprint analysis? Or more precisely, given that fingerprint examiners, unlike sentencing judges or underwriters, do not produce a number but make a categorical judgment, how often do they disagree, and why? This question is what Itiel Dror, a cognitive neuroscience researcher at University College London, was the first to set out to study. He conducted what amounts to a series of noise audits in a field that had assumed it did not have a noise problem.

Occasion Noise in Fingerprint Analysis

It may seem odd for a cognitive scientist — a psychologist — to challenge fingerprint examiners. After all, as you may have seen on TV shows like *CSI: Crime Scene Investigation* and subsequent series of the CSI franchise, these are latex-glove-wearing, microscope-wielding hard-science types. But Dror realized that examining fingerprints was clearly a matter of judgment. And as a cognitive neuroscientist, he reasoned that wherever there is judgment, there must be noise.

To test this hypothesis, Dror focused first on occasion noise: the variability between the judgments of *the same* experts looking at *the same* evidence twice. As Dror puts it, "If experts are not reliable in the sense that they are not consistent with themselves, then the basis of their judgments and professionalism is in question."

Fingerprints provide a perfect test bed for an audit of occasion noise because unlike the cases that a physician or a judge encounters, pairs of prints are not easily memorable. Of course, a suitable interval of time must be allowed to pass to ensure that examiners do not remember the prints. (In Dror's studies, some brave, open-minded experts agreed that, *at any time in the next five years,* they would take part in studies, without their knowledge.) Additionally, the experiment must happen in the course of the experts' routine casework, so that they are not aware that their skills are being tested. If, under these circumstances, the examiners' judgments change from one test to the next, we are in the presence of occasion noise.

The Forensic Confirmation Bias

In two of his original studies, Dror added an important twist. When seeing the prints for the second time, some of the examiners were exposed to additional biasing information about the case. For instance, fingerprint examiners who had earlier found the prints to be a match were told, this time, that "the suspect has an alibi" or that "firearms evidence suggests it's not him." Others, who had first concluded that a suspect was innocent or that the prints were inconclusive, were told the second time that "the detective believes the suspect is guilty," "eyewitnesses identified him," or "he confessed to the crime." Dror called this experiment a test of the experts' "biasability," because the contextual information supplied activated a psychological bias (a confirmation bias) in a given direction.

Indeed, the examiners turned out to be susceptible to bias. When the same examiners considered the same prints they had seen earlier, but this time with biasing information, their judgments changed. In the first study, four out of five experts altered their previous identification decision when presented with strong contextual information that suggested an exclusion. In the second study, six experts reviewed four pairs of prints; biasing information led to changes in four of the twenty-four decisions. To be sure, most of their decisions did not change, but for these kinds of decisions, a shift of one in six can be counted as large. These findings have since been replicated by other researchers.

Predictably, the examiners were more likely to change their minds when the decision was a difficult one to start with, when the biasing information was strong, and when the change was from a conclusive to an inconclusive decision. It is, nonetheless, troubling that "expert fingerprint examiners made decisions on the basis of the context, rather than on the basis of the actual information contained in the print."

The effect of biasing information is not restricted to the examiner's conclusion (identification, inconclusive, or exclusion). Biasing information actually changes *what* the examiner perceives, in addition to *how* that perception is interpreted. In a separate study, Dror and colleagues showed that examiners who have been placed in a biased context literally do not see the same things as those who have not been exposed to biasing information. When the latent print is accompanied by a target exemplar print, the examiners observe significantly fewer details (called *minutiae*) than they do when they see the latent print alone. A later, independent study confirmed this conclusion and added that "how [it] occurs is not obvious."

Dror coined a term for the impact of biasing information: the *forensic confirmation bias*. This bias has since been documented with other forensic techniques, including blood pattern analysis, arson investigation, the analysis of skeletal remains, and forensic pathology. Even DNA analysis — widely regarded as the new gold standard in forensic science — can be susceptible to confirmation bias, at least when experts must assess complex DNA mixtures.

The susceptibility of forensic experts to confirmation bias is not just a theoretical concern because, in reality, no systematic precautions are in place to make sure that forensic experts are not exposed to biasing information. Examiners often receive such information in the transmittal letters that accompany the evidence submitted to them. Examiners are also often in direct communication with police, prosecutors, and other examiners.

Confirmation bias raises another problem. An important safeguard against errors, built into the ACE-V procedure, is the independent verification by another expert before an identification can be confirmed. But most often, only identifications are independently verified. The result is a strong risk of confirmation bias, as the verifying examiner knows that the initial conclusion was an identification. The verification step therefore does not provide the benefit normally expected from the aggregation of independent judgments, because verifications are not, in fact, independent.

A cascade of confirmation biases seems to have been at work in the Mayfield case, in which not two but three FBI experts concurred on the erroneous identification. As the later investigation of the error noted, the first examiner appears to have been impressed by "the power of the correlation" from the automated system searching the databases of fingerprints for a possible match. Although he was, apparently, not exposed to Mayfield's biographical details, the results provided by the computerized system performing the initial search, "coupled with the inherent pressure of working an extremely high-profile case," were enough to produce the initial confirmation bias. Once the first examiner made an erroneous identification, the report continues, "the subsequent examinations were tainted." As the first examiner was a highly respected supervisor, "it became increasingly difficult for others in the agency to disagree." The initial error was replicated and amplified, resulting in a near-certainty that Mayfield was guilty. Tellingly, even a highly respected independent expert, appointed by the court to examine the evidence on behalf of Mayfield's defense, concurred with the FBI in confirming the identification.

The same phenomenon can be at work in other forensic disciplines and across them. Latent print identification is reputed to be among the most objective of the forensic disciplines. If fingerprint examiners can be biased, so can experts in other fields. Moreover, if a firearms expert knows that the fingerprints are a match, this knowledge may bias that expert's judgment, too. And if a forensic odontologist knows that DNA analysis has identified a suspect, that expert is probably less likely to suggest that the bite marks do not match the suspect. These examples raise the specter of bias cascades: just as in the group decisions we described in chapter 8, an initial error prompted by confirmation bias becomes the biasing information that influences a second expert, whose judgment biases a third one, and so on.

Having established that biasing information creates variability, Dror and his colleagues uncovered more evidence of occasion noise. Even when fingerprint experts are not exposed to biasing information, they sometimes change their minds about a set of prints they have seen before. As we would expect, changes are less frequent when no biasing information is supplied, but they happen nonetheless. A 2012 study commissioned by the FBI replicated this finding on a larger scale by asking seventy-two examiners to look again at twenty-five pairs of prints they had evaluated about seven months earlier. With a large sample of highly qualified examiners, the study confirmed that fingerprint experts are sometimes susceptible to occasion noise. About one decision in ten was altered. Most of the changes were to or from the inconclusive category, and none resulted in false identifications. The study's most troubling implication is that some fingerprint identifications that led to convictions could potentially have been judged inconclusive at another time. When the same examiners are looking at the same prints, even when the context is not designed to bias them but is instead meant to be as constant as possible, there is inconsistency in their decisions.

Some Noise, but How Much Error?

The practical question raised by these findings is the possibility of judicial errors. We cannot ignore questions about the reliability of experts who testify in court: validity requires reliability because, quite simply, it is hard to agree with reality if you cannot agree with yourself.

How many errors, exactly, are caused by faulty forensic science? A review of 350 exonerations obtained by the Innocence Project, a non-profit that works to overturn wrongful convictions, concluded that the misapplication of forensic science was a contributing cause in 45% of cases. This statistic sounds bad, but the question that matters to judges and jurors is different: To know how much trust they should accord the examiner taking the stand to testify, they need to know how likely forensic scientists, including fingerprint examiners, are to make consequential errors.

The most robust set of answers to this question can be found in a report by the President's Council of Advisors on Science and Technology (PCAST), an advisory group of the nation's leading scientists and engineers, which in 2016 produced an in-depth review of forensic science in criminal courts. The report summarizes the available evidence on the validity of fingerprint analysis and especially on the likelihood of erroneous identifications (false positives) such as the one involving Mayfield.

This evidence is surprisingly sparse, and as PCAST notes, it is "distressing" that work to produce it did not begin until recently. The most credible data come from the only published large-scale study of fingerprint identification accuracy, which was conducted by FBI scientists themselves in 2011. The study involved 169 examiners, each comparing approximately one hundred pairs of latent and exemplar fingerprints. Its central finding was that very few erroneous identifications occurred: the false-positive rate was about one in six hundred.

An error rate of one in six hundred is low but, as the report noted, is *much higher* than the general public (and, by extension, most jurors) would likely believe based on longstanding claims about the accuracy of fingerprint analysis." Furthermore, this study contained no biasing contextual information, and the participating examiners knew they were taking part in a test — which may have caused the study to underestimate the errors that occur in real casework. A subsequent study conducted in Florida arrived at much higher numbers of false positives. The varied findings in the literature suggest that we need more research on the accuracy of fingerprint examiner decisions and how these decisions are reached.

One reassuring finding that does seem consistent across all studies, however, is that the examiners appear to err on the side of caution. Their accuracy is not perfect, but they are aware of the consequences of their judgments, and they take into account the asymmetrical cost of possible errors. Because of the very high credibility of fingerprinting, an erroneous identification can have tragic effects. Other types of error are less consequential. For instance, FBI experts observe, "in most casework, an exclusion has the same operational implications as an inconclusive." In other words, the fact that a fingerprint is found on the murder weapon is sufficient to convict, but the absence of that print is not sufficient to exonerate a suspect.

Consistent with our observation of examiner caution, the evidence suggests that experts think twice — or much more than twice — before making an identification decision. In the FBI study of identification accuracy, less than one-third of "mated" pairs (where the latent and the exemplar are from the same person) were judged (accurately) as identifications. Examiners also make far fewer false-positive identifications than false-negative exclusions. They are susceptible to bias, but not equally in both directions. As Dror notes, "It is easier to bias forensic experts towards the non-committal conclusion of 'inconclusive' than to the definitive 'identification' conclusion."

Examiners are trained to consider erroneous identification as the deadly sin to be avoided at all costs. To their credit, they act in accordance with this principle. We can only hope that their level of care keeps erroneous identifications, like those in the Mayfield case and a handful of other high-profile cases, extremely rare.

Listening to Noise

To observe that there is noise in forensic science should not be seen as a criticism of forensic scientists. It is merely a consequence of the observation we have made repeatedly: Wherever there is judgment, there is noise, and more of it than you think. A task like the analysis of fingerprints seems objective, so much so that many of us would not spontaneously regard it as a form of judgment. Yet it leaves room for inconsistency, disagreement, and, occasionally, error. However low the error rate of fingerprint identification may be, it is not zero, and as PCAST noted, juries should be made aware of that.

The first step to reduce noise must be, of course, to acknowledge its possibility. This admission does not come naturally to members of the fingerprint community, many of whom were initially highly skeptical of Dror's noise audit. The notion that an examiner can be unwittingly influenced by information about the case irked many experts. In a reply to Dror's study, the chair of the Fingerprint Society wrote that "any fingerprint examiner who...is swayed either way in that decision making process...is so immature he/she should seek employment in Disneyland." A director of a major forensic laboratory noted that having access to case information — precisely the sort of information that could bias the examiner —"provides some personal satisfaction which allows [examiners] to enjoy their job *without actually altering their judgment*." Even the FBI, in its internal investigation of the Mayfield case, noted that "latent print examiners routinely conduct verifications in which they know the previous examiners' results *and yet those results do not influence the examiner's conclusions.*" These remarks essentially amount to a denial of the existence of confirmation bias.

Even when they are aware of the risk of bias, forensic scientists are not immune to the bias blind spot: the tendency to acknowledge the presence of bias in others, but not in oneself. In a survey of four hundred professional forensic scientists in twenty-one countries, 71% agreed that "cognitive bias is a cause for concern in the forensic sciences as a whole," but only 26% thought that their "own judgments are influenced by cognitive bias." In other words, about half of these forensic professionals believe that their colleagues' judgments are noisy but that their own are not. Noise can be an invisible problem, even to people whose job is to see the invisible.

Sequencing Information

Thanks to the persistence of Dror and his colleagues, attitudes are slowly changing and a growing number of forensic laboratories have begun taking new measures to reduce error in their analyses. For example, the PCAST report commended the FBI laboratory for redesigning its procedures to minimize the risk of confirmation bias.

The necessary methodological steps are relatively simple. They illustrate a decision hygiene strategy that has applicability in many domains: *sequencing information to limit the formation of premature intuitions.* In any judgment, some information is relevant, and some is not. More information is not always better, especially if it has the potential to bias judgments by leading the judge to form a premature intuition.

In that spirit, the new procedures deployed in forensic laboratories aim to protect the independence of the examiners' judgments by giving the examiners only the information they need, when they need it. In other words, the laboratory keeps them as much in the dark about the case as possible and reveals information only gradually. To do that, the approach Dror and colleagues codified is called *linear sequential unmasking.*

Dror has another recommendation that illustrates the same decision hygiene strategy: examiners should document their judgments at each step. They should document their analysis of a latent fingerprint *before* they look at exemplar fingerprints to decide whether they are a match. This sequence of steps helps experts avoid the risk that they see only what they are looking for. And they should record their judgment on the evidence before they have access to contextual information that risks biasing them. If they change their mind after they are exposed to contextual information, these changes, and the rationale for them, should be documented. This requirement limits the risk that an early intuition biases the entire process.

The same logic inspires a third recommendation, which is an important part of decision hygiene. When a different examiner is called on to verify the identification made by the first person, the second person should not be aware of the first judgment.

The presence of noise in forensic science is, of course, of concern because of its potential life-or-death consequences. But it is also revealing. That we remained for so long entirely unaware of the possibility of error in fingerprint identification shows how our confidence in expert human judgment can sometimes be exaggerated and how a noise audit can reveal an unexpected amount of noise. The ability to mitigate these shortcomings through relatively simple process changes should be encouraging to all those who care about improving the quality of decisions.

The main decision hygiene strategy this case illustrates — sequencing information — has broad applicability as a safeguard against occasion noise. As we have noted, occasion noise is driven by countless triggers, including mood and even outside temperature. You cannot hope to control all these triggers, but you can attempt to shield judgments from the most obvious ones. You already know, for instance, that judgments can be altered by anger, fear, or other emotions, and perhaps you have noted that it is a good practice, if you can, to revisit your judgment at different points in time, when the triggers of occasion noise are likely to be different.

Less obvious is the possibility that your judgment can be altered by another trigger of occasion noise: information — even when it is accurate information. As in the example of the fingerprint examiners, as soon as you know what others think, confirmation bias can lead you to form an overall impression too early and to ignore contradictory information. The titles of two Hitchcock movies sum it up: a good decision maker should aim to keep a "shadow of a doubt," not to be "the man who knew too much."

Speaking of Sequencing Information

"Wherever there is judgment, there is noise — and that includes reading fingerprints."

"We have more information about this case, but let's not tell the experts everything we know before they make their judgment, so as not to bias them. In fact, let's tell them only what they absolutely need to know."

"The second opinion is not independent if the person giving it knows what the first opinion was. And the third one, even less so: there can be a bias cascade."

"To fight noise, they first have to admit that it exists."

CHAPTER 21

Selection and Aggregation in Forecasting

Many judgments involve forecasting. What is the unemployment rate likely to be in the next quarter? How many electric cars will be sold next year? What will be the effects of climate change in 2050? How long will it take to complete a new building? What will be the annual earnings of a particular company? How will a new employee perform? What will be the cost of a new air pollution regulation? Who will win an election? The answers to such questions have major consequences. Fundamental choices of private and public institutions often depend on them.

Analysts of forecasting — of when it goes wrong and why — make a sharp distinction between bias and noise (also called inconsistency or unreliability). Everyone agrees that in some contexts, forecasters are biased. For example, official agencies show unrealistic optimism in their budget forecasts. On average, they project unrealistically high economic growth and unrealistically low deficits. For practical purposes, it matters little whether their unrealistic optimism is a product of a cognitive bias or political considerations.

In addition, forecasters tend to be overconfident: if asked to formulate their forecasts as confidence intervals rather than as point estimates, they tend to pick narrower intervals than they should. For instance, an ongoing quarterly survey asks the chief financial officers of US companies to estimate the annual return of the S&P 500 index for the next year. The CFOs provide two numbers: a minimum, below which they think there is a one-in-ten chance the actual return will be, and a maximum, which they believe the actual return has a one-in-ten chance of exceeding. Thus the two numbers are the bounds of an 80% confidence interval. Yet the realized returns fall in that interval only 36% of the time. The CFOs are far too confident in the precision of their forecasts.

Forecasters are also noisy. A reference text, J. Scott Armstrong's *Principles of Forecasting*, points out that even among experts, "unreliability is a source of error in judgmental forecasting." In fact noise is a major source of error. Occasion noise is common; forecasters do not always agree with themselves. Between-person noise is also pervasive; forecasters disagree with one another, even if they are specialists. If you ask law professors to predict Supreme Court rulings, you will find a great deal of noise. If you ask specialists to project the annual benefits of air pollution regulation, you will find massive variability, with ranges of, for example, $3 billion to $9 billion. If you ask a group of economists to make forecasts about unemployment and growth, you will also find great variability. We have already seen many examples of noisy forecasts, and research on forecasting uncovers many more.

Improving Forecasts

The research also offers suggestions for reducing noise and bias. We will not review them exhaustively here, but we will focus on two noise-reduction strategies that have broad applicability. One is an application of the principle we mentioned in chapter 18: selecting better judges produces better judgments. The other is one of the most universally applicable decision hygiene strategies: aggregating multiple independent estimates.

The easiest way to aggregate several forecasts is to average them. Averaging is mathematically guaranteed to reduce noise: specifically, it divides it by the square root of the number of judgments averaged. This means that if you average one hundred judgments, you will reduce noise by 90%, and if you average four hundred judgments, you will reduce it by 95% — essentially eliminating it. This statistical law is the engine of the wisdom-of-crowds approach, discussed in chapter 7.

Because averaging does nothing to reduce bias, its effect on total error (MSE) depends on the proportions of bias and noise in it. That is why the wisdom of crowds works best when judgments are independent, and therefore less likely to contain shared biases. Empirically, ample evidence suggests that averaging multiple forecasts greatly increases accuracy, for instance in the "consensus" forecast of economic forecasters of stock analysts. With respect to sales forecasting, weather forecasting, and economic forecasting, the unweighted average of a group of forecasters outperforms most and sometimes all individual forecasts. Averaging forecasts obtained by different methods has the same effect: in an analysis of thirty empirical comparisons in diverse domains, combined forecasts reduced errors by an average of 12.5%.

Straight averaging is not the only way to aggregate forecasts. A *select-crowd* strategy, which selects the best judges according to the accuracy of their recent judgments and averages the judgments of a small number of judges (e.g., five), can be as effective as straight averaging. It is also easier for decision makers who respect expertise to understand and adopt a strategy that relies not only on aggregation but also on selection.

One method to produce aggregate forecasts is to use *prediction markets,* in which individuals bet on likely outcomes and are thus incentivized to make the right forecasts. Much of the time, prediction markets have been found to do very well, in the sense that if the prediction market price suggests that events are, say, 70% likely to happen, they happen about 70% of the time. Many companies in various industries have used prediction markets to aggregate diverse views.

Another formal process for aggregating diverse views is known as the Delphi method. In its classic form, this method involves multiple rounds during which the participants submit estimates (or votes) to a moderator and remain anonymous to one another. At each new round, the participants provide reasons for their estimates and respond to the reasons given by others, still anonymously. The process encourages estimates to converge (and sometimes forces them to do so by requiring new judgments to fall within a specific range of the distribution of previous-round judgments). The method benefits both from aggregation and social learning.

The Delphi method has worked well in many situations, but it can be challenging to implement. A simpler version, *mini-Delphi,* can be deployed within a single meeting. Also called *estimate-talk-estimate,* it requires participants first to produce separate (and silent) estimates, then to explain and justify them, and finally to make a new estimate in response to the estimates and explanations of others. The consensus judgment is the average of the individual estimates obtained in that second round.

The Good Judgment Project

Some of the most innovative work on the quality of forecasting, going well beyond what we have explored thus far, started in 2011, when three prominent behavioral scientists founded the Good Judgment Project. Philip Tetlock (whom we encountered in chapter 11 when we discussed his assessment of long-term forecasts of political events); his spouse, Barbara Mellers; and Don Moore teamed up to improve our understanding of forecasting and, in particular, why some people are good at it.

The Good Judgment Project started with the recruitment of tens of thousands of volunteers — not specialists or experts but ordinary people from many walks of life. They were asked to answer hundreds of questions, such as these:

- ❑ *Will North Korea detonate a nuclear device before the end of the year?*
- ❑ *Will Russia officially annex additional Ukrainian territory in the next three months?*
- ❑ *Will India or Brazil become a permanent member of the UN Security Council in the next two years?*
- ❑ *In the next year, will any country withdraw from the eurozone?*

As these examples show, the project has focused on large questions about world events. Importantly, efforts to answer such questions raise many of the same problems that more mundane forecasts do. If a lawyer is asking whether a client will win in court, or if a television studio is asked whether a proposed show will be a big hit, forecasting skills are involved. Tetlock and his colleagues wanted to learn whether some people are especially good forecasters. They also wanted to learn whether the ability to forecast could be taught or at least improved.

To understand the central findings, we need to explain some key aspects of the method adopted by Tetlock and his team to evaluate forecasters. First, they used a large number of forecasts, not just one or a few, where luck might be responsible for success or failure. If you predict that your favorite sports team will win its next game, and it does, you are not necessarily a good forecaster. Maybe you *always* predict that your favorite team will win: if that's your strategy, and if they win only half the time, your forecasting ability is not especially impressive. To reduce the role of luck, the researchers examined how participants did, on average, across numerous forecasts.

Second, the researchers asked participants to make their forecasts in terms of probabilities that an event would happen, rather than a binary "it will happen" or "it will not happen." To many people, forecasting means the latter — taking a stand one way or the other. However, given our objective ignorance of future events, it is much better to formulate probabilistic forecasts. If someone said in 2016, "Hillary Clinton is 70% likely to be elected president," he is not necessarily a bad forecaster. Things that are correctly said to be 70% likely will not happen 30% of the time. To know whether forecasters are good, we should ask whether their probability estimates map onto reality. Suppose that a particular forecaster named Margaret says that 500 different events are 60% likely. If 300 of them actually happen, then we can conclude that Margaret's confidence is well *calibrated*. Good calibration is one requirement for good forecasting.

Third, as an added refinement, Tetlock and colleagues did not just ask their forecasters to make *one* probability estimate about whether an event would happen in, say, twelve months. They gave the participants the opportunity to revise their forecasts continuously in light of new information. Suppose that you had estimated, back in 2016, that the United Kingdom had only a 30% chance of leaving the European Union before the end of 2019. As new polls came out, suggesting that the "Leave" vote was gaining ground, you probably would have revised your forecast upward. When the result of the referendum was known, it was still uncertain whether the United Kingdom would leave the union within that time frame, but it certainly looked a lot more probable. (Brexit technically happened in 2020.)

With each new piece of information, Tetlock and his colleagues allowed the forecasters to update their forecasts. For scoring purposes, each one of these updates is treated as a new forecast. That way, participants in the Good Judgment Project are incentivized to monitor the news and update their forecasts continuously. This approach mirrors what is expected of forecasters in business and government, who should also be updating their forecasts frequently on the basis of new information, despite the risk of being criticized for changing their minds. (A well-known response to this criticism, sometimes attributed to John Maynard Keynes, is, "When the facts change, I change my mind. What do *you* do?")

Fourth, to score the performance of the forecasters, the Good Judgment Project used a system developed by Glenn W. Brier in 1950. *Brier scores,* as they are known, measure the distance between what people forecast and what actually happens.

Brier scores are a clever way to get around a pervasive problem associated with probabilistic forecasts: the incentive for forecasters to hedge their bets by never taking a bold stance. Think again of Margaret, whom we described as a well-calibrated forecaster because she rated 500 events as 60% likely, and 300 of those events did happen. This result may not be as impressive as it seems. If Margaret is a weather forecaster who *always* predicts a 60% chance of rain and there are 300 rainy days out of 500, Margaret's forecasts are well calibrated but also practically useless. Margaret, in essence, is telling you that, just in case, you might want to carry an umbrella every day. Compare her with Nicholas, who predicts a 100% chance of rain on the 300 days when it will rain, and a 0% chance of rain on the 200 dry days. Nicholas has the same perfect calibration as Margaret: when either forecaster predicts that X% of the days will be rainy, rain falls precisely X% of the time. But Nicholas's forecasts are much more valuable: instead of hedging his bets, he is willing to tell you whether you should take an umbrella. Technically, Nicholas is said to have a high *resolution* in addition to good calibration.

Brier scores reward both good calibration and good resolution. To produce a good score, you have not only to be right on average (i.e., well calibrated) but also to be willing to take a stand and differentiate among forecasts (i.e., have high resolution). Brier scores are based on the logic of mean squared errors, and lower scores are better: a score of 0 would be perfect.

So, now that we know how they were scored, how well did the Good Judgment Project volunteers do? One of the major findings was that the overwhelming majority of the volunteers did poorly, but about 2% stood out. As mentioned earlier, Tetlock calls these well-performing people superforecasters. They were hardly unerring, but their predictions were much better than chance. Remarkably, one government official said that the group did significantly "better than the average for intelligence community analysts who could read intercepts and other secret data." This comparison is worth pausing over. Intelligence community analysts are trained to make accurate forecasts; they are not amateurs. In addition, they have access to classified information. And yet they do not do as well as the superforecasters do.

Perpetual Beta

What makes superforecasters so good? Consistent with our argument in chapter 18, we could reasonably speculate that they are unusually intelligent. That speculation is not wrong. On GMA tests, the superforecasters do better than the average volunteer in the Good Judgment Project (and the average volunteer is significantly above the national average). But the difference isn't all that large, and many volunteers who do extremely well on intelligence tests do not qualify as superforecasters. Apart from general intelligence, we could reasonably expect that superforecasters are unusually good with numbers. And they are. But their real advantage is not their talent at math; it is their ease in thinking analytically and probabilistically.

Consider superforecasters' willingness and ability to structure and disaggregate problems. Rather than form a holistic judgment about a big geopolitical question (whether a nation will leave the European Union, whether a war will break out in a particular place, whether a public official will be assassinated), they break it up into its component parts. They ask, "What would it take for the answer to be yes? What would it take for the answer to be no?" Instead of offering a gut feeling or some kind of global hunch, they ask and try to answer an assortment of subsidiary questions.

Superforecasters also excel at taking the outside view, and they care a lot about base rates. As explained for the Gambardi problem in chapter 13, before you focus on the specifics of Gambardi's profile, it helps to know the probability that the average CEO will be fired or quit in the next two years. Superforecasters systematically look for base rates. Asked whether the next year will bring an armed clash between China and Vietnam over a border dispute, superforecasters do not focus only or immediately on whether China and Vietnam are getting along right now. They might have an intuition about this, in light of the news and analysis they have read. But they know that their intuition about one event is generally not a good guide. Instead they start by looking for a base rate: they ask how often past border disputes have escalated into armed clashes. If such clashes are rare, superforecasters will begin by incorporating that fact and only then turn to the details of the China–Vietnam situation.

In short, what distinguishes the superforecasters isn't their sheer intelligence; it's *how* they apply it. The skills they bring to bear reflect the sort of cognitive style we described in chapter 18 as likely to result in better judgments, particularly a high level of "active open-mindedness." Recall the test for actively open-minded thinking: it includes such statements as "People should take into consideration evidence that goes against their beliefs" and "It is more useful to pay attention to people who disagree with you than to pay attention to those who agree." Clearly, people who score high on this test are not shy about updating their judgments (without overreacting) when new information becomes available.

To characterize the thinking style of superforecasters, Tetlock uses the phrase "perpetual beta," a term used by computer programmers for a program that is not meant to be released in a final version but that is endlessly used, analyzed, and improved. Tetlock finds that "the strongest predictor of rising into the ranks of superforecasters is perpetual beta, the degree to which one is committed to belief updating and self-improvement." As he puts it, "What makes them so good is less what they are than what they do — the hard work of research, the careful thought and self-criticism, the gathering and synthesizing of other perspectives, the granular judgments and relentless updating." They like a particular cycle of thinking: "try, fail, analyze, adjust, try again."

Noise and Bias in Forecasting

At this point, you might be tempted to think that people can be trained to be superforecasters or at least to perform more like them. And indeed, Tetlock and his collaborators have worked to do exactly that. Their efforts should be considered the second stage of under-standing why superforecasters perform so well and how to make them perform better.

In an important study, Tetlock and his team randomly assigned regular (nonsuper) forecasters to three groups, in which they tested the effect of different interventions on the quality of subsequent judgments. These interventions exemplify three of the strategies we have described to improve judgments:

1. *Training:* Several forecasters completed a tutorial designed to improve their abilities by teaching them probabilistic reasoning. In the tutorial, the forecasters learned about various biases (including base-rate neglect, overconfidence, and confirmation bias); the impor-tance of averaging multiple predictions from diverse sources; and considering reference classes.

2. *Teaming (a form of aggregation):* Some forecasters were asked to work in teams in which they could see and debate one another's predictions. Teaming could increase accuracy by encouraging forecast-ers to deal with opposing arguments and to be actively open-minded.

3. *Selection:* All forecasters were scored for accuracy, and at the end of a full year, the top 2% were designated as superforecasters and given the opportunity to work together in elite teams the follow-ing year.

As it turns out, all three interventions worked, in the sense that they improved people's Brier scores. Training made a difference, teaming made a larger one, and selection had an even larger effect.

This important finding confirms the value of aggregating judg-ments and selecting good judges. But it is not the full story. Armed with data about the effects of each intervention, Ville Satopää, who collaborated with Tetlock and Mellers, developed a sophisticated sta-tistical technique to tease out how, exactly, each intervention improved forecasts. In principle, he reasoned, there are three major reasons why some forecasters can perform better or worse than others:

1. They can be more skilled at finding and analyzing data in the environment that are relevant to the prediction they have to make. This explanation points to the importance of information.

2. Some forecasters may have a general tendency to err on a particular side of the true value of a forecast. If, out of hundreds of forecasts, you systematically overestimate or underestimate the probability that certain changes from the status quo will occur, you can be said to suffer from a form of bias, in favor of either change or stability.

3. Some forecasters may be less susceptible to noise (or random errors). In forecasting, as in any judgment, noise can have many triggers. Forecasters may overreact to a particular piece of news (this is an example of what we have called pattern noise), they may be subject to occasion noise, or they may be noisy in their use of the probability scale. All these errors (and many more) are unpredictable in their size and direction.

Satopää, Tetlock, Mellers, and their colleague Marat Salikhov called their model the BIN (bias, information, and noise) model for forecasting. They set out to measure how much each of the three components was responsible for the performance improvement in each of the three interventions.

Their answer was simple: all three interventions worked primarily by reducing noise. As the researchers put it, "Whenever an intervention boosted accuracy, it worked mainly by suppressing random errors in judgment. Curiously, the original intent of the training intervention was to reduce bias."

Since the training was designed to reduce biases, a less-than-super forecaster would have predicted that bias reduction would be the major effect of the training. Yet the training worked by reducing noise. The surprise is easily explained. Tetlock's training is designed to fight *psychological* biases. As you now know, the effect of psychological biases is not always a statistical bias. When they affect different individuals on different judgments in different ways, psychological biases produce noise. This is clearly the case here, as the events being forecast are quite varied. The same biases can lead a forecaster to overreact or underreact, depending on the topic. We should not expect them to produce a *statistical* bias, defined as the general tendency of a forecaster to believe that events will happen or not happen. As a result, training forecasters to fight their psychological biases works — by reducing noise.

Teaming had a comparably large effect on noise reduction, but it also significantly improved the ability of the teams to extract information. This result is consistent with the logic of aggregation: several brains that work together are better at finding information than one is. If Alice and Brian are working together, and Alice has spotted signals that Brian has missed, their joint forecast will be better. When working in groups, the superforecasters seem capable of avoiding the dangers of group polarization and information cascades. Instead, they pool their data and insights and, in their actively open-minded way, make the most of the combined information. Satopää and his colleagues explain this advantage: "Teaming — unlike training... allows forecasters to harness the information."

Selection had the largest total effect. Some of the improvement comes from a better use of information. Superforecasters are better than others at finding relevant information — possibly because they are smarter, more motivated, and more experienced at making these kinds of forecasts than is the average participant. But the main effect of selection is, again, to reduce noise. Superforecasters are less noisy than regular players or even trained teams. This finding, too, was a surprise to Satopää and the other researchers: " 'Superforecasters' may owe their success more to superior discipline in tamping down measurement error, than to incisive readings of the news" that others cannot replicate.

Where Selection and Aggregation Work

The success of the superforecasting project highlights the value of two decision hygiene strategies: *selection* (the superforecasters are, well, super) and *aggregation* (when they work in teams, forecasters perform better). The two strategies are broadly applicable in many judgments. Whenever possible, you should aim to combine the strategies, by constructing teams of judges (e.g., forecasters, investment professionals, recruiting officers) who are selected for being both good at what they do *and* complementary to one another.

So far, we have considered the improved precision that is achieved by averaging multiple independent judgments, as in the wisdom-of-crowds experiments. Aggregating the estimates of higher-validity judges will further improve accuracy. Yet another gain in accuracy can be obtained by combining judgments that are both independent and complementary. Imagine that four people are witnesses to a crime: it is essential, of course, to make sure that they do not influence one another. If, in addition, they have seen the crime from four different angles, the quality of the information they provide will be much better.

The task of assembling a team of professionals to make judgments together resembles the task of assembling a battery of tests to predict the future performance of candidates at school or on the job. The standard tool for that task is multiple regression (introduced in chapter 9). It works by selecting variables in succession. The test that best predicts the outcome is selected first. However, the next test to be included is not necessarily the second most valid. Instead, it is the one that *adds* the most predictive power to the first test, by providing predictions that are both valid and not redundant with the first. For example, suppose you have two tests of mental aptitude, which correlate .50 and .45 with future performance, and a test of personality that correlates only .30 with performance but is uncorrelated with aptitude tests. The optimal solution is to pick the more valid aptitude test first, then the personality test, which brings more new information.

Similarly, if you are assembling a team of judges, you should of course pick the best judge first. But your next choice may be a moderately valid individual who brings some new skill to the table rather than a more valid judge who is highly similar to the first one. A team selected in this manner will be superior because the validity of pooled judgments increases faster when the judgments are uncorrelated with one another than when they are redundant. Pattern noise will be relatively high in such a team because individual judgments of each case will differ. Paradoxically, the average of that noisy group will be more accurate than the average of a unanimous one.

An important caveat is in order. Regardless of diversity, aggregation can only reduce noise if judgments are truly independent. As our discussion of noise in groups has highlighted, group deliberation often adds more error in bias than it removes in noise. Organizations that want to harness the power of diversity must welcome the disagreements that will arise when team members reach their judgments independently. Eliciting and aggregating judgments that are both independent and diverse will often be the easiest, cheapest, and most broadly applicable decision hygiene strategy.

Speaking of Selection and Aggregation

"Let's take the average of four independent judgments — this is guaranteed to reduce noise by half."

"We should strive to be in perpetual beta, like the superforecasters."

"Before we discuss this situation, what is the relevant base rate?"

"We have a good team, but how can we ensure more diversity of opinions?"

CHAPTER 22

Guidelines in Medicine

Some years ago, a good friend of ours (let's call him Paul) was diagnosed with high blood pressure by his primary care doctor (we will call him Dr. Jones). The doctor advised Paul to try medication. Dr. Jones prescribed a diuretic, but it had no effect; Paul's blood pressure remained high. A few weeks later, Dr. Jones responded with a second medication, a calcium channel blocker. Its effect was also modest.

These results baffled Dr. Jones. After three months of weekly office visits, Paul's high blood pressure readings had dropped slightly, but they were still too high. It wasn't clear what the next steps would be. Paul was anxious and Dr. Jones was troubled, not least because Paul was a relatively young man in good health. Dr. Jones contemplated trying a third medication.

At that point, Paul happened to move to a new city, where he consulted a new primary care doctor (we will call him Dr. Smith). Paul told Dr. Smith the story of his continuing struggles with high blood pressure. Dr. Smith immediately responded, "Buy a home blood pressure kit, and see what the readings are. I don't think you have high blood pressure at all. You probably just have white coat syndrome — your blood pressure goes up in doctors' offices!"

Paul did as he was told, and sure enough, his blood pressure was normal at home. It has been normal ever since (and a month after Dr. Smith told him about white coat syndrome, it became normal in doctors' offices as well).

A central task of doctors is to make diagnoses — to decide whether a patient has some kind of illness and, if so, to identify it. Diagnosis often requires some kind of judgment. For many conditions, the diagnosis is routine and largely mechanical, and rules and procedures are in place to minimize noise. It's usually easy for a doctor to determine whether someone has a dislocated shoulder or a broken toe. Something similar can be said about problems that are more technical. Quantifying tendon degeneration produces little noise. When pathologists evaluate core needle biopsies of breast lesions, their evaluations are relatively straightforward, with little noise.

Importantly, some diagnoses do not involve judgment at all. Health care often progresses by removing the element of judgment — by shifting from judgment to calculation. For strep throat, a doctor will begin with a rapid antigen test on a swab sample from a patient's throat. In a short period, the test can detect strep bacteria. (Without the rapid antigen result, and to some extent even with it, there is noise in diagnosis of strep throat.) If you have a fasting blood sugar level of 126 milligrams per deciliter or higher or an HbA1c (an average measure of blood sugar over the prior three months) of at least 6.5, you are considered to have diabetes. During the early stages of the COVID-19 pandemic, some doctors initially made diagnoses as a result of judgments reached after considering symptoms; as the pandemic progressed, testing became much more common, and the tests made judgment unnecessary.

Many people know that when doctors do exercise judgment, they can be noisy, and they might err; a standard practice is to advise patients to get a second opinion. In some hospitals, a second opinion is even mandatory. Whenever the second opinion diverges from the first, we have noise — though of course it may not be clear which doctor has it right. Some patients (including Paul) have been astonished to see how much the second opinion diverges from the first. But the surprise is not the existence of noise in the medical profession. It is its sheer magnitude.

Our goals in this chapter are to elaborate that claim and to describe some of the approaches to noise reduction used by the medical profession. We will focus on one decision hygiene strategy: the development of diagnostic guidelines. We are keenly aware that an entire book could easily be written about noise in medicine and the various steps that doctors, nurses, and hospitals have been taking by way of remedy. Notably, noise in medicine is hardly limited to noise in diagnostic judgments, which is our focus here. Treatments can also be noisy, and an extensive literature addresses this topic as well. If a patient has a heart problem, doctors' judgments about the best treatment are shockingly variable, whether the question involves the right medication, the right kind of surgery, or whether to get surgery at all. The Dartmouth Atlas Project has dedicated itself, for more than twenty years, to documenting "glaring variations in how medical resources are distributed and used in the United States." Similar conclusions hold in numerous nations. For our purposes, however, a brief exploration of noise in diagnostic judgments will be sufficient.

A Tour of the Horizon

There is an immense literature on noise in medicine. While much of the literature is empirical, testing for the presence of noise, much of it is also prescriptive. Those involved in health care are continuing to search for noise-reduction strategies, which take many forms and are a gold mine of ideas worth considering in many fields.

When there is noise, one physician may be clearly right and the other may be clearly wrong (and may suffer from some kind of bias). As might be expected, skill matters a lot. A study of pneumonia diagnoses by radiologists, for instance, found significant noise. Much of it came from differences in skill. More specifically, "variation in skill can explain 44% of the variation in diagnostic decisions," suggesting that "policies that improve skill perform better than uniform decision guidelines." Here as elsewhere, training and selection are evidently crucial to the reduction of error, and to the elimination of both noise and bias.

In some specialties, such as radiology and pathology, doctors are well aware of the presence of noise. Radiologists, for example, call diagnostic variation their "Achilles' heel." It is not clear whether noise in the fields of radiology and pathology receives particular attention because there is truly more noise in these fields than in others or simply because noise is more easily documented there. We suspect that ease of documentation may be more important. Clean, simple tests of noise (and sometimes error) are easier to conduct in radiology. For example, you can return to scans or slides to reevaluate a previous assessment.

In medicine, between-person noise, or *interrater reliability*, is usually measured by the *kappa statistic*. The higher the kappa, the less noise. A kappa value of 1 reflects perfect agreement; a value of 0 reflects exactly as much agreement as you would expect between monkeys throwing darts onto a list of possible diagnoses. In some domains of medical diagnosis, reliability as measured by this coefficient has been found to be "slight" or "poor," which means that noise is very high. It is often found to be "fair," which is of course better but which also indicates significant noise. On the important question of which drug-drug interactions are clinically significant, generalist physicians, reviewing one hundred randomly selected drug-drug interactions, showed "poor agreement." To outsiders and to many doctors, diagnosis of the various stages of kidney disease might seem relatively straightforward. But nephrologists show only "slight to moderate agreement" in their judgments about the meaning of standard tests used in the evaluation of patients with kidney disease.

On the question of whether a breast lesion was cancerous, one study found only "fair" agreement among pathologists. In diagnosing breast proliferative lesions, agreement was again only "fair." Agreement was also "fair" when physicians assessed MRI scans for the degree of spinal stenosis. It is worth pausing over these findings. We have said that in some domains, the level of noise in medicine is very low. But in some areas that are fairly technical, doctors are far from noise-free. Whether a patient will be diagnosed with a serious disease, such as cancer, might depend on a kind of lottery, determined by the particular doctor that she will see.

Consider just a few other findings from the literature, drawn from areas in which the volume of noise seems especially noteworthy. We describe these findings not to give authoritative statements about the current state of medical practice, which continues to evolve and improve (in some cases rapidly), but to convey a general sense of the pervasiveness of noise, both in the relatively recent past and in the present.

1. Heart disease is the leading cause of death in both men and women in the United States. Coronary angiograms, a primary method used to test for heart disease, assess the degree of blockage in the heart's arteries in both acute and nonacute settings. In nonacute settings, when a patient presents with recurrent chest pain, treatment — such as stent placement — is often pursued if more than 70% of one or more arteries is found to be blocked. However, a degree of variability in interpreting angiograms has been documented, potentially leading to unnecessary procedures. An early study found that 31% of the time, physicians evaluating angiograms disagreed on whether a major vessel was more than 70% blocked. Despite widespread awareness by cardiologists of potential variability in reading angiograms, and despite continuing efforts and corrective steps, the problem has yet to be solved.

2. Endometriosis is a disorder in which endometrial tissue, normally lining the inside of the uterus, grows outside the uterus. The disorder can be painful and lead to fertility problems. It is often diagnosed through laparoscopy, in which a small camera is surgically inserted into the body. Digital videos of laparoscopies in three patients, two of whom had endometriosis of varying degrees of severity and one of whom did not, were shown to 108 gynecological surgeons. The surgeons were asked to judge the number and location of endometriotic lesions. They disagreed dramatically, with weak correlations on both number and location.

3. Tuberculosis (TB) is one of the most widespread and deadly diseases worldwide — in 2016 alone, it infected more than 10 million people and killed almost 2 million. A widely used method for detecting TB is a chest X-ray, which allows examination of the lungs for the empty space caused by the TB bacteria. Variability in diagnosis of TB has been well documented for almost seventy-five years. Despite improvements over the decades, studies have continued to find significant variability in diagnosis of TB, with "moderate" or just "fair" interrater agreement. There is also variability in TB diagnoses between radiologists in different countries.

4. When pathologists analyzed skin lesions for the presence of melanoma — the most dangerous form of skin cancer — there was only "moderate" agreement. The eight pathologists reviewing each case were unanimous or showed only one disagreement just 62% of the time. Another study at an oncology center found that the diagnostic accuracy of melanomas was only 64%, meaning that doctors misdiagnosed melanomas in one of every three lesions. A third study found that dermatologists at New York University failed to diagnose melanoma from skin biopsies 36% of the time. The authors of the study conclude that "the clinical failure to diagnose melanoma correctly has grievous implications for survival of patients with that potentially fatal disease."

5. There is variability in radiologists' judgments with respect to breast cancer from screening mammograms. A large study found that the range of false negatives among different radiologists varied from 0% (the radiologist was correct every time) to greater than 50% (the radiologist incorrectly identified the mammogram as normal more than half of the time). Similarly, false-positive rates ranged from less than 1% to 64% (meaning that nearly two-thirds of the time, the radiologist said the mammogram showed cancer when cancer was not present). False negatives and false positives, from different radiologists, ensure that there is noise.

These cases of interpersonal noise dominate the existing research, but there are also findings of occasion noise. Radiologists sometimes offer a different view when assessing the same image again and thus disagree with themselves (albeit less often than they disagree with others). When assessing the degree of blockage in angiograms, twenty-two physicians disagreed with themselves between 63 and 92% of the time. In areas that involve vague criteria and complex judgments, intrarater reliability, as it is called, can be poor.

These studies offer no clear explanation of this occasion noise. But another study, not involving diagnosis, identifies a simple source of occasion noise in medicine — a finding worth bearing in mind for both patients and doctors. In short, doctors are significantly more likely to order cancer screenings early in the morning than late in the afternoon. In a large sample, the order rates of breast and colon screening tests were highest at 8 a.m., at 63.7%. They decreased throughout the morning to 48.7% at 11 a.m. They increased to 56.2% at noon — and then decreased to 47.8% at 5 p.m. It follows that patients with appointment times later in the day were less likely to receive guideline-recommended cancer screening.

How can we explain such findings? A possible answer is that physicians almost inevitably run behind in clinic after seeing patients with complex medical problems that require more than the usual twenty-minute slot. We already mentioned the role of stress and fatigue as triggers of occasion noise (see chapter 7), and these elements seem to be at work here. To keep up with their schedules, some doctors skip discussions about preventive health measures. Another illustration of the role of fatigue among clinicians is the lower rate of appropriate handwashing during the end of hospital shifts. (Handwashing turns out to be noisy, too.)

Less Noisy Doctors: The Value of Guidelines

It would be a major contribution not only to medicine but also to human knowledge to provide a comprehensive account of the existence and magnitude of noise in the context of different medical problems. We are unaware of any such account; we hope that it will be produced in the fullness of time. But even now, existing findings provide some clues.

At one extreme, diagnosis for some problems and illnesses is essentially mechanical and allows no room for judgment. In other cases, the diagnosis is not mechanical but straightforward; anyone with medical training is highly likely to reach the same conclusion. In still other cases, a degree of specialization — among, say, lung cancer specialists — will be sufficient to ensure that noise exists but is minimal. At the other extreme, some cases present a great deal of room for judgment, and the relevant criteria for diagnosis are so open-ended that noise will be substantial and difficult to reduce. As we will see, this is the case in much of psychiatry.

What might work to reduce noise in medicine? As we mentioned, training can increase skill, and skill certainly helps. So does the aggregation of multiple expert judgments (second opinions and so forth). Algorithms offer an especially promising avenue, and doctors are now using deep-learning algorithms and artificial intelligence to reduce noise. For example, such algorithms have been used to detect lymph node metastases in women with breast cancer. The best of these have been found to be superior to the best pathologist, and, of course, algorithms are not noisy. Deep-learning algorithms have also been used, with considerable success, for the detection of eye problems associated with diabetes. And AI now performs at least as well as radiologists do in detecting cancer from mammograms; further advances in AI will probably demonstrate its superiority.

The medical profession is likely to rely on algorithms more and more in the future; they promise to reduce both bias and noise and to save lives and money in the process. But our emphasis here will be on human-judgment guidelines, because the domain of medicine helpfully illustrates how they produce good or even excellent results in some applications and more mixed results in others.

Perhaps the most famous example of a guideline for diagnosis is the Apgar score, developed in 1952 by the obstetric anesthesiologist

Virginia Apgar. Assessing whether a newborn baby is in distress used to be a matter of clinical judgment for physicians and midwives. Apgar's score gave them a standard guideline instead. The evaluator measures the baby's color, heart rate, reflexes, muscle tone, and respiratory effort, sometimes summarized as a "backronym" for Apgar's name: *appearance* (skin color), *pulse* (heart rate), *grimace* (reflexes), *activity* (muscle tone), and *respiration* (breathing rate and effort). In the Apgar test, each of these five measures is given a score of 0, 1, or 2. The highest possible total score is 10, which is rare. A score of 7 or above is considered indicative of good health (table 3).

Table 3: *Apgar Scoring Guidelines*

Category	Number of points assigned
Appearance (skin color)	0: Entire body is blue or pale 1: Good color in body but blue hands or feet 2: Completely pink or normal color
Pulse (heart rate)	0: No heart rate 1: <100 beats per minute 2: >100 beats per minute
Grimace (reflexes)	0: No response to airways being stimulated 1: Grimace during stimulation 2: Grimace and cough or sneeze during stimulation
Activity (muscle tone)	0: Limp 1: Some flexing (bending) of arms and legs 2: Active motion
Respiration (breathing rate and effort)	0: Not breathing 1: Weak cry (whimpering, grunting) 2: Good, strong cry

Note that heart rate is the only strictly numerical component of the score and that all the other items involve an element of judgment. But because the judgment is decomposed into individual elements, each of which is straightforward to assess, practitioners with even a modest degree of training are unlikely to disagree a great deal — and hence Apgar scoring produces little noise.

The Apgar score exemplifies how guidelines work and why they reduce noise. Unlike rules or algorithms, guidelines do not eliminate the need for judgment: the decision is not a straightforward computation. Disagreement remains possible on each of the components and hence on the final conclusion. Yet guidelines succeed in reducing noise because they decompose a complex decision into a number of easier subjudgments on predefined dimensions.

The benefits of this approach are clear when we view the problem in terms of the simple prediction models discussed in chapter 9. A clinician making a judgment about a newborn's health is working from several predictive cues. Occasion noise might be at work: on one day but not another, or in one mood but not another, a clinician could pay attention to relatively unimportant predictors or ignore important ones. The Apgar score focuses the health professional on the five that are empirically known to matter. Then, the score provides a clear description of how to evaluate each cue, which greatly simplifies each cue-level judgment and hence reduces its noise. Finally, the Apgar score specifies how to weight the predictors mechanically to produce the overall judgment required, whereas human clinicians would otherwise differ on the weights they assign to the cues. A focus on the relevant predictors, simplification of the predictive model, and mechanical aggregation — all of these reduce noise.

Analogous approaches have been used in many medical domains. One example is the Centor score to guide diagnosis of strep throat. A patient is given one point for each of the following symptoms or signs (whose terms, like the Apgar score, constitute a backronym for the last name of Robert Centor, who with his colleagues first summarized this guideline): absence of a *cough*, presence of *exudates* (white patches on the back of throat), tender or swollen lymph *nodes* in the neck, and a *temperature* greater than 100.4 degrees. Depending on the number of points a patient is assigned, a throat swab to diagnose strep pharyngitis may be recommended. Assessment and scoring are relatively straightforward using this scale, which has effectively reduced the number of people undergoing unnecessary testing and treatment for strep throat.

Similarly, guidelines have been developed for breast cancer diagnosis with the Breast Imaging Reporting and Data System (BI-RADS), which reduces noise in the interpretations of mammograms. One study found that BI-RADS increased interrater agreement on the assessments of mammograms, demonstrating that guidelines can be effective in reducing noise in an area where variability has been significant. In pathology, there have been many successful efforts to use guidelines for the same purpose.

The Depressing Case of Psychiatry

In terms of noise, psychiatry is an extreme case. When diagnosing the same patient using the same diagnostic criteria, psychiatrists frequently disagree with one another. For that reason, noise reduction has been a major priority for the psychiatric community since at least the 1940s. And as we will see, despite being constantly refined, guidelines have provided only modest help in reducing noise.

A 1964 study involving 91 patients and ten experienced psychiatrists found that the likelihood of an agreement between two opinions was just 57%. Another early study, involving 426 state hospital patients diagnosed independently by two psychiatrists, found agreement merely 50% of the time in their diagnosis of the kind of mental illness that was present. Yet another early study, involving 153 outpatients, found 54% agreement. In these studies, the source of the noise was not specified. Interestingly, however, some psychiatrists were found to be inclined to assign patients to specific diagnostic categories. For example, some psychiatrists were especially likely to diagnose patients with depression, and others with anxiety.

As we shall soon see, levels of noise continue to be high in psychiatry. Why is this? Specialists lack a single, clear answer (which means that the explanations for noise are themselves noisy). The large set of diagnostic categories is undoubtedly one factor. But in a preliminary effort to answer that question, researchers asked one psychiatrist to interview a patient first, and then had a second psychiatrist conduct another interview after a short resting period. The two psychiatrists met afterward and, if they disagreed, discussed why they did so.

One frequent reason was "inconstancy of the physician": different schools of thought, different training, different clinical experiences, different interview styles. While a "clinician with developmental training might explain the hallucinatory experience as part of post-traumatic experience of past abuse," a different clinician "with a bio-medical orientation might explain the same hallucinations as part of a schizophrenic process." Such differences are examples of pattern noise.

Beyond physician differences, however, the main reason for noise was "inadequacy of the nomenclature." Such observations and wide-spread professional dissatisfaction with psychiatric nomenclature helped motivate the 1980 revision (the third edition) of the *Diagnostic and Statistical Manual of Mental Disorders* (DSM-III). The manual included, for the first time, explicit and detailed criteria for diagnosing mental disorders, a first step in the direction of introducing diagnostic guidelines.

DSM-III led to a dramatic increase in the research on whether diagnoses were noisy. It also proved helpful in reducing noise. But the manual was far from a complete success. Even after a significant 2000 revision of the fourth edition, DSM-IV (originally published in 1994), research showed that the level of noise remained high. On the one hand, Ahmed Aboraya and his colleagues conclude that "the use of diagnostic criteria for psychiatric disorders has been shown to increase the reliability of psychiatric diagnoses." On the other hand, there continues to be a serious risk that "admissions of a single patient will reveal multiple diagnoses for the same patient."

Another version of the manual, DSM-5, was released in 2013. The American Psychiatric Association had hoped that DSM-5 would reduce noise because the new edition relied on more objective, clearly scaled criteria. But psychiatrists continue to show significant noise. For example, Samuel Lieblich and his colleagues find that "psychiatrists have a hard time agreeing on who does and does not have major depressive disorder." Field trials for DSM-5 found "minimal agreement," which "means that highly trained specialist psychiatrists under study conditions were only able to agree that a patient has depression between 4 and 15% of the time." According to some field trials, DSM-5 actually made things worse, showing increased noise "in all major domains, with some diagnoses, such as mixed anxiety-depressive disorder ... so unreliable as to appear useless in clinical practice."

The major reason for the limited success of guidelines seems to be that, in psychiatry, "the diagnostic criteria of some disorders are still vague and difficult to operationalize." Some guidelines reduce noise by decomposing judgment into criteria on which disagreement is reduced, but to the extent that such criteria are relatively open-ended, noise remains likely. With this point in mind, prominent proposals call for more standardized diagnostic guidelines. These include (1) clarifying diagnostic criteria, moving away from vague standards; (2) producing "reference definitions" of symptoms and their level of severity, on the theory that when "clinicians agree on the presence or absence of symptoms, they are more likely to agree on the diagnosis"; and (3) using structured interviews of patients in addition to open conversation. One proposed interview guide includes twenty-four screening questions that allow for more reliable diagnosis of, for example, anxiety, depression, and eating disorders.

These steps sound promising, but it is an open question to what extent they would succeed in reducing noise. In the words of one observer, "the reliance on the patient's subjective symptoms, the clinician's interpretation of the symptoms, and the absence of objective measure (such as a blood test) implant the seeds of diagnostic unreliability of psychiatric disorders." In this sense, psychiatry may prove especially resistant to attempts at noise reduction.

On that particular question, it is too soon to make a confident prediction. But one thing is clear. In medicine in general, guidelines have been highly successful in reducing both bias and noise. They have helped doctors, nurses, and patients and greatly improved public health in the process. The medical profession needs more of them.

Speaking of Guidelines in Medicine

"Among doctors, the level of noise is far higher than we might have suspected. In diagnosing cancer and heart disease — even in reading X-rays — specialists sometimes disagree. That means that the treatment a patient gets might be a product of a lottery."

"Doctors like to think that they make the same decision whether it's Monday or Friday or early in the morning or late in the afternoon. But it turns out that what doctors say and do might well depend on how tired they are."

"Medical guidelines can make doctors less likely to blunder at a patient's expense. Such guidelines can also help the medical profession as a whole, because they reduce variability."

CHAPTER 23

Defining the Scale in Performance Ratings

L et's start with an exercise. Take three people you know; they might be friends or colleagues. Rate them on a scale of 1 to 5, where 1 is the lowest and 5 is the highest, in terms of three characteristics: kindness, intelligence, and diligence. Now ask someone who knows them well — your spouse, best friend, or closest colleague — to do the same thing with respect to the same three people.

There is a good chance that on some of the ratings, you and the other rater came up with different numbers. If you (and your counterpart) are willing, please discuss the reasons for the differences. You might find that the answer lies in how you used the scale — what we have called level noise. Perhaps you thought a 5 requires something truly extraordinary, whereas the other rater thought that it merely requires something unusually good. Or perhaps you differed because of your differing views of the people being rated: your understanding of whether they are kind, and how exactly to define that virtue, might be different from that of the other rater.

Now imagine that for the three people you rated, a promotion or bonus is at stake. Suppose that you and the other rater are engaged in performance ratings at a company that values kindness (or collegiality), intelligence, and diligence. Would there be a difference between your ratings? Would it be as large as in the earlier exercise? Even larger? However those questions are answered, differences in policies and scaling are likely to produce noise. And in fact, that is what is pervasively observed in performance ratings across organizational settings.

A Judgment Task

In almost all large organizations, performance is formally evaluated on a regular basis. Those who are rated do not enjoy the experience. As one newspaper headline put it, "Study Finds That Basically Every Single Person Hates Performance Reviews." Every single person also knows (we think) that performance reviews are subject to both bias and noise. But most people do not know just how noisy they are.

In an ideal world, evaluating people's performance would not be a judgment task; objective facts would be sufficient to determine how well people are doing. But most modern organizations have little in common with Adam Smith's pin factory, in which every worker had a measurable output. What would that output be for a chief financial officer or for a head of research? Today's knowledge workers balance multiple, sometimes contradictory objectives. Focusing on only one of them might produce erroneous evaluations and have harmful incentive effects. The number of patients a doctor sees every day is an important driver of hospital productivity, for example, but you would not want physicians to focus single-mindedly on that indicator, much less to be evaluated and rewarded only on that basis. Even quantifiable performance metrics — say, sales for a salesperson or number of lines of code written for a programmer — must be evaluated in context: not all customers are equally difficult to serve, and not all software development projects are identical. In light of these challenges, many people cannot be evaluated entirely on the basis of objective performance metrics. Hence the ubiquity of judgment-based performance reviews.

DEFINING THE SCALE IN PERFORMANCE RATINGS

One-Quarter Signal, Three-Quarters Noise

Thousands of research articles have been published on the practice of performance appraisals. Most researchers find that such appraisals are exceedingly noisy. This sobering conclusion comes mostly from studies based on 360-degree performance reviews, in which multiple raters provide input on the same person being rated, usually on multiple dimensions of performance. When this analysis is conducted, the result is not pretty. Studies often find that true variance, that is, variance attributable to the person's performance, accounts for no more than 20 to 30% of the total variance. The rest, 70 to 80% of the variance in the ratings, is system noise.

Where does this noise come from? Thanks to multiple studies of variance in job performance ratings, we know that all the components of system noise are present.

These components are quite easy to picture in the context of a performance rating. Consider two raters, Lynn and Mary. If Lynn is lenient and Mary tough, in the sense that Lynn gives higher ratings than Mary does, on average, to all people being evaluated, then we have level noise. As noted in our discussion of judges, this noise may mean either that Lynn and Mary form truly different impressions or that the two raters merely use the rating scale differently to express the same impression.

Now, if Lynn is evaluating you and happens to have a distinctly poor opinion of you and your contributions, her general leniency may be offset by her idiosyncratic (and negative) reaction to you. This is what we have called a stable pattern: a specific rater's reaction to a specific person being rated. Because the pattern is unique to Lynn (and to her judgment of you), it is a source of pattern noise.

Finally, Mary may have discovered that someone dented her car in the company parking lot just before she filled in a rating form, or Lynn may just have received her own, surprisingly generous, bonus, which put her in an unusually good mood as she evaluated your performance. Such events may, of course, produce occasion noise.

Different studies come to different conclusions on the breakdown of system noise into these three components (level, pattern, and occasion), and we can certainly imagine reasons why it should vary from one organization to the next. But all forms of noise are undesirable. The basic message that emerges from this research is a simple one: most ratings of performance have much less to do with the performance of the person being rated than we would wish. As one review summarizes it, "the relationship between job performance and ratings of job performance is likely to be weak or at best uncertain."

In addition, there are many reasons why ratings in organizations might not reflect the rater's perception of an employee's true performance. For example, raters might not in fact attempt to evaluate performance accurately but might rate people "strategically." Among other motives, the evaluators might intentionally inflate a rating to avoid a difficult feedback conversation, to favor a person who is seeking a long-awaited promotion, or even, paradoxically, to get rid of an underperforming team member who needs a good evaluation to be allowed to transfer to another division.

These strategic calculations certainly affect ratings, but they are not the only source of noise. We know this thanks to a sort of natural experiment: some 360-degree feedback systems are used solely for developmental purposes. With these systems, the respondents are told that the feedback will not be used for evaluation purposes. To the extent that the raters actually believe what they are told, this approach discourages them from inflating — or deflating — ratings. As it turns out, the developmental review does make a difference in the quality of the feedback, but system noise remains high and still accounts for much more variance than does the performance of the person being rated. Even when the feedback is purely developmental, ratings remain noisy.

A Problem Long Recognized but Not Solved

If performance rating systems are so badly broken, the people who measure performance should take notice and improve them. Indeed, over the past several decades, organizations have experimented with countless reforms to those systems. The reforms have employed some of the noise-reduction strategies we have outlined. In our view, much more could be done.

Almost all organizations use the noise-reduction strategy of *aggregation.* Aggregate ratings are often associated with 360-degree rating systems, which became the standard in large corporations in the 1990s. (The journal *Human Resources Management* had a special issue on 360-degree feedback in 1993.)

While averaging ratings from several raters should help to reduce system noise, it is worth noting that 360-degree feedback systems were not invented as a remedy for that problem. Their primary purpose is to measure much more than what a boss sees. When your peers and subordinates, and not just your boss, are asked to contribute to your performance evaluation, the nature of what is valued is changed. The theory is that this shift is for the better, because today's jobs entail more than pleasing your boss. The rise in popularity of 360-degree feedback coincided with the generalization of fluid, project-based organizations.

Some evidence suggests that 360-degree feedback is a useful tool in that it predicts objectively measurable performance. Unfortunately, the use of this feedback system has created its own problems. As computerization made it effortless to add more questions to feedback systems, and as the proliferation of multiple corporate objectives and constraints added dimensions to job descriptions, many feedback questionnaires became absurdly complex. Overengineered questionnaires abound (one example involves forty-six ratings on eleven dimensions for each rater and person being rated). It would take a superhuman rater to recall and process accurate, relevant facts about numerous people being evaluated on so many dimensions. In some ways, this overly complicated approach is not only useless but also pernicious. As we have seen, the halo effect implies that supposedly separate dimensions will in fact not be treated separately. A strong positive or negative rating on one of the first questions will tend to pull answers to subsequent questions in the same direction.

Even more importantly, the development of 360-degree systems has exponentially increased the amount of time devoted to providing feedback. It is not uncommon for middle managers to be asked to complete dozens of questionnaires on their colleagues at all levels — and sometimes on their counterparts in other organizations, because many companies now request feedback from customers, vendors, and other business partners. However well intentioned, this explosion in the demands placed on time-constrained raters cannot be expected to improve the quality of the information they supply. In this case, the reduction of noise may not be worth the cost — a problem that we will discuss in part 6.

Finally, 360-degree systems are not immune to a near-universal disease of all performance measurement systems: creeping ratings inflation. One large industrial company once observed that 98% of its managers had been rated as "fully meeting expectations." When almost everyone receives the highest possible rating, it is fair to question the value of these ratings.

In Praise of Relative Judgments

A theoretically effective solution to the problem of ratings inflation is to introduce some standardization in ratings. One popular practice that aims to do this is *forced ranking*. In a forced ranking system, raters are not only prevented from giving everyone the highest possible rating but also forced to abide by a predetermined distribution. Forced ranking was advocated by Jack Welch when he was CEO of General Electric, as a way to stop inflation in ratings and to ensure "candor" in performance reviews. Many companies adopted it, only to abandon it later, citing undesirable side effects on morale and teamwork.

Whatever their flaws, rankings are less noisy than ratings. We saw in the example of punitive damages that there is much less noise in relative judgments than in absolute ones, and this relationship has been shown to apply in performance ratings, too.

Panel A

Work quality of Employee A: _____

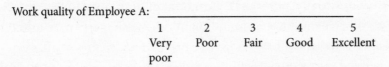

	1	2	3	4	5
	Very poor	Poor	Fair	Good	Excellent

Panel B

Please rate your subordinates on *safety*. *Safety* refers to how well the employees follow the proper rules and regulations; behave in a safe manner on the job; and demonstrate awareness and understanding of safe work practices.

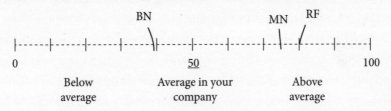

FIGURE 17: *Examples of absolute and relative rating scales*

To appreciate why, consider figure 17, which shows two examples of scales for evaluating employees. Panel A, in which an employee is rated on an absolute scale, requires what we have called a matching operation: finding the score that most closely matches your impression of the employee's "work quality." Panel B, by contrast, requires each individual to be compared with a group of others on a specific dimension — safety. The supervisor is asked to state the rank (or percentile) of an employee in a specified population, using a percentile scale. We can see that a supervisor has placed three employees on this common scale.

The approach in panel B has two advantages. First, rating all employees on one dimension at a time (in this example, safety) exemplifies a noise-reduction strategy we will discuss in more detail in the next chapter: *structuring* a complex judgment into several dimensions. Structuring is an attempt to limit the halo effect, which usually keeps the ratings of one individual on different dimensions within a small range. (Structuring, of course, works only if the ranking is done on each dimension separately, as in this example: ranking employees on an ill-defined, aggregate judgment of "work quality" would not reduce the halo effect.)

Second, as we discussed in chapter 15, a ranking reduces both pattern noise and level noise. You are less likely to be inconsistent (and to create pattern noise) when you compare the performance of two members of your team than when you separately give each one a grade. More importantly, rankings mechanically eliminate level noise. If Lynn and Mary are evaluating the same group of twenty employees, and Lynn is more lenient than Mary, their average ratings will be different, but their average rankings will not. A lenient ranker and a tough ranker use the same ranks.

Indeed, noise reduction is the main stated objective of forced ranking, which ensures that all raters have the same mean and the same distribution of evaluations. Rankings are "forced" when a distribution of ratings is mandated. For instance, a rule might state that no more than 20% of the people being rated can be put in the top category and that no less than 15% can be put in the bottom one.

Rank but Do Not Force

In principle, therefore, forced ranking should bring about much-needed improvements. Yet it often backfires. We do not intend here to review all its possible unwanted effects (which are often related to poor implementation rather than principle). But two issues with forced ranking systems offer some general lessons.

The first is the confusion between absolute and relative performance. It is certainly impossible for 98% of the managers of any company to be in the top 20%, 50%, or even 80% of their peer group. But it is not impossible that they all "meet expectations," if these expectations have been defined ex ante *and in absolute terms.*

Many executives object to the notion that nearly all employees can meet expectations. If so, they argue, the expectations must be too low, perhaps because of a culture of complacency. Admittedly this interpretation may be valid, but it is also possible that most employees really do meet *high* expectations. Indeed, this is exactly what we would expect to find in a high-performance organization. You would not sneer at the leniency of the National Aeronautics and Space Administration's performance management procedures if you heard that all the astronauts on a successful space mission have fully met expectations.

The upshot is that a system that depends on relative evaluations is appropriate only if an organization cares about relative performance. For example, relative ratings might make sense when, regardless of people's absolute performance, only a fixed percentage of them can be promoted — think of colonels being evaluated for promotion to general. But forcing a relative ranking on what purports to measure an *absolute* level of performance, as many companies do, is illogical. And mandating that a set percentage of employees be rated as failing to meet (absolute) expectations is not just cruel; it is absurd. It would be foolish to say that 10% of an elite unit of the army must be graded "unsatisfactory."

The second problem is that the forced distribution of the ratings is assumed to reflect the distribution of the underlying true performances — typically, something close to a normal distribution. Yet even if the distribution of performances in the population being rated is known, the same distribution may not be reproduced in a smaller group, such as those assessed by a single evaluator. If you randomly pick ten people from a population of several thousand, there is no guarantee that exactly two of them will belong to the top 20% of the general population. ("No guarantee" is an understatement: the probability that this will be the case is just 30%.) In practice, the problem is even worse, because the composition of teams is not random. Some units may be staffed almost entirely with high performers, and others with subpar employees.

Inevitably, forced ranking in such a setting is a source of error and unfairness. Suppose that one rater's team is composed of five people whose performances are indistinguishable. Forcing a differentiated distribution of ratings on this undifferentiated reality does not reduce error. It increases it.

Critics of forced ranking have often focused their attacks on the principle of ranking, which they decry as brutal, inhumane, and ultimately counterproductive. Whether or not you accept these arguments, the fatal flaw of forced ranking is not the "ranking," but the "forced." Whenever judgments are forced onto an inappropriate scale, either because a relative scale is used to measure an absolute performance or because judges are forced to distinguish the indistinguishable, the choice of the scale mechanically adds noise.

What's Next?

In light of all the efforts that organizations have made to improve performance measurement, it is an understatement to say that the results have been disappointing. As a result of those efforts, the cost of performance evaluations skyrocketed. In 2015, Deloitte calculated that it was spending 2 million hours each year evaluating its sixty-five thousand people. Performance reviews continue to be one of the most dreaded rituals of organizations, hated almost as much by those who have to perform them as by those who receive them. One study found that a staggering 90% of managers, employees, and HR heads believe that their performance management processes fail to deliver the results they expected. Research has confirmed what most managers have experienced. Although performance feedback, when associated with a development plan for the employee, can bring about improvements, performance ratings as they are most often practiced demotivate as often as they motivate. As one review article summarized, "No matter what has been tried over decades to improve [performance management] processes, they continue to generate inaccurate information and do virtually nothing to drive performance."

In despair, a small but growing number of companies are now considering the radical option of eliminating evaluation systems altogether. Proponents of this "performance management revolution," including many technology companies, some professional services organizations, and a handful of companies in traditional sectors, aim to focus on developmental, future-oriented feedback rather than on evaluative, backward-looking assessment. A few have even made their evaluations numberless, which means that they abandon traditional performance ratings.

For companies that are not giving up on performance ratings (and they are the overwhelming majority), what can be done to improve them? One noise-reduction strategy has to do, again, with picking the right scale. The aim is to ensure a *common frame of reference*. Research suggests that a combination of improved rating formats and training of the raters can help achieve more consistency between raters in their use of the scale.

At a minimum, performance rating scales must be anchored on descriptors that are sufficiently specific to be interpreted consistently. Many organizations use *behaviorally anchored rating scales* in which each degree on the scale corresponds to a description of specific behaviors. The left panel of figure 18 provides an example.

Evidence suggests, however, that behaviorally anchored rating scales are not sufficient to eliminate noise. A further step, *frame-of-reference training,* has been shown to help ensure consistency between raters. In this step, raters are trained to recognize different dimensions of performance. They practice rating performance using videotaped vignettes and then learn how their ratings compare with "true" ratings provided by experts. The performance vignettes act as reference cases; each vignette defines an anchor point on the performance scale, which becomes a *case scale*, such as the one shown on the right panel of figure 18.

With a case scale, each rating of a new individual is a comparison with the anchor cases. It becomes a relative judgment. Because comparative judgments are less susceptible to noise than ratings are, case scales are more reliable than scales that use numbers, adjectives, or behavioral descriptions.

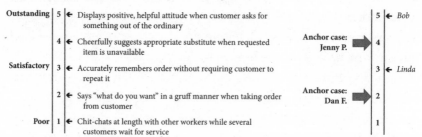

Customer Relations: Serves customers in a courteous and respectful manner. Appropriately uses knowledge of food items to help customers make choices. Listens carefully and makes effort to be cheerful, positive, and helpful.

Outstanding	5	← Displays positive, helpful attitude when customer asks for something out of the ordinary	5 ← Bob
	4	← Cheerfully suggests appropriate substitute when requested item is unavailable	Anchor case: Jenny P. → 4
Satisfactory	3	← Accurately remembers order without requiring customer to repeat it	3 ← Linda
	2	← Says "what do you want" in a gruff manner when taking order from customer	Anchor case: Dan F. → 2
Poor	1	← Chit-chats at length with other workers while several customers wait for service	1

FIGURE 18: *Example of a behaviorally anchored rating scale (left) and case scale (right)*

Frame-of-reference training has been known for decades and provides demonstrably less noisy and more accurate ratings. Yet it has gained little ground. It is easy to guess why. Frame-of-reference training, case scales, and other tools that pursue the same goals are complex and time-consuming. To be valuable, they usually need to be customized for the company and even for the unit conducting the evaluations, and they must be frequently updated as job requirements evolve. These tools require a company to add to its already-large investment in its performance management systems. Current fashion goes in the opposite direction. (In part 6, we shall have more to say about the costs of reducing noise.)

In addition, any organization that tames the noise attributable to raters also reduces their ability to influence ratings in pursuit of their own goals. Requiring managers to undergo additional rater training, to invest more effort in the rating process, and to give up some of the control they have over outcomes is certain to generate considerable resistance. Tellingly, the majority of studies of frame-of-reference rater training have so far been conducted on students, not on actual managers.

The large subject of performance evaluation raises many questions, both practical and philosophical. Some people ask, for instance, to what extent the notion of individual performance is meaningful in today's organizations, where outcomes often depend on how people interact with one another. If we believe the notion is indeed meaningful, we must wonder how levels of individual performance are distributed among people in a given organization — for instance, whether performance follows a normal distribution or whether there exists "star talent" making a hugely disproportionate contribution. And if your goal is to bring out the best in people, you can reasonably ask whether measuring individual performance and using that measurement to motivate people through fear and greed is the best approach (or even an effective one).

If you are designing or revising a performance management system, you will need to answer these questions and many more. Our aspiration here is not to examine these questions but to make a more modest suggestion: if you do measure performance, your performance ratings have probably been pervaded by system noise and, for that reason, they might be essentially useless and quite possibly counterproductive. Reducing this noise is a challenge that cannot be solved by simple technological fixes. It requires clear thinking about the judgments that raters are expected to make. Most likely, you will find that you can improve judgments by clarifying the rating scale and training people to use it consistently. This noise-reduction strategy is applicable in many other fields.

Speaking of Defining the Scale

"We spend a lot of time on our performance ratings, and yet the results are one-quarter performance and three-quarters system noise."

"We tried 360-degree feedback and forced ranking to address this problem, but we may have made things worse."

"If there is so much level noise, it is because different raters have completely different ideas of what 'good' or 'great' means. They will only agree if we give them concrete cases as anchors on the rating scale."

CHAPTER 24

Structure in Hiring

If you have ever held a job of any kind, the words *recruiting interview* might evoke some vivid and stressful memories. Job interviews, in which a candidate meets with a future supervisor or an HR professional, are a rite of passage required to enter many organizations.

In most cases, interviews follow a well-rehearsed routine. After exchanging some pleasantries, interviewers ask candidates to describe their experience or elaborate on specific aspects of it. Questions are asked about achievements and challenges, motivations for the job, or improvement ideas for the company. Often the interviewers ask candidates to describe their personality and explain why they would be a good fit for the position or the company's culture. Hobbies and interests are sometimes discussed. Toward the end, the candidate usually gets to ask a few questions, which are duly evaluated for relevance and insightfulness.

If you are now in a position to hire employees, your selection methods probably include some version of this ritual. As one organizational psychologist noted, "It is rare, even unthinkable, for someone to be hired without some type of interview." And almost all professionals rely to some degree on their intuitive judgments when making hiring decisions in these interviews.

The ubiquity of the employment interview reflects a deep-seated belief in the value of judgment when it comes to choosing the people we will work with. And as a judgment task, personnel selection has a great advantage: because it is so ubiquitous and so important, organizational psychologists have studied it in great detail. The inaugural issue of the *Journal of Applied Psychology*, published in 1917, identified hiring as the "supreme problem... because human capacities are after all the chief national resources." A century later, we know a lot about the effectiveness of various selection techniques (including standard interviews). No complex judgment task has been the focus of so much field research. This makes it a perfect test case, offering lessons that can be extrapolated to many judgments involving a choice among several options.

The Dangers of Interviews

If you are unfamiliar with research on the employment interview, what follows may surprise you. In essence, if your goal is to determine which candidates will succeed in a job and which will fail, standard interviews (also called unstructured interviews to distinguish them from structured interviews, to which we will turn shortly) are not very informative. To put it more starkly, they are often useless.

To reach this conclusion, innumerable studies estimated the correlation between the rating an evaluator gives a candidate after an interview and the candidate's eventual success on the job. If the correlation between the interview rating and success is high, then interviews — or any other recruiting techniques for which correlation is computed in the same manner — can be assumed to be a good predictor of how candidates will perform.

A caveat is needed here. The definition of success is a nontrivial problem. Typically, performance is evaluated on the basis of supervisor ratings. Sometimes, the metric is length of employment. Such measures raise questions, of course, especially given the questionable validity of performance ratings, which we noted in the previous chapter. However, for the purpose of evaluating the quality of an employer's judgments when selecting employees, it seems reasonable to use the judgments that the same employer makes when evaluating the employees thus hired. Any analysis of the quality of hiring decisions must make this assumption.

So what do these analyses conclude? In chapter 11, we mentioned a correlation between typical interview ratings and job performance ratings of .28. Other studies report correlations that range between .20 and .33. As we have seen, this is a very good correlation by social science standards — but not a very good one on which to base your decisions. Using the percent concordant (PC) we introduced in part 3, we can calculate a probability: given the preceding levels of correlation, if all you know about two candidates is that one appeared better than the other in the interview, the chances that this candidate will indeed perform better are about 56 to 61%. Somewhat better than flipping a coin, for sure, but hardly a fail-safe way to make important decisions.

Admittedly, interviews serve other purposes besides making a judgment about a candidate. Notably, they provide an opportunity to sell the company to promising candidates and to start building rapport with future colleagues. Yet from the perspective of an organization that invests time and effort in talent selection, the main purpose of interviews is clearly one of selection. And at that task, they are not exactly a terrific success.

Noise in Interviewing

We can easily see why traditional interviews produce error in their prediction of job performance. Some of this error has to do with what we have termed objective ignorance (see chapter 11). Job performance depends on many things, including how quickly the person you hire adjusts to her new position or how various life events affect her work. Much of this is unpredictable at the time of hiring. This uncertainty limits the predictive validity of interviews and, indeed, any other personnel selection technique.

Interviews are also a minefield of psychological biases. In recent years, people have become well aware that interviewers tend, often unintentionally, to favor candidates who are culturally similar to them or with whom they have something in common, including gender, race, and educational background. Many companies now recognize the risks posed by biases and try to address them through specific training of recruiting professionals and other employees. Other biases have also been known for decades. For instance, physical appearance plays a large part in the evaluation of candidates, even for positions where it should matter little or not at all. Such biases are shared by all or most recruiters and, when applied to a given candidate, will thus tend to produce a shared error — a negative or positive bias in the candidate's evaluation.

You will not be surprised to hear that there is noise as well: Different interviewers respond differently to the same candidate and reach different conclusions. Measures of the correlation between the ratings that two interviewers produce after interviewing the same candidate range between .37 and .44 (PC = 62–65%). One reason is that the candidate may not behave in exactly the same way with different interviewers. But even in panel interviews, where several interviewers are exposed to the same interviewee behavior, the correlation between their ratings is far from perfect. One meta-analysis estimates a correlation of .74 (PC = 76%). This means that you and another interviewer, after seeing the *same* two candidates in the *same* panel interview, will still disagree about which of two candidates is better about one-quarter of the time.

This variability is largely the product of pattern noise, the difference in interviewers' idiosyncratic reactions to a given interviewee. Most organizations fully expect this variability and, for that reason, require several interviewers to meet the same candidate, with the results aggregated in some way. (Typically, the aggregate opinion is formed through a discussion in which some sort of consensus must be reached — a procedure that creates its own problems, as we have already noted.)

A more surprising finding is the presence of much occasion noise in interviews. There is strong evidence, for instance, that hiring recommendations are linked to impressions formed in the informal rapport-building phase of an interview, those first two or three minutes where you just chat amicably to put the candidate at ease. First impressions turn out to matter — a lot.

Perhaps you think that judging on first impressions is unproblematic. At least some of what we learn from first impressions is meaningful. All of us know that we do learn something in the first seconds of interaction with a new acquaintance. It stands to reason that this may be particularly true of skilled interviewers. But the first seconds of an interview reflect exactly the sort of superficial qualities you associate with first impressions: early perceptions are based mostly on a candidate's extraversion and verbal skills. Even the quality of a handshake is a significant predictor of hiring recommendations! We may all like a firm handshake, but few recruiters would consciously choose to make it a key hiring criterion.

The Psychology of Interviewers

Why do first impressions end up driving the outcome of a much longer interview? One reason is that in a traditional interview, interviewers are at liberty to steer the interview in the direction they see fit. They are likely to ask questions that confirm an initial impression. If a candidate seems shy and reserved, for instance, the interviewer may want to ask tough questions about the candidate's past experiences of working in teams but perhaps will neglect to ask the same questions of someone who seems cheerful and gregarious. The evidence collected about these two candidates will not be the same. One study that tracked the behavior of interviewers who had formed a positive or negative initial impression from résumés and test scores found that initial impressions have a deep effect on the way the interview proceeds. Interviewers with positive first impressions, for instance, ask fewer questions and tend to "sell" the company to the candidate.

The power of first impressions is not the only problematic aspect of interviews. Another is that as interviewers, we want the candidate sitting in front of us to *make sense* (a manifestation of our excessive tendency, discussed in chapter 13, to seek and find coherence). In one striking experiment, researchers assigned students to play the role of interviewer or interviewee and told both that the interview should consist only of closed-ended, yes-or-no questions. They then asked some of the interviewees to answer questions *randomly*. (The first letter of the questions as formulated determined if they should answer yes or no.) As the researchers wryly note, "Some of the interviewees were initially concerned that the random interview would break down and be revealed to be nonsense. No such problems occurred, and the interviews proceeded." You read that right: *not a single interviewer* realized that the candidates were giving random answers. Worse, when asked to estimate whether they were "able to infer a lot about this person given the amount of time we spent together," interviewers in this "random" condition were as likely to agree as those who had met candidates responding truthfully. Such is our ability to create coherence. As we can often find an imaginary pattern in random data or imagine a shape in the contours of a cloud, we are capable of finding logic in perfectly meaningless answers.

For a less extreme illustration, consider the following case. One of the present authors had to interview a candidate who was, in his former position, chief financial officer at a midsize company. He noticed that the candidate had left this position after a few months and asked him why. The candidate explained that the reason was a "strategic disagreement with the CEO." A colleague also interviewed the candidate, asked the same question, and got the same answer. In the debrief that followed, however, the two interviewers had radically different views. One, having so far formed a positive evaluation of the candidate, saw the candidate's decision to leave the company as an indication of integrity and courage. The other, who had formed a negative first impression, construed the same fact as a sign of inflexibility, perhaps even of immaturity. The story illustrates that however much we would like to believe that our judgment about a candidate is based on facts, our interpretation of facts is colored by prior attitudes.

The limitations of traditional interviews cast serious doubt on our ability to draw any meaningful conclusions from them. Yet impressions formed in an interview are vivid, and the interviewer is usually confident about them. When combining the conclusions reached in an interview with other cues about the candidate, we tend to give too much weight to the interview and too little to other data that may be more predictive, such as test scores.

A story may help bring this observation to life. Professors who interview for a faculty position are often asked to teach in front of a panel of their peers to ensure that their teaching skills are up to the institution's standards. It is, of course, a higher-stakes situation than an ordinary class. One of us once witnessed a candidate making a bad impression in this exercise, clearly because of the stress of the situation: the candidate's résumé mentioned outstanding teaching evaluations and several awards for teaching excellence. Yet the vivid impression produced by his failure in one highly artificial situation weighed more heavily in the final decision than did the abstract data about his excellent past teaching performance.

A final point: when interviews are not the only source of information about candidates — for instance, when there are also tests, references, or other inputs — these various inputs must be combined into an overall judgment. The question this raises is one you now recognize: should the inputs be combined using judgment (a clinical aggregation) or a formula (a mechanical aggregation)? As we saw in chapter 9, the mechanical approach is superior both in general and in the specific case of work performance prediction. Unfortunately, surveys suggest that the overwhelming majority of HR professionals favor clinical aggregation. This practice adds yet another source of noise to an already-noisy process.

Improving Personnel Selection Through Structure

If traditional interviews and judgment-based hiring decisions have limited predictive validity, what can we do about them? Fortunately, research has also produced some advice on how to improve personnel selection, and some companies are paying attention.

One example of a company that has upgraded its personnel selection practices and reported on the results is Google. Laszlo Bock, its former senior vice president of People Operations, tells the tale in his book *Work Rules!* Despite being focused on hiring talent of the highest caliber and devoting considerable resources to finding the right people, Google was struggling. An audit of the predictive validity of its recruiting interviews found "zero relationship (...), a complete random mess." The changes Google implemented to address this situation reflect principles that have emerged from decades of research. They also illustrate decision hygiene strategies.

One of these strategies should be familiar by now: aggregation. Its use in this context is not a surprise. Almost all companies aggregate the judgments of multiple interviewers on the same candidate. Not to be outdone, Google sometimes had candidates suffer through twenty-five interviews! One of the conclusions of Bock's review was to reduce that number to four, as he found that additional interviews added almost no predictive validity to what was achieved by the first four. To ensure this level of validity, however, Google stringently enforces a rule that not all companies observe: the company makes sure that the interviewers rate the candidate separately, *before* they communicate with one another. Once more: aggregation works — but only if the judgments are independent.

Google also adopted a decision hygiene strategy we haven't yet described in detail: *structuring complex judgments.* The term *structure* can mean many things. As we use the term here, a structured complex judgment is defined by three principles: decomposition, independence, and delayed holistic judgment.

The first principle, *decomposition*, breaks down the decision into components, or *mediating assessments*. This step serves the same purpose as the identification of the subjudgments in a guideline: it focuses the judges on the important cues. Decomposition acts as a road map to specify what data is needed. And it filters out irrelevant information.

In Google's case, there are four mediating assessments in the decomposition: general cognitive ability, leadership, cultural fit (called "googleyness"), and role-related knowledge. (Some of these assessments are then broken down into smaller components.) Note that a candidate's good looks, smooth talk, exciting hobbies, and any other aspects, positive or negative, that a recruiter might notice in an unstructured interview are not on the list.

Creating this sort of structure for a recruiting task may seem like mere common sense. Indeed, if you are hiring an entry-level accountant or an administrative assistant, standard job descriptions exist and specify the competencies needed. As professional recruiters know, however, defining the key assessments gets difficult for unusual or senior positions, and this step of definition is frequently overlooked. One prominent headhunter points out that defining the required competencies in a sufficiently specific manner is a challenging, often overlooked task. He highlights the importance for decision makers of "investing in the problem definition": spending the necessary time up front, before you meet any candidates, to agree on a clear and detailed job description. The challenge here is that many interviewers use bloated job descriptions produced by consensus and compromise. The descriptions are vague wish lists of all the characteristics an ideal candidate would possess, and they offer no way to calibrate the characteristics or make trade-offs among them.

The second principle of structured judgment, *independence*, requires that information on each assessment be collected independently. Just listing the components of the job description is not enough: most recruiters conducting traditional interviews also know the four or five things they look for in a candidate. The problem is that, in the conduct of the interview, they do not evaluate these elements separately. Each assessment influences the others, which makes each assessment very noisy.

To overcome this problem, Google orchestrated ways to make assessments in a fact-based manner and independently of one another. Perhaps its most visible move was to introduce *structured behavioral interviews*. The interviewers' task in such interviews is not to decide whether they like a candidate overall; it is to collect data about each assessment in the evaluation structure and to assign a score to the candidate on each assessment. To do so, interviewers are required to ask predefined questions about the candidate's behaviors in past situations. They must also record the answers and score them against a predetermined rating scale, using a unified rubric. The rubric gives examples of what average, good, or great answers look like for each question. This shared scale (an example of the behaviorally anchored rating scales we introduced in the preceding chapter) helps reduce noise in judgments.

If this approach sounds different from a traditional, chatty interview, it is. In fact, it can feel more like an exam or interrogation than a business encounter, and there is some evidence that both interviewees and interviewers dislike structured interviews (or at least prefer unstructured ones). There is continuing debate about exactly what an interview must include to qualify as structured. Still, one of the most consistent findings to emerge from the literature on interviewing is that structured interviews are far more predictive of future performance than are traditional, unstructured ones. Correlations with job performance range between .44 and .57. Using our PC metric, your chances of picking the better candidate with a structured interview are between 65 and 69%, a marked improvement over the 56 to 61% chance an unstructured interview would give you.

Google uses other data as inputs on some of the dimensions it cares about. To test job-related knowledge, it relies in part on *work sample tests*, such as asking a candidate for a programming job to write some code. Research has shown that work sample tests are among the best predictors of on-the-job performance. Google also uses "backdoor references," supplied not by someone the candidate has nominated but by Google employees with whom the candidate has crossed paths.

The third principle of structured judgment, *delayed holistic judgment,* can be summarized in a simple prescription: do not exclude intuition, but delay it. At Google, the final hiring recommendation is made collegially by a hiring committee, which reviews a complete file of all the ratings the candidates have obtained on each assessment in each interview and other relevant information in support of these assessments. On the basis of that information, the committee then decides whether to extend an offer.

Despite the famously data-driven culture of this company, and despite all the evidence that a mechanical combination of data out-performs a clinical one, the final hiring decision is *not* mechanical. It remains a judgment, in which the committee takes all the evidence into account and weighs it holistically, engaging in a discussion of the question "Will this person be successful at Google?" The decision is not merely computed.

In the next chapter, we will explain why we believe that this approach to making the final decision is a sensible one. But note that while they are not mechanical, Google's final hiring decisions are anchored on the average score assigned by the four interviewers. They are also informed by the underlying evidence. In other words, Google allows judgment and intuition in its decision-making process only after all the evidence has been collected and analyzed. Thus, the tendency of each interviewer (and hiring committee member) to form quick, intuitive impressions and rush to judgment is kept in check.

The three principles — once more, decomposition, independent assessment on each dimension, and delayed holistic judgment — do not necessarily provide a template for all organizations trying to improve their selection processes. But the principles are broadly con-sistent with the recommendations that organizational psychologists have formulated over the years. In fact, the principles bear some resemblance to the selection method that one of us (Kahneman) implemented in the Israeli army as early as 1956 and described in *Thinking, Fast and Slow*. That process, like the one Google put in place, formalized an evaluation structure (the list of personality and competence dimensions that had to be evaluated). It required inter-viewers to elicit objective evidence relevant to each dimension in turn and to score that dimension before moving on to the next. And it allowed recruiters to use judgment and intuition to reach a final decision — but only after the structured evaluation had taken place.

———

There is overwhelming evidence of the superiority of structured judgment processes (including structured interviews) in hiring. Practical advice is available to guide executives who want to adopt them. As the example of Google illustrates and as other researchers have noted, structured judgment methods are also less costly — because few things are as costly as face time.

Nevertheless, most executives remain convinced of the irreplaceable value of informal, interview-based methods. Remarkably, so do many candidates who believe that only a face-to-face interview will enable them to show a prospective employer their true mettle. Researchers have called this "the persistence of an illusion." One thing is clear: recruiters and candidates severely underestimate the noise in hiring judgments.

Speaking of Structure in Hiring

"In traditional, informal interviews, we often have an irresistible, intuitive feeling of understanding the candidate and knowing whether the person fits the bill. We must learn to distrust that feeling."

"Traditional interviews are dangerous not only because of biases but also because of noise."

"We must add structure to our interviews and, more broadly, to our selection processes. Let's start by defining much more clearly and specifically what we are looking for in candidates, and let's make sure we evaluate the candidates independently on each of these dimensions."

CHAPTER 25

The Mediating Assessments Protocol

S ome time ago, two of us (Kahneman and Sibony), together with our friend Dan Lovallo, described a method of decision making in organizations. We called the method, which was designed with noise mitigation as a primary objective, the *mediating assessments protocol.* It incorporates most of the decision hygiene strategies that we have introduced in the preceding chapters. The protocol can be applied broadly and whenever the evaluation of a plan or an option requires considering and weighting multiple dimensions. It can be used, and adapted in various ways, by organizations of all kinds, including diverse companies, hospitals, universities, and government agencies.

We illustrate the protocol here with a stylized example that is a composite of several real cases: a fictitious corporation we'll call Mapco. We will follow the steps Mapco takes as it studies the opportunity to make a major, transformative acquisition, and we will highlight how these differ from the usual steps a company takes in such a situation. As you will see, the differences are significant, but subtle — an inattentive observer might not even notice them.

The First Meeting: Agreeing on the Approach

The idea of acquiring Roadco, a competitor, had been percolating at Mapco, and had matured sufficiently so that the company's leaders were contemplating a board meeting to discuss it. Joan Morrison, the CEO of Mapco, convened a meeting of the board's strategy committee for a preliminary discussion of the possible acquisition and of what should be done to improve the board's deliberations about it. Early in the meeting, Joan surprised the committee with a proposal:

"I would like to propose that we try a new procedure for the board meeting where we will decide on the Roadco acquisition. The new procedure has an unappealing name, the mediating assessments protocol, but the idea is really quite simple. It is inspired by the similarity between the evaluation of a strategic option and the evaluation of a job candidate.

"You are certainly familiar with the research that shows that structured interviews produce better results than unstructured ones, and more broadly with the idea that structuring a hiring decision improves it. You know that our HR department has adopted these principles for its hiring decisions. A vast amount of research shows that structure in interviews leads to much higher accuracy — unstructured interviews as we used to practice them don't even come close.

"I see a clear similarity between the evaluation of candidates and the evaluation of options in big decisions: *options are like candidates.* And this similarity leads me to the idea that we should adapt the method that works for evaluating candidates to our task, which is to evaluate strategic options."

The committee members were initially puzzled by the analogy. The recruiting process, they argued, is a well-oiled machine that makes numerous, similar decisions and is not under severe time pressure. A strategic decision, on the other hand, requires a great deal of ad hoc work and must be made quickly. Some committee members made clear to Joan that they would be hostile to any proposal that delayed the decision. They were also worried about adding to the due-diligence requirements from Mapco's research staff.

Joan responded directly to these objections. She assured her colleagues that the structured process would not delay the decision. "This is all about setting the agenda for the board meeting in which we will discuss the deal," she explained. "We should decide in advance on a list of assessments of different aspects of the deal, just as an interviewer starts with a job description that serves as a checklist of traits or attributes a candidate must possess. We will make sure the board discusses these assessments separately, one by one, just as interviewers in structured interviews evaluate the candidate on the separate dimensions in sequence. Then, and only then, will we turn to a discussion of whether to accept or reject the deal. This procedure will be a much more effective way to take advantage of the collective wisdom of the board.

"If we agree on this approach, of course, it has implications for how the information should be presented and for how the deal team should work to prepare the meeting. That's why I wanted to get your thoughts now."

One committee member, still skeptical, asked Joan what benefits the structure brought to the quality of decision making in hiring and why she believed these benefits would transfer to a strategic decision. Joan walked him through the logic. Using the mediating assessments protocol, she explained, maximizes the value of information by keeping the dimensions of the evaluation independent of each other. "The board discussions we usually have look a lot like unstructured interviews," she observed. "We are constantly aware of the final goal of reaching a decision, and we process all the information in light of that goal. We start out looking for closure, and we achieve it as soon as we can. Just like a recruiter in an unstructured interview, we are at risk of using all the debate to confirm our first impressions.

"Using a structured approach will force us to postpone the goal of reaching a decision until we have made all the assessments. We will take on the separate assessments as intermediate goals. This way, we will consider all the information available and make sure that our conclusion on one aspect of the deal does not change our reading on another, unrelated aspect."

The committee members agreed to try out the approach. But, they asked, what were the mediating assessments? Was there a pre-defined checklist that Joan had in mind? "No," she replied. "That might be the case if we applied the protocol to a routine decision, but in this case, we need to define the mediating assessments ourselves. This is critically important: deciding on the major aspects of the acquisition that should be assessed is up to us." The strategy committee agreed to meet again the next day to do that.

The Second Meeting: Defining the Mediating Assessments

"The first thing we are going to do," Joan explained, "is draw up a comprehensive list of independent assessments about the deal. These will be assessed by Jeff Schneider's research team. Our task today is to construct the list of assessments. It should be comprehensive in the sense that any relevant fact you can think of should find its place and should influence at least one of the assessments. And what I mean by 'independent' is that a relevant fact should preferably influence only one of the assessments, to minimize redundancy."

The group got to work and generated a long list of facts and data that seemed relevant. It then organized them into a list of assessments. The challenge, the participants soon discovered, was to make the list short, comprehensive, and composed of nonoverlapping assessments. But the task was manageable. Indeed, the group's final list of seven assessments was superficially similar to the table of contents the board would expect in a regular report presenting an acquisition proposal. In addition to the expected financial modeling, the list included, for instance, an evaluation of the quality of the target's management team and an assessment of the likelihood that the anticipated synergies would be captured.

Some of the strategy committee members were disappointed that the meeting did not produce novel insights about Roadco. But, Joan explained, that was not the goal. The immediate objective was to brief the deal team in charge of studying the acquisition. Each assessment, she said, would be the subject of a different chapter in the deal team's report and would be discussed separately by the board.

The deal team's mission, as Joan saw it, was not to tell the board what it thought of the deal as a whole — at least, not yet. It was to provide an objective, independent evaluation on each of the mediating assessments. Ultimately, Joan explained, each chapter in the deal team's report should end with a rating that answers a simple question: "Leaving aside the weight we should give this topic in the final decision, how strongly does the evidence on this assessment argue for or against the deal?"

The Deal Team

The leader of the team in charge of evaluating the deal, Jeff Schneider, got his team together that afternoon to organize the work. The changes from the team's usual way of working were not many, but he stressed their importance.

First, he explained, the team's analysts should try to make their analyses as objective as possible. The evaluations should be based on facts — nothing new about that — but they should also use an *outside view* whenever possible. Since the team members were unsure of what he meant by "outside view," Jeff gave them two examples, using two of the mediating assessments Joan had identified. To evaluate the probability that the deal would receive regulatory approval, he said, they would need to start by finding out the *base rate*, the percentage of comparable transactions that are approved. This task would, in turn, require them to define a relevant *reference class*, a group of deals considered comparable enough.

Jeff then explained how to evaluate the technological skills of the target's product development department — another important assessment Joan had listed. "It is not enough to describe the company's recent achievements in a fact-based way and to call them 'good' or 'great.' What I expect is something like, 'This product development department is in the second quintile of its peer group, as measured by its recent track record of product launches.'" Overall, he explained, the goal was to make evaluations as comparative as possible, because relative judgments are better than absolute ones.

Jeff had another request. In keeping with Joan's instructions, he said, assessments should be as independent of one another as possible, to reduce the risk that one assessment would influence the others. Accordingly, he assigned different analysts to the different assessments, and he instructed them to work independently.

Some of the analysts expressed surprise. "Isn't teamwork better?" they asked him. "What's the point of assembling a team if you don't want us to communicate?"

Jeff realized he needed to explain the need for independence. "You probably know about the halo effect in recruiting," he said. "That is what happens when the general impression of a candidate influences your assessment of the candidate's skills on a specific dimension. That's what we are trying to avoid." Since some of the analysts seemed to think that this effect was not a serious problem, Jeff used another analogy: "If you have four witnesses to a crime, would you let them talk to each other before testifying? Obviously not! You don't want one witness to influence the others." The analysts did not find the comparison particularly flattering, but it got the message across, Jeff thought.

As it happened, Jeff did not have enough analysts to achieve the goal of perfectly independent assessments. Jane, an experienced member of the team, was charged with two assessments. Jeff chose the two to be as different from each other as possible, and he instructed Jane to complete the first assessment and prepare the report on it before turning to the other. Another concern was the evaluation of the quality of the management team; Jeff was worried that his analysts would struggle to dissociate their assessment of the team's intrinsic quality from judgments about the company's recent results (which the team would, of course, study in detail). To address this issue, Jeff asked an outside HR expert to weigh in on the quality of the management team. This way, he thought, he would obtain a more independent input.

Jeff had another instruction that the team found somewhat unusual. Each chapter should focus on one assessment and, as requested by Joan, lead to a conclusion in the form of a rating. However, Jeff added, the analysts should include in each chapter all the relevant factual information about the assessment. "Don't hide anything," he instructed them. "The general tone of the chapter will be consistent with the proposed rating, of course, but if there is information that seems inconsistent or even contradictory with the main rating, don't sweep anything under the rug. Your job is not to sell your recommendation. It is to represent the truth. If it is complicated, so be it — it often is."

In the same spirit, Jeff encouraged the analysts to be transparent about their level of confidence in each assessment. "The board knows that you do not have perfect information; it will help them if you tell them when you're really in the dark. And if you run into something that really gives you pause — a potential deal breaker — you should, of course, report it immediately."

The deal team proceeded as instructed. Fortunately, it found no major deal breakers. It assembled a report for Joan and the board, covering all the assessments identified.

The Decision Meeting

As she read the team's report to prepare for the decision meeting, Joan immediately noticed something important: while most of the assessments supported doing the deal, they did not paint a simple, rosy, all-systems-go picture. Some of the ratings were strong; others were not. These differences, she knew, were a predictable result of keeping the assessments independent of one another. When excessive coherence is kept in check, reality is not as coherent as most board presentations make it seem. "Good," Joan thought. "These discrepancies between assessments will raise questions and trigger discussions. That's just what we need to have a good debate in the board. The diverse results will not make the decision easier, for sure — but they will make it better."

Joan convened a meeting of the board to review the report and come to a decision. She explained the approach that the deal team followed, and she invited the board members to apply the same principle. "Jeff and his team have worked hard to keep the assessments independent of each other," she said, "and our task now is to review them independently, too. This means we will consider each assessment separately, before we start discussing the final decision. We are going to treat each assessment as a distinct agenda item."

The board members knew that following this structured approach would be difficult. Joan was asking them not to form a holistic view of the deal before all assessments were discussed, but many of them were industry insiders. They *had* a view on Roadco. Not discussing it felt a bit artificial. Nevertheless, because they understood what Joan was trying to achieve, they agreed to play by her rules and refrain temporarily from discussing their overall views.

To their surprise, the board members found that this practice was highly valuable. During the meeting, some of them even changed their mind about the deal (although no one would ever know, since they had kept their views to themselves). The way Joan ran the meeting played a large part: she used the *estimate-talk-estimate* method, which combines the advantages of deliberation and those of averaging independent opinions.

Here is how she proceeded. On each assessment, Jeff, on behalf of the deal team, briefly summarized the key facts (which the board members had read in detail beforehand). Then Joan asked the board members to use a voting app on their phones to give their own rating on the assessment — either the same as the deal team's proposed rating or a different one. The distribution of ratings was projected immediately on the screen, without identifying the raters. "This is not a vote," Joan explained. "We are just taking the temperature of the room on each topic." By getting an immediate read on each board member's independent opinion before starting a discussion, Joan reduced the danger of social influence and information cascades.

On some assessments, there was immediate consensus, but on others, the process revealed opposing views. Naturally, Joan managed the discussion to spend more time on the latter. She made sure that board members on each side of the divide spoke up, encouraging them to express their viewpoints with facts and arguments but also with nuance and humility. Once, when a board member who felt strongly about the deal got carried away, she reminded him that "we are all reasonable people and we disagree, so this must be a subject on which reasonable people can disagree."

When the discussion of an assessment drew to a close, Joan asked the board members to vote again on a rating. Most of the time, there was more convergence than in the initial round. The same sequence — a first estimate, a discussion, and a second estimate — was repeated for each assessment.

Finally, it was time to reach a conclusion about the deal. To facilitate the discussion, Jeff showed the list of assessments on the whiteboard, with, for each assessment, the average of the ratings that the board had assigned to it. The board members were looking at the profile of the deal. How should they decide?

One board member had a simple suggestion: use a straight average of the ratings. (Perhaps he knew about the superiority of mechanical aggregation over holistic, clinical judgment, as discussed in chapter 9.) Another member, however, immediately objected that, in her view, some of the assessments should be given a much higher weight than others. A third person disagreed, suggesting a different hierarchy of the assessments.

Joan interrupted the discussion. "This is not just about computing a simple combination of the assessment ratings," she said. "We have delayed intuition, but now is the time to use it. What we need now is your judgment."

Joan did not explain her logic, but she had learned this lesson the hard way. She knew that, particularly with important decisions, people reject schemes that tie their hands and do not let them use their judgment. She had seen how decision makers game the system when they know that a formula will be used. They change the ratings to arrive at the desired conclusion — which defeats the purpose of the entire exercise. Furthermore, although this was not the case here, she remained alert to the possibility that decisive considerations could emerge that were not anticipated in the definition of assessments (the broken-leg factors discussed in chapter 10). If such unanticipated deal breakers (or, conversely, deal clinchers) appeared, a purely mechanical decision process based on the average of the assessments might lead to a serious mistake.

Joan also knew that letting the board members use their intuition at this stage was very different from having them use it earlier in the process. Now that the assessments were available and known to all, the final decision was safely anchored on these fact-based, thoroughly discussed ratings. A board member would need to come up with strong reasons to be against the deal while staring at a list of mediating assessments that mostly supported it. Following this logic, the board discussed the deal and voted on it, in much the same way all boards do.

The Mediating Assessments Protocol in Recurring Decisions

We have described the mediating assessments protocol in the context of a one-off, singular decision. But the procedure applies to recurring decisions, too. Imagine that Mapco is not making a single acquisition but is a venture capital fund that makes repeated investments in start-ups. The protocol would be just as applicable and the story would be much the same, with just two twists that, if anything, make it simpler.

First, the initial step — defining the list of mediating assessments — needs to be done only once. The fund has investment criteria, which it applies to all its prospective investments: these are the assessments. There is no need to reinvent them each time.

Second, if the fund makes many decisions of the same type, it can use its experience to calibrate its judgments. Consider, for instance, an assessment that every fund will want to make: evaluating the quality of the management team. We suggested that such evaluations should be made relative to a reference class. Perhaps you sympathized with the analysts of Mapco: gathering data about comparable companies, in addition to evaluating a specific target, is challenging.

Comparative judgments become much easier in the context of a recurring decision. If you have evaluated the management teams of dozens, even hundreds of companies, you can use this shared experience as a reference class. A practical way to do this is to create a case scale defined by anchor cases. You might say, for instance, that the target management team is "as good as the management team of ABC Company when we acquired it" but not quite "as good as the management team of DEF Company." The anchor cases must, of course, be known to all the participants (and periodically updated). Defining them requires an up-front investment of time. But the value of this approach is that relative judgments (comparing this team to the ones at ABC and DEF) are much more reliable than are absolute ratings on a scale defined by numbers or adjectives.

What the Protocol Changes

For ease of reference, we summarize the main changes that the mediating assessments protocol entails in table 4.

Table 4: *Main steps of the mediating assessments protocol*

1. At the beginning of the process, structure the decision into mediating assessments. *(For recurring judgments, this is done only once.)*

2. Ensure that whenever possible, mediating assessments use an outside view. *(For recurring judgments: use relative judgments, with a case scale if possible.)*

3. In the analytical phase, keep the assessments as independent of one another as possible.

4. In the decision meeting, review each assessment separately.

5. On each assessment, ensure that participants make their judgments individually; then use the estimate-talk-estimate method.

6. To make the final decision, delay intuition, but don't ban it.

You may have recognized here an implementation of several of the decision hygiene techniques we presented in the preceding chapters: sequencing information, structuring the decision into independent assessments, using a common frame of reference grounded in the outside view, and aggregating the independent judgments of multiple individuals. By implementing these techniques, the mediating assessments protocol aims to change the decision *process* to introduce as much decision hygiene as possible.

No doubt this emphasis on process, as opposed to the content of decisions, may raise some eyebrows. The reactions of the research team members and the board members, as we have described them, are not unusual. Content is specific; process is generic. Using intuition and judgment is fun; following process is not. Conventional wisdom holds that good decisions — especially the very best ones — emerge from the insight and creativity of great leaders. (We especially like to believe this when we are the leader in question.) And to many, the word *process* evokes bureaucracy, red tape, and delays.

Our experience with companies and government agencies that have implemented all or some of the components of the protocol suggests that these concerns are misguided. To be sure, adding complexity to the decision-making processes of an organization that is already bureaucratic will not make things better. But decision hygiene need not be slow and certainly doesn't need to be bureaucratic. On the contrary, it promotes challenge and debate, not the stifling consensus that characterizes bureaucracies.

The case for decision hygiene is clear. Leaders in business and in the public sector are usually entirely unaware of noise in their largest and most important decisions. As a result, they take no specific measures to reduce it. In that respect, they are just like the recruiters who continue to rely on unstructured interviews as their sole personnel selection tool: oblivious to the noise in their own judgment, more confident in its validity than they should be, and unaware of procedures that could improve it.

Handwashing does not prevent all diseases. Likewise, decision hygiene will not prevent all mistakes. It will not make every decision brilliant. But like handwashing, it addresses an invisible yet pervasive and damaging problem. Wherever there is judgment, there is noise, and we propose decision hygiene as a tool to reduce it.

Speaking of the Mediating Assessments Protocol

"We have a structured process to make hiring decisions. Why don't we have one for strategic decisions? After all, options are like candidates."

"This is a difficult decision. What are the mediating assessments it should be based on?"

"Our intuitive, holistic judgment about this plan is very important — but let's not discuss it yet. Our intuition will serve us much better once it is informed by the separate assessments we have asked for."

PART VI

Optimal Noise

In 1973, Judge Marvin Frankel was right to call for a sustained effort to reduce noise in criminal sentencing. His informal, intuitive noise audit, followed by more formal and systematic efforts, uncovered unjustified disparities in the treatment of similar people. Those disparities were outrageous. They were also startling.

Much of this book can be understood as an effort to generalize Frankel's arguments and to offer an understanding of their psychological foundations. To some people, noise in the criminal justice system seems uniquely intolerable, even scandalous. But in countless other contexts, it is not exactly tolerable, as supposedly interchangeable people in the private and public sectors make different judgments on the job. In insurance, recruitment and evaluation of employees, medicine, forensic science, education, business, and government, interpersonal noise is a major source of error. We have also seen that each of us is subject to occasion noise, in the sense that supposedly irrelevant factors can lead us to make different judgments in the morning and in the afternoon, or on Monday and Thursday.

But as the intensely negative judicial reaction to the sentencing guidelines suggests, noise-reduction efforts often run into serious and even passionate objections. Many people have argued that the guidelines are rigid, dehumanizing, and unfair in their own way. Almost everyone has had the experience of making a reasonable request to a company, an employer, or a government, only to be met with the response "We really would love to help you, but our hands are tied. We have clear rules here." The rules in question may seem stupid and even cruel, but they may have been adopted for a good reason: to reduce noise (and perhaps bias as well).

Even so, some efforts to reduce noise raise serious concerns, perhaps above all if they make it difficult or impossible for people to get a fair hearing. The use of algorithms and machine learning has put that objection in a new light. No one is marching under a banner that says "Algorithms now!"

An influential critique comes from Kate Stith of Yale Law School and José Cabranes, a federal judge. They offered a vigorous attack on the sentencing guidelines and, in a sense, on one of our central arguments here. Their argument was limited to the area of criminal sentencing, but it can be offered as an objection to many noise-reduction strategies in education, business, sports, and everywhere else. Stith and Cabranes maintain that the sentencing guidelines are animated "by a fear of the exercise of discretion — by a fear of judging — and by a technocratic faith in experts and central planning." They argue that "fear of judging" operates to forbid consideration of "the particulars of each case at hand." In their view, "no mechanical solution can satisfy the demands of justice."

These objections are worth examining. In settings that involve judgments of all kinds, people often view the "demands of justice" as forbidding any sort of mechanical solution — and hence allowing or even mandating processes and approaches that turn out to guarantee noise. Many people call for attention to "the particulars of each case at hand." In hospitals, schools, and firms large and small, this call has deep intuitive appeal. We have seen that decision hygiene includes diverse strategies for reducing noise, and most of them do not involve mechanical solutions; when people decompose a problem into its component parts, their judgments need not be mechanical. Even so, many people would not welcome the use of decision hygiene strategies.

We have defined noise as unwanted variability, and if something is unwanted, it should probably be eliminated. But the analysis is more complicated and more interesting than that. Noise may be unwanted, other things being equal. But other things might not be equal, and the costs of eliminating noise might exceed the benefits. And even when an analysis of costs and benefits suggests that noise is costly, eliminating it might produce a range of awful or even unacceptable consequences for both public and private institutions.

There are seven major objections to efforts to reduce or eliminate noise.

First, reducing noise can be expensive; it might not be worth the trouble. The steps that are necessary to reduce noise might be highly burdensome. In some cases, they might not even be feasible.

Second, some strategies introduced to reduce noise might introduce errors of their own. Occasionally, they might produce systematic bias. If all forecasters in a government office adopted the same unrealistically optimistic assumptions, their forecasts would not be noisy, but they would be wrong. If all doctors at a hospital prescribed aspirin for every illness, they would not be noisy, but they would make plenty of mistakes.

We explore these objections in chapter 26. In chapter 27, we turn to five more objections, which are also common and which are likely to be heard in many places in coming years, especially with increasing reliance on rules, algorithms, and machine learning.

Third, if we want people to feel that they have been treated with respect and dignity, we might have to tolerate some noise. Noise can be a by-product of an imperfect process that people end up embracing because the process gives everyone (employees, customers, applicants, students, those accused of crime) an individualized hearing, an opportunity to influence the exercise of discretion, and a sense that they have had a chance to be seen and heard.

Fourth, noise might be essential to accommodate new values and hence to allow moral and political evolution. If we eliminate noise, we might reduce our ability to respond when moral and political commitments move in new and unexpected directions. A noise-free system might freeze existing values.

Fifth, some strategies designed to reduce noise might encourage opportunistic behavior, allowing people to game the system or evade prohibitions. A little noise, or perhaps a lot of it, might be necessary to prevent wrongdoing.

Sixth, a noisy process might be a good deterrent. If people know that they could be subject to either a small penalty or a large one, they might steer clear of wrongdoing, at least if they are risk-averse. A system might tolerate noise as a way of producing extra deterrence.

Finally, people do not want to be treated as if they are mere things, or cogs in some kind of machine. Some noise-reduction strategies might squelch people's creativity and prove demoralizing.

Although we will address these objections as sympathetically as we can, we by no means endorse them, at least not if they are taken as reasons to reject the general goal of reducing noise. To presage a point that will recur throughout: whether an objection is convincing depends on the particular noise-reduction strategy to which it is meant to apply. You might, for example, object to rigid guidelines while also agreeing that aggregation of independent judgments is a good idea. You might object to the use of the mediating assessments protocol while strongly favoring the use of a shared scale grounded in the outside view. With these points in mind, our general conclusion is that even when the objections are given their due, noise reduction remains a worthy and even an urgent goal. In chapter 28, we defend this conclusion by exploring a dilemma that people face every day, even if they are not always aware of it.

CHAPTER 26

The Costs of Noise Reduction

Whenever people are asked to eliminate noise, they might object that the necessary steps are just too expensive. In extreme circumstances, noise reduction is simply not possible. We have heard this objection in business, education, government, and elsewhere. There is a legitimate concern here, but it is easily overstated, and it is often just an excuse.

To put the objection in its most appealing light, consider the case of a high school teacher who grades twenty-five essays by tenth-graders during each week of the school year. If the teacher spends no more than fifteen minutes on each essay, the grading might be noisy and therefore inaccurate and unfair. The teacher might consider a little decision hygiene, perhaps reducing the noise by asking a colleague to grade the essays as well, so that two people are reading every paper. Perhaps the teacher could accomplish the same goal by spending more time reading each essay, structuring the relatively complex process of assessment, or by reading the essays more than once and in different orders. A detailed grading guideline used as a checklist might help. Or perhaps the educator could make sure to read each essay at the same time of day, so as to reduce occasion noise.

But if the teacher's own judgments are pretty accurate and not terribly noisy, it might be sensible not to do any of these things. It might not be worth the bother. The teacher might think that using a checklist or asking a colleague to read the same papers would be a form of overkill. To know whether it is, a disciplined analysis might be necessary: how much more accuracy would the teacher gain, how important is more accuracy, and how much time and money would be required by the effort to reduce noise? We could easily imagine a limit on how much to invest in noise reduction. We could just as easily see that this limit should be different when the essays are written by ninth-graders or as senior theses, where university admission may be on the line and the stakes are higher.

The basic analysis might be extended to more complex situations faced by private and public organizations of all kinds, leading them to reject some noise-reduction strategies. For some diseases, hospitals and doctors might struggle to identify simple guidelines to eliminate variability. In the case of divergent medical diagnoses, efforts to reduce noise have particular appeal; they might save lives. But the feasibility and costs of those efforts need to be taken into account. A test might eliminate noise in diagnoses, but if the test is invasive, dangerous, and costly, and if variability in diagnoses is modest and has only mild consequences, then it might not be worthwhile for all doctors to require all patients to take the test.

Rarely does the evaluation of employees involve life and death. But noise can result in unfairness for employees and high costs for the firm. We have seen that efforts to reduce noise should be feasible. Are they worthwhile? Cases involving clearly mistaken evaluations might get noticed and seem embarrassing, shameful, or worse. Nonetheless, an institution might think that elaborate corrective steps are not worth the effort. Sometimes that conclusion is shortsighted, self-serving, and wrong, even catastrophically so. Some form of decision hygiene might well be worthwhile. But the belief that it is too expensive to reduce noise is not always wrong.

In short, we have to compare the benefits of noise reduction with the costs. That is fair, and it is one reason noise audits are so important. In many situations, the audits reveal that noise is producing outrageous levels of unfairness, very high costs, or both. If so, the cost of noise reduction is hardly a good reason not to make the effort.

Less Noise, More Mistakes?

A different objection is that some noise-reduction efforts might themselves produce unacceptably high levels of error. The objection might be convincing if the instruments used to reduce noise are too blunt. In fact, some efforts at noise reduction might even increase bias. If a social media platform such as Facebook or Twitter introduced firm guidelines that call for removing all posts containing certain vulgar words, its decisions will be less noisy, but it will be taking down numerous posts that should be allowed to stay up. These false positives are a directional error — a bias.

Life is full of institutional reforms that are designed to reduce the discretion of people and practices that generate noise. Many such reforms are well motivated, but some cures are worse than the disease. In *The Rhetoric of Reaction,* economist Albert Hirschman points to three common objections to reform efforts. First, such efforts might be perverse, in the sense that they will aggravate the very problem they are intended to solve. Second, they might be futile; they might not change things at all. Third, they put other important values in jeopardy (such as when an effort to protect labor unions and the right to unionize is said to hurt economic growth). Perversity, futility, and jeopardy might be offered as objections to noise reduction, and of the three, claims of perversity and jeopardy tend to be the most powerful. Sometimes these objections are just rhetoric — an effort to derail a reform that will actually do a great deal of good. But some noise-reduction strategies could jeopardize important values, and for others the risk of perversity might not be readily dismissed.

The judges who objected to the sentencing guidelines were

pointing to that risk. They were well aware of Judge Frankel's work, and they did not deny that discretion produces noise. But they thought that reducing discretion would produce more mistakes, not fewer. Quoting Václav Havel, they insisted, "We have to abandon the arrogant belief that the world is merely a puzzle to be solved, a machine with instructions for use waiting to be discovered, a body of information to be fed into a computer in the hope that, sooner or later, it will spit out a universal solution." One reason for rejecting the idea of universal solutions is an insistent belief that human situations are highly varied and that good judges address the variations — which might mean tolerating noise, or at least rejecting some noise-reduction strategies.

In the early days of computer chess, a large airline offered a chess program for international passengers, who were invited to play against a computer. The program had several levels. At the lowest level, the program used a simple rule: place your opponent's king in check whenever you can. The program was not noisy. It played the same way every time; it would always follow its simple rule. But the rule ensured a great deal of error. The program was terrible at chess. Even inexperienced chess players could defeat it (which was undoubtedly the point; winning air travelers are happy air travelers).

Or consider the criminal sentencing policy adopted in some US states and called "three strikes and you're out." The idea is that if you commit three felonies, your sentence is life imprisonment — period. The policy reduces the variability that comes from random assignment of the sentencing judge. Some of its proponents were especially concerned about level noise and the possibility that some judges were too lenient with hardened criminals. Eliminating noise is the central point of the three-strikes legislation.

But even if the three-strikes policy succeeds in its noise-reduction goal, we can reasonably object that the price of this success is too high. Some people who have committed three felonies should not be put away for life. Perhaps their crimes were not violent. Or their awful life circumstances might have helped lead them to crime. Maybe they show a capacity for rehabilitation. Many people think that a life sentence, inattentive to the particular circumstances, is not only too harsh but also intolerably rigid. For that reason, the price of that noise-reduction strategy is too high.

Consider the case of *Woodson v. North Carolina,* in which the US Supreme Court held that a mandatory death sentence was unconstitutional not because it was too brutal but *because it was a rule.* The whole point of the mandatory death sentence was to ensure against noise — to say that under specified circumstances, murderers would have to be put to death. Invoking the need for individualized treatment, the court said that "the belief no longer prevails that every offense in a like legal category calls for an identical punishment without regard to the past life and habits of a particular offender." According to the Supreme Court, a serious constitutional shortcoming of the mandatory death sentence is that it "treats all persons convicted of a designated offense not as uniquely individual human beings, but as members of a faceless, undifferentiated mass to be subjected to the blind infliction of the penalty of death."

The death penalty involves especially high stakes, of course, but the court's analysis can be applied to many other situations, most of them not involving law at all. Teachers evaluating students, doctors evaluating patients, employers evaluating employees, underwriters setting insurance premiums, coaches evaluating athletes — all these people might make mistakes if they apply overly rigid, noise-reducing rules. If employers use simple rules for evaluating, promoting, or suspending employees, those rules might eliminate noise while neglecting important aspects of the employees' performance. A noise-free scoring system that fails to take significant variables into account might be worse than reliance on (noisy) individual judgments.

Chapter 27 considers the general idea of treating people as "uniquely individual," rather than as "members of a faceless, undifferentiated mass." For now, we are focusing on a more prosaic point. Some noise-reduction strategies ensure too many mistakes. They might be a lot like that foolish chess program.

Still, the objection seems far more convincing than it actually is. If one noise-reduction strategy is error-prone, we should not rest content with high levels of noise. We should instead try to devise a better noise-reduction strategy — for example, aggregating judgments rather than adopting silly rules or developing wise guidelines or rules rather than foolish ones. In the interest of noise reduction, a university could say, for example, that people with the highest test scores will be admitted, and that's it. If that rule seems too crude, the school could create a formula that takes account of test scores, grades, age, athletic achievements, family background, and more. Complex rules might be more accurate — more attuned to the full range of relevant factors. Similarly, doctors have complex rules for diagnosing some illnesses. The guidelines and rules used by professionals are not always simple or crude, and many of them help reduce noise without creating intolerably high costs (or bias). And if guidelines or rules will not work, perhaps we could introduce other forms of decision hygiene, suited to the particular situation, that will; recall aggregating judgments or using a structured process such as the mediating assessments protocol.

Noiseless, Biased Algorithms

The potentially high costs of noise reduction often come up in the context of algorithms, where there are growing objections to "algorithmic bias." As we have seen, algorithms eliminate noise and often seem appealing for that reason. Indeed, much of this book might be taken as an argument for greater reliance on algorithms, simply because they are noiseless. But as we have also seen, noise reduction can come at an intolerable cost if greater reliance on algorithms increases discrimination on the basis of race and gender, or against members of disadvantaged groups.

There are widespread fears that algorithms will in fact have that discriminatory consequence, which is undoubtedly a serious risk. In *Weapons of Math Destruction,* mathematician Cathy O'Neil urges that reliance on big data and decision by algorithm can embed prejudice, increase inequality, and threaten democracy itself. According to another skeptical account, "potentially biased mathematical models are remaking our lives — and neither the companies responsible for developing them nor the government is interested in addressing the problem." According to ProPublica, an independent investigative journalism organization, COMPAS, an algorithm widely used in recidivism risk assessments, is strongly biased against members of racial minorities.

No one should doubt that it is possible — even easy — to create an algorithm that is noise-free but also racist, sexist, or otherwise biased. An algorithm that explicitly uses the color of a defendant's skin to determine whether that person should be granted bail would discriminate (and its use would be unlawful in many nations). An algorithm that takes account of whether job applicants might become pregnant would discriminate against women. In these and other cases, algorithms could eliminate unwanted variability in judgment but also embed unacceptable bias.

In principle, we should be able to design an algorithm that does *not* take account of race or gender. Indeed, an algorithm could be designed that disregards race or gender entirely. The more challenging problem, now receiving a great deal of attention, is that an algorithm could discriminate and, in that sense, turn out to be biased, even when it does not overtly use race and gender as predictors.

As we have suggested, an algorithm might be biased for two main reasons. First, by design or not, it could use predictors that are highly correlated with race or gender. For example, height and weight are correlated with gender, and the place where people grew up or where they live might well be correlated with race.

Second, discrimination could also come from the source data. If an algorithm is trained on a data set that is biased, it will be biased, too. Consider "predictive policing" algorithms, which attempt to predict crime, often in order to improve the allocation of police resources. If the existing data about crime reflects the overpolicing of certain neighborhoods or the comparative overreporting of certain types of offenses, then the resulting algorithms will perpetuate or exacerbate discrimination. Whenever there is bias in the training data, it is quite possible to design, intentionally or unintentionally, an algorithm that encodes discrimination. It follows that even if an algorithm does not expressly consider race or gender, it could turn out to be as biased as human beings are. Indeed, in this regard, algorithms could be worse: since they eliminate noise, they could be more *reliably* biased than human judges.

For many people, a key practical consideration is whether an algorithm has a disparate impact on identifiable groups. Exactly how to test for disparate impact, and how to decide what constitutes discrimination, bias, or fairness for an algorithm, are surprisingly complex topics, well beyond the scope of this book.

The fact that this question can be raised at all, however, is a distinct advantage of algorithms over human judgments. For starters, we recommend careful assessment of algorithms to ensure that they do not consider inadmissible inputs and to test whether they discriminate in an objectionable way. It is much harder to subject individual human beings, whose judgments are often opaque, to the same kind of scrutiny; people sometimes discriminate unconsciously and in ways that outside observers, including the legal system, cannot easily see. So in some ways, an algorithm can be more transparent than human beings are.

Undoubtedly, we need to draw attention to the costs of noiseless but biased algorithms, just as we need to consider the costs of noiseless but biased rules. The key question is whether we can design algorithms that do better than real-world human judges on a combination of criteria that matter: accuracy and noise reduction, and nondiscrimination and fairness. A great deal of evidence suggests that algorithms can outperform human beings on whatever combination of criteria we select. (Note that we said *can* and not *will*.) For instance, as described in chapter 10, an algorithm can be more accurate than human judges with respect to bail decisions while producing less racial discrimination than human beings do. Similarly, a résumé-selection algorithm can select a better *and more diverse* pool of talent than human résumé screeners do.

These examples and many others lead to an inescapable conclusion: although a predictive algorithm in an uncertain world is unlikely to be perfect, it can be far less imperfect than noisy and often-biased human judgment. This superiority holds in terms of both validity (good algorithms almost always predict better) and discrimination (good algorithms can be less biased than human judges). If algorithms make fewer mistakes than human experts do and yet we have an intuitive preference for people, then our intuitive preferences should be carefully examined.

Our broader conclusions are simple and extend well beyond the topic of algorithms. It is true that noise-reduction strategies can be costly. But much of the time their costs are merely an excuse — and not a sufficient reason to tolerate the unfairness and costs of noise. Of course, efforts to reduce noise might produce errors of their own, perhaps in the form of bias. In that case we have a serious problem, but the solution is not to abandon noise-reduction efforts; it is to come up with better ones.

Speaking of the Costs of Noise Reduction

"If we tried to eliminate noise in education, we would have to spend a lot of money. When they grade students, teachers are noisy. We can't have five teachers grading the same paper."

"If, instead of relying on human judgment, a social network decides that no one may use certain words, whatever the context, it will eliminate noise, but also create a lot of errors. The cure might be worse than the disease."

"True, there are rules and algorithms that are biased. But people have biases, too. What we should ask is, can we design algorithms that are both noise-free and less biased?"

"It might be costly to remove noise — but the cost is often worth incurring. Noise can be horribly unfair. And if one effort to reduce noise is too crude — if we end up with guidelines or rules that are unacceptably rigid or that inadvertently produce bias — we shouldn't just give up. We have to try again."

CHAPTER 27

Dignity

Suppose you have been denied a mortgage, not because any person has studied your situation but because a bank has a firm rule that people with your credit rating simply cannot get a mortgage. Or suppose you have terrific qualifications and an interviewer at a firm was greatly impressed with you, but your application for employment is rejected because you were convicted of a drug offense fifteen years ago — and the firm has a flat prohibition on hiring anyone who has been convicted of a crime. Or maybe you are accused of a crime and denied bail not after an individualized hearing before an actual human being but because an algorithm has decided that people with your characteristics have a flight risk that exceeds the threshold that would allow for bail.

In such cases, many people would object. They want to be treated as individuals. They want a real human being to look at their particular circumstances. They may or may not be aware that individualized treatment would produce noise. But if that is the price of such treatment, they insist that it is a price worth paying. They might complain whenever people are treated, in the Supreme Court's words, "not as uniquely individual human beings, but as members of a faceless,

339

undifferentiated mass to be subjected to the blind infliction" of some penalty (see chapter 26).

Many people insist on an individualized hearing, free from what they see as the tyranny of rules, to give people a sense that they are being treated as individuals and hence with a kind of respect. The idea of due process, taken as part of ordinary life, might seem to require an opportunity for a face-to-face interaction in which a human being, authorized to exercise discretion, considers a wide range of factors.

In many cultures, this argument for case-by-case judgment has deep moral foundations. It can be found in politics, law, theology, and even literature. Shakespeare's *Merchant of Venice* is easily read as an objection to noise-free rules and a plea for a role of mercy in law and in human judgment generally. Hence Portia's closing argument:

> *The quality of mercy is not strained;*
> *It droppeth as the gentle rain from heaven*
> *Upon the place beneath. It is twice blest;*
> *It blesseth him that gives and him that takes:*
> *(...)*
> *It is enthroned in the hearts of kings,*
> *It is an attribute to God himself;*
> *And earthly power doth then show likest God's*
> *When mercy seasons justice.*

Because it is not bound by rules, mercy is noisy. Nonetheless, Portia's plea can be made in many situations and in countless organizations. It often resonates. An employee might be seeking a promotion. A would-be homeowner might be applying for a loan. A student might be applying to university. Those who are making decisions about such cases might reject some noise-reduction strategies, above all firm rules. If they do not, it might be because they think, with Portia, that the quality of mercy is not strained. They might know that their own approach is noisy, but if it ensures that people feel that they have been treated with respect and that someone has listened to them, they might embrace it anyway.

Some noise-reduction strategies do not run into this objection. If three people, rather than merely one, are making a decision, people are still given an individualized hearing. Guidelines may leave decision makers with significant discretion. But some efforts to reduce noise, including rigid rules, do eliminate that discretion and might lead people to object that the resulting process offends their sense of dignity.

Are they right? Certainly, people often care about whether they receive an individualized hearing. There is an unquestionable human value in the opportunity to be heard. But if individualized hearings produce more deaths, more unfairness, and much higher costs, they should not be celebrated. We have emphasized that in situations like hiring, admissions, and medicine, some noise-reduction strategies might turn out to be crude; they might forbid forms of individualized treatment that, while noisy, would produce fewer errors on balance. But if a noise-reduction strategy is crude, then, as we have urged, the best response is to try to come up with a better strategy — one attuned to a wide range of relevant variables. And if that better strategy eliminates noise and produces fewer errors, it would have obvious advantages over individualized treatment, even if it reduces or eliminates the opportunity to be heard.

We are not saying that the interest in individualized treatment does not matter. But there is a high price to pay if such treatment leads to all sorts of terrible consequences, including palpable unfairness.

Changing Values

Imagine that a public institution succeeds in eliminating noise. Let's say that a university defines *misconduct* so that every faculty member and every student knows what it does and does not include. Or suppose that a large firm specifies exactly what *corruption* means, so that anyone in the firm would know what is permitted and what is forbidden. Or imagine that a private institution reduces noise significantly, perhaps by saying that it will not hire anyone who has not majored in certain subjects. What happens if an organization's values change? Some noise-reduction strategies would seem unable to make space for them, and their inflexibility might be a problem, one that is closely connected with the interest in individualized treatment and dignity.

A famously puzzling decision in American constitutional law helps make the point. Decided in 1974, the case involved a school system's firm rule requiring pregnant teachers to take unpaid leave five months before the expected date of childbirth. Jo Carol LaFleur, a teacher, argued that she was perfectly fit to teach, that the rule was discriminatory, and that five months was excessive.

The US Supreme Court agreed. But it did not speak of sex discrimination, and it did not say that five months was necessarily excessive. Instead it objected that LaFleur had not been given an opportunity to show that there was no physical need for her, in particular, to stop working. In the court's own words,

> there is no individualized determination by the teacher's doctor — or the school board's — as to any particular teacher's ability to continue at her job. The rules contain an irrebuttable presumption of physical incompetency, and that presumption applies even when the medical evidence as to an individual woman's physical status might be wholly to the contrary.

A mandatory period of five months off does seem absurd. But the court did not emphasize that point. Instead it complained of the "irrebuttable presumption" and the absence of an "individualized determination." In so saying, the court was apparently arguing, with Portia, that the quality of mercy is not strained and that a particular person should be required to look at LaFleur's particular circumstances.

But without some decision hygiene, that is a recipe for noise. Who decides LaFleur's case? Will the decision be the same for her as for many other, similarly situated women? In any case, many rules amount to irrebuttable presumptions. Is a specified speed limit unacceptable? A minimum age for voting or drinking? A flat prohibition on drunk driving? With such examples in mind, critics objected that an argument against "irrebuttable presumptions" would prove too much — not least because their purpose and effect are to reduce noise.

Influential commentators at the time defended the court's decision by emphasizing that moral values change over time and hence the need to avoid rigid rules. They argued that with respect to women's role in society, social norms were in a state of great flux. They contended that individualized determinations were especially suitable in that context because they would allow for incorporation of those changing norms. A rule-bound system might eliminate noise, which is good, but it might also freeze existing norms and values, which is not so good.

In sum, some people might insist that an advantage of a noisy system is that it will allow people to accommodate new and emerging values. As values change, and if judges are allowed to exercise discretion, they might begin to give, for example, lower sentences to those convicted of drug offenses or higher sentences to those convicted of rape. We have emphasized that if some judges are lenient and others are not, then there will be a degree of unfairness; similarly situated people will be treated differently. But unfairness might be tolerated if it allows room for novel or emerging social values.

The problem is hardly limited to the criminal justice system or even to law. With respect to any number of policies, companies might decide to allow some flexibility in their judgments and decisions, even if doing so produces noise, because flexibility ensures that as new beliefs and values arise, they can change policies over time. We offer a personal example: when one of us joined a large consulting firm some years ago, the not-so-recent welcome pack he received specified the travel expenses for which he was allowed to claim reimbursement ("one phone call home on safe arrival; a pressing charge for a suit; tips for bellboys"). The rules were noise-free but clearly

343

outdated (and sexist). They were soon replaced with standards that can evolve with the times. For example, expenses must now be "proper and reasonable."

The first answer to this defense of noise is simple: Some noise-reduction strategies do not run into this objection at all. If people use a shared scale grounded in an outside view, they can respond to changing values over time. In any event, noise-reduction efforts need not and should not be permanent. If such efforts take the form of firm rules, those who make them should be willing to make changes over time. They might revisit them annually. They might decide that because of new values, new rules are essential. In the criminal justice system, the rule makers might reduce sentences for certain crimes and increase them for others. They might decriminalize some activity altogether — and criminalize an activity that had previously been considered perfectly acceptable.

But let's step back. Noisy systems can make room for emerging moral values, and that can be a good thing. But in many spheres, it is preposterous to defend high levels of noise with this argument. Some of the most important noise-reduction strategies, such as aggregating judgments, do allow for emerging values. And if different customers, complaining of a malfunctioning laptop, are treated differently by a computer company, the inconsistency is unlikely to be because of emerging values. If different people get different medical diagnoses, it is rarely because of new moral values. We can do a great deal to reduce noise or even eliminate it while still designing processes to allow values to evolve.

Gaming the System, Evading the Rules

In a noisy system, judges of all kinds can adapt as the situation requires — and respond to unexpected developments. By eliminating the power of adaptation, some noise-reduction strategies can have the unintended consequence of giving people an incentive to game the system. A potential argument for tolerating noise is that it may turn out to be a by-product of approaches that private and public institutions adopt to prevent that kind of gaming.

The tax code is a familiar example. On the one hand, the tax system should not be noisy. It should be clear and predictable; identical taxpayers ought not to be treated differently. But if we eliminated noise in the tax system, clever taxpayers would inevitably find a way to evade the rules. Among tax specialists, there is a lively debate about whether it is best to have clear rules, eliminating noise, or instead to have a degree of vagueness, allowing for unpredictability but also reducing the risk that clear rules will produce opportunistic or self-interested behavior.

Some companies and universities forbid people to engage in "wrongdoing," without specifying what that means. The inevitable result is noise, which is not good and may even be very bad. But if there is a specific list of what counts as wrongdoing, then terrible behavior that is not explicitly covered by the list will end up being tolerated.

Because rules have clear edges, people can evade them by engaging in conduct that is technically exempted but that creates the same or analogous harms. (Every parent of a teenager knows this!) When we cannot easily design rules that ban all conduct that ought to be prohibited, we have a distinctive reason to tolerate noise, or so the objection goes.

In some circumstances, clear, defined rules eliminating noise do give rise to the risk of evasion. And this risk might be a reason to adopt some other strategy for reducing noise, such as aggregation, and perhaps to tolerate an approach that allows for some noise. But the words *might be* are crucial. We need to ask how much evasion there would be — and how much noise there would be. If there is only a little evasion and a lot of noise, then we are better off with approaches that reduce noise. We will return to this question in chapter 28.

Deterrence and Risk Aversion

Suppose that the goal is to deter misconduct — by employees, by students, by ordinary citizens. A little unpredictability, or even a lot of it, might not be the worst thing. An employer might think, "If the punishment of certain kinds of wrongdoing is a fine, a suspension, or a dismissal, then my employees will not engage in those kinds of wrongdoing." Those who run a criminal justice system might think, "We don't much mind if would-be criminals have to guess about the likely punishment. If the prospect of a punishment lottery discourages people from crossing the line, maybe the resulting noise can be tolerated."

In the abstract, these arguments cannot be dismissed, but they are not terribly convincing. At first glance, what matters is the expected value of the punishment, and a 50% chance of a $5,000 fine is equivalent to the certainty of a $2,500 fine. Of course, some people might focus on the worst-case scenario. Risk-averse people might be more deterred by the 50% chance of a $5,000 fine — but risk-seeking people will be less deterred by it. To know whether a noisy system imposes more deterrence, we need to know whether potential wrongdoers are risk-averse or risk-seeking. And if we want to increase deterrence, wouldn't it be better to increase the penalty and eliminate the noise? Doing that would eliminate unfairness as well.

Creativity, Morale, and Fresh Ideas

Might some noise-reduction efforts squelch motivation and engagement? Might they affect creativity and prevent people from making big breakthroughs? Many organizations think so. In some cases, they might be right. To know whether they are, we need to specify the noise-reduction strategy to which they are objecting.

Recall the intensely negative reaction of many judges to the sentencing guidelines. As one judge put it, "We must learn once again to trust the exercise of judgment in the courtroom." In general, people in positions of authority do not like to have their discretion taken away. They may feel diminished as well as constrained — even humiliated. When steps are taken to reduce their discretion, many people will rebel. They value the opportunity to exercise judgment; they might even cherish it. If their discretion is removed so that they will do what everyone else does, they might feel like cogs in a machine.

In short, a noisy system might be good for morale not because it is noisy but because it allows people to decide as they see fit. If employees are allowed to respond to customer complaints in their own way, evaluate their subordinates as they think best, or establish premiums as they deem appropriate, then they might enjoy their jobs more. If the company takes steps to eliminate noise, employees might think that their own agency has been compromised. Now they are following rules rather than exercising their own creativity. Their jobs look more mechanical, even robotic. Who wants to work in a place that squelches your own capacity to make independent decisions?

Organizations might respond to these feelings not only because they honor them but also because they want to give people space to come up with new ideas. If a rule is in place, it might reduce ingenuity and invention.

These points apply to many people in organizations but, of course, not all of them. Different tasks must be evaluated differently; noisy diagnoses of strep throat or hypertension might not be a good place to exercise creativity. But we might be willing to tolerate noise if it makes for a happier and more inspired workforce. Demoralization is itself a cost and leads to other costs, such as poor performance. To be sure, we should be able to reduce noise while remaining receptive to fresh ideas. Some noise-reduction strategies, such as structuring complex judgments, do exactly that. If we want to reduce noise while maintaining good morale, we might select decision hygiene strategies that have that consequence. And those who are in charge might make it clear that even when firm rules are in place, a process exists to challenge and rethink them — but not to break them by exercising case-by-case discretion.

In a series of energetic books, Philip Howard, a distinguished lawyer and thinker, makes similar points in favor of allowing more flexible judgments. Howard wants policies to take the form not of prescriptive rules, which eliminate noise, but of general principles: "be reasonable," "act prudently," "do not impose excessive risks."

In Howard's view, the modern world of government regulation has gone mad, simply because it is so rigid. Teachers, farmers, developers, nurses, doctors — all of these experts, and many more, are burdened by rules that tell them what to do and exactly how to do it. Howard thinks that it would be much better to allow people to use their own creativity to figure out how to achieve the relevant goals, whether the goals are better educational outcomes, reduced accidents, cleaner water, or healthier patients.

Howard makes some appealing arguments, but it is important to ask about the consequences of the approaches he favors, including potential increases in noise and bias. Most people do not love rigidity in the abstract, but it might be the best way of reducing noise and eliminating bias and error. If only general principles are in place, noise in their interpretation and enforcement will follow. That noise might well be intolerable, even scandalous. At the very least, the costs of noise have to be given careful consideration — and they usually are not. Once we see that noise produces widespread unfairness and high costs of its own, we will often conclude that it is unacceptable and that we should identify noise-reduction strategies that do not compromise important values.

Speaking of Dignity

"People value and even need face-to-face interactions. They want a
real human being to listen to their concerns and complaints and
to have the power to make things better. Sure, those interactions
will inevitably produce noise. But human dignity is priceless."
"Moral values are constantly evolving. If we lock everything down,
we won't make space for changing values. Some efforts to reduce
noise are just too rigid; they would prevent moral change."

"If you want to deter misconduct, you should tolerate some noise. If students are left wondering about the penalty for plagiarism, great — they will avoid plagiarizing. A little uncertainty in the form of noise can magnify deterrence."

"If we eliminate noise, we might end up with clear rules, which wrongdoers will find ways to avoid. Noise can be a price worth paying if it is a way of preventing strategic or opportunistic behavior."

"Creative people need space. People aren't robots. Whatever your job, you deserve some room to maneuver. If you're hemmed in, you might not be noisy, but you won't have much fun and you won't be able to bring your original ideas to bear."

"In the end, most of the efforts to defend noise aren't convincing. We can respect people's dignity, make plenty of space for moral evolution, and allow for human creativity without tolerating the unfairness and cost of noise."

CHAPTER 28

Rules or Standards?

If the goal is to reduce noise or decide how and whether to do so (and to what degree), it is useful to distinguish between two ways of regulating behavior: rules and standards. Organizations of all kinds often choose one or the other or some combination of the two.

In business, a company might say that employees have to be at work between specified hours, that no one may take vacations of more than two weeks, and that if anyone leaks to the press, the person will be fired. Alternatively, it might say that employees must be at work "for a reasonable working day," that vacations will be decided "on a case-by-case basis, consistent with the needs of the firm," and that leaks "will be punished appropriately."

In law, a rule might say that no one may exceed a numerical speed limit, that workers may not be exposed to carcinogens, or that all prescription drugs must come with specific warnings. By contrast, a standard might say that people must drive "prudently," that employers must provide safe workplaces "to the extent feasible," or that in deciding whether to offer warnings for prescription drugs, companies must act "reasonably."

These examples illustrate the central distinction between rules and standards. Rules are meant to eliminate discretion by those who apply them; standards are meant to grant such discretion. Whenever rules are in place, noise ought to be severely reduced. Those who interpret rules must answer a question of fact: How fast did the driver go? Was a worker exposed to a carcinogen? Did the drug have the required warnings?

Under rules, the enterprise of fact-finding may itself involve judgment and so produce noise or be affected by bias. We have encountered many examples. But people who design rules aim to reduce those risks, and when a rule consists of a number ("no one may vote until they reach the age of eighteen" or "the speed limit is sixty-five miles per hour"), noise should be reduced. Rules have an important feature: *they reduce the role of judgment.* On that count, at least, judges (understood to include all those who apply rules) have less work to do. They follow the rules. For better or worse, they have far less room to maneuver.

Standards are altogether different. When standards are in place, judges have to do a lot of work to specify the meaning of open-ended terms. They might have to make numerous judgments to decide what counts as (for example) "reasonable" and "feasible." In addition to finding facts, they must give content to relatively vague phrases. Those who devise standards effectively export decision-making authority to others. They delegate power.

The kinds of guidelines discussed in chapter 22 might be rules or standards. If they are rules, they dramatically constrain judgment. Even if they are standards, they might be far from open-ended. Apgar scores are guidelines and not rules. They do not forbid some exercise of discretion. When guidelines are tightened so as to eliminate that discretion, they turn into rules. Algorithms work as rules, not standards.

Divisions and Ignorance

It should be clear at the outset that whenever firms, organizations, societies, or groups are sharply divided, it might be far easier to generate standards than rules. Company leaders might agree that managers should not act abusively, without knowing precisely what the proscription means. Managers might oppose sexual harassment in the workplace without deciding whether flirtatious behavior is acceptable. A university might prohibit students from engaging in plagiarism, without specifying the exact meaning of that term. People might agree that a constitution should protect freedom of speech, without deciding whether it should protect commercial advertising, threats, or obscenity. People might agree that environmental regulators should issue prudent rules to reduce greenhouse gas emissions, without defining what constitutes prudence.

Setting standards without specifying details can lead to noise, which might be controlled through some of the strategies we have discussed, such as aggregating judgments and using the mediating assessments protocol. Leaders might want to come up with rules but, as a practical matter, might not be able to agree on them. Constitutions themselves include many standards (protecting, for example, freedom of religion). The same is true of the Universal Declaration of Human Rights ("All human beings are born free and equal in dignity and rights").

The great difficulty of getting diverse people to agree on noise-reducing rules is one reason why standards, and not rules, are put in place. The leaders of a company might be unable to agree on specific words to govern how employees must deal with customers. Standards might be the best that such leaders can do. There are analogies in the public sector. Lawmakers might reach a compromise on a standard (and tolerate the resulting noise) if that is the price of enacting law at all. In medicine, doctors might agree on standards for diagnosing illnesses; attempts to devise rules, on the other hand, might cause intractable disagreement.

But social and political divisions are not the only reason that people resort to standards instead of rules. Sometimes, the real problem is that people lack the information that would enable them to produce sensible rules. A university might be unable to produce rules to govern its decisions about whether to promote a faculty member. An employer might struggle to foresee all the circumstances that would lead it to retain or discipline employees. A national legislature might not know about the appropriate level of air pollutants — particulate matter, ozone, nitrogen dioxide, lead. The best it can do is issue some kind of standard and rely on trusted experts to specify its meaning, even if the consequence is noise.

Rules can be biased in many ways. A rule might forbid women from becoming police officers. It might say that Irish need not apply. Even if they create a large bias, rules will sharply reduce noise (if everyone follows them). If a rule says that everyone over the age of twenty-one is permitted to buy alcoholic beverages and that no one under that age can do so, there will probably be little noise, at least as long as people follow the rule. By contrast, standards invite noise.

Bosses, Controlling Subordinates

The distinction between rules and standards has great importance for all public and private institutions, including businesses of all kinds. The choice between the two arises whenever a principal is trying to control an agent. As described in chapter 2, insurance underwriters work hard to charge the Goldilocks premium (one neither too high nor too low) to benefit their company. Would their bosses give these underwriters standards or rules to guide them? Any leader in a company might direct employees very specifically or more generally ("use your common sense" or "exercise your best judgment"). A doctor might use one or the other approach when offering instructions to a patient. "Take a pill every morning and every night" is a rule; "take a pill whenever you feel you need it" is a standard.

We have noted that a social media company such as Facebook will inevitably be concerned with noise and how to reduce it. The company might tell its employees to take down content when a post violates a clear rule (forbidding, say, nudity). Or it might tell its employees to enforce a standard (such as forbidding bullying or patently offensive materials). Facebook's Community Standards, first made public in 2018, are a fascinating mix of rules and standards, with plenty of both. After they were released, numerous complaints were made by Facebook's users, who argued that the company's standards produced excessive noise (and therefore created both errors and unfairness). A recurring concern was that because many thousands of Facebook's reviewers had to make judgments, the decisions could be highly variable. In deciding whether to take down posts that they reviewed, the reviewers made different decisions about what was allowed and what was forbidden. To see why such variability was inevitable, consider these words from Facebook's Community Standards in 2020:

> *We define hate speech as a direct attack on people based on what we call protected characteristics — race, ethnicity, national origin, religious affiliation, sexual orientation, caste, sex, gender, gender identity, and serious disease or disability. We also provide some protections for immigration status. We define attack as violent or dehumanizing speech, statements of inferiority, or calls for exclusion or segregation.*

In implementing a definition of this kind, reviewers will inevitably be noisy. What, exactly, counts as "violent or dehumanizing speech"? Facebook was aware of such questions, and in response to them, it moved in the direction of blunt rules, precisely to reduce noise. Those rules were cataloged in a nonpublic document called the Implementation Standards, consisting of about twelve thousand words, which *The New Yorker* obtained. In the public Community Standards, the text governing graphic content started with a standard "We remove content that glorifies violence." (What's that, exactly?) By contrast, the Implementation Standards listed graphic images and explicitly told the content moderators what to do about these images. Examples included "charred or burning human beings" and "the detachment of non-generating body parts." To summarize a complicated story, the Community Standards look more like standards whereas the Implementation Standards look more like rules.

In the same vein, an airline might ask its pilots to abide by either rules or standards. The question might be whether to go back to the gate after ninety minutes on the tarmac or when, exactly, to turn on the seatbelt sign. The airline might like rules because they limit pilots' discretion, thus reducing error. But it might also believe that under some circumstances, pilots ought to use their best judgment. In these situations, standards might be much better than rules, even if they produce some noise.

In all these cases and many more, those who decide between rules and standards must focus on the problem of noise, the problem of bias, or both. Businesses, both large and small, have to make that decision all the time. Sometimes they do so intuitively and without much of a framework.

Standards come in many shapes and sizes. They can have essentially no content: "do what is appropriate, under the circumstances." They can be written so as to approach rules — as, for example, when what is appropriate is specifically defined, to limit judges' discretion. Rules and standards can also be mixed and matched. For example, a personnel office might adopt a rule ("all applicants must have a college degree") to precede the application of the standard ("subject to that constraint, choose people who will do a terrific job").

We have said that rules should reduce or possibly even eliminate noise and that standards will often produce a great deal of it (unless some noise-reduction strategy is adopted). In private and public organizations, noise is often a product of a failure to issue rules. When the noise is loud enough — when everyone can see that similarly situated people are not being treated similarly — there is often a movement in the direction of rules. As in the case of criminal sentencing, the movement might turn into an outcry. Some sort of noise audit typically precedes that outcry.

The Return of the Repressed

Consider an important question: who counts as disabled, such that they should qualify for economic benefits reserved for those who are unable to work? If the question is phrased that way, judges will make ad hoc decisions that will be noisy and therefore unfair. In the United States, such noisy, unfair decisions were once the norm, and the results were scandalous. Two seemingly identical people in wheelchairs or with severe depression or chronic pain would be treated differently. In response, public officials shifted to something far more like a rule — a *disability matrix*. The matrix calls for relatively mechanical judgments on the basis of education, geographical location, and remaining physical capacities. The goal is to make the decisions less noisy.

The leading discussion of the problem, written by law professor Jerry Mashaw, gives a name to the effort to eliminate noisy judgments: *bureaucratic justice*. The term is worth remembering. Mashaw celebrates the creation of the matrix as fundamentally just, precisely because it promises to eliminate noise. In some situations, however, the promise of bureaucratic justice might not be realized. Whenever an institution shifts to rule-bound decisions, there is a risk that noise will reemerge.

Suppose that rules produce terrible results in particular cases. If so, judges might simply ignore the rules, thinking that they are far too harsh. For that reason, they might exercise discretion through a mild form of civil disobedience, which can be hard to police or even see. In private companies, employees ignore firm rules that seem stupid. Similarly, administrative agencies charged with protecting public safety and health can simply refuse to enforce statutes when they are too rigid and rule-like. In criminal law, *jury nullification* refers to situations in which juries simply refuse to follow the law, on the ground that it is senselessly rigid and harsh.

Whenever a public or private institution tries to control noise through firm rules, it must always be alert to the possibility that the rules will simply drive discretion underground. With the three-strikes policy, the frequent response of prosecutors — to avoid making a felony charge against people who had been convicted twice — was extremely difficult to control and even see.

When such things happen, there will be noise, but no one will hear it. We need to monitor our rules to make sure they are operating as intended. If they are not, the existence of noise might be a clue, and the rules should be revised.

A Framework

In business and in government, the choice between rules and standards is often made intuitively, but it can be made more disciplined. As a first approximation, the choice depends on just two factors: (1) the costs of decisions and (2) the costs of errors.

With standards, the costs of decisions can be very high for judges of all kinds, simply because they have to work to give them content. Exercising judgment can be burdensome. If doctors are told to make their best judgment, they might have to spend time thinking about each case (and the judgments might well be noisy). If doctors are given clear guidelines to decide whether patients have strep throat, their decisions might be fast and relatively straightforward. If the speed limit is sixty-five miles per hour, police officers do not have to think hard about how fast people are allowed to go, but if the standard is that people may not drive "unreasonably fast," officers have to do a lot more thinking (and the enforcement will almost certainly be noisy). With rules, the costs of decisions are typically much lower.

Still, it's complicated. Rules may be straightforward to apply once they are in place, but before a rule is put in place, *someone has to decide what it is.* Producing a rule can be hard. Sometimes it is prohibitively costly. Legal systems and private companies therefore often use words such as *reasonable, prudent,* and *feasible.* This is also why terms like these play an equally important role in fields such as medicine and engineering.

The costs of errors refer to the number and the magnitude of mistakes. A pervasive question is whether agents are knowledgeable and reliable, and whether they practice decision hygiene. If they are, and if they do, then a standard might work just fine — and there might be little noise. Principals need to impose rules when they have reason to distrust their agents. If agents are incompetent or biased and if they cannot feasibly implement decision hygiene, then they should be constrained by rules. Sensible organizations well understand that the amount of discretion they grant is closely connected with the level of trust they have in their agents.

Of course there is a continuum from perfect trust to complete distrust. A standard might lead to numerous errors by less-than-trustworthy agents, but if those errors are minor, they might be tolerable. A rule might lead to only a few mistakes, but if they are catastrophic, we might want a standard. We should be able to see that there is no *general* reason to think that the costs of errors are larger with either rules or standards. If a rule is perfect, of course, it will produce no errors. But rules are rarely perfect.

Suppose that the law says that you can buy liquor only if you are 21 or older. The law aims to protect young people from the various risks associated with alcohol consumption. Understood in this way, the law will produce plenty of mistakes. Some people who are 20 or 19 or 18 or even 17 can do just fine with liquor. Some people who are 22 or 42 or 62 cannot. A standard would produce fewer errors — if we could find a suitable form of words and if people could apply these words accurately. Of course, that is very hard to do, which is why we almost always see simple rules, based on age, for liquor sales.

This example suggests a much larger point. Whenever numerous decisions must be made, there might well be a lot of noise, and there is a strong argument for clear rules. If dermatologists are seeing a large number of patients with itchy rashes and moles, they might make fewer errors if their judgments are constrained by sensible rules. Without such rules, and with open-ended standards, the costs of decisions tend to become impossibly large. For repeated decisions, there are real advantages to moving in the direction of mechanical rules rather than ad hoc judgments. The burdens of exercising discretion turn out to be great, and the costs of noise, or the unfairness it creates, might well be intolerable.

Smart organizations are keenly aware of the disadvantages of both ways of regulating behavior. They enlist rules, or standards that are close to rules, as a way of reducing noise (and bias). And to minimize the costs of errors, they are willing to devote considerable time and attention, in advance, to ensuring that the rules are accurate (enough).

Outlawing Noise?

In many situations, noise should be a scandal. People live with it, but they should not have to do that. A simple response is to shift from open-ended discretion or a vague standard to a rule or something close to it. We now have a sense of when the simple response is the right response. But even when a rule is not feasible or not a good idea, we have identified an assortment of strategies to reduce noise.

All this raises a large question: should the legal system outlaw noise? It would be too simple to answer yes, but the law should be doing much more than it now does to control noise. Here is one way to think about the problem. The German sociologist Max Weber complained of "Kadi justice," which he understood as informal, ad hoc judgments undisciplined by general rules. In Weber's view, Kadi justice was intolerably case by case; it was a violation of the rule of law. As Weber put it, the judge "precisely did not adjudicate according to formal rules and 'without regard to persons.' Just the reverse largely obtained; he judged persons according to their concrete qualities and in terms of the concrete situation, or according to equity and the appropriateness of the concrete result."

This approach, Weber argued, "knows no rational rules of decision." We can easily see Weber as complaining about intolerable noise that Kadi justice ensured. Weber celebrated the rise of bureaucratic judgments, disciplined in advance. (Recall the idea of bureaucratic justice.) He saw specialized, professional, and rule-bound approaches as the final stage in the evolution of law. But long after Weber wrote, it is clear that Kadi justice, or something like it, remains pervasive. The question is what to do about it.

We would not go so far as to say that noise reduction should be part of the Universal Declaration of Human Rights, but in some cases, noise can be counted as a rights violation, and in general, legal systems all over the world should be making much greater efforts to control noise. Consider criminal sentencing; civil fines for wrongdoing; and the grant or denial of asylum, educational opportunities, visas, building permits, and occupational licenses. Or suppose that a large government agency is hiring hundreds or even thousands of people and that its decisions have no rhyme or reason; there is a cacophony of noise. Or suppose that a child custody agency treats young children very differently, depending on whether one or another employee is assigned to the case. How is it acceptable that a child's life and future depend on that lottery?

In many cases, variability in such decisions is clearly driven by biases, including identifiable cognitive biases and certain forms of discrimination. When that is so, people tend to find the situation intolerable, and the law may be invoked as a corrective, requiring new and different practices. Organizations all over the world see bias as a villain. They are right. They do not see noise that way. They should.

In many areas, the current level of noise is far too high. It is imposing high costs and producing terrible unfairness. What we have cataloged here is the tip of the iceberg. The law should do much more to reduce those costs. It should combat that unfairness.

Speaking of Rules and Standards

"Rules simplify life, and reduce noise. But standards allow people to adjust to the particulars of the situations."

"Rules or standards? First, ask which produces more mistakes. Then, ask which is easier or more burdensome to produce or work with."

"We often use standards when we should embrace rules — simply because we don't pay attention to noise."

"Noise reduction shouldn't be part of the Universal Declaration of Human Rights — at least not yet. Still, noise can be horribly unfair. All over the world, legal systems should consider taking strong steps to reduce it."

REVIEW AND CONCLUSION

Taking Noise Seriously

Noise is the unwanted variability of judgments, and there is too much of it. Our central goals here have been to explain why that is so and to see what might be done about it. We have covered a great deal of material in this book, and by way of conclusion, we offer here a brisk review of the main points, as well as a broader perspective.

Judgments

As we use the term, *judgment* should not be confused with "thinking." It is a much narrower concept: judgment is a form of measurement in which the instrument is a human mind. Like other measurements, a judgment assigns a score to an object. The score need not be a number. "Mary Johnson's tumor is probably benign" is a judgment, as are statements like "The national economy is very unstable," "Fred Williams would be the best person to hire as our new manager," and "The premium to insure this risk should be $12,000." Judgments informally integrate diverse pieces of information into an overall assessment. They are not computations, and they do not follow exact rules. A teacher uses judgment to grade an essay, but not to score a multiple-choice test.

Many people earn a living by making professional judgments, and everyone is affected by such judgments in important ways. Professional *judges,* as we call them here, include football coaches and cardiologists, lawyers and engineers, Hollywood executives and insurance underwriters, and many more. Professional judgments have been the focus of this book, both because they have been extensively studied and because their quality has such a large impact on all of us. We believe that what we have learned applies to judgments that people make in other parts of their lives, too.

Some judgments are *predictive,* and some predictive judgments are verifiable; we will eventually know whether they were accurate. This is generally the case for short-term forecasts of outcomes such as the effects of a medication, the course of a pandemic, or the results of an election. But many judgments, including long-term forecasts and answers to fictitious questions, are unverifiable. The quality of such judgments can be assessed only by the quality of the thought process that produces them. Furthermore, many judgments are not predictive but *evaluative:* the sentence set by a judge or the rank of a painting in a prize competition cannot easily be compared to an objective true value.

Strikingly, however, people who make judgments behave as if a true value exists, regardless of whether it does. They think and act as if there were an invisible bull's-eye at which to aim, one that they and others should not miss by much. The phrase *judgment call* implies both the possibility of disagreement and the expectation that it will be limited. Matters of judgment are characterized by an expectation of *bounded disagreement.* They occupy a space between matters of computation, where disagreement is not allowed, and matters of taste, where there is little expectation of agreement except in extreme cases.

Errors: Bias and Noise

We say that *bias* exists when most errors in a set of judgments are in the same direction. Bias is the *average error,* as, for example, when a team of shooters consistently hits below and to the left of the target;

when executives are too optimistic about sales, year after year; or when a company keeps reinvesting money in failing projects that it should write off.

Eliminating bias from a set of judgments will not eliminate all error. The errors that remain when bias is removed are not shared. They are the unwanted divergence of judgments, the unreliability of the measuring instrument we apply to reality. They are *noise*. Noise is variability in judgments that should be identical. We use the term *system noise* for the noise observed in organizations that employ interchangeable professionals to make decisions, such as physicians in an emergency room, judges imposing criminal penalties, and underwriters in an insurance company. Much of this book has been concerned with system noise.

Measuring Bias and Noise

The *mean of squared errors (MSE)* has been the standard of accuracy in scientific measurement for two hundred years. The main features of MSE are that it yields the sample mean as an unbiased estimate of the population mean, treats positive and negative errors equally, and disproportionately penalizes large errors. MSE does not reflect the real costs of judgment errors, which are often asymmetric. However, professional decisions always require accurate predictions. For a city facing a hurricane, the costs of under- and overestimating the threat are clearly not the same, but you would not want these costs to influence the meteorologists' forecast of the storm's speed and trajectory. MSE is the appropriate standard for making such predictive judgments, where objective accuracy is the goal.

As measured by MSE, bias and noise are independent and additive sources of error. Obviously, bias is always bad and reducing it always improves accuracy. Less intuitive is the fact that noise is equally bad and that reducing noise is always an improvement. The best amount of scatter is zero, even when the judgments are clearly biased. The goal, of course, is to minimize both bias and noise.

Bias in a set of verifiable judgments is defined by the difference between the average judgment of a case and the corresponding true value. This comparison is impossible for unverifiable judgments. For example, the true value of a premium that an underwriter sets for a particular risk will never be known. Nor can we easily know the true value of the just sentence for a particular crime. Lacking that knowledge, a frequent and convenient (though not always correct) assumption is that judgments are unbiased and that the average of many judges is the best estimate of the true value.

Noise in a system can be assessed by a *noise audit*, an experiment in which several professionals make independent judgments of the same cases (real or fictitious). We can measure noise without knowing a true value, just as we can see, from the back of the target, the scatter of a set of shots. Noise audits can measure the variability of judgments in many systems, including a radiology department and the system of criminal justice. They may sometimes call attention to deficiencies in skill or training. And they will quantify system noise — for instance, when underwriters in the same team differ in their assessments of risks.

Of bias and noise, which is the larger problem? It depends on the situation. The answer might well turn out to be noise. Bias and noise make equal contributions to overall error (MSE) when the mean of errors (the bias) is equal to the standard deviations of errors (the noise). When the distribution of judgments is normal (the standard bell-shaped curve), the effects of bias and noise are equal when 84% of judgments are above (or below) the true value. This is a substantial bias, which will often be detectable in a professional context. When the bias is smaller than one standard deviation, noise is the bigger source of overall error.

Noise Is a Problem

Variability as such is unproblematic in some judgments, even welcome. Diversity of opinions is essential for generating ideas and options. Contrarian thinking is essential to innovation. A plurality of opinions among movie critics is a feature, not a bug. Disagreements among traders make markets. Strategy differences among competing start-ups enable markets to select the fittest. In what we call matters of judgment, however, system noise is always a problem. If two doctors give you different diagnoses, at least one of them is wrong.

The surprises that motivated this book are the sheer magnitude of system noise and the amount of damage that it does. Both of these far exceed common expectations. We have given examples from many fields, including business, medicine, criminal justice, fingerprint analysis, forecasting, personnel ratings, and politics. Hence our conclusion: wherever there is judgment, there is noise, and more of it than you think.

The large role of noise in error contradicts a commonly held belief that random errors do not matter, because they "cancel out." This belief is wrong. If multiple shots are scattered around the target, it is unhelpful to say that, on average, they hit the bull's-eye. If one candidate for a job gets a higher rating than she deserves and another gets a lower one, the wrong person may be hired. If one insurance policy is overpriced and another is underpriced, both errors are costly to the insurance company; one makes it lose business, the other makes it lose money.

In short, we can be sure that there is error if judgments vary for no good reason. Noise is detrimental even when judgments are not verifiable and error cannot be measured. It is unfair for similarly situated people to be treated differently, and a system in which professional judgments are seen as inconsistent loses credibility.

Types of Noise

System noise can be broken down into *level noise* and *pattern noise*. Some judges are generally more severe than others, and others are more lenient; some forecasters are generally bullish and others bearish about market prospects; some doctors prescribe more antibiotics than others do. *Level noise* is the variability of the average judgments made by different individuals. The ambiguity of judgment scales is one of the sources of level noise. Words such as *likely* or numbers (e.g., "4 on a scale of 0 to 6") mean different things to different people. Level noise is an important source of error in judgment systems and an important target for interventions aimed at noise reduction.

System noise includes another, generally larger component. Regardless of the average level of their judgments, two judges may differ in their views of which crimes deserve the harsher sentences. Their sentencing decisions will produce a different *ranking* of cases. We call this variability *pattern noise* (the technical term is *statistical interaction*).

The main source of pattern noise is stable: it is the difference in the personal, idiosyncratic responses of judges to the same case. Some of these differences reflect principles or values that the individuals follow, whether consciously or not. For example, one judge might be especially severe with shoplifters and unusually lenient with traffic offenders; another might show the opposite pattern. Some of the underlying principles or values may be quite complex, and the judge may be unaware of them. For example, a judge could be relatively lenient toward older shoplifters without realizing it. Finally, a highly personal reaction to a particular case could also be stable. A defendant who resembles the judge's daughter might well have evoked the same feeling of sympathy, and hence leniency, on another day.

This *stable pattern noise* reflects the uniqueness of judges: their response to cases is as individual as their personality. The subtle differences among people are often enjoyable and interesting, but the differences become problematic when professionals operate within a system that assumes consistency. In the studies we have examined, the stable pattern noise that such individual differences produce is generally the single largest source of system noise.

Still, judges' distinctive attitudes to particular cases are not perfectly stable. Pattern noise also has a transient component, called *occasion noise*. We detect this kind of noise if a radiologist assigns different diagnoses to the same image on different days or if a fingerprint examiner identifies two prints as a match on one occasion but not on another. As these examples illustrate, occasion noise is most easily measured when the judge does not recognize the case as one seen before. Another way to demonstrate occasion noise is to show the effect of an irrelevant feature of the context on judgments, such as when judges are more lenient after their favorite football team won, or when doctors prescribe more opioids in the afternoon.

The Psychology of Judgment and Noise

The judges' cognitive flaws are not the only cause of errors in predictive judgments. *Objective ignorance* often plays a larger role. Some facts are actually unknowable — how many grandchildren a baby born yesterday will have seventy years from now, or the number of a winning lottery ticket in a drawing to be held next year. Others are perhaps knowable but are not known to the judge. People's exaggerated confidence in their predictive judgment underestimates their objective ignorance as well as their biases.

There is a limit to the accuracy of our predictions, and this limit is often quite low. Nevertheless, we are generally comfortable with our judgments. What gives us this satisfying confidence is an *internal signal,* a self-generated reward for fitting the facts and the judgment into a coherent story. Our subjective confidence in our judgments is not necessarily related to their objective accuracy.

Most people are surprised to hear that the accuracy of their predictive judgments is not only low but also inferior to that of formulas. Even simple linear models built on limited data, or simple rules that can be sketched on the back of an envelope, consistently outperform human judges. The critical advantage of rules and models is that they are noise-free. As we subjectively experience it, judgment is a subtle and complex process; we have no indication that the subtlety may be mostly noise. It is difficult for us to imagine that mindless adherence to simple rules will often achieve higher accuracy than we can — but this is by now a well-established fact.

Psychological biases are, of course, a source of systematic error, or statistical bias. Less obviously, they are also a source of noise. When biases are not shared by all judges, when they are present to different degrees, and when their effects depend on extraneous circumstances, psychological biases produce noise. For instance, if half the managers who make hiring decisions are biased against women and half are biased in their favor, there will be no overall bias, but system noise will cause many hiring errors. Another example is the disproportionate effect of first impressions. This is a psychological bias, but that bias will produce occasion noise when the order in which the evidence is presented varies randomly.

We have described the process of judgment as the informal integration of a set of cues to produce a judgment on a scale. The elimination of system noise would therefore require judges to maintain uniformity in their use of cues, in the weights they assign to cues, and in their use of the scale. Even leaving aside the random effects of occasion noise, these conditions are rarely met.

Agreement is often fairly high in judgments on single dimensions. Different recruiters will often agree on their evaluations of which of two candidates is more charismatic or more diligent. The shared intuitive process of *matching* across intensity dimensions — such as when people match a high GPA to a precocious reading age — will generally produce similar judgments. The same is true of judgments based on a small number of cues that point in the same general direction.

Large individual differences emerge when a judgment requires the *weighting of multiple, conflicting cues.* Looking at the same candidate, some recruiters will give more weight to evidence of brilliance or charisma; others will be more influenced by concerns about diligence or calm under pressure. When cues are inconsistent and do not fit a coherent story, different people will inevitably give more weight to certain cues and ignore others. Pattern noise will result.

The Obscurity of Noise

Noise is not a prominent problem. It is rarely discussed, and it is certainly less salient than bias. You probably had not given it much thought. Given its importance, the obscurity of noise is an interesting phenomenon in and of itself.

Cognitive biases and other emotional or motivated distortions of thinking are often used as explanations for poor judgments. Analysts invoke overconfidence, anchoring, loss aversion, availability bias, and other biases to explain decisions that turned out badly. Such bias-based explanations are satisfying, because the human mind craves causal explanations. Whenever something goes wrong, we look for a cause — and often find it. In many cases, the cause will appear to be a bias.

Bias has a kind of explanatory charisma, which noise lacks. If we try to explain, in hindsight, why a particular decision was wrong, we will easily find bias and never find noise. Only a *statistical view* of the world enables us to see noise, but that view does not come naturally — we prefer causal stories. The absence of statistical thinking from our intuitions is one reason that noise receives so much less attention than bias does.

Another reason is that professionals seldom see a need to confront noise in their own judgments and in those of their colleagues. After a period of training, professionals often make judgments on their own. Fingerprint experts, experienced underwriters, and veteran patent officers rarely take time to imagine how colleagues might disagree with them — and they spend even less time imagining how they might disagree with themselves.

Most of the time, professionals have confidence in their own judgment. They expect that colleagues would agree with them, and they never find out whether they actually do. In most fields, a judgment may never be evaluated against a true value and will at most be subjected to vetting by another professional who is considered a *respect-expert*. Only occasionally will professionals be faced with a surprising disagreement, and when that happens, they will generally find reasons to view it as an isolated case. The routines of organizations also tend to ignore or suppress evidence of divergence among experts in their midst. This is understandable; from an organizational perspective, noise is an embarrassment.

How to Reduce Noise (and Bias, Too)

There is reason to believe that some people make better judgments than others do. Task-specific skill, intelligence, and a certain cognitive style — best described as being *actively open-minded* — characterize the best judges. Unsurprisingly, good judges will make few egregious mistakes. Given the multiple sources of individual differences, however, we should not expect even the best judges to be in perfect agreement on complex judgment problems. The infinite variety of backgrounds, personalities, and experiences that make each of us unique is also what makes noise inevitable.

One strategy for error reduction is debiasing. Typically, people attempt to remove bias from their judgments either by correcting judgments after the fact or by taming biases before they affect judgments. We propose a third option, which is particularly applicable to decisions made in a group setting: detect biases in real time, by designating a *decision observer* to identify signs of bias (see appendix B).

Our main suggestion for reducing noise in judgment is *decision hygiene.* We chose this term because noise reduction, like health hygiene, is prevention against an unidentified enemy. Handwashing, for example, prevents unknown pathogens from entering our bodies. In the same way, decision hygiene will prevent errors without knowing what they are. Decision hygiene is as unglamorous as its name and certainly less exciting than a victorious fight against predictable biases. There may be no glory in preventing an unidentified harm, but it is very much worth doing.

A noise-reduction effort in an organization should always begin with a noise audit (see appendix A). An important function of the audit is to obtain a commitment of the organization to take noise seriously. An essential benefit is the assessment of separate types of noise.

We described the successes and limitations of noise reduction efforts in various domains. We now recapitulate six principles that define decision hygiene, describe how they address the psychological mechanisms that cause noise, and show how they relate to the specific decision hygiene techniques we have discussed

The goal of judgment is accuracy, not individual expression. This statement is our candidate for the first principle of decision hygiene in judgment. It reflects the narrow, specific way we have defined judgment in this book. We have shown that stable pattern noise is a large component of system noise and that it is a direct consequence of individual differences, of judgment personalities that lead different people to form different views of the same problem. This observation leads to a conclusion that will be as unpopular as it is inescapable: judgment is not the place to express your individuality.

To be clear, personal values, individuality, and creativity are needed, even essential, in many phases of thinking and decision making, including the choice of goals, the formulation of novel ways to approach a problem, and the generation of options. But when it comes to making a judgment about these options, expressions of individuality are a source of noise. When the goal is accuracy and you expect others to agree with you, you should also consider what other competent judges would think if they were in your place.

A radical application of this principle is the replacement of judgment with rules or algorithms. Algorithmic evaluation is guaranteed to eliminate noise — indeed, it is the only approach that can eliminate noise completely. Algorithms are already in use in many important domains, and their role is increasing. But it is unlikely that algorithms will replace human judgment in the final stage of important decisions — and we consider this good news. However, judgment can be improved, by both the appropriate use of algorithms and the adoption of approaches that make decisions less dependent on the idiosyncrasies of one professional. We have seen, for instance, how decision guidelines can help constrain the discretion of judges or promote homogeneity in the diagnoses of physicians and thus reduce noise and improve decisions.

Think statistically, and take the outside view of the case. We say that a judge takes the outside view of a case when she considers it as a member of a reference class of similar cases rather than as a unique problem. This approach diverges from the default mode of thinking, which focuses firmly on the case at hand and embeds it in a causal story. When people apply their unique experiences to form a unique view of the case, the result is pattern noise. The outside view is a remedy for this problem: professionals who share the same reference class will be less noisy. In addition, the outside view often yields valuable insights.

The outside-view principle favors the anchoring of predictions in the statistics of similar cases. It also leads to the recommendation that predictions should be moderate (the technical term is *regressive;* see appendix C). Attention to the wide range of past outcomes and to their limited predictability should help decision makers calibrate their confidence in their judgments. People cannot be faulted for failing to predict the unpredictable, but they can be blamed for a lack of predictive humility.

Structure judgments into several independent tasks. This divide-and-conquer principle is made necessary by the psychological mechanism we have described as *excessive coherence,* which causes people to distort or ignore information that does not fit a preexisting or emerging story. Overall accuracy suffers when impressions of distinct aspects of a case contaminate each other. For an analogy, think of what happens to the evidentiary value of a set of witnesses when they are allowed to communicate.

People can reduce excessive coherence by breaking down the judgment problem into a series of smaller tasks. This technique is analogous to the practice of structured interviews, in which interviewers evaluate one trait at a time and score it before moving to the next one. The principle of structuring inspires diagnostic guidelines, such as the Apgar score. It is also at the heart of the approach we have called the *mediating assessments protocol.* This protocol breaks down a complex judgment into multiple fact-based assessments and aims to ensure that each one is evaluated independently of the others. Whenever possible, independence is protected by assigning assessments to different teams and minimizing communication among them.

Resist premature intuitions. We have described the internal signal of judgment completion that gives decision makers confidence in their judgment. The unwillingness of decision makers to give up this rewarding signal is a key reason for the resistance to the use of guidelines and algorithms and other rules that tie their hands. Decision makers clearly need to be comfortable with their eventual choice and to attain the rewarding sense of intuitive confidence. But they should not grant themselves this reward prematurely. An intuitive choice that is informed by a balanced and careful consideration of the evidence is far superior to a snap judgment. Intuition need not be banned, but it should be informed, disciplined, and delayed.

This principle inspires our recommendation to *sequence the information:* professionals who make judgments should not be given information that they don't need and that could bias them, even if that information is accurate. In forensic science, for example, it is good practice to keep examiners unaware of other information about a suspect. Control of discussion agendas, a key element of the mediating assessments protocol, also belongs here. An efficient agenda will ensure that different aspects of the problem are considered separately and that the formation of a holistic judgment is delayed until the profile of assessments is complete.

Obtain independent judgments from multiple judges, then consider aggregating those judgments. The requirement of independence is routinely violated in the procedures of organizations, notably in meetings in which participants' opinions are shaped by those of others. Because of cascade effects and group polarization, group discussions often increase noise. The simple procedure of collecting participants' judgments *before* the discussion both reveals the extent of noise and facilitates a constructive resolution of differences.

Averaging independent judgments is guaranteed to reduce system noise (but not bias). A single judgment is a sample of one, drawn from the population of all possible judgments; and increasing sample size improves the precision of estimates. The advantage of averaging is further enhanced when judges have diverse skills and complementary judgment patterns. The average of a noisy group may end up being more accurate than a unanimous judgment.

Favor relative judgments and relative scales. Relative judgments are less noisy than absolute ones, because our ability to categorize objects on a scale is limited, while our ability to make pairwise comparisons is much better. Judgment scales that call for comparisons will be less noisy than scales that require absolute judgments. For example, a *case scale* requires judges to locate a case on a scale that is defined by instances familiar to everyone.

———

The decision hygiene principles we have just listed are applicable not only to recurrent judgments but also to one-off major decisions, or what we call *singular decisions*. The existence of noise in singular decisions may seem counterintuitive: by definition, there is no variability to measure if you decide only once. Yet noise is there, causing errors. The noise in a team of shooters is invisible if we see only the first shooter in action, but the scatter would become apparent if we saw the other shooters. Similarly, the best way to think about singular judgments is to treat them as *recurrent judgments that are made only once.* That is why decision hygiene should improve them, too.

Enforcing decision hygiene can be thankless. Noise is an invisible enemy, and a victory against an invisible enemy can only be an invisible victory. But like physical health hygiene, decision hygiene is vital. After a successful operation, you like to believe that it is the surgeon's skill that saved your life — and it did, of course — but if the surgeon and all the personnel in the operating room had not washed their hands, you might be dead. There may not be much glory to be gained in hygiene, but there are results.

How Much Noise?

Of course, the battle against noise is not the only consideration for decision makers and organizations. Noise may be too costly to reduce: a high school could eliminate noise in grading by having five teachers read each and every paper, but that burden is hardly justified. Some noise may be inevitable in practice, a necessary side effect of a system of due process that gives each case individualized consideration, that does not treat people like cogs in a machine, and that grants decision makers a sense of agency. Some noise may even be desirable, if the variation it creates enables a system to adapt over time — as when noise reflects changing values and goals and triggers a debate that leads to change in practice or in the law.

Perhaps most importantly, noise-reduction strategies may have unacceptable downsides. Many concerns about algorithms are overblown, but some are legitimate. Algorithms may produce stupid mistakes that a human would never make, and therefore lose credibility even if they also succeed in preventing many errors that humans do make. They may be biased by poor design or by training on inadequate data. Their facelessness may inspire distrust. Decision hygiene practices also have their downsides: if poorly managed, they risk bureaucratizing decisions and demoralizing professionals who feel their autonomy is being undermined.

All these risks and limitations deserve full consideration. However, whether an objection to noise reduction makes sense depends on the particular noise-reduction strategy that is under discussion. An objection to aggregating judgments — perhaps on the ground that it is too costly — may not apply to the use of guidelines. To be sure, whenever the costs of noise reduction exceed its benefits, it should not be pursued. Once the cost-benefit calculation is made, it may reveal an optimal level of noise that is not zero. The problem is that in the absence of noise audits, people are unaware of how much noise there is in their judgments. When that is the case, invoking the difficulty of reducing noise is nothing but an excuse not to measure it.

Bias leads to errors and unfairness. Noise does too — and yet, we do a lot less about it. Judgment error may seem more tolerable when it is random than when we attribute it to a cause; but it is no less damaging. If we want better decisions about things that matter, we should take noise reduction seriously.

EPILOGUE

A Less Noisy World

I magine what organizations would look like if they were redesigned to reduce noise. Hospitals, hiring committees, economic forecasters, government agencies, insurance companies, public health authorities, criminal justice systems, law firms, and universities would be keenly alert to the problem of noise and strive to reduce it. Noise audits would be routine; they might be undertaken every year.

Leaders of organizations would use algorithms either to replace human judgment or to supplement it in far more areas than they do today. People would break down complex judgments into simpler mediating assessments. They would know about decision hygiene and follow its prescriptions. Independent judgments would be elicited and aggregated. Meetings would look very different; discussions would be more structured. An outside view would be more systematically integrated into the decision process. Overt disagreements would be both more frequent and more constructively resolved.

The result would a be less noisy world. It would save a great deal of money, improve public safety and health, increase fairness, and prevent many avoidable errors. Our aim in writing this book has been to draw attention to this opportunity. We hope that you will be among those who seize it.

APPENDIX A

How to Conduct a Noise Audit

This appendix provides a practical guide for conducting a noise audit. You should read it from the perspective of a consultant who has been engaged by an organization to examine the quality of the professional judgments its employees produce by conducting a noise audit in one of its units.

As implied by its name, the focus of the audit is the prevalence of noise. However, a well-conducted audit will provide valuable information about biases, blind spots, and specific deficiencies in the training of employees and in the supervision of their work. A successful audit should stimulate changes in the operations of the unit, including in the doctrine that guides professionals' judgments, the training they receive, the tools they use to support their judgments, and the routine supervision of their work. If the effort is considered successful, it may be extended to other units of the organization.

A noise audit requires a substantial amount of work and much attention to detail because its credibility will surely be questioned if its findings reveal significant flaws. Every detail of the cases and the procedure should therefore be considered with hostile scrutiny in mind. The process we describe aims to reduce opposition by enlisting the professionals who are the most significant potential critics of the audit to be its authors.

Alongside the consultant (who may be external or internal), the relevant cast of characters includes the following:

- *Project team.* The project team will be responsible for all phases of the study. If the consultants are internal, they will form the core of the project team. If the consultants are external, an internal project team will work closely with them. This will ensure that people in the company view the audit as *their* project and consider the consultants as playing a supporting role. In addition to the consultants who administer the collection of data, analyze the results, and prepare a final report, the project team should include subject matter experts who can construct the cases that the judges will assess. All the members of the project team should have high professional credibility.

- *Clients.* A noise audit will only be useful if it leads to significant changes, which requires early involvement of the leadership of the organization, which is the "client" of the project. You can expect clients to be initially skeptical about the prevalence of noise. This initial skepticism is actually an advantage if it is accompanied by an open-minded attitude, curiosity about the results of the audit, and a commitment to remedy the situation if the consultant's pessimistic expectations are confirmed.

- *Judges.* The clients will designate one or more units to be audited. The selected unit should consist of a substantial number of "judges," the professionals who make similar judgments and decisions on behalf of the company. The judges should be effectively interchangeable; i.e., if one person was unavailable to handle a case, another would be assigned to it and expected to arrive at a similar judgment. The examples that introduced this book were sentencing decisions of federal judges and the setting of risk premiums and claims reserves in an insurance company. For a noise audit, it is best to select a judgment task that (1) can be completed on the basis of written information, and (2) is expressed numerically (e.g., in dollars, probabilities, or ratings).

- *Project manager.* A high-level manager in the administrative staff should be designated as project manager. Specific professional expertise is not required for that task. However, a high position in the organization is of practical significance in overcoming administrative hurdles and is also a demonstration of the importance that the company attaches to the project. The task of the project manager is to provide administrative support to facilitate all phases of the project, including the preparation of the final report and the communication of its conclusions to the leadership of the company.

Construction of Case Materials

The subject matter experts who are part of the project team should have recognized expertise in the task of the unit (e.g., setting premiums for risks or evaluating the potential of possible investments). They will be in charge of developing the cases that will be used in the audit. Designing a credible simulation of the judgments professionals make on the job is a delicate task — especially given the scrutiny that the study will undergo if it reveals serious problems. The team must consider this question: if the results of our simulation indicate a high level of noise, will people in the company accept that there is noise in the actual judgments of the unit? The noise audit is only worth carrying out if the answer is a clear yes.

There is more than one way to achieve a positive response. The noise audit of sentencing described in chapter 1 summarized each case by a brief schematic list of relevant attributes and obtained assessments of sixteen cases in ninety minutes. The noise audit in the insurance company described in chapter 2 used detailed and realistic summaries of complex cases. Findings of high noise in both instances provided acceptable evidence because of the argument that if much disagreement was found in simplified cases, noise could only be worse in real cases.

A questionnaire should be prepared for each case, to provide a deeper understanding of the reasoning that led each judge to a judgment of that case. The questionnaire should be administered only after the completion of all cases. It should include:

- Open questions about the key factors that led the participant to her response.

- A list of the facts of the case, allowing the participant to rate their importance.

- Questions that call for an "outside view" of the category to which the case belongs. For instance, if the cases call for dollar valuations, participants should provide an estimate of how much below or above average the case is compared to all valuations for cases of the same category.

Prelaunch Meeting with Executives

When the case materials to be used in the audit are assembled, a meeting should be scheduled in which the project team will present the audit to the leadership of the company. The discussion in that meeting should consider possible outcomes of the study, including a finding of unacceptable system noise. The purpose of the meeting is to hear objections to the planned study and to obtain from the leadership a commitment to accept its results, whatever they are: there is no point moving on to the next stage without such a commitment. If serious objections are raised, the project team may be required to improve the case materials and try again.

Once the executives accept the design of the noise audit, the project team should ask them to state their expectations about the results of the study. They should discuss questions such as:

- "What level of disagreement do you expect between a randomly selected pair of answers to each case?"
- "What is the maximum level of disagreement that would be acceptable from a business perspective?"
- "What is the estimated cost of getting an evaluation wrong in either direction (too high or low) by a specified amount (e.g., 15%)?"

The answers to these questions should be documented to ensure that they are remembered and believed when the actual results of the audit come in.

Administration of the Study

The managers of the audited unit should be, from the beginning, informed in general terms that their unit has been selected for special study. However, it is important that the term *noise audit* not be used to describe the project. The words *noise* and *noisy* should be avoided, especially as descriptions of people. A neutral term such as *decision-making study* should be used instead.

The managers of the unit will be immediately in charge of the data collection and responsible for briefing the participants about the task, with the participation of the project manager and members of the project team. The intent of the exercise should be described to the participants in general terms, as in *"The organization is interested in how [decision makers] reach their conclusions."*

It is essential to reassure the professionals who participate in the study that individual answers will not be known to anyone in the organization, including the project team. If necessary, an outside firm may be hired to anonymize the data. It is also important to stress that there will be no specific consequences for the unit, which was merely selected as representative of units that perform judgment tasks on behalf of the organization. To ensure the credibility of the results, all qualified professionals in the unit should participate in the study. The allocation of half a working day to the exercise will help convince the participants of its importance.

All participants should complete the exercise at the same time, but they should be kept physically separate and asked not to communicate while the study is in progress. The project team will be available to answer questions during the study.

Analyses and Conclusions

The project team will be in charge of the statistical analyses of the multiple cases evaluated by each participant, including the measurement of the overall amount of noise and its constituents, level noise and pattern noise. If the case materials allow it, it will also identify statistical biases in the responses. The project team will have the equally important task of trying to understand the sources of variability in judgments by examining responses to the questionnaire in which participants explained their reasoning and identified the facts that most influenced their decisions. Focusing mainly on extreme responses at both ends of the distribution, the team will search for patterns in the data. It will look for indications of possible deficiencies in the training of employees, the procedures of the organization, and the information that it provides to its employees.

The consultant and the internal project team will work together to develop tools and procedures that apply principles of decision hygiene and debiasing to improve the judgments and decisions made in the unit. This step of the process is likely to extend over several months. In parallel, the consultant and the professional team will also prepare a report on the project, which they will present to the leadership of the organization.

At this point, the organization will have carried out a sample noise audit in one of its units. If the effort is considered successful, the executive team may decide on a broader effort to evaluate and improve the quality of the judgments and decisions that are produced in the organization.

APPENDIX B

A Checklist for a Decision Observer

This appendix presents a generic example of a checklist to be used by a decision observer (see chapter 19). The checklist presented here roughly follows the chronological sequence of the discussion that leads to an important decision.

The suggested questions that follow each item in the checklist bring additional clarifications. Decision observers should ask themselves these questions while observing the decision process.

This checklist is not intended to be used as it stands. Rather, we hope that it will serve as an inspiration and a starting point for decision observers who will design a custom bias observation checklist of their own.

Bias Observation Checklist

1. APPROACH TO JUDGMENT
1a. Substitution
___ "Did the group's choice of evidence and the focus of their discussion indicate substitution of an easier question for the difficult one they were assigned?"

___ "Did the group neglect an important factor (or appear to give weight to an irrelevant one)?"

1b. Inside view
___ "Did the group adopt the outside view for part of its deliberations and seriously attempt to apply comparative rather than absolute judgment?"

1c. Diversity of views
___ "Is there any reason to suspect that members of the group share biases, which could lead their errors to be correlated? Conversely, can you think of a relevant point of view or expertise that is not represented in this group?

2. PREJUDGMENTS AND PREMATURE CLOSURE
2a. Initial prejudgments
___ "Do (any of) the decision makers stand to gain more from one conclusion than another?"

___ "Was anyone already committed to a conclusion? Is there any reason to suspect prejudice?"

___ "Did dissenters express their views?"

___ "Is there a risk of escalating commitment to a losing course of action?"

2b. Premature closure; excessive coherence
___ "Was there accidental bias in the choice of considerations that were discussed early?"

___ "Were alternatives fully considered, and was evidence that would support them actively sought?"

___ "Were uncomfortable data or opinions suppressed or neglected?"

3. INFORMATION PROCESSING

3a. Availability and salience

___ "Are the participants exaggerating the relevance of an event because of its recency, its dramatic quality, or its personal relevance, even if it is not diagnostic?"

3b. Inattention to quality of information

___ "Did the judgment rely heavily on anecdotes, stories, or analogies? Did the data confirm them?"

3c. Anchoring

___ "Did numbers of uncertain accuracy or relevance play an important role in the final judgment?"

3d. Nonregressive prediction

___ "Did the participants make nonregressive extrapolations, estimates, or forecasts?"

4. DECISION

4a. Planning fallacy

___ "When forecasts were used, did people question their sources and validity? Was the outside view used to challenge the forecasts?"

___ "Were confidence intervals used for uncertain numbers? Are they wide enough?"

4b. Loss aversion

___ "Is the risk appetite of the decision makers aligned with that of the organization? Is the decision team overly cautious?"

4c. Present bias

___ "Do the calculations (including the discount rate used) reflect the organization's balance of short- and long-term priorities?"

APPENDIX C

Correcting Predictions

Matching predictions are errors caused by our reliance on the intuitive matching process (see chapter 14). We make matching predictions when we rely on the information we have to make a forecast and behave as if this information were perfectly (or very highly) predictive of the outcome.

Recall the example of Julie, who could "read fluently when she was four years old." The question was, what is her GPA? If you predicted 3.8 for Julie's college GPA, you intuitively judged that the four-year-old Julie was in the top 10% of her age group by reading age (although not in the top 3–5%). You then, implicitly, assumed that Julie would also rank somewhere around the 90th percentile of her class in terms of GPA. This corresponds to a GPA of 3.7 or 3.8 — hence the popularity of these answers.

What makes this reasoning statistically incorrect is that it grossly overstates the diagnostic value of the information available about Julie. A precocious four-year-old does not always become an academic overachiever (and, fortunately, a child who initially struggles with reading will not languish at the bottom of the class forever).

More often than not, in fact, outstanding performance will

become less outstanding. Conversely, very poor performance will improve. It is easy to imagine social, psychological, or even political reasons for this observation, but reasons are not required. The phenomenon is purely statistical. Extreme observations in one direction or the other will tend to become less extreme, simply because past performance is not perfectly correlated with future performance. This tendency is called *regression to the mean* (hence the technical term *nonregressive* for matching predictions, which fail to take it into account).

To put it quantitatively, the judgment you made about Julie would be correct if reading age were a perfect predictor of GPA, that is, if there were a correlation of 1 between the two factors. That is obviously not the case.

There is a statistical way to make a judgment that is likely to be more accurate. It is nonintuitive and difficult to find, even for people with some statistical training. Here is the procedure. Figure 19 illustrates it with Julie's example.

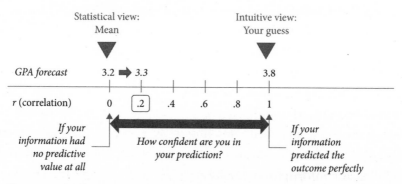

FIGURE 19: *Adjusting an intuitive prediction for regression to the mean*

1. Make your intuitive guess.

Your intuition about Julie, or about any case about which you have information, is not worthless. Your fast, system 1 thinking easily places the information you have onto the scale of your prediction and produces a GPA score for Julie. This guess is the prediction you would make if the information you have were perfectly predictive. Write it down.

2. *Look for the mean.*

Now, step back and forget what you know about Julie for a moment. What would you say about Julie's GPA *if you knew absolutely nothing about her*? The answer, of course, is straightforward: in the absence of any information, your best guess of Julie's GPA would have to be the mean GPA in her graduating class — probably somewhere around 3.2.

Looking at Julie this way is an application of the broader principle we have discussed above, the *outside view*. When we take the outside view, we think of the case we are considering as an instance of a class, and we think about that class in statistical terms. Recall, for instance, how taking the outside view about the Gambardi problem leads us to ask what the base rate of success is for a new CEO (see chapter 4).

3. *Estimate the diagnostic value of the information you have.*

This is the difficult step, where you need to ask yourself, "What is the predictive value of the information I have?" The reason this question matters should be clear by now. If all you knew about Julie was her shoe size, you would correctly give this information zero weight and stick to the mean GPA prediction. If, on the other hand, you had the list of grades Julie has obtained in every subject, this information would be perfectly predictive of her GPA (which is their average). There are many shades of gray between these two extremes. If you had data about Julie's exceptional intellectual achievements in high school, this information would be much more diagnostic than her reading age, but less than her college grades.

Your task here is to quantify the diagnostic value of the data you have, expressed as a correlation with the outcome you are predicting. Except in rare cases, this number will have to be a back-of-the-envelope estimate.

To make a sensible estimate, remember some of the examples we listed in chapter 12. In the social sciences, correlations of more than

.50 are very rare. Many correlations that we recognize as meaningful are in the .20 range. In Julie's case, a correlation of .20 is probably an upper bound.

4. *Adjust from the outside view in the direction of your intuitive guess, to an extent that reflects the diagnostic value of the information you have.*

The final step is a simple arithmetic combination of the three numbers you have now produced: you must adjust from the mean, in the direction of your intuitive guess, in proportion to the correlation you have estimated.

This step simply extends the observation we have just made: if the correlation were 0, you would stick to the mean; if it were 1, you would disregard the mean and happily make a matching prediction. In Julie's case, then, the best prediction you can make of GPA is one that lies no more than 20% of the way from the mean of the class in the direction of the intuitive estimate that her reading age suggested to you. This computation leads you to a prediction of about 3.3.

We have used Julie's example, but this method can be applied just as easily to many of the judgment problems we have discussed in this book. Consider, for instance, a vice president of sales who is hiring a new salesperson and has just had an interview with an absolutely outstanding candidate. Based on this strong impression, the executive estimates that the candidate should book sales of $1 million in the first year on the job — twice the mean amount achieved by new hires during their first year on the job. How could the vice president make this estimate regressive? The calculation depends on the diagnostic value of the interview. How well does a recruiting interview predict on-the-job success in this case? Based on the evidence we have reviewed, a correlation of .40 is a very generous estimate. Accordingly, a regressive estimate of the new hire's first-year sales would be, at most, $500K + ($1 million − $500K) × .40 = $700K.

This process, again, is not at all intuitive. Notably, as the examples illustrate, corrected predictions will always be more conservative than intuitive ones: they will never be as extreme as intuitive predictions, but instead closer, often *much* closer, to the mean. If you correct your predictions, you will never bet that the tennis champion who has won ten Grand Slam titles will win another ten. Neither will you foresee that a highly successful start-up worth $1 billion will become a behemoth worth several hundred times that. Corrected predictions do not take bets on outliers.

This means that, in hindsight, corrected predictions will inevitably result in some highly visible failures. However, prediction is not done in hindsight. You should remember that outliers are, by definition, extremely rare. The opposite error is much more frequent: when we predict that outliers will remain outliers, they generally don't, because of regression to the mean. That is why, whenever the aim is to maximize accuracy (i.e., minimize MSE), corrected predictions are superior to intuitive, matching predictions.

Acknowledgments

We have many people to thank. Linnea Gandhi has served as our chief of staff, offering substantive guidance and help, keeping us organized, making us smile and laugh, and basically running the show. Aside from all that, she offered numerous valuable suggestions on the manuscript. We couldn't have done it without her. Dan Lovallo played a major part by coauthoring one of the articles that seeded this book. John Brockman, our agent, was enthusiastic, hopeful, sharp, and wise at every stage. We are grateful to him. Tracy Behar, our principal editor and guide, made the book better in ways large and small. Arabella Pike and Ian Straus also provided superb editorial suggestions.

Special thanks too to Oren Bar-Gill, Maya Bar-Hillel, Max Bazerman, Tom Blaser, David Budescu, Jeremy Clifton, Anselm Dannecker, Vera Delaney, Itiel Dror, Angela Duckworth, Annie Duke, Dan Gilbert, Adam Grant, Anupam Jena, Louis Kaplow, Gary Klein, Jon Kleinberg, Nathan Kuncel, Kelly Leonard, Daniel Levin, Sara McLanahan, Barbara Mellers, Josh Miller, Sendhil Mullainathan, Scott Page, Eric Posner, Lucia Reisch, Matthew Salganik, Eldar Shafir, Tali Sharot, Philip Tetlock, Richard Thaler, Barbara Tversky,

Peter Ubel, Crystal Wang, Duncan Watts, and Caroline Webb, who read and commented on draft chapters, and in some cases a draft of the full text. We are grateful for their generosity and help.

We were lucky to benefit from the advice of many great researchers. Julian Parris offered invaluable help on many statistical issues. Our chapters on the achievements of machine learning would not have been possible without Sendhil Mullainathan, Jon Kleinberg, Jens Ludwig, Gregory Stoddard, and Hye Chang. And our discussion of the consistency of judgment owes a lot to Alex Todorov and his Princeton colleagues Joel Martinez, Brandon Labbree, and Stefan Uddenberg, as well as Scott Highhouse and Alison Broadfoot. These amazing teams of researchers not only graciously shared their insights but were kind enough to run special analyses for us. Of course, any misunderstandings or errors are our responsibility. In addition, we thank Laszlo Bock, Bo Cowgill, Jason Dana, Dan Goldstein, Harold Goldstein, Brian Hoffman, Alan Krueger, Michael Mauboussin, Emily Putnam-Horstein, Charles Scherbaum, Anne-Laure Sellier, and Yuichi Shoda for sharing their expertise.

We are also thankful to a veritable army of researchers over the years, including Shreya Bhardwaj, Josie Fisher, Rohit Goyal, Nicole Grabel, Andrew Heinrich, Meghann Johnson, Sophie Mehta, Eli Nachmany, William Ryan, Evelyn Shu, Matt Summers, and Noam Ziv-Crispel. Many of the discussions here involve substantive areas in which we lack expertise, and because of their excellent work, the book has less bias, and less noise, than it otherwise would have.

Finally, collaborating as a three-author, two-continent team is challenging at the best of times, and the year 2020 was not the best of times. We would not have finished this book without the technological magic of Dropbox and Zoom. We are thankful to the people behind these great products.

Notes

INTRODUCTION

4. *The targets illustrate:* Using bows and arrows rather than guns, Swiss mathematician Daniel Bernoulli offered the same analogy in 1778 in an essay on problems of estimation. Bernoulli, "The Most Probable Choice Between Several Discrepant Observations and the Formation Therefrom of the Most Likely Induction," *Biometrika* 48, no. 1–2 (June 1961): 3–18, https://doi.org/10.1093/biomet/48.1-2.3.

6. *Child custody decisions:* Joseph J. Doyle Jr., "Child Protection and Child Outcomes: Measuring the Effects of Foster Care," *American Economic Review* 95, no. 5 (December 2007): 1583–1610.

6. *the same software developers:* Stein Grimstad and Magne Jørgensen, "Inconsistency of Expert Judgment-Based Estimates of Software Development Effort," *Journal of Systems and Software* 80, no. 11 (2007): 1770–1777.

6. *Asylum decisions:* Andrew I. Schoenholtz, Jaya Ramji-Nogales, and Philip G. Schrag, "Refugee Roulette: Disparities in Asylum Adjudication," *Stanford Law Review* 60, no. 2 (2007).

7. *Decisions to grant patents:* Mark A. Lemley and Bhaven Sampat, "Examiner Characteristics and Patent Office Outcomes," *Review of Economics and Statistics* 94, no. 3 (2012): 817–827. See also Iain Cockburn, Samuel Kortum, and Scott Stern, "Are All Patent Examiners Equal? The Impact of Examiner Characteristics," working paper 8980, June 2002, www.nber.org/papers/w8980; and Michael D. Frakes and Melissa F. Wasserman, "Is the Time Allocated to Review

Patent Applications Inducing Examiners to Grant Invalid Patents? Evidence from Microlevel Application Data," *Review of Economics and Statistics* 99, no. 3 (July 2017): 550–563.

CHAPTER 1

14. *described his motivation:* Marvin Frankel, *Criminal Sentences: Law Without Order,* 25 Inst. for Sci. Info. Current Contents / Soc. & Behavioral Scis.: This Week's Citation Classic 14, 2A-6 (June 23, 1986), available at http://www.garfield.library.upenn.edu/classics1986/A1986C697400001.pdf.

14. *"almost wholly unchecked":* Marvin Frankel, *Criminal Sentences: Law Without Order* (New York: Hill and Wang, 1973), 5.

14. *"arbitrary cruelties perpetrated daily":* Frankel, *Criminal Sentences,* 103.

15. *"government of laws, not of men":* Frankel, 5.

15. *"idiosyncratic ukases":* Frankel, 11.

15. *"some form of numerical or other objective grading":* Frankel, 114.

15. *"computers as an aid":* Frankel, 115.

15. *a commission on sentencing:* Frankel, 119.

15. *"absence of consensus was the norm":* Anthony Partridge and William B. Eldridge, *The Second Circuit Sentence Study: A Report to the Judges of the Second Circuit August 1974* (Washington, DC: Federal Judicial Center, August 1974), 9.

16. *"astounding":* US Senate, "Comprehensive Crime Control Act of 1983: Report of the Committee on the Judiciary, United States Senate, on S. 1762, Together with Additional and Minority Views" (Washington, DC: US Government Printing Office, 1983). Report No. 98-225.

16. *A heroin dealer:* Anthony Partridge and Eldridge, *Second Circuit Sentence Study,* A-11.

16. *a bank robber:* Partridge and Eldridge, *Second Circuit Sentence Study,* A-9.

16. *an extortion case:* Partridge and Eldridge, A-5–A-7

16. *a survey of forty-seven judges:* William Austin and Thomas A. Williams III, "A Survey of Judges' Responses to Simulated Legal Cases: Research Note on Sentencing Disparity," *Journal of Criminal Law & Criminology* 68 (1977): 306.

16. *A much larger study:* John Bartolomeo et al., "Sentence Decisionmaking: The Logic of Sentence Decisions and the Extent and Sources of Sentence Disparity," *Journal of Criminal Law and Criminology* 72, no. 2 (1981). (See chapter 6 for a full discussion.) See also Senate Report, 44.

17. *If judges are hungry:* Shai Danziger, Jonathan Levav, and Liora Avnaim-Pesso, "Extraneous Factors in Judicial Decisions," *Proceedings of the National Academy of Sciences of the United States of America* 108, no. 17 (2011): 6889-92.

17. *juvenile court decisions:* Ozkan Eren and Naci Mocan, "Emotional Judges and

Unlucky Juveniles," *American Economic Journal: Applied Economics* 10, no. 3 (2018): 171–205.

17. *more severe on days that follow a loss:* Daniel L. Chen and Markus Loecher, "Mood and the Malleability of Moral Reasoning: The Impact of Irrelevant Factors on Judicial Decisions," *SSRN Electronic Journal* (September 21, 2019): 1–70, http://users.nber.org/dlchen/papers/Mood_and_the_Malleability _of_Moral_Reasoning.pdf.

17. *more leniency on their birthday:* Daniel L. Chen and Arnaud Philippe, "Clash of Norms: Judicial Leniency on Defendant Birthdays," (2020) available at SSRN: https://ssrn.com/abstract=3203624.

17. *something as irrelevant as outside temperature:* Anthony Heyes and Soodeh Saberian, "Temperature and Decisions: Evidence from 207,000 Court Cases," *American Economic Journal: Applied Economics* 11, no. 2 (2018): 238–265.

18. *"the unfettered discretion":* Senate Report, 38.

18. *"unjustifiably wide" sentencing disparity:* Senate Report, 38.

18. *the use of past practice:* Justice Breyer is quoted in Jeffrey Rosen, "Breyer Restraint," *New Republic*, July 11, 1994, at 19, 25.

19. *departures must be justified:* United States Sentencing Commission, Guidelines Manual (2018), www.ussc.gov/sites/default/files/pdf/guidelines-manual /2018/GLMFull.pdf.

19. *"reduced the net variation":* James M. Anderson, Jeffrey R. Kling, and Kate Stith, "Measuring Interjudge Sentencing Disparity: Before and After the Federal Sentencing Guidelines," *Journal of Law and Economics* 42, no. S1 (April 1999): 271–308.

19. *the commission itself:* US Sentencing Commission, *The Federal Sentencing Guidelines: A Report on the Operation of the Guidelines System and Short-Term Impacts on Disparity in Sentencing, Use of Incarceration, and Prosecutorial Discretion and Plea Bargaining,* vols. 1 & 2 (Washington, DC: US Sentencing Commission, 1991).

19. *According to another study:* Anderson, Kling, and Stith, "Interjudge Sentencing Disparity."

19. *An independent study:* Paul J. Hofer, Kevin R. Blackwell, and R. Barry Ruback, "The Effect of the Federal Sentencing Guidelines on Inter-Judge Sentencing Disparity," *Journal of Criminal Law and Criminology* 90 (1999): 239, 241.

20. *"the need is not for blindness…":* Kate Stith and José Cabranes, *Fear of Judging: Sentencing Guidelines in the Federal Courts* (Chicago: University of Chicago Press, 1998), 79.

20. *the Supreme Court struck the guidelines down:* 543 U.S. 220 (2005).

20. *Seventy-five percent preferred the advisory regime:* US Sentencing Commission,

"Results of Survey of United States District Judges, January 2010 through March 2010" (June 2010) (question 19, table 19), www.ussc.gov/sites/default/files/pdf /research-and-publications/research-projects-and-surveys/surveys/20100608 _Judge_Survey.pdf.

20. *"findings raise..."*: Crystal Yang, "Have Interjudge Sentencing Disparities Increased in an Advisory Guidelines Regime? Evidence from Booker," *New York University Law Review* 89 (2014): 1268–1342; pp. 1278, 1334.

CHAPTER 2

26. *To prepare for the noise audit:* Executives of the company constructed detailed descriptions of representative cases, similar to the risks and claims that employees dealt with every day. Six cases were prepared for claims adjusters in the Property and Casualty Division, and four for underwriters specializing in financial risk. The employees were given half a day off from their regular workload to evaluate two or three cases each. They were instructed to work independently and were not told that the purpose of the study was to examine the variability of their judgments. Altogether, we obtained eight-six judgments from forty-eight underwriters and one hundred thirteen judgments from sixty-eight claims adjusters.

31. *naive realism:* Dale W. Griffin and Lee Ross, "Subjective Construal, Social Inference, and Human Misunderstanding," *Advances in Experimental Social Psychology* 24 (1991): 319–359; Robert J. Robinson, Dacher Keltner, Andrew Ward, and Lee Ross, "Actual Versus Assumed Differences in Construal: 'Naive Realism' in Intergroup Perception and Conflict," *Journal of Personality and Social Psychology* 68, no. 3 (1995): 404; and Lee Ross and Andrew Ward, "Naive Realism in Everyday Life: Implications for Social Conflict and Misunderstanding," *Values and Knowledge* (1997).

PART 2

41. *the most common measure of variability:* The standard deviation of a set of numbers is derived from another statistical quantity, called the *variance.* To compute the variance, we first obtain the distribution of deviations from the mean and then take the square of each of these deviations. Variance is the mean of these squared deviations, and the standard deviation is the square root of the variance.

CHAPTER 4

44. *Judges at wine competitions:* R. T. Hodgson, "An Examination of Judge Reliability at a Major U.S. Wine Competition," *Journal of Wine Economics* 3, no. 2 (2008): 105–113.

52. *trade-offs are resolved by evaluative judgments:* Some students of decision making define decisions as choices between options and view quantitative judgments as a special case of decision, in which there is a continuum of possible choices. In that view, judgments are a special case of decision. Our approach here is different: we view decisions that call for a choice between options as stemming from an underlying evaluative judgment about each option. That is, we regard decisions as a special case of judgment.

CHAPTER 5

59. *invented in 1795:* The method of least squares was first published by Adrien-Marie Legendre in 1805. Gauss claimed that he had first used it ten years earlier, and he later linked it to the development of a theory of error and to the normal error curve that bears his name. The priority dispute has been much discussed, and historians are inclined to believe Gauss's claim (Stephen M. Stigler, "Gauss and the Invention of Least Squares," *Annals of Statistics* 9 [1981]: 465–474; and Stephen M. Stigler, *The History of Statistics: The Measurement of Uncertainty Before 1900* [Cambridge, MA: Belknap Press of Harvard University Press, 1986]).

62. *Using some simple algebra:* We have defined *noise* as the standard deviation of errors; therefore noise squared is the variance of errors. The definition of *variance* is "the mean of the squares minus the square of the mean." Since the mean error is bias, "the square of the mean" is bias squared. Therefore: $\text{Noise}^2 = \text{MSE} - \text{Bias}^2$.

65. *intuitions in this regard:* Berkeley J. Dietvorst and Soaham Bharti, "People Reject Algorithms in Uncertain Decision Domains Because They Have Diminishing Sensitivity to Forecasting Error," *Psychological Science* 31, no. 10 (2020): 1302–1314.

CHAPTER 6

69. *an exceptionally detailed study:* Kevin Clancy, John Bartolomeo, David Richardson, and Charles Wellford, "Sentence Decisionmaking: The Logic of Sentence Decisions and the Extent and Sources of Sentence Disparity," *Journal of Criminal Law and Criminology* 72, no. 2 (1981): 524–554; and INSLAW, Inc. et al., "Federal Sentencing: Towards a More Explicit Policy of Criminal Sanctions III-4," (1981).

70. *asked to set a sentence:* the sentence could include any combination of prison time, supervised time, and fines. For simplicity, we focus here mostly on the main component of the sentences — the prison time — and leave aside the other two components.

71. *This variance is what is often…:* In a multiple-case, multiple-judge setting, the

extended version of the error equation we introduced in chapter 5 includes a term that reflects this variance. Specifically, if we define a *grand bias* as the average error over all cases, and if this error is not identical across cases, there will be a variance of case biases. The equation becomes: MSE = Grand Bias^2 + Variance of Case Biases + System Noise^2.

71. *The average prison term:* The numbers mentioned in this chapter are derived from the original study as follows.

First, the authors report the main effect of the *offense and offender* as accounting for 45% of the total variance (John Bartolomeo et al., "Sentence Decision-making: The Logic of Sentence Decisions and the Extent and Sources of Sentence Disparity," *Journal of Criminal Law and Criminology* 72, no. 2 [1981], table 6). However, we are concerned here more broadly with the effect of each case, including all the features presented to the judges — such as whether the defendant had a criminal record or whether a weapon was used in the commission of the crime. By our definition, all these features are part of *true case variance*, not noise. Accordingly, we reintegrated interactions between features of each case in the case variance (these account for 11% of total variance; see Bartolomeo et al., table 10). As a result, we redefine the shares of case variance as 56%, judge main effect (level noise) as 21%, and interactions in total variance as 23%. System noise is therefore 44% of total variance.

The variance of just sentences can be computed from Bartolomeo et al., 89, in the table listing mean sentences for each case: the variance is 15. If this is 56 % of total variance, then total variance is 26.79 and the variance of system noise is 11.79. The square root of that variance is the standard deviation for a representative case, or 3.4 years.

Judge main effect, or level noise, is 21% of total variance. The square root of that variance is the standard deviation that is attributable to judge level noise, or 2.4 years.

72. *3.4 years:* This value is the square root of the average of the variances of sentences for the sixteen cases. We calculated it as explained in the preceding note.

75. *simple, additive logic:* The additivity hypothesis effectively assumes that the harshness of a judge adds a constant amount of prison time. This hypothesis is unlikely to be correct: the harshness of the judge is more likely to add an amount that is proportional to the average sentence. This issue was ignored in the original report, which provides no way of assessing its importance.

76. *"Patterned differences between judges":* Bartolomeo et al., "Sentence Decision-making," 23.

76. *approximately equally:* The following equation holds: (System Noise)^2 = (Level

Noise)^2 + (Pattern Noise)^2. The table shows that system noise is 3.4 years and level noise is 2.4 years. It follows that pattern noise is also about 2.4 years. The calculation is shown as an illustration — the actual values are slightly different because of rounding errors.

CHAPTER 7

79. *The all-time best:* See http://www.iweblists.com/sports/basketball/FreeThrow Percent_c.html, consulted Dec. 27, 2020.

79. *Shaquille O'Neal:* See https://www.basketball-reference.com/players/o/onealsh01 .html, consulted Dec. 27, 2020.

80. *wine experts:* R. T. Hodgson, "An Examination of Judge Reliability at a Major U.S. Wine Competition," *Journal of Wine Economics* 3, no. 2 (2008): 105–113.

80. *software consultants:* Stein Grimstad and Magne Jørgensen, "Inconsistency of Expert Judgment-Based Estimates of Software Development Effort," *Journal of Systems and Software* 80, no. 11 (2007): 1770–1777.

82. *agree with themselves:* Robert H. Ashton, "A Review and Analysis of Research on the Test–Retest Reliability of Professional Judgment," *Journal of Behavioral Decision Making* 294, no. 3 (2000): 277–294. Incidentally, the author then noted that not a single one of the forty-one studies he reviewed was designed to evaluate occasion noise: "In all cases, the measurement of reliability was a by-product of some other research objectives" (Ashton, 279). This comment suggests that the interest in studying occasion noise is relatively recent.

83. *correct answer:* Central Intelligence Agency, *The World Factbook* (Washington, DC: Central Intelligence Agency, 2020). The figure cited includes all airports or airfields recognizable from the air. The runway or runways may be paved or unpaved and may include closed or abandoned installations.

83. *Edward Vul and Harold Pashler:* Edward Vul and Harold Pashler, "Crowd Within: Probabilistic Representations Within Individuals,"

83. *closer to the truth:* James Surowiecki, *The Wisdom of Crowds: Why the Many Are Smarter Than the Few and How Collective Wisdom Shapes Business, Economies, Societies, and Nations* (New York: Doubleday, 2004).

84. *less noisy:* The standard deviation of the averaged judgments (our measure of noise) decreases in proportion to the square root of the number of judgments.

84. *"You can gain":* Vul and Pashler, "Crowd Within," 646.

84. *Stefan Herzog and Ralph Hertwig:* Stefan M. Herzog and Ralph Hertwig, "Think Twice and Then: Combining or Choosing in Dialectical Bootstrapping?," *Journal*

of Experimental Psychology: Learning, Memory, and Cognition 40, no. 1 (2014): 218–232.

85. *"Responses made":* Vul and Pashler, "Measuring the Crowd Within," 647.

86. *Joseph Forgas:* Joseph P. Forgas, "Affective Influences on Interpersonal Behavior," *Psychological Inquiry* 13, no. 1 (2002): 1–28.

86. *"The same smile…":* Forgas, "Affective Influences," 10.

87. *negotiators who shift:* A. Filipowicz, S. Barsade, and S. Melwani, "Understanding Emotional Transitions: The Interpersonal Consequences of Changing Emotions in Negotiations," *Journal of Personality and Social Psychology* 101, no. 3 (2011): 541–556.

87. *participants read a short philosophical essay:* Joseph P. Forgas, "She Just Doesn't Look like a Philosopher…? Affective Influences on the Halo Effect in Impression Formation," *European Journal of Social Psychology* 41, no. 7 (2011): 812–817.

87. *pseudo-profound statements:* Gordon Pennycook, James Allan Cheyne, Nathaniel Barr, Derek J. Koehler, and Jonathan A. Fugelsang, "On the Reception and Detection of Pseudo-Profound Bullshit," *Judgment and Decision Making* 10, no. 6 (2015): 549–563.

87–88. On Bullshit: Harry Frankfurt, *On Bullshit* (Princeton, NJ: Princeton University Press, 2005).

88. *"seemingly impressive assertions":* Pennycook et al., "Pseudo-Profound Bullshit," 549.

88. *more gullible:* Joseph P. Forgas, "Happy Believers and Sad Skeptics? Affective Influences on Gullibility," *Current Directions in Psychological Science* 28, no. 3 (2019): 306–313.

88. *eyewitnesses:* Joseph P. Forgas, "Mood Effects on Eyewitness Memory: Affective Influences on Susceptibility to Misinformation," *Journal of Experimental Social Psychology* 41, no. 6 (2005): 574–588.

88. *footbridge problem:* Piercarlo Valdesolo and David Desteno, "Manipulations of Emotional Context Shape Moral Judgment," *Psychological Science* 17, no. 6 (2006): 476–477.

89. *opioids at the end of a long day:* Hannah T. Neprash and Michael L. Barnett, "Association of Primary Care Clinic Appointment Time with Opioid Prescribing," *JAMA Network Open* 2, no. 8 (2019); Lindsey M. Philpot, Bushra A. Khokhar, Daniel L. Roellinger, Priya Ramar, and Jon O. Ebbert, "Time of Day Is Associated with Opioid Prescribing for Low Back Pain in Primary Care," *Journal of General Internal Medicine* 33 (2018): 1828.

89. *antibiotics:* Jeffrey A. Linder, Jason N. Doctor, Mark W. Friedberg, Harry Reyes Nieva, Caroline Birks, Daniella Meeker, and Craig R. Fox, "Time of Day and the

Decision to Prescribe Antibiotics," *JAMA Internal Medicine* 174, no. 12 (2014): 2029–2031.

89. *flu shots:* Rebecca H. Kim, Susan C. Day, Dylan S. Small, Christopher K. Snider, Charles A. L. Rareshide, and Mitesh S. Patel, "Variations in Influenza Vaccination by Clinic Appointment Time and an Active Choice Intervention in the Electronic Health Record to Increase Influenza Vaccination," *JAMA Network Open* 1, no. 5 (2018): 1–10.

90. *Bad weather:* For comment on improved memory, see Joseph P. Forgas, Liz Goldenberg, and Christian Unkelbach, "Can Bad Weather Improve Your Memory? An Unobtrusive Field Study of Natural Mood Effects on Real-Life Memory," *Journal of Experimental Social Psychology* 45, no. 1 (2008): 254–257. For comment on sunshine, see David Hirshleifer and Tyler Shumway, "Good Day Sunshine: Stock Returns and the Weather," *Journal of Finance* 58, no. 3 (2003): 1009–1032.

90. *"Clouds Make Nerds Look Good":* Uri Simonsohn, "Clouds Make Nerds Look Good: Field Evidence of the Impact of Incidental Factors on Decision Making," *Journal of Behavioral Decision Making* 20, no. 2 (2007): 143–152.

90. *gambler's fallacy:* Daniel Chen et al., "Decision Making Under the Gambler's Fallacy: Evidence from Asylum Judges, Loan Officers, and Baseball Umpires," *Quarterly Journal of Economics* 131, no. 3 (2016): 1181–1242.

91. *grant asylum:* Jaya Ramji-Nogales, Andrew I. Schoenholtz, and Philip Schrag, "Refugee Roulette: Disparities in Asylum Adjudication," *Stanford Law Review* 60, no. 2 (2007).

91. *memory performance:* Michael J. Kahana et al., "The Variability Puzzle in Human Memory," *Journal of Experimental Psychology: Learning, Memory, and Cognition* 44, no. 12 (2018): 1857–1863.

CHAPTER 8

95. *study of music downloads:* Matthew J. Salganik, Peter Sheridan Dodds, and Duncan J. Watts, "Experimental Study of Inequality and Unpredictability in an Artificial Cultural Market," *Science* 311 (2006): 854–856. See also Matthew Salganik and Duncan Watts, "Leading the Herd Astray: An Experimental Study of Self-Fulfilling Prophecies in an Artificial Cultural Market," *Social Psychology Quarterly* 71 (2008): 338–355; and Matthew Salganik and Duncan Watts, "Web-Based Experiments for the Study of Collective Social Dynamics in Cultural Markets," *Topics in Cognitive Science* 1 (2009): 439–468.

96. *popularity is self-reinforcing:* Salganik and Watts, "Leading the Herd Astray."

97. *in many other areas:* Michael Macy et al., "Opinion Cascades and the Unpredictability of Partisan Polarization," *Science Advances* (2019): 1–8. See also

Helen Margetts et al., *Political Turbulence* (Princeton: Princeton University Press, 2015).

97. *sociologist Michael Macy:* Michael Macy et al., "Opinion Cascades."

98. *comments on websites:* Lev Muchnik et al., "Social Influence Bias: A Randomized Experiment," *Science* 341, no. 6146 (2013): 647–651.

99. *Research has revealed:* Jan Lorenz et al., "How Social Influence Can Undermine the Wisdom of Crowd Effect," *Proceedings of the National Academy of Sciences* 108, no. 22 (2011): 9020–9025.

104. *an experiment that compares:* Daniel Kahneman, David Schkade, and Cass Sunstein, "Shared Outrage and Erratic Awards: The Psychology of Punitive Damages," *Journal of Risk and Uncertainty* 16 (1998): 49–86.

104. *five hundred mock juries:* David Schkade, Cass R. Sunstein, and Daniel Kahneman, "Deliberating about Dollars: The Severity Shift," *Columbia Law Review* 100 (2000): 1139–1175.

PART 3

108. *percent concordant:* percent concordant (PC) is closely related to Kendall's *W*, also known as the coefficient of concordance.

108. *height and foot size:* Kanwal Kamboj et al., "A Study on the Correlation Between Foot Length and Height of an Individual and to Derive Regression Formulae to Estimate the Height from Foot Length of an Individual," *International Journal of Research in Medical Sciences* 6, no. 2 (2018): 528.

108. *Table 1 presents the PC:* PC is calculated on the assumption that the joint distribution is bivariate-normal. The values shown in the table are approximations based on that assumption. We thank Julian Parris for producing this table.

CHAPTER 9

112. *actual study of performance prediction:* Martin C. Yu and Nathan R. Kuncel, "Pushing the Limits for Judgmental Consistency: Comparing Random Weighting Schemes with Expert Judgments," *Personnel Assessment and Decisions* 6, no. 2 (2020): 1–10. The .15 correlation achieved by experts is the unweighted average of the three samples studied, including 847 cases in total. The real study differs from this simplified description in several respects.

113. *a weighted average:* A prerequisite for constructing a weighted average is that all predictors must be measured in comparable units. This requirement was satisfied in our introductory example, where all ratings were made on a 0-to-10 scale, but this is not always the case. For example, the predictors of performance might be an interviewer's assessment on a 0-to-10 scale, the number of years of relevant experience, and a score on a test of proficiency. The multiple

regression program transforms all predictors into *standard scores* before combining them. A standard score measures the distance of an observation from the mean of a population, with the standard deviation as a unit. For example, if the mean of the proficiency test is 55 and the standard deviation is 8, a standard score of +1.5 corresponds to a test result of 67. Notably, standardization of each individual's data eliminates any trace of error in the mean or in the variance of individuals' judgments.

113. *gets a large weight:* An important feature of multiple regression is that the optimal weight for each predictor depends on the other predictors. If a predictor is highly correlated with another one, it should not get an equally large weight — this would be a form of "double counting."

113. *"the workhorse…":* Robin M. Hogarth and Natalia Karelaia, "Heuristic and Linear Models of Judgment: Matching Rules and Environments," *Psychological Review* 114, no. 3 (2007): 734.

113. *a simple structure:* A research framework that has been extensively used in this context is the *lens model of judgment,* on which this discussion is based. See Kenneth R. Hammond, "Probabilistic Functioning and the Clinical Method," *Psychological Review* 62, no. 4 (1955): 255–262; Natalia Karelaia and Robin M. Hogarth, "Determinants of Linear Judgment: A Meta-Analysis of Lens Model Studies," *Psychological Bulletin* 134, no. 3 (2008): 404–426.

114. Paul E. Meehl, *Clinical Versus Statistical Prediction: A Theoretical Analysis and a Review of the Evidence* (Minneapolis: University of Minnesota Press, 1954).

116. *A picture of Freud:* Paul E. Meehl, *Clinical Versus Statistical Prediction: A Theoretical Analysis and a Review of the Evidence* (Northvale, NJ: Aronson, 1996), preface.

116. *a polymath:* "Paul E. Meehl," in Ed Lindzey (ed.), *A History of Psychology in Autobiography,* 1989.

116. *"massive and consistent":* "Paul E. Meehl," in *A History of Psychology in Autobiography,* ed. Ed Lindzey (Washington, DC: American Psychological Association, 1989), 362.

116. *A 2000 review:* William M. Grove et al., "Clinical Versus Mechanical Prediction: A Meta-Analysis," *Psychological Assessment* 12, no. 1 (2000): 19–30.

116. *access to "private" information:* William M. Grove and Paul E. Meehl, "Comparative Efficiency of Informal (Subjective, Impressionistic) and Formal (Mechanical, Algorithmic) Prediction Procedures: The Clinical-Statistical Controversy," *Psychology, Public Policy, and Law* 2, no. 2 (1996): 293–323.

117. *In the late 1960s:* Lewis Goldberg, "Man Versus Model of Man: A Rationale, plus Some Evidence, for a Method of Improving on Clinical Inferences," *Psychological Bulletin* 73, no. 6 (1970): 422–432.

118. *nothing of the kind:* Milton Friedman and Leonard J. Savage, "The Utility Analysis of Choices Involving Risk," *Journal of Political Economy* 56, no. 4 (1948): 279–304.

118. *this correlation:* Karelaia and Hogarth, "Determinants of Linear Judgment," 411, table 1.

118. *An early replication:* Nancy Wiggins and Eileen S. Kohen, "Man Versus Model of Man Revisited: The Forecasting of Graduate School Success," *Journal of Personality and Social Psychology* 19, no. 1 (1971): 100–106.

118. *a review of fifty years:* Karelaia and Hogarth, "Determinants of Linear Judgment."

120. *improvement of your predictive accuracy:* The correction of a correlation coefficient for the imperfect reliability of the predictor is known as *correction for attenuation.* The formula is Corrected $r_{xy} = r_{xy}/\sqrt{r_{xx}}$, where r_{xx} is the reliability coefficient (the proportion of true variance in the observed variance of the predictor).

121. *A study by Martin Yu and Nathan Kuncel:* Yu and Kuncel, "Judgmental Consistency."

121. *random formulas:* We discuss equal-weight and random-weight models in greater detail in the next chapter. The weights are constrained to a range of small numbers, and they are constrained to have the right sign.

CHAPTER 10

124. *far superior to clinical judgments:* Robyn M. Dawes and Bernard Corrigan, "Linear Models in Decision Making," *Psychological Bulletin* 81, no. 2 (1974): 95–106. Dawes and Corrigan also proposed using random weights. The study of managerial performance prediction, described in chapter 9, is an application of this idea.

124. *"contrary to statistical intuition":* Jason Dana, "What Makes Improper Linear Models Tick?," in *Rationality and Social Responsibility: Essays in Honor of Robyn M. Dawes,* ed. Joachim I. Krueger, 71–89 (New York: Psychology Press, 2008), 73.

126. *Similar results:* Jason Dana and Robyn M. Dawes, "The Superiority of Simple Alternatives to Regression for Social Sciences Prediction," *Journal of Educational and Behavior Statistics* 29 (2004): 317–331; Dana, "What Makes Improper Linear Models Tick?"

126. *"It Don't Make":* Howard Wainer, "Estimating Coefficients in Linear Models: It Don't Make No Nevermind," *Psychological Bulletin* 83, no. 2 (1976): 213–217.

126. *"we do not need":* Dana, "What Makes Improper Linear Models Tick?," 72.

126. *correlation with the outcome:* Martin C. Yu and Nathan R. Kuncel, "Pushing

the Limits for Judgmental Consistency: Comparing Random Weighting Schemes with Expert Judgments," *Personnel Assessment and Decisions* 6, no. 2 (2020): 1–10. As in the previous chapter, the reported correlation is the unweighted average of the three samples studied. The comparison holds in each of the three samples: the validity of clinical expert judgment was .17, .16, and .13, and the validity of equal-weight models was .19, .33, and .22, respectively.

126. *"robust beauty":* Robyn M. Dawes, "The Robust Beauty of Improper Linear Models in Decision Making," *American Psychologist* 34, no. 7 (1979): 571–582.

127. *"The whole trick":* Dawes and Corrigan, "Linear Models in Decision Making," 105.

127. *A team of researchers:* Jongbin Jung, Conner Concannon, Ravi Shroff, Sharad Goel, and Daniel G. Goldstein, "Simple Rules to Guide Expert Classifications," *Journal of the Royal Statistical Society, Statistics in Society,* no. 183 (2020): 771–800.

128. *a separate team:* Julia Dressel and Hany Farid, "The Accuracy, Fairness, and Limits of Predicting Recidivism," *Science Advances* 4, no. 1 (2018): 1–6.

128. *only two inputs:* these two examples are linear models based on an extremely small set of variables (and, in the case of the bail model, on an approximation of the linear weights obtained by a rounding method that transforms the model into a back-of-the-envelope calculation). Another type of "improper model" is a *single-variable rule,* which considers only one predictor and ignores all others. *See* Peter M. Todd and Gerd Gigerenzer, "Précis of Simple Heuristics That Make Us Smart," *Behavioral and Brain Sciences* 23, no. 5 (2000): 727–741.

128. *well documented:* P. Gendreau, T. Little, and C. Goggin, "A Meta-Analysis of the Predictors of Adult Offender Recidivism: What Works!," *Criminology* 34 (1996).

129. *Very large data sets:* Size in this context should be understood as the ratio of the number of observations to predictors. Dawes, "Robust Beauty," suggested that it must be as high as 15 or 20 to 1 before the optimal weights do better on cross-validation than do unit weights. Dana and Dawes, "Superiority of Simple Alternatives," using many more case studies, raised the bar to a ratio of 100 to 1.

130. *another team:* J. Kleinberg, H. Lakkaraju, J. Leskovec, J. Ludwig, and S. Mullainathan, "Human Decisions and Machine Predictions," *Quarterly Journal of Economics* 133 (2018): 237–293.

130. *trained a machine-learning algorithm:* The algorithm was trained on a subset of training data and then evaluated on its ability to predict outcomes on a different, randomly chosen subset.

131. *"The machine-learning algorithm finds":* Kleinberg et al., "Human Decisions," 16.

131. *System noise included:* Gregory Stoddard, Jens Ludwig, and Sendhil Mullainathan, e-mail exchanges with the authors, June–July 2020.

132. *the recruitment of software engineers:* B. Cowgill, "Bias and Productivity in Humans and Algorithms: Theory and Evidence from Résumé Screening," paper presented at Smith Entrepreneurship Research Conference, College Park, MD, April 21, 2018.

134. *a 1996 article:* William M. Grove and Paul E. Meehl, "Comparative Efficiency of Informal (Subjective, Impressionistic) and Formal (Mechanical, Algorithmic) Prediction Procedures: The Clinical-Statistical Controversy," *Psychology, Public Policy, and Law* 2, no. 2 (1996): 293–323.

135. *prefer the algorithm:* Jennifer M. Logg, Julia A. Minson, and Don A. Moore, "Algorithm Appreciation: People Prefer Algorithmic to Human Judgment," *Organizational Behavior and Human Decision Processes* 151 (April 2018): 90–103.

135. *as soon as they see that it makes mistakes:* B. J. Dietvorst, J. P. Simmons, and C. Massey, "Algorithm Aversion: People Erroneously Avoid Algorithms After Seeing Them Err," *Journal of Experimental Psychology General* 144 (2015): 114–126. See also A. Prahl and L. Van Swol, "Understanding Algorithm Aversion: When Is Advice from Automation Discounted?," *Journal of Forecasting* 36 (2017): 691–702.

135. *If this expectation is violated:* M. T. Dzindolet, L. G. Pierce, H. P. Beck, and L. A. Dawe, "The Perceived Utility of Human and Automated Aids in a Visual Detection Task," *Human Factors: The Journal of the Human Factors and Ergonomics Society* 44, no. 1 (2002): 79–94; K. A. Hoff and M. Bashir, "Trust in Automation: Integrating Empirical Evidence on Factors That Influence Trust," *Human Factors: The Journal of the Human Factors and Ergonomics Society* 57, no. 3 (2015): 407–434; and P. Madhavan and D. A. Wiegmann, "Similarities and Differences Between Human–Human and Human–Automation Trust: An Integrative Review," *Theoretical Issues in Ergonomics Science* 8, no. 4 (2007): 277–301.

CHAPTER 11

137. *Research in managerial decision making:* E. Dane and M. G. Pratt, "Exploring Intuition and Its Role in Managerial Decision Making," *Academy of Management Review* 32, no. 1 (2007): 33–54; Cinla Akinci and Eugene Sadler-Smith, "Intuition in Management Research: A Historical Review," *International Journal of Management Reviews* 14 (2012): 104–122; and Gerard P. Hodgkinson et al., "Intuition in Organizations: Implications for Strategic Management," *Long Range Planning* 42 (2009): 277–297.

137. *One review:* Hodgkinson et al., "Intuition in Organizations," 279.

139. *a recent review:* Nathan Kuncel et al., "Mechanical Versus Clinical Data Combination in Selection and Admissions Decisions: A Meta-Analysis," *Journal of*

Applied Psychology 98, no. 6 (2013): 1060–1072. See also chapter 24 for further discussion of personnel decisions.

140. *Overconfidence:* Don A. Moore, *Perfectly Confident: How to Calibrate Your Decisions Wisely* (New York: HarperCollins, 2020).

141. *"commenting or offering advice":* Philip E. Tetlock, *Expert Political Judgment: How Good Is It? How Can We Know?* (Princeton, NJ: Princeton University Press, 2005), 239 and 233.

143. *a review of 136 studies:* William M. Grove et al., "Clinical Versus Mechanical Prediction: A Meta-Analysis," *Psychological Assessment* 12, no. 1 (2000): 19–30.

143. *heart attacks:* Sendhil Mullainathan and Ziad Obermeyer, "Who Is Tested for Heart Attack and Who Should Be: Predicting Patient Risk and Physician Error," 2019. NBER Working Paper 26168, National Bureau of Economic Research.

145. *in situations that they perceive as highly uncertain:* Weston Agor, "The Logic of Intuition: How Top Executives Make Important Decisions," *Organizational Dynamics* 14, no. 3 (1986): 5–18; Lisa A. Burke and Monica K. Miller, "Taking the Mystery Out of Intuitive Decision Making," *Academy of Management Perspectives* 13, no. 4 (1999): 91–99.

146. *prepared to trust an algorithm:* Poornima Madhavan and Douglas A. Wiegmann, "Effects of Information Source, Pedigree, and Reliability on Operator Interaction with Decision Support Systems," *Human Factors: The Journal of the Human Factors and Ergonomics Society* 49, no. 5 (2007).

CHAPTER 12

148. *an unusual article:* Matthew J. Salganik et al., "Measuring the Predictability of Life Outcomes with a Scientific Mass Collaboration," *Proceedings of the National Academy of Sciences* 117, no. 15 (2020): 8398–8403.

150. *total sample:* this included 4,242 families, as some of the families in the Fragile Families study were excluded from this analysis for privacy reasons.

150. *correlation of .22:* To score accuracy, the competition's organizers used the same metric we introduced in part 1: mean squared error, or MSE. For ease of comparability, they also benchmarked the MSE of each model against a "useless" prediction strategy: a one-size-fits-all prediction that each individual case is not different from the mean of the training set. For convenience, we have converted their results to correlation coefficients. MSE and correlation are related by the expression $r^2 = (\text{Var}(Y) - \text{MSE}) / \text{Var}(Y)$, where Var (Y) is the variance of the outcome variable and (Var (Y) – MSE) is the variance of the predicted outcomes.

151. *An extensive review of research in social psychology:* F. D. Richard et al., "One

Hundred Years of Social Psychology Quantitatively Described," *Review of General Psychology* 7, no. 4 (2003): 331–363.

151. *A review of 708 studies:* Gilles E. Gignac and Eva T. Szodorai, "Effect Size Guidelines for Individual Differences Researchers," *Personality and Individual Differences* 102 (2016): 74–78.

152. *"Researchers must reconcile":* One caveat is in order. By design, this study uses an existing descriptive data set, which is very large, but not specifically tailored to predict specific outcomes. This is an important difference with the experts in Tetlock's study, who were free to use any information they saw fit. It may be possible, for instance, to identify predictors of eviction that are not in the database but that could conceivably be collected. Hence, the study does not prove how *intrinsically* unpredictable evictions and other outcomes are but how unpredictable they are *based on this data set,* which is used by numerous social scientists.

152. *a causal chain:* Jake M. Hofman et al., "Prediction and Explanation in Social Systems," *Science* 355 (2017): 486–488; Duncan J. Watts et al., "Explanation, Prediction, and Causality: Three Sides of the Same Coin?," October 2018, 1–14, available through Center for Open Science, https://osf.io/bgwjc.

154. *comes more naturally to our minds:* A closely related distinction contrasts *extensional* from *non-extensional,* or *intentional,* thinking. Amos Tversky and Daniel Kahneman, "Extensional Versus Intuitive Reasoning: The Conjunction Fallacy in Probability Judgment," *Psychological Review* 4 (1983): 293–315.

155. *backward-looking:* Daniel Kahneman and Dale T. Miller, "Norm Theory: Comparing Reality to Its Alternatives," *Psychological Review* 93, no. 2 (1986): 136–153.

156. *classic research on hindsight:* Baruch Fischhoff, "An Early History of Hindsight Research," *Social Cognition* 25, no. 1 (2007): 10–13, doi:10.1521/soco.2007.25.1.10; Baruch Fischhoff, "Hindsight Is Not Equal to Foresight: The Effect of Outcome Knowledge on Judgment Under Uncertainty," *Journal of Experimental Psychology: Human Perception and Performance* 1, no. 3 (1975): 288.

157. *System 2:* Daniel Kahneman, *Thinking, Fast and Slow.* New York: Farrar, Straus and Giroux, 2011.

Chapter 13

161. *The first four decades:* Daniel Kahneman, *Thinking, Fast and Slow* (New York: Farrar, Straus and Giroux, 2011).

163. *the evidence suggests:* A caveat is in order. Psychologists who study judgment biases are not content with five participants in each group, as shown in figure 10, for a very good reason: because judgments are noisy, the results for each experimental group will rarely cluster as closely as figure 11 suggests. People

vary in their susceptibility to each bias and do not *completely* neglect relevant variables. For example, with a very large number of participants, you could almost certainly confirm that scope insensitivity is imperfect: the average probability assigned to Gambardi's leaving the position is very slightly higher for three years than it is for two. Still, the description of scope insensitivity is appropriate because the difference is a tiny fraction of what it should be.

165. *multiple experiments:* Daniel Kahneman et al., eds., *Judgment Under Uncertainty: Heuristics and Biases* (New York: Cambridge University Press, 1982), chap. 6; Daniel Kahneman and Amos Tversky, "On the Psychology of Prediction," *Psychological Review* 80, no. 4 (1973): 237–251.

167. *estimates of CEO turnover:* See, for example, Steven N. Kaplan and Bernadette A. Minton, "How Has CEO Turnover Changed?," *International Review of Finance* 12, no. 1 (2012): 57–87. See also Dirk Jenter and Katharina Lewellen, "Performance-Induced CEO Turnover," Harvard Law School Forum on Corporate Governance, September 2, 2020, https://corpgov.law.harvard.edu/2020/09/02/performance-induced-ceo-turnover.

168. *At a key moment:* J. W. Rinzler, *The Making of Star Wars: Return of the Jedi: The Definitive Story* (New York: Del Rey, 2013), 64.

168. *development of the screenplay:* Cass Sunstein, *The World According to Star Wars* (New York: HarperCollins, 2016).

169. *selective and distorted:* We are highlighting here the simple case in which a prejudgment exists when the judgment begins. In fact, even in the absence of such a prejudgment, a bias toward a particular conclusion can develop as evidence accumulates, because of the tendency toward simplicity and coherence. As a tentative conclusion emerges, the confirmation bias tilts the collection and interpretation of new evidence in its favor.

170. *even when the reasoning:* This observation has been called the *belief bias.* See J. St. B. T. Evans, Julie L. Barson, and Paul Pollard, "On the Conflict between Logic and Belief in Syllogistic Reasoning," *Memory & Cognition* 11, no. 3 (1983): 295–306.

170. *In a typical demonstration:* Dan Ariely, George Loewenstein, and Drazen Prelec, "'Coherent Arbitrariness': Stable Demand Curves Without Stable Preferences," *Quarterly Journal of Economics* 118, no. 1 (2003): 73–105.

171. *in negotiations:* Adam D. Galinsky and T. Mussweiler, "First Offers as Anchors: The Role of Perspective-Taking and Negotiator Focus," *Journal of Personality and Social Psychology* 81, no. 4 (2001): 657–669.

172. *excessive coherence:* Solomon E. Asch, "Forming Impressions of Personality," *Journal of Abnormal and Social Psychology* 41, no. 3 (1946): 258–290, first used a series of adjectives in different orders to illustrate this phenomenon.

172. *in a revealing study:* Steven K. Dallas et al., "Don't Count Calorie Labeling Out: Calorie Counts on the Left Side of Menu Items Lead to Lower Calorie Food Choices," *Journal of Consumer Psychology* 29, no. 1 (2019): 60–69.

CHAPTER 14

178. *one intensity scale onto another:* S. S. Stevens, "On the Operation Known as Judgment," *American Scientist* 54, no. 4 (December 1966): 385–401. Our use of the term *matching* is more expansive than Stevens's which was restricted to ratio scales, to which we return in chapter 15.

179. *systematic judgment error:* The example was first introduced in Daniel Kahneman, *Thinking, Fast and Slow* (New York: Farrar, Straus and Giroux, 2011).

180. *exactly the same numbers:* Daniel Kahneman and Amos Tversky, "On the Psychology of Prediction," *Psychological Review* 80 (1973): 237–251.

183. *"The Magical Number Seven":* G. A. Miller, "The Magical Number Seven, Plus or Minus Two: Some Limits on Our Capacity for Processing Information," *Psychological Review* (1956): 63–97.

185. *scales that compel comparisons:* R. D. Goffin and J. M. Olson, "Is It All Relative? Comparative Judgments and the Possible Improvement of Self-Ratings and Ratings of Others," *Perspectives on Psychological Science* 6 (2011): 48–60.

CHAPTER 15

189. *reported in 1998:* Daniel Kahneman, David Schkade, and Cass Sunstein, "Shared Outrage and Erratic Awards: The Psychology of Punitive Damages," *Journal of Risk and Uncertainty* 16 (1998): 49–86, https://link.springer.com /article/10.1023/A:1007710408413; and Cass Sunstein, Daniel Kahneman, and David Schkade, "Assessing Punitive Damages (with Notes on Cognition and Valuation in Law)," *Yale Law Journal* 107, no. 7 (May 1998): 2071–2153. The costs of the research were covered by Exxon in a one-off arrangement, but the company did not pay the researchers and had neither control of the data nor advance knowledge of the results before publication in academic journals.

189. *"reasonable doubt":* A. Keane and P. McKeown, *The Modern Law of Evidence* (New York: Oxford University Press, 2014).

189. *"unlikely to happen":* Andrew Mauboussin and Michael J. Mauboussin, "If You Say Something Is 'Likely,' How Likely Do People Think It Is?," *Harvard Business Review,* July 3, 2018.

190. *new BMW: BMW v. Gore,* 517 U.S. 559 (1996), https://supreme.justia .com/cases/federal/us/517/559.

191. *the emotion of outrage:* For discussions of the role of emotion in moral judgments, see J. Haidt, "The Emotional Dog and Its Rational Tail: A Social

Intuitionist Approach to Moral Judgment," *Psychological Review* 108, no. 4 (2001): 814–834; Joshua Greene, *Moral Tribes: Emotion, Reason, and the Gap Between Us and Them* (New York: Penguin Press, 2014).

193. *Figure 13 shows the results:* Given the large amount of noise in these ratings, you may be puzzled by the very high correlation (.98) between outrage and punitive intent judgments, which provided the support for the outrage hypothesis. The puzzle vanishes when you recall that the correlation was computed between *averages* of judgments. For an average of 100 judgments, noise (the standard deviation of judgments) is reduced by a factor of 10. Noise ceases to be a factor when many judgments are aggregated. See chapter 21.

195. ratios *of intensity:* S. S. Stevens, *Psychophysics: Introduction to Its Perceptual, Neural and Social Prospects* (New York: John Wiley & Sons, 1975).

196. *"coherent arbitrariness":* Dan Ariely, George Loewenstein, and Drazen Prelec, " 'Coherent Arbitrariness': Stable Demand Curves Without Stable Preferences," *Quarterly Journal of Economics* 118, no. 1 (2003): 73–106.

197. *Transforming the dollar awards into rankings:* A transformation into rankings entails a loss of information, as the distances between judgments are not preserved. Suppose that there are only three cases and one juror recommends damages of $10 million, $2 million, and $1 million. Clearly, the juror intends to convey a greater difference in punitive intent between the first two cases than between the second and the third. Once converted to ranks, however, the difference will be the same—a difference of one rank only. This problem could be solved by converting the judgments into standard scores.

CHAPTER 16

202. *process in perception:* R. Blake and N. K. Logothetis, "Visual competition," *Nature Reviews Neuroscience* 3 (2002) 13–21; M. A. Gernsbacher and M. E. Faust, "The Mechanism of Suppression: A Component of General Comprehension Skill," *Journal of Experimental Psychology: Learning, Memory, and Cognition* 17 (March 1991): 245–262; and M. C. Stites and K. D. Federmeier, "Subsequent to Suppression: Downstream Comprehension Consequences of Noun/Verb Ambiguity in Natural Reading," *Journal of Experimental Psychology: Learning, Memory, and Cognition* 41 (September 2015): 1497–1515.

203. *more confident than we should be:* D. A. Moore and D. Schatz, "The three faces of overconfidence," *Social and Personality Psychology Compass* 11, no. 8 (2017), article e12331.

204. *A study of corporate reputation:* S. Highhouse, A. Broadfoot, J. E. Yugo, and S. A. Devendorf, "Examining Corporate Reputation Judgments with Generalizability Theory," *Journal of Applied Psychology* 94 (2009): 782–789. We

thank Scott Highhouse and Alison Broadfoot for providing their original data, and Julian Parris for some supplemental analyses.

205. *construct teams:* P. J. Lamberson and Scott Page, "Optimal forecasting groups," *Management Science* 58, no. 4 (2012): 805–10. We thank Scott Page for drawing our attention to this source of pattern noise.

207. *an early attempt to scan:* The work of Allport and Odbert (1936) on English personality-relevant vocabulary is cited in Oliver P. John and Sanjay Srivastava, "The Big-Five Trait Taxonomy: History, Measurement, and Theoretical Perspectives," in *Handbook of Personality: Theory and Research,* 2nd ed., ed. L. Pervin and Oliver P. John (New York: Guilford, 1999).

207. *considered high:* Ian W. Eisenberg, Patrick G. Bissett, A. Zeynep Enkavi et al., "Uncovering the structure of self-regulation through data-driven ontology discovery," *Nature Communications* 10 (2019): 2319.

208. *when physically threatened:* Walter Mischel, "Toward an integrative science of the person," *Annual Review of Psychology* 55 (2004): 1–22.

CHAPTER 17

211. *how MSE breaks down:* Whereas there is no general rule about the breakdown of bias and noise, the proportions in this figure are roughly representative of some of the examples, real or fictitious, that we have reviewed. Specifically, in this figure, bias and noise are equal (as they were in GoodSell's sales forecasts). The square of level noise accounts for 37% of the square of system noise (as it did in the punitive damages study). The square of occasion noise, as shown, is about 35% of the square of pattern noise.

213. *patent offices:* See references in introduction. Mark A. Lemley and Bhaven Sampat, "Examiner Characteristics and Patent Office Outcomes," *Review of Economics and Statistics* 94, no. 3 (2012): 817–827. See also Iain Cockburn, Samuel Kortum, and Scott Stern, "Are All Patent Examiners Equal? The Impact of Examiner Characteristics," working paper 8980, June 2002, www.nber.org /papers/w8980; and Michael D. Frakes and Melissa F. Wasserman, "Is the Time Allocated to Review Patent Applications Inducing Examiners to Grant Invalid Patents? Evidence from Microlevel Application Data," *Review of Economics and Statistics* 99, no. 3 (July 2017): 550–563.

213. *child protection services:* Joseph J. Doyle Jr., "Child Protection and Child Outcomes: Measuring the Effects of Foster Care," *American Economic Review* 95, no. 5 (December 2007): 1583–1610.

213. *asylum judges:* Andrew I. Schoenholtz, Jaya Ramji-Nogales, and Philip G. Schrag, "Refugee Roulette: Disparities in Asylum Adjudication," *Stanford Law Review* 60, no. 2 (2007).

214. *about 2.8 years:* This value is estimated from calculations presented in chapter 6, where the interaction variance is 23% of total variance. On the assumption that sentences are normally distributed, the mean absolute difference between two randomly selected observations is 1.128 SD.

214. *A group of researchers at Princeton:* J. E. Martinez, B. Labbree, S. Uddenberg, and A. Todorov, "Meaningful 'noise': Comparative judgments contain stable idiosyncratic contributions" (unpublished ms.).

215. *study of bail judges:* J. Kleinberg, H. Lakkaraju, J. Leskovec, J. Ludwig, and S. Mullainathan, "Human Decisions and Machine Predictions," *Quarterly Journal of Economics* 133 (2018): 237–293.

215. *applied the simulated judges:* The model produced for each judge both an ordering of the 141,833 cases and a threshold beyond which bail would be granted. Level noise reflects the variability of the thresholds, while pattern noise reflects variability in the ordering of cases.

216. *stable pattern noise:* Gregory Stoddard, Jens Ludwig, and Sendhil Mullainathan, e-mail exchanges with authors, June–July 2020.

219. *Phil Rosenzweig has convincingly argued:* Phil Rosenzweig. *Left Brain, Right Stuff: How Leaders Make Winning Decisions* (New York: PublicAffairs, 2014).

CHAPTER 18

225. *crowd is composed of more able people:* Albert E. Mannes et al., "The Wisdom of Select Crowds," *Journal of Personality and Social Psychology* 107, no. 2 (2014): 276–299; Jason Dana et al., "The Composition of Optimally Wise Crowds," *Decision Analysis* 12, no. 3 (2015): 130–143.

228. *confidence heuristic:* Briony D. Pulford, Andrew M. Colmna, Eike K. Buabang, and Eva M. Krockow, "The Persuasive Power of Knowledge: Testing the Confidence Heuristic," *Journal of Experimental Psychology: General* 147, no. 10 (2018): 1431–1444.

229. *it is associated not only:* Nathan R. Kuncel and Sarah A. Hezlett, "Fact and Fiction in Cognitive Ability Testing for Admissions and Hiring Decisions," *Current Directions in Psychological Science* 19, no. 6 (2010): 339–345.

229. *lingering misconceptions:* Kuncel and Hezlett, "Fact and Fiction."

229. *As one review put it:* Frank L. Schmidt and John Hunter, "General Mental Ability in the World of Work: Occupational Attainment and Job Performance," *Journal of Personality and Social Psychology* 86, no. 1 (2004): 162.

229. *conscientiousness and* grit: Angela L. Duckworth, David Weir, Eli Tsukayama, and David Kwok, "Who Does Well in Life? Conscientious Adults Excel in Both Objective and Subjective Success," *Frontiers in Psychology* 3 (September 2012). For grit, see Angela L. Duckworth, Christopher Peterson, Michael D. Matthews,

and Dennis Kelly, "Grit: Perseverance and Passion for Long-Term Goals," *Journal of Personality and Social Psychology* 92, no. 6 (2007): 1087–1101.

229. *fluid intelligence:* Richard E. Nisbett et al., "Intelligence: New Findings and Theoretical Developments," *American Psychologist* 67, no. 2 (2012): 130–159.

229. *"larger than most":* Schmidt and Hunter, "Occupational Attainment," 162.

230. *in the .50 range:* Kuncel and Hezlett, "Fact and Fiction."

230. *by social-science standards:* These correlations are derived from meta-analyses that correct the observed correlations for measurement error in the criterion and range restriction. There is some debate among researchers about whether these corrections overstate the predictive value of GMA. However, since these methodological debates apply to other predictors, too, experts generally agree that GMA (along with work sample tests; see chapter 24) is the best available predictor of job success. See Kuncel and Hezlett, "Fact and Fiction."

230. *almost no people with below-average GMA:* Schmidt and Hunter, "Occupational Attainment," 162.

230. *Even among the top 1%:* David Lubinski, "Exceptional Cognitive Ability: The Phenotype," *Behavior Genetics* 39, no. 4 (2009): 350–358.

231. *a 2013 study focused on the CEOs of Fortune 500 companies:* Jonathan Wai, "Investigating America's Elite: Cognitive Ability, Education, and Sex Differences," *Intelligence* 41, no. 4 (2013): 203–211.

232. *Other questions that have been proposed:* Keela S. Thomson and Daniel M. Oppenheimer, "Investigating an Alternate Form of the Cognitive Reflection Test," *Judgment and Decision Making* 11, no. 1 (2016): 99–113.

232. *Lower CRT scores are associated:* Gordon Pennycook et al., "Everyday Consequences of Analytic Thinking," *Current Directions in Psychological Science* 24, no. 6 (2015): 425–432.

232. *fall for blatantly inaccurate "fake news":* Gordon Pennycook and David G. Rand, "Lazy, Not Biased: Susceptibility to Partisan Fake News Is Better Explained by Lack of Reasoning than by Motivated Reasoning," *Cognition* 188 (June 2018): 39–50.

232. *how much people will use their smartphones:* Nathaniel Barr et al., "The Brain in Your Pocket: Evidence That Smartphones Are Used to Supplant Thinking," *Computers in Human Behavior* 48 (2015): 473–480.

232. *the propensity to use reflective:* Niraj Patel, S. Glenn Baker, and Laura D. Scherer, "Evaluating the Cognitive Reflection Test as a Measure of Intuition/Reflection, Numeracy, and Insight Problem Solving, and the Implications for Understanding Real-World Judgments and Beliefs," *Journal of Experimental Psychology: General* 148, no. 12 (2019): 2129–2153.

232. *need-for-cognition scale:* John T. Cacioppo and Richard E. Petty, "The Need for Cognition," *Journal of Personality and Social Psychology* 42, no. 1 (1982): 116–131.

233. *less susceptible to known cognitive biases:* Stephen M. Smith and Irwin P. Levin, "Need for Cognition and Choice Framing Effects," *Journal of Behavioral Decision Making* 9, no. 4 (1996): 283–290.

233. *spoiler alert:* Judith E. Rosenbaum and Benjamin K. Johnson, "Who's Afraid of Spoilers? Need for Cognition, Need for Affect, and Narrative Selection and Enjoyment," *Psychology of Popular Media Culture* 5, no. 3 (2016): 273–289.

233. *Adult Decision Making Competence scale:* Wandi Bruine De Bruin et al., "Individual Differences in Adult Decision-Making Competence," *Journal of Personality and Social Psychology* 92, no. 5 (2007): 938–956.

233. *Halpern Critical Thinking:* Heather A. Butler, "Halpern Critical Thinking Assessment Predicts Real-World Outcomes of Critical Thinking," *Applied Cognitive Psychology* 26, no. 5 (2012): 721–729.

234. *might predict forecasting ability:* Uriel Haran, Ilana Ritov, and Barbara Mellers, "The Role of Actively Open-Minded Thinking in Information Acquisition, Accuracy, and Calibration," *Judgment and Decision Making* 8, no. 3 (2013): 188–201.

234. *"actively open-minded thinking":* Haran, Ritov, and Mellers, "Role of Actively Open-Minded Thinking."

234. *a teachable skill:* J. Baron, "Why Teach Thinking? An Essay," *Applied Psychology: An International Review* 42 (1993): 191–214; J. Baron, *The Teaching of Thinking: Thinking and Deciding,* 2nd ed. (New York: Cambridge University Press, 1994), 127–148.

CHAPTER 19

236. *their central findings:* For an excellent review, see Jack B. Soll et al., "A User's Guide to Debiasing," in *The Wiley Blackwell Handbook of Judgment and Decision Making,* ed. Gideon Keren and George Wu, vol. 2 (New York: John Wiley & Sons, 2015), 684.

237. The Green Book: HM Treasury, *The Green Book: Central Government Guidance on Appraisal and Evaluation* (London: UK Crown, 2018), https://assets.publishing.service.gov.uk/government/uploads/system/uploads/attachment_data/file/685903/The_Green_Book.pdf.

237. nudges: Richard H. Thaler and Cass R. Sunstein, *Nudge: Improving Decisions about Health, Wealth, and Happiness* (New Haven, CT: Yale University Press, 2008).

238. boosting: Ralph Hertwig and Till Grüne-Yanoff, "Nudging and Boosting: Steering or Empowering Good Decisions," *Perspectives on Psychological Science* 12, no. 6 (2017).

238. *education is useful:* Geoffrey T. Fong et al., "The Effects of Statistical Training on Thinking About Everyday Problems," *Cognitive Psychology* 18, no. 3 (1986): 253–292.

238. *just as overconfident:* Willem A. Wagenaar and Gideon B. Keren, "Does the

Expert Know? The Reliability of Predictions and Confidence Ratings of Experts," *Intelligent Decision Support in Process Environments* (1986): 87–103.

239. *reduced the number of errors:* Carey K. Morewedge et al., "Debiasing Decisions: Improved Decision Making with a Single Training Intervention," *Policy Insights from the Behavioral and Brain Sciences* 2, no. 1 (2015): 129–140.

239. *applied this learning:* Anne-Laure Sellier et al., "Debiasing Training Transfers to Improve Decision Making in the Field," *Psychological Science* 30, no. 9 (2019): 1371–1379.

240. *bias blind spot:* Emily Pronin et al., "The Bias Blind Spot: Perceptions of Bias in Self Versus Others," *Personality and Social Psychology Bulletin* 28, no. 3 (2002): 369–381.

241. *biases that may have affected:* Daniel Kahneman, Dan Lovallo, and Olivier Sibony, "Before You Make That Big Decision…," *Harvard Business Review* 89, no. 6 (June 2011): 50–60.

242. *checklists have a long history:* Atul Gawande, *Checklist Manifesto: How to Get Things Right* (New York: Metropolitan Books, 2010).

242. *a simple checklist:* Office of Information and Regulatory Affairs, "Agency Checklist: Regulatory Impact Analysis," no date, www.whitehouse.gov/sites/whitehouse.gov/files/omb/inforeg/inforeg/regpol/RIA_Checklist.pdf.

242. *we have included:* This checklist is partly adapted from Daniel Kahneman et al., "Before You Make That Big Decision," *Harvard Business Review.*

242. *facilitate its adoption:* See Gawande, *Checklist Manifesto.*

CHAPTER 20

246. *"a human error":* R. Stacey, "A Report on the Erroneous Fingerprint Individualisation in the Madrid Train Bombing Case," *Journal of Forensic Identification* 54 (2004): 707–718.

248. *The FBI website:* Michael Specter, "Do Fingerprints Lie?," *The New Yorker,* May 27, 2002. Emphasis added.

249. *As Dror puts it:* I. E. Dror and R. Rosenthal, "Meta-analytically Quantifying the Reliability and Biasability of Forensic Experts," *Journal of Forensic Science* 53 (2008): 900–903.

250. *In the first study:* I. E. Dror, D. Charlton, and A. E. Péron, "Contextual Information Renders Experts Vulnerable to Making Erroneous Identifications," *Forensic Science International* 156 (2006): 74–78.

250. *In the second study:* I. E. Dror amd D. Charlton, "Why Experts Make Errors," *Journal of Forensic Identification* 56 (2006): 600–616.

250. *"expert fingerprint examiners":* I. E. Dror and S. A. Cole, "The Vision in 'Blind' Justice: Expert Perception, Judgment, and Visual Cognition in Forensic Pattern

Recognition," *Psychonomic Bulletin and Review* 17 (2010): 161–167, 165. See also I. E. Dror, "A Hierarchy of Expert Performance (HEP)," *Journal of Applied Research in Memory and Cognition* (2016): 1–6.

250. *In a separate study:* I. E. Dror et al., "Cognitive Issues in Fingerprint Analysis: Inter- and Intra-Expert Consistency and the Effect of a 'Target' Comparison," *Forensic Science International* 208 (2011): 10–17.

250. *A later, independent study:* B. T. Ulery, R. A. Hicklin, M. A. Roberts, and J. A. Buscaglia, "Changes in Latent Fingerprint Examiners' Markup Between Analysis and Comparison," *Forensic Science International* 247 (2015): 54–61.

251. *Even DNA analysis:* I. E. Dror and G. Hampikian, "Subjectivity and Bias in Forensic DNA Mixture Interpretation," *Science and Justice* 51 (2011): 204–208.

251. *Examiners often receive:* M. J. Saks, D. M. Risinger, R. Rosenthal, and W. C. Thompson, "Context Effects in Forensic Science: A Review and Application of the Science of Science to Crime Laboratory Practice in the United States," *Science Justice Journal of Forensic Science Society* 43 (2003): 77–90.

251. *the verifying examiner knows:* President's Council of Advisors on Science and Technology (PCAST), *Report to the President: Forensic Science in Criminal Courts: Ensuring Scientific Validity of Feature-Comparison Methods* (Washington, DC: Executive Office of the President, PCAST, 2016).

251. *the later investigation of the error:* Stacey, "Erroneous Fingerprint."

252. *a highly respected independent expert:* Dror and Cole, "Vision in 'Blind' Justice."

252. *bias cascades:* I. E. Dror, "Biases in Forensic Experts," *Science* 360 (2018): 243.

252. *sometimes change their minds:* Dror and Charlton, "Why Experts Make Errors."

252. *A 2012 study:* B. T. Ulery, R. A. Hicklin, J. A. Buscaglia, and M. A. Roberts, "Repeatability and Reproducibility of Decisions by Latent Fingerprint Examiners," *PLoS One* 7 (2012).

253. *the Innocence Project:* Innocence Project, "Overturning Wrongful Convictions Involving Misapplied Forensics," *Misapplication of Forensic Science* (2018): 1–7, www.innocenceproject.org/causes/misapplication-forensic-science. See also S. M. Kassin, I. E. Dror, J. Kukucka, and L. Butt, "The Forensic Confirmation Bias: Problems, Perspectives, and Proposed Solutions," *Journal of Applied Research in Memory and Cognition* 2 (2013): 42–52.

253. *an in-depth review:* PCAST, *Report to the President.*

253. *large-scale study of fingerprint:* B. T. Ulery, R. A. Hicklin, J. Buscaglia, and M. A. Roberts, "Accuracy and Reliability of Forensic Latent Fingerprint Decisions," *Proceedings of the National Academy of Sciences* 108 (2011): 7733–7738.

254. *"much higher":* (PCAST), *Report to the President*, p. 95. Emphasis in original.

254. *subsequent study conducted in Florida:* Igor Pacheco, Brian Cerchiai, and Stephanie Stoiloff, "Miami-Dade Research Study for the Reliability of the ACE-V Process: Accuracy & Precision in Latent Fingerprint Examinations," final report, Miami-Dade Police Department Forensic Services Bureau, 2014, www.ncjrs.gov/pdffiles1/nij/grants/248534.pdf.

254. *"in most casework":* B. T. Ulery, R. A. Hicklin, M. A. Roberts, and J. A. Buscaglia, "Factors Associated with Latent Fingerprint Exclusion Determinations," *Forensic Science International* 275 (2017): 65–75.

254. *far fewer false-positive identifications:* R. N. Haber and I. Haber, "Experimental Results of Fingerprint Comparison Validity and Reliability: A Review and Critical Analysis," *Science & Justice* 54 (2014): 375–389.

254–5. *"It is easier to bias":* Dror, "Hierarchy of Expert Performance," 3.

255. *"seek employment in Disneyland":* M. Leadbetter, letter to the editor, *Fingerprint World* 33 (2007): 231.

255. *"without actually altering their judgment":* L. Butt, "The Forensic Confirmation Bias: Problems, Perspectives and Proposed Solutions — Commentary by a Forensic Examiner," *Journal of Applied Research in Memory and Cognition* 2 (2013): 59–60. Emphasis added.

255. *Even the FBI:* Stacey, "Erroneous Fingerprint," 713. Emphasis added.

256. *In a survey of four hundred:* J. Kukucka, S. M. Kassin, P. A. Zapf, and I. E. Dror, "Cognitive Bias and Blindness: A Global Survey of Forensic Science Examiners," *Journal of Applied Research in Memory and Cognition* 6 (2017).

257. linear sequential unmasking: I. E. Dror et al., letter to the editor: "Context Management Toolbox: A Linear Sequential Unmasking (LSU) Approach for Minimizing Cognitive Bias in Forensic Decision Making," *Journal of Forensic Science* 60 (2015): 1111–1112.

CHAPTER 21

259. *official agencies:* Jeffrey A. Frankel, "Over-optimism in Forecasts by Official Budget Agencies and Its Implications," working paper 17239, National Bureau of Economic Research, December 2011, www.nber.org/papers/w17239.

259. *tend to be overconfident:* H. R. Arkes, "Overconfidence in Judgmental Forecasting," in *Principles of Forecasting: A Handbook for Researchers and Practitioners,* ed. Jon Scott Armstrong, vol. 30, International Series in Operations Research & Management Science (Boston: Springer, 2001).

260. *an ongoing quarterly survey:* Itzhak Ben-David, John Graham, and Campell Harvey, "Managerial Miscalibration," *The Quarterly Journal of Economics* 128, no. 4 (November 2013): 1547–1584.

260. *"unreliability is a source":* T. R. Stewart, "Improving Reliability of Judgmental

Forecasts," in *Principles of Forecasting: A Handbook for Researchers and Practitioners,* ed. Jon Scott Armstrong, vol. 30, International Series in Operations Research & Management Science (Boston: Springer, 2001) (hereafter cited as *Principles of Forecasting*), 82.

260. *to predict Supreme Court rulings:* Theodore W. Ruger, Pauline T. Kim, Andrew D. Martin, and Kevin M. Quinn, "The Supreme Court Forecasting Project: Legal and Political Science Approaches to Predicting Supreme Court Decision-Making," *Columbia Law Review* 104 (2004): 1150–1209.

260. *air pollution regulation:* Cass Sunstein, "Maximin," *Yale Journal of Regulation* (draft; May 3, 2020), https://papers.ssrn.com/sol3/papers.cfm?abstract_id =3476250.

260. *many examples:* For numerous examples, see Armstrong, *Principles of Forecasting.*

261. *averaging multiple forecasts:* Jon Scott Armstrong, "Combining Forecasts," in *Principles of Forecasting*, 417–439.

261. *outperforms most:* T. R. Stewart, "Improving Reliability of Judgmental Forecasts," in *Principles of Forecasting,* 95.

261. *an average of 12.5%:* Armstrong, "Combining Forecasts."

261. select-crowd: Albert E. Mannes et al., "The Wisdom of Select Crowds," *Journal of Personality and Social Psychology* 107, no. 2 (2014): 276–299.

261. *prediction markets have been found to do very well:* Justin Wolfers and Eric Zitzewitz, "Prediction Markets," *Journal of Economic Perspectives* 18 (2004): 107–126.

262. *used prediction markets:* Cass R. Sunstein and Reid Hastie, *Wiser: Getting Beyond Groupthink to Make Groups Smarter* (Boston: Harvard Business Review Press, 2014).

262. *Delphi method:* Gene Rowe and George Wright, "The Delphi Technique as a Forecasting Tool: Issues and Analysis," *International Journal of Forecasting* 15 (1999): 353–375. See also Dan Bang and Chris D. Frith, "Making Better Decisions in Groups," *Royal Society Open Science* 4, no. 8 (2017).

262. *challenging to implement:* R. Hastie, "Review Essay: Experimental Evidence on Group Accuracy," in B. Grofman and G. Guillermo, eds., *Information Pooling and Group Decision Making* (Greenwich, CT: JAI Press, 1986), 129–157.

262. mini-Delphi: Andrew H. Van De Ven and André L. Delbecq, "The Effectiveness of Nominal, Delphi, and Interacting Group Decision Making Processes," *Academy of Management Journal* 17, no. 4 (2017).

265. *"better than the average":* Superforecasting, 95.

267. *"the strongest predictor":* Superforecasting, 231.

267. *"try, fail, analyze":* Superforecasting, 273.

268. *a sophisticated statistical technique:* Ville A. Satopää, Marat Salikhov, Philip

E. Tetlock, and Barb Mellers, "Bias, Information, Noise: The BIN Model of Forecasting," February 19, 2020, 23, https://dx.doi.org/10.2139/ssrn.3540864.

269. *"Whenever an intervention":* Satopää et al., "Bias, Information, Noise," 23.

270. *"Teaming—unlike training":* Satopää et al., 22.

270. *"'Superforecasters' may owe":* Satopää et al., 24.

271. *both independent and complementary:* Clintin P. Davis-Stober, David V. Budescu, Stephen B. Broomell, and Jason Dana. "The composition of optimally wise crowds." *Decision Analysis* 12, no. 3 (2015): 130–143.

CHAPTER 22

274. *Quantifying tendon degeneration produces:* Laura Horton et al., "Development and Assessment of Inter- and Intra-Rater Reliability of a Novel Ultrasound Tool for Scoring Tendon and Sheath Disease: A Pilot Study," *Ultrasound* 24, no. 3 (2016): 134, www.ncbi.nlm.nih.gov/pmc/articles/PMC5105362.

274. *When pathologists evaluate core:* Laura C. Collins et al., "Diagnostic Agreement in the Evaluation of Image-guided Breast Core Needle Biopsies," *American Journal of Surgical Pathology* 28 (2004): 126, https://journals.lww.com/ajsp/Abstract/2004/01000/Diagnostic_Agreement_in_the_Evaluation_of.15.aspx.

274. *Without the rapid antigen result:* Julie L. Fierro et al., "Variability in the Diagnosis and Treatment of Group A Streptococcal Pharyngitis by Primary Care Pediatricians," *Infection Control and Hospital Epidemiology* 35, no. S3 (2014): S79, www.jstor.org/stable/10.1086/677820.

274. *you are considered to have diabetes:* Diabetes Tests, Centers for Disease Control and Prevention, https://www.cdc.gov/diabetes/basics/getting-tested.html (last accessed January 15, 2020).

274. *In some hospitals, a second:* Joseph D. Kronz et al., "Mandatory Second Opinion Surgical Pathology at a Large Referral Hospital," *Cancer* 86 (1999): 2426, https://onlinelibrary.wiley.com/doi/full/10.1002/(SICI)1097-0142(19991201)86:11%3C2426::AID-CNCR34%3E3.0.CO;2-3.

275. *The Dartmouth Atlas Project has dedicated:* Most of the material can be found online; a book-length outline is Dartmouth Medical School, *The Quality of Medical Care in the United States: A Report on the Medicare Program; the Dartmouth Atlas of Health Care 1999* (American Hospital Publishers, 1999).

275. *Similar conclusions hold in:* See, for example, OECD, *Geographic Variations in Health Care: What Do We Know and What Can Be Done to Improve Health System Performance?* (Paris: OECD Publishing, 2014), 137–169; Michael P. Hurley et al., "Geographic Variation in Surgical Outcomes and Cost Between the United States and Japan," *American Journal of Managed Care* 22 (2016): 600, www.ajmc.com/journals/issue/2016/2016-vol22-n9/geographic-variation-in-surgical

-outcomes-and-cost-between-the-united-states-and-japan; and John Appleby, Veena Raleigh, Francesca Frosini, Gwyn Bevan, Haiyan Gao, and Tom Lyscom, *Variations in Health Care: The Good, the Bad and the Inexplicable* (London: The King's Fund, 2011), www.kingsfund.org.uk/sites/default/files/Variations-in -health-care-good-bad-inexplicable-report-The-Kings-Fund-April-2011.pdf.

275. *A study of pneumonia diagnoses:* David C. Chan Jr. et al., "Selection with Variation in Diagnostic Skill: Evidence from Radiologists," National Bureau of Economic Research, NBER Working Paper No. 26467, November 2019, www.nber .org/papers/w26467.

275. *Here as elsewhere, training:* P. J. Robinson, "Radiology's Achilles' Heel: Error and Variation in the Interpretation of the Röntgen Image," *British Journal of Radiology* 70 (1997): 1085, www.ncbi.nlm.nih.gov/pubmed/9536897. A relevant study is Yusuke Tsugawa et al., "Physician Age and Outcomes in Elderly Patients in Hospital in the US: Observational Study," *BMJ* 357 (2017), www.bmj.com /content/357/bmj.j1797, which finds that doctors' outcomes get worse the further they are out from training. It follows that there is a trade-off between developing experience, which comes from years of practice, and having familiarity with the most recent evidence and guidelines. The study finds that the best outcomes come from doctors who are in the first few years out of residency, when they have that evidence in mind.

276. *Radiologists, for example, call:* Robinson, "Radiology's Achilles' Heel."

276. the kappa statistic: Like the correlation coefficient, kappa can be negative, although that is rare in practice. Here is one characterization of the meaning of different kappa statistics: "slight (κ = 0.00 to 0.20), fair (κ = 0.21 to 0.40), moderate (κ = 0.41 to 0.60), substantial (κ = 0.61 to 0.80), and almost perfect (κ > 0.80)" (Ron Wald, Chaim M. Bell, Rosane Nisenbaum, Samuel Perrone, Orfeas Liangos, Andreas Laupacis, and Bertrand L. Jaber, "Interobserver Reliability of Urine Sediment Interpretation," *Clinical Journal of the American Society of Nephrology* 4, no. 3 [March 2009]: 567–571, https://cjasn.asnjournals.org/content/4/3/567).

276. *drug-drug interactions:* Howard R. Strasberg et al., "Inter-Rater Agreement Among Physicians on the Clinical Significance of Drug-Drug Interactions," *AMIA Annual Symposium Proceedings* (2013): 1325, www.ncbi.nlm.nih.gov /pmc/articles/PMC3900147.

276. *But nephrologists show only:* Wald et al., "Interobserver Reliability of Urine Sediment Interpretation," https://cjasn.asnjournals.org/content/4/3/567.

276. *whether a breast lesion:* Juan P. Palazzo et al., "Hyperplastic Ductal and Lobular Lesions and Carcinomas in Situ of the Breast: Reproducibility of Current Diagnostic Criteria Among Community- and Academic-Based Pathologists," *Breast Journal* 4 (2003): 230, www.ncbi.nlm.nih.gov/pubmed/21223441.

276. *breast proliferative lesions:* Rohit K. Jain et al., "Atypical Ductal Hyperplasia: Interobserver and Intraobserver Variability," *Modern Pathology* 24 (2011): 917, www.nature.com/articles/modpathol201166.

276. *degree of spinal stenosis:* Alex C. Speciale et al., "Observer Variability in Assessing Lumbar Spinal Stenosis Severity on Magnetic Resonance Imaging and Its Relation to Cross-Sectional Spinal Canal Area," *Spine* 27 (2002): 1082, www.ncbi.nlm.nih.gov/pubmed/12004176.

277. *Heart disease is the leading cause:* Centers for Disease Control and Prevention, "Heart Disease Facts," accessed June 16, 2020, www.cdc.gov/heartdisease /facts.htm.

277. *An early study found that 31%:* Timothy A. DeRouen et al., "Variability in the Analysis of Coronary Arteriograms," *Circulation* 55 (1977): 324, www.ncbi .nlm.nih.gov/pubmed/832349.

277. *They disagreed dramatically:* Olaf Buchweltz et al., "Interobserver Variability in the Diagnosis of Minimal and Mild Endometriosis," *European Journal of Obstetrics & Gynecology and Reproductive Biology* 122 (2005): 213, www.ejog .org/article/S0301-2115(05)00059-X/pdf.

278. *significant variability in diagnosis of TB:* Jean-Pierre Zellweger et al., "Intra-observer and Overall Agreement in the Radiological Assessment of Tuberculosis," *International Journal of Tuberculosis & Lung Disease* 10 (2006): 1123, www.ncbi .nlm.nih.gov/pubmed/17044205. For "fair" interrater agreement, see Yanina Balabanova et al., "Variability in Interpretation of Chest Radiographs Among Russian Clinicians and Implications for Screening Programmes: Observational Study," *BMJ* 331 (2005): 379, www.bmj.com/content/331/7513/379.short.

278. *between radiologists in different countries:* Shinsaku Sakurada et al., "Inter-Rater Agreement in the Assessment of Abnormal Chest X-Ray Findings for Tuberculosis Between Two Asian Countries," *BMC Infectious Diseases* 12, article 31 (2012), https://bmcinfectdis.biomedcentral.com/articles/10.1186/1471-2334-12-31.

278. *The eight pathologists reviewing:* Evan R. Farmer et al., "Discordance in the Histopathologic Diagnosis of Melanoma and Melanocytic Nevi Between Expert Pathologists," *Human Pathology* 27 (1996): 528, www.ncbi.nlm.nih.gov /pubmed/8666360.

278. *Another study at an oncology center:* Alfred W. Kopf, M. Mintzis, and R. S. Bart, "Diagnostic Accuracy in Malignant Melanoma," *Archives of Dermatology* 111 (1975): 1291, www.ncbi.nlm.nih.gov/pubmed/1190800.

278. *The authors of the study conclude that:* Maria Miller and A. Bernard Ackerman, "How Accurate Are Dermatologists in the Diagnosis of Melanoma? Degree of Accuracy and Implications," *Archives of Dermatology* 128 (1992): 559, https://jamanetwork.com/journals/jamadermatology/fullarticle/554024.

278. *Similarly, false-positive rates ranged:* Craig A. Beam et al., "Variability in the Interpretation of Screening Mammograms by US Radiologists," *Archives of Internal Medicine* 156 (1996): 209, www.ncbi.nlm.nih.gov/pubmed/8546556.

278–279. *Radiologists sometimes offer:* P. J. Robinson et al., "Variation Between Experienced Observers in the Interpretation of Accident and Emergency Radiographs," *British Journal of Radiology* 72 (1999): 323, www.birpublications .org/doi/pdf/10.1259/bjr.72.856.10474490.

279. *the degree of blockage in angiograms:* Katherine M. Detre et al., "Observer Agreement in Evaluating Coronary Angiograms," *Circulation* 52 (1975): 979, www.ncbi.nlm.nih.gov/pubmed/1102142.

279. *In areas that involve vague criteria:* Horton et al., "Inter- and Intra-Rater Reliability"; and Megan Banky et al., "Inter- and Intra-Rater Variability of Testing Velocity When Assessing Lower Limb Spasticity," *Journal of Rehabilitation Medicine* 51 (2019), www.medicaljournals.se/jrm/content/abstract/10.2340 /16501977-2496.

279. *But another study, not involving:* Esther Y. Hsiang et al., "Association of Primary Care Clinic Appointment Time with Clinician Ordering and Patient Completion of Breast and Colorectal Cancer Screening," *JAMA Network Open* 51 (2019), https://jamanetwork.com/journals/jamanetworkopen/fullarticle/2733171.

279. *Another illustration of the role:* Hengchen Dai et al., "The Impact of Time at Work and Time Off from Work on Rule Compliance: The Case of Hand Hygiene in Health Care," *Journal of Applied Psychology* 100 (2015): 846, www.ncbi.nlm .nih.gov/pubmed/25365728.

279. *a major contribution:* Ali S. Raja, "The HEART Score Has Substantial Interrater Reliability," *NEJM J Watch,* December 5, 2018, www.jwatch.org/na47998/2018/12 /05/heart-score-has-substantial-interrater-reliability (reviewing Colin A. Gershon et al., "Inter-rater Reliability of the HEART Score," *Academic Emergency Medicine* 26 [2019]: 552).

280. *As we mentioned, training:* Jean-Pierre Zellweger et al., "Intra-observer and Overall Agreement in the Radiological Assessment of Tuberculosis," *International Journal of Tuberculosis & Lung Disease* 10 (2006): 1123, www.ncbi.nlm. nih.gov/pubmed/17044205; Ibrahim Abubakar et al., "Diagnostic Accuracy of Digital Chest Radiography for Pulmonary Tuberculosis in a UK Urban Population," *European Respiratory Journal* 35 (2010): 689, https://erj.ersjournals.com/ content/35/3/689.short.

280. *So does the aggregation of multiple:* Michael L. Barnett et al., "Comparative Accuracy of Diagnosis by Collective Intelligence of Multiple Physicians vs Individual Physicians," *JAMA Network Open* 2 (2019): e19009, https://jamanetwork .com/journals/jamanetworkopen/fullarticle/2726709; Kimberly H. Allison et

al., "Understanding Diagnostic Variability in Breast Pathology: Lessons Learned from an Expert Consensus Review Panel," *Histopathology* 65 (2014): 240, https://onlinelibrary.wiley.com/doi/abs/10.1111/his.12387.

280. *The best of these have been found:* Babak Ehteshami Bejnordi et al., "Diagnostic Assessment of Deep Learning Algorithms for Detection of Lymph Node Metastases in Women with Breast Cancer," *JAMA* 318 (2017): 2199, https://jamanetwork.com/journals/jama/fullarticle/2665774.

280. *Deep-learning algorithms have:* Varun Gulshan et al., "Development and Validation of a Deep Learning Algorithm for Detection of Diabetic Retinopathy in Retinal Fundus Photographs," *JAMA* 316 (2016): 2402, https://jamanetwork.com/journals/jama/fullarticle/2588763.

280. *AI now performs at least:* Mary Beth Massat, "A Promising Future for AI in Breast Cancer Screening," *Applied Radiology* 47 (2018): 22, www.appliedradiology.com/articles/a-promising-future-for-ai-in-breast-cancer-screening; Alejandro Rodriguez-Ruiz et al., "Stand-Alone Artificial Intelligence for Breast Cancer Detection in Mammography: Comparison with 101 Radiologists," *Journal of the National Cancer Institute* 111 (2019): 916, https://academic.oup.com/jnci/advance-article-abstract/doi/10.1093/jnci/djy222/5307077.

281 Table 3: Apgar Score, Medline Plus, https://medlineplus.gov/ency/article/003402.htm (last accessed February 4, 2020).

282. *Apgar scoring produces little noise:* L. R. Foster et al., "The Interrater Reliability of Apgar Scores at 1 and 5 Minutes," *Journal of Investigative Medicine* 54, no. 1 (2006): 293, https://jim.bmj.com/content/54/1/S308.4.

283. *Assessment and scoring are relatively:* Warren J. McIsaac et al., "Empirical Validation of Guidelines for the Management of Pharyngitis in Children and Adults," *JAMA* 291 (2004): 1587, www.ncbi.nlm.nih.gov/pubmed/15069046.

283. *One study found that BI-RADS:* Emilie A. Ooms et al., "Mammography: Interobserver Variability in Breast Density Assessment," *Breast* 16 (2007): 568, www.sciencedirect.com/science/article/abs/pii/S0960977607000793.

283. *In pathology, there have been:* Frances P. O'Malley et al., "Interobserver Reproducibility in the Diagnosis of Flat Epithelial Atypia of the Breast," *Modern Pathology* 19 (2006): 172, www.nature.com/articles/3800514.

283. *For that reason, noise reduction:* See Ahmed Aboraya et al., "The Reliability of Psychiatric Diagnosis Revisited," *Psychiatry (Edgmont)* 3 (2006): 41, www.ncbi.nlm.nih.gov/pmc/articles/PMC2990547. For an overview, see N. Kreitman, "The Reliability of Psychiatric Diagnosis," *Journal of Mental Science* 107 (1961): 876–886, www.cambridge.org/core/journals/journal-of-mental-science/article/reliability-of-psychiatric-diagnosis/92832FFA170F4FF41189428C6A3E6394.

283. *A 1964 study involving 91 patients:* Aboraya et al., "Reliability of Psychiatric Diagnosis Revisited," 43.

284. *But in a preliminary effort to:* C. H. Ward et al., "The Psychiatric Nomenclature: Reasons for Diagnostic Disagreement," *Archives of General Psychiatry* 7 (1962): 198.

284. *While a "clinician with developmental training":* Aboraya et al., "Reliability of Psychiatric Diagnosis Revisited."

284. *DSM-III led to a dramatic:* Samuel M. Lieblich, David J. Castle, Christos Pantelis, Malcolm Hopwood, Allan Hunter Young, and Ian P. Everall, "High Heterogeneity and Low Reliability in the Diagnosis of Major Depression Will Impair the Development of New Drugs," *British Journal of Psychiatry Open* 1 (2015): e5–e7, www.ncbi.nlm.nih.gov/pmc/articles/PMC5000492/pdf/bjporcpsych_1_2_e5.pdf.

284. *But the manual was far:* Lieblich et al., "High Heterogeneity."

284. *Even after a significant 2000 revision:* See Elie Cheniaux et al., "The Diagnoses of Schizophrenia, Schizoaffective Disorder, Bipolar Disorder and Unipolar Depression: Interrater Reliability and Congruence Between DSM-IV and ICD-10," *Psychopathology* 42 (2009): 296–298, especially 293; and Michael Chmielewski et al., "Method Matters: Understanding Diagnostic Reliability in DSM-IV and DSM-5," *Journal of Abnormal Psychology* 124 (2015): 764, 768–769.

284. *"increase the reliability of psychiatric diagnoses":* Aboraya et al., "Reliability of Psychiatric Diagnosis Revisited," 47.

284. *a serious risk:* Aboraya et al., 47.

285. *Another version of the manual:* See Chmielewski et al., "Method Matters."

285. *The American Psychiatric Association:* See, for example, Helena Chmura Kraemer et al., "DSM-5: How Reliable Is Reliable Enough?," *American Journal of Psychiatry* 169 (2012): 13–15.

285. *psychiatrists continue to show:* Lieblich et al., "High Heterogeneity."

285. *"psychiatrists have a hard time":* Lieblich et al., "High Heterogeneity," e-5.

285. *Field trials for DSM-5 found:* Lieblich et al., e-5.

285. *According to some field trials:* Lieblich et al., e-6.

285. *The major reason for the limited:* Aboraya et al., "Reliability of Psychiatric Diagnosis Revisited," 47.

285. *These include (1) clarifying:* Aboraya et al.

285. *In the words of one observer:* Aboraya et al.

286. *The medical profession needs more:* Some valuable cautionary notes can be found in Christopher Worsham and Anupam B. Jena, "The Art of Evidence-Based Medicine," *Harvard Business Review,* January 30, 2019, https://hbr.org/2019/01/the-art-of-evidence-based-medicine.

CHAPTER 23

288. *one newspaper headline:* Jena McGregor, "Study Finds That Basically Every Single Person Hates Performance Reviews," *Washington Post,* January 27, 2014.

288. *ubiquity of judgment-based:* The digital transformation that many organizations are undergoing may create new possibilities here. In theory, companies can now collect great amounts of granular, real-time information about the performance of every worker. This data may make entirely algorithmic performance evaluations possible for some positions. We focus here, however, on the positions for which judgment cannot be entirely eliminated from the measurement of performance. See E. D. Pulakos, R. Mueller-Hanson, and S. Arad, "The Evolution of Performance Management: Searching for Value," *Annual Review of Organizational Psychology and Organizational Behavior* 6 (2018): 249–271.

289. *Most researchers find:* S. E. Scullen, M. K. Mount, and M. Goff, "Understanding the Latent Structure of Job Performance Ratings," *Journal of Applied Psychology* 85 (2000): 956–970.

289. *The rest, 70 to 80% variance:* A small component — 10% of total variance in some studies — is what researchers call the *rater perspective,* or the *level* effect, in the sense of level in the organization, not of the *level noise* as we define it here. The rater perspective reflects that, in rating the same person, a boss differs systematically from a peer, and a peer from a subordinate. Under a charitable interpretation of results from 360-degree rating systems, one could argue that this is not noise. If people at different levels of the organization systematically see different facets of the same person's performance, their judgment on that person should differ systematically, and their ratings should reflect it.

289. *multiple studies:* Scullen, Mount, and Goff, "Latent Structure"; C. Viswesvaran, D. S. Ones, and F. L. Schmidt, "Comparative Analysis of the Reliability of Job Performance Ratings," *Journal of Applied Psychology* 81 (1996): 557–574. G. J. Greguras and C. Robie, "A New Look at Within-Source Interrater Reliability of 360-Degree Feedback Ratings," *Journal of Applied Psychology* 83 (1998): 960–968; G. J. Greguras, C. Robie, D. J. Schleicher, and M. A. Goff, "A Field Study of the Effects of Rating Purpose on the Quality of Multisource Ratings," *Personnel Psychology* 56 (2003): 1–21; C. Viswesvaran, F. L. Schmidt, and D. S. Ones, "Is There a General Factor in Ratings of Job Performance? A Meta-Analytic Framework for Disentangling Substantive and Error Influences," *Journal of Applied Psychology* 90 (2005): 108–131; and B. Hoffman, C. E. Lance, B. Bynum, and W. A. Gentry, "Rater Source Effects Are Alive and Well After All," *Personnel Psychology* 63 (2010): 119–151.

290. *"the relationship between job performance":* K. R. Murphy, "Explaining the

Weak Relationship Between Job Performance and Ratings of Job Performance," *Industrial and Organizational Psychology* 1 (2008): 148–160, especially 151.

290. *an employee's true performance:* In the discussion of sources of noise, we ignored the possibility of case noise arising from systematic biases in the rating of certain employees or categories of employees. None of the studies we could locate on the variability of performance ratings compared them with an externally assessed "true" performance.

290. *rate people "strategically":* E. D. Pulakos and R. S. O'Leary, "Why Is Performance Management Broken?," *Industrial and Organizational Psychology* 4 (2011): 146–164; M. M. Harris, "Rater Motivation in the Performance Appraisal Context: A Theoretical Framework," *Journal of Management* 20 (1994): 737–756; and K. R. Murphy and J. N. Cleveland, *Understanding Performance Appraisal: Social, Organizational, and Goal-Based Perspectives* (Thousand Oaks, CA: Sage, 1995).

290. *purely developmental:* Greguras et al., "Field Study."

291. *predicts objectively measurable:* P. W. Atkins and R. E. Wood, "Self- Versus Others' Ratings as Predictors of Assessment Center Ratings: Validation Evidence for 360-Degree Feedback Programs," *Personnel Psychology* (2002).

291. *Overengineered questionnaires:* Atkins and Wood, "Self- Versus Others' Ratings."

292. *98%:* Olson and Davis, cited in Peter G. Dominick, "Forced Ranking: Pros, Cons and Practices," in *Performance Management: Putting Research into Action,* ed. James W. Smither and Manuel London (San Francisco: Jossey-Bass, 2009), 411–443.

292. *forced ranking:* Dominick, "Forced Ranking."

292. *to apply in performance ratings:* Barry R. Nathan and Ralph A. Alexander, "A Comparison of Criteria for Test Validation: A Meta-Analytic Investigation," *Personnel Psychology* 41, no. 3 (1988): 517–535.

293. *Figure 17:* Adapted from Richard D. Goffin and James M. Olson, "Is It All Relative? Comparative Judgments and the Possible Improvement of Self-Ratings and Ratings of Others," *Perspectives on Psychological Science* 6, no. 1 (2011): 48–60.

296. *Deloitte:* M. Buckingham and A. Goodall, "Reinventing Performance Management," *Harvard Business Review,* April 1, 2015, 1–16, doi:ISSN: 0017-8012.

296. *One study:* Corporate Leadership Council, cited in S. Adler et al., "Getting Rid of Performance Ratings: Genius or Folly? A Debate," *Industrial and Organizational Psychology* 9 (2016): 219–252.

296. *"No matter":* Pulakos, Mueller-Hanson, and Arad, "Evolution of Performance Management," 250.

297. *"performance management revolution":* A. Tavis and P. Cappelli, "The Performance Management Revolution," *Harvard Business Review,* October 2016, 1–17.

297. *Evidence suggests:* Frank J. Landy and James L. Farr, "Performance Rating," *Psychological Bulletin* 87, no. 1 (1980): 72–107.

297. *They practice rating performance:* D. J. Woehr and A. I. Huffcutt, "Rater Training for Performance Appraisal: A Quantitative Review," *Journal of Occupational and Organizational Psychology* 67 (1994): 189–205; S. G. Roch, D. J. Woehr, V. Mishra, and U. Kieszczynska, "Rater Training Revisited: An Updated Meta-Analytic Review of Frame-of-Reference Training," *Journal of Occupational and Organizational Psychology* 85 (2012): 370–395; and M. H. Tsai, S. Wee, and B. Koh, "Restructured Frame-of-Reference Training Improves Rating Accuracy," *Journal of Organizational Behavior* (2019): 1–18, doi:10.1002/job.2368.

298. *Figure 18:* Left panel is adapted from Richard Goffin and James M. Olson, "Is It All Relative? Comparative Judgments and the Possible Improvement of Self-Ratings and Ratings of Others," *Perspectives on Psychological Science* 6, no. 1 (2011): 48–60.

298. *the majority of studies:* Roch et al., "Rater Training Revisited."

299. *"star talent":* Ernest O'Boyle and Herman Aguinis, "The Best and the Rest: Revisiting the Norm of Normality of Individual Performance," *Personnel Psychology* 65, no. 1 (2012): 79–119; and Herman Aguinis and Ernest O'Boyle, "Star Performers in Twenty-First Century Organizations," *Personnel Psychology* 67, no. 2 (2014): 313–350.

CHAPTER 24

300. *"It is rare":* A. I. Huffcutt and S. S. Culbertson, "Interviews," in S. Zedeck, ed., *APA Handbook of Industrial and Organizational Psychology* (Washington, DC: American Psychological Association, 2010), 185–203.

301. *rely to some degree on their intuitive judgments:* N. R. Kuncel, D. M. Klieger, and D. S. Ones, "In Hiring, Algorithms Beat Instinct," *Harvard Business Review* 92, no. 5 (2014): 32.

301. *"supreme problem":* R. E. Ployhart, N. Schmitt, and N. T. Tippins, "Solving the Supreme Problem: 100 Years of Selection and Recruitment at the *Journal of Applied Psychology*," *Journal of Applied Psychology* 102 (2017): 291–304.

302. *Other studies report:* M. McDaniel, D. Whetzel, F. L. Schmidt, and S. Maurer, "Meta Analysis of the Validity of Employment Interviews," *Journal of Applied Psychology* 79 (1994): 599–616; A. Huffcutt and W. Arthur, "Hunter and Hunter (1984) Revisited: Interview Validity for Entry-Level Jobs," *Journal of Applied Psychology* 79 (1994): 2; F. L. Schmidt and J. E. Hunter, "The Validity and Utility of Selection Methods in Personnel Psychology: Practical and Theoretical Implications of 85 Years of Research Findings," *Psychology Bulletin* 124 (1998): 262–274; and F. L. Schmidt and R. D. Zimmerman, "A Counterintuitive Hypothesis About Employment Interview Validity and Some Supporting Evidence," *Journal*

of *Applied Psychology* 89 (2004): 553–561. Note that validities are higher when certain subsets of studies are considered, especially if research uses performance ratings specifically created for this purpose, rather than existing administrative ratings.

302. *objective ignorance:* S. Highhouse, "Stubborn Reliance on Intuition and Subjectivity in Employee Selection," *Industrial and Organizational Psychology* 1 (2008): 333–342; D. A. Moore, "How to Improve the Accuracy and Reduce the Cost of Personnel Selection," *California Management Review* 60 (2017): 8–17.

303. *culturally similar to them:* L. A. Rivera, "Hiring as Cultural Matching: The Case of Elite Professional Service Firms," *American Sociology Review* 77 (2012): 999–1022.

303. *Measures of the correlation:* Schmidt and Zimmerman, "Counterintuitive Hypothesis"; Timothy A. Judge, Chad A. Higgins, and Daniel M. Cable, "The Employment Interview: A Review of Recent Research and Recommendations for Future Research," *Human Resource Management Review* 10 (2000): 383–406; and A. I. Huffcutt, S. S. Culbertson, and W. S. Weyhrauch, "Employment Interview Reliability: New Meta-Analytic Estimates by Structure and Format," *International Journal of Selection and Assessment* 21 (2013): 264–276.

304. *matter — a lot:* M. R. Barrick et al., "Candidate Characteristics Driving Initial Impressions During Rapport Building: Implications for Employment Interview Validity," *Journal of Occupational and Organizational Psychology* 85 (2012): 330–352; M. R. Barrick, B. W. Swider, and G. L. Stewart, "Initial Evaluations in the Interview: Relationships with Subsequent Interviewer Evaluations and Employment Offers," *Journal of Applied Psychology* 95 (2010): 1163.

304. *quality of a handshake:* G. L. Stewart, S. L. Dustin, M. R. Barrick, and T. C. Darnold, "Exploring the Handshake in Employment Interviews," *Journal of Applied Psychology* 93 (2008): 1139–1146.

304. *positive first impressions:* T. W. Dougherty, D. B. Turban, and J. C. Callender, "Confirming First Impressions in the Employment Interview: A Field Study of Interviewer Behavior," *Journal of Applied Psychology* 79 (1994): 659–665.

305. *In one striking experiment:* J. Dana, R. Dawes, and N. Peterson, "Belief in the Unstructured Interview: The Persistence of an Illusion," *Judgment and Decision Making* 8 (2013): 512–520.

306. *HR professionals favor:* Nathan R. Kuncel et al., "Mechanical versus Clinical Data Combination in Selection and Admissions Decisions: A Meta-Analysis," *Journal of Applied Psychology* 98, no. 6 (2013): 1060–1072.

307. *"zero relationship":* Laszlo Bock, interview with Adam Bryant, *The New York Times*, June 19, 2013. See also Laszlo Bock, *Work Rules!: Insights from Inside Google That Will Transform How You Live and Lead* (New York: Hachette, 2015).

308. *One prominent headhunter:* C. Fernández-Aráoz, "Hiring Without Firing," *Harvard Business Review,* July 1, 1999.

308. *structured behavioral interviews:* For an accessible guide to structured interviews, see Michael A. Campion, David K. Palmer, and James E. Campion, "Structuring Employment Interviews to Improve Reliability, Validity and Users' Reactions," *Current Directions in Psychological Science* 7, no. 3 (1998): 77–82.

309. *must include to qualify:* J. Levashina, C. J. Hartwell, F. P. Morgeson, and M. A. Campion, "The Structured Employment Interview: Narrative and Quantitative Review of the Research Literature," *Personnel Psychology* 67 (2014): 241–293.

309. *structured interviews are far more predictive:* McDaniel et al., "Meta Analysis"; Huffcutt and Arthur, "Hunter and Hunter (1984) Revisited"; Schmidt and Hunter, "Validity and Utility"; and Schmidt and Zimmerman, "Counterintuitive Hypothesis."

309. *work sample tests:* Schmidt and Hunter, "Validity and Utility."

310. *Israeli Army:* Kahneman, *Thinking, Fast and Slow,* 229.

311. *Practical advice:* Kuncel, Klieger, and Ones, "Algorithms Beat Instinct." See also Campion, Palmer, and Campion, "Structuring Employment Interviews."

311. *"the persistence of an illusion":* Dana, Dawes, and Peterson, "Belief in the Unstructured Interview."

CHAPTER 25

312. *mediating assessments protocol:* Daniel Kahneman, Dan Lovallo, and Olivier Sibony, "A Structured Approach to Strategic Decisions: Reducing Errors in Judgment Requires a Disciplined Process," *MIT Sloan Management Review* 60 (2019): 67–73.

319. estimate-talk-estimate: Andrew H. Van De Ven and André Delbecq, "The Effectiveness of Nominal, Delphi, and Interacting Group Decision Making Processes," *Academy of Management Journal* 17, no. 4 (1974): 605–621. See also chapter 21.

PART 6

326. *In their view:* Kate Stith and José A. Cabranes, *Fear of Judging: Sentencing Guidelines in the Federal Courts* (Chicago: University of Chicago Press, 1998), 177.

CHAPTER 26

331. *First, such efforts might:* Albert O. Hirschman, *The Rhetoric of Reaction: Perversity, Futility, Jeopardy* (Cambridge, MA: Belknap Press, 1991).

332. *Quoting Václav Havel, they:* Stith and Cabranes, *Fear of Judging.*

332. *"three strikes and you're out"*: See, for example, Three Strikes Basics, Stanford Law School, https://law.stanford.edu/stanford-justice-advocacy-project/three-strikes-basics/.

333. *"Woodson v. North Carolina"*: 428 U.S. 280 (1976).

355. *can embed prejudice:* Cathy O'Neil, *Weapons of Math Destruction: How Big Data Increases Inequality and Threatens Democracy* (New York: Crown, 2016).

355. *"potentially biased"*: Will Knight, "Biased Algorithms Are Everywhere, and No One Seems to Care," *MIT Technology Review,* July 12, 2017.

355. *ProPublica:* Jeff Larson, Surya Mattu, Lauren Kirchner, and Julia Angwin, "How We Analyzed the COMPAS Recidivism Algorithm," *ProPublica,* May 23, 2016, www.propublica.org/article/how-we-analyzed-the-compas-recidivism-algorithm. The claim of bias in this example is disputed, and different definitions of bias may lead to opposite conclusions. For views on this case and more broadly on the definition and measurement of algorithmic bias, see later note, *"Exactly how to test."*

355. *"predictive policing"*: Aaron Shapiro, "Reform Predictive Policing," *Nature* 541, no. 7638 (2017): 458–460.

336. *Indeed, in this regard, algorithms:* Although this concern is resurfacing in the context of AI-based models, it is not specific to AI. As early as 1972, Paul Slovic noted that modeling intuition would preserve and reinforce, and perhaps even magnify, existing cognitive biases. Paul Slovic, "Psychological Study of Human Judgment: Implications for Investment Decision Making," *Journal of Finance* 27 (1972): 779.

336. *Exactly how to test:* For an introduction to this debate in the context of the controversy over the COMPAS recidivism-prediction algorithm, see Larson et al., "COMPAS Recidivism Algorithm"; William Dieterich et al., "COMPAS Risk Scales: Demonstrating Accuracy Equity and Predictive Parity," Northpointe, Inc., July 8, 2016, http://go.volarisgroup.com/rs/430-MBX-989/images/ProPublica_Commentary_Final_070616.pdf; Julia Dressel and Hany Farid, "The Accuracy, Fairness, and Limits of Predicting Recidivism," *Science Advances* 4, no. 1 (2018): 1–6; Sam Corbett-Davies et al., "A Computer Program Used for Bail and Sentencing Decisions Was Labeled Biased Against Blacks. It's Actually Not That Clear," *Washington Post,* October 17, 2016, www.washingtonpost.com/news/monkey-cage/wp/2016/10/17/can-an-algorithm-be-racist-our-analysis-is-more-cautious-than-propublicas; Alexandra Chouldechova, "Fair Prediction with Disparate Impact: A Study of Bias in Recidivism Prediction Instruments," *Big Data* 153 (2017): 5; and Jon Kleinberg, Sendhil Mullainathan, and Manish Raghavan, "Inherent Trade-Offs in the Fair Determination of Risk Scores," Leibniz International Proceedings in Informatics, January 2017.

CHAPTER 27

340. *They might know that their:* Tom R. Tyler, *Why People Obey the Law*, 2nd ed. (New Haven, CT: Yale University Press, 2020).

342. *A famously puzzling decision in American: Cleveland Bd. of Educ. v. LaFleur*, 414 U.S. 632 (1974).

343. *Influential commentators at the time:* Laurence H. Tribe, "Structural Due Process," *Harvard Civil Rights–Civil Liberties Law Review* 10, no. 2 (spring 1975): 269.

346. *Recall the intensely negative:* Stith and Cabranes, *Fear of Judging*, 177.

347. *In a series of energetic:* See, for example, Philip K. Howard, *The Death of Common Sense: How Law Is Suffocating America* (New York: Random House, 1995); and Philip K. Howard, *Try Common Sense: Replacing the Failed Ideologies of Right and Left* (New York: W. W. Norton & Company, 2019).

CHAPTER 28

354. *Facebook's Community Standards in 2020* 12. Hate Speech, Facebook: Community Standards, www.facebook.com/communitystandards/hate_speech.

354. *The New Yorker:* Andrew Marantz, "Why Facebook Can't Fix Itself," *The New Yorker*, October 12, 2020.

356. *noisy judgments:* bureaucratic justice: Jerry L. Mashaw, *Bureaucratic Justice* (New Haven, CT: Yale University Press, 1983).

359. *Just the reverse largely obtained:* David M. Trubek, "Max Weber on Law and the Rise of Capitalism," *Wisconsin Law Review* 720 (1972): 733, n. 22 (quoting Max Weber, *The Religion of China* [1951], 149).

Index

A

Aboraya, Ahmed, 284

absence of consensus *See* disagreement

absolute judgment, limitations of, 183–184

absolute ratings, performance evaluation, 292–296

accuracy
  as goal of judgment, 40, 371
  natural variability of, 40–41

actively open-minded thinking, 234, 267, 370

Adult Decision Making Competence scale, 233

affect heuristic, 170

aggregation
  decision hygiene, 373–374
  forecasting, 260, 271–272
    averaging, 261
    Delphi method, 262
    estimate-talk-estimate, 262
    prediction markets, 261–262
  job interviews, 307–308
  performance evaluation, 291–292

AI (artificial intelligence), 143. *See also* machine learning models

airline industry
  chess program, 332
  rules vs. standards, 355

algorithms. *See also* machine learning models; rule-based approaches

algorithm aversion, 135

algorithmic bias, 334
  defined, 128–133
  predictive policing, 335–336

Amazon Mechanical Turk, 214

anchoring effect, 170–171, 183, 195–197

Apgar, Virginia, 280–281

Apgar score, 280–282, 351, 372

arbitrary cruelties, criminal sentencing, 14–15, 53

arithmetic mean *See* averaging

Armstrong, J. Scott, 260

artificial intelligence (AI), 143. *See also* machine learning models

as-if model, predictive judgment, 118

asylum decisions
  conclusion biases, 174
  effect of irrelevant information on, 17
  level noise and, 213
  noise in, 6–7
  order of cases and, 90–91

Austin, William, 16

availability heuristic, 167

averaging, 66, 373
  dialectical bootstrapping, 84–85
  forecasting, 261
  mean sentences, 71
  mean squared error, 59–61

averaging *(cont.)*
    select-crowd strategy, 261
    straight averaging, 261
    wisdom-of-crowds effect, 83–84, 223

B
bail decisions
    frugal models, 127–128
    machine learning models, 130, 143
    noise in, 7
Baron, Jonathan, 234
base-rate information, 166
behavior regulation, 350–360
behaviorally anchored rating scales,
    performance evaluation, 297–298
Bentham, Jeremy, 88
Bertillon, Alphonse, 246
between-person noise, 47, 173, 276, 279
bias. *See also* psychological biases
    bias cascades, 252
    bias checklist, 242–243
    bias observation checklist, 387–389
    broad usage of word, 163–164
    cognitive bias, 90, 239–240, 256
    conclusion bias, 168–171, 174
    confirmation bias, 169, 172
    contribution to error, 55–56, 62–66
    criminal sentencing, 15, 19
    debiasing, 222, 236–244, 370, 387–389
    defined, 3–4, 163–164
    desirability bias, 169
    diagnosing, 162–164
    equality with noise, 58
    errors and, 362–363
    excessive coherence, 171–173, 174
    forensic confirmation bias, 249–253,
        255–256
    hiring decisions, 303
    lap duration exercise, 40
    measuring, 363–364
    noise reduction and, 334–337
    noise vs., 4–6, 8, 53
    overall error equation, 62–66
    overconfidence, 140–142, 144–145,
        239–240, 259–260
    planning fallacy, 162
    reducing, 58, 64
    rules vs. standards, 353, 360
    shooting range metaphor, 3–5
    statistical bias, 161–162, 173

    status quo bias, 240
    substitution bias, 164–168, 173–174
bias, information, and noise (BIN)
    forecasting model, 269
bias blind spot, 240
Big Five model of personality, 117, 207
BIN (bias, information, and noise)
    forecasting model, 269
BI-RADS (Breast Imaging Reporting and
    Data System), 283
Bock, Laszlo, 307
boosting, 238–239
brain function, variability in, 92–93
breast cancer, diagnostic variability for,
    276, 278
Breast Imaging Reporting and Data System
    (BI-RADS), 283
Breyer, Stephen, 18
Brier, Glenn W., 264
Brier scores, 264–265
broken-leg principle
    machine learning models, 129
    simple models, 129
bullshit receptivity, 87–88
bureaucratic justice, 356

C
Cabranes, José, 20, 326
calorie listings on menus, 172
case scales
    defined, 374
    mediating assessments protocol, 322
    performance evaluation, 297–298
case-by-case judgment, 339–348
    creativity, 346
    deterrence, 346
    gaming the system, 344–345
    moral values and, 341–344
    morale, 347
    overview, 339–340
    risk aversion, 346
causal thinking, 153–154, 157–158, 219
causation vs. correlation, 152–153
Centor, Robert, 282
Centor score, 282–283
Ceres, 61–62
child protection and custody decisions, 6, 360
claims adjusters, insurance, 24–27
clients, noise audit, 380
clinical judgment *See* judgment

Clinical Versus Statistical Prediction (Meehl), 114
clinical-versus-mechanical debate, 114–116, 134, 142–144
"Clouds Make Nerds Look Good" (Simonsohn), 90
cognitive biases
  fingerprint analysis, 256
  gambler's fallacy, 90
  overconfidence, 239–240
    forecasting, 259–260
    objective ignorance and, 140–142, 144–145
cognitive reflection test (CRT), 232
cognitive style, respect-experts, 232–235
coherent arbitrariness, 195–197
COMPAS algorithm, 335
comprehensive coherence, 202
conclusion biases, 168–171
  affect heuristic, 170
  anchoring effect, 170–171
  confirmation bias, 169
  desirability bias, 169
  noise, 174
confidence, respect-experts, 228
confirmation bias, 169, 172
constitutions, 352
corrected predictions, 391–395
  conservative nature of, 394–395
  intuition and, 392–393
  matching predictions vs., 391–392
  outliers, 395
  quantifying diagnostic value of available data, 393–394
  regression to the mean, 392
  taking outside view, 393
corrective (ex post) debiasing, 237
correlation
  causation vs., 152–153
  cross-validated correlation, 125–126
  interview-performance correlation, 138–139, 302
Corrigan, Bernard, 124–125
counterfactual thinking, 37–38
Cowgill, Bo, 132
creativity, 328, 346–348
criminal sentencing
  arbitrary cruelties, 14–15, 53
  bias, 15, 19
  death penalty, 333

evaluative judgment, 51
external factors influencing judges' decisions, 16–17
idiosyncratic ukases, 15
interjudge disparities, 14–18, 20–21
judge-by-case, 76
judicial discretion, 13–14
level errors, 73–74
level noise, 74
mandatory death sentence, 333
mean sentences, 71–72
noise audit of, 8, 69–76
pattern errors, 75, 203
pattern noise, 74–77
sentencing guidelines, 18–21
  advisory, 20–21
  mandatory, 18–20
Sentencing Reform Act of 1984, 18
three-strikes policy, 332, 356
US Sentencing Commission, 18, 19
weather and, 89–90
Woodson v. North Carolina, 333
cross-validated correlation, 125–126
crowd within, 84–85
CRT (cognitive reflection test), 232
crystallized intelligence, 229
Curry, Stephen, 79

D
Dartmouth Atlas Project, 275
Dawes, Robyn, 124–126
death penalty, 333
debiasing, 370
  bias blind spot, 240
  decision observers, 222, 240–243, 370, 387–389
  ex ante, 237–240
    boosting, 238–239
    nudges, 237–238
  ex post, 237
  limitations of, 239–240
  overview, 236–237
decision hygiene, 326–327. *See also* mediating assessments protocol; noise reduction
  costs of errors, 357–359
  debiasing and, 243–244
  forecasting, 271–272
  linear sequential unmasking, 256–257
  overview, 9

decision hygiene *(cont.)*
  principles of, 370–374
    aggregation, 373–374
    divide-and-conquer principle, 372
    goal of judgment accuracy, 371
    outside-view principle, 371–372
    relative judgments, 374
    sequencing information, 256–258, 373
  singular decisions, 374
  structuring complex judgments, 307
decision making. *See also* group dynamics
    and decision making
  costs of decisions, 357–359
  evaluative judgment and, 67–68
  not mixing values and facts, 67
  recurrent decisions, 34–36
  singular decisions, 34–38, 374
decision observers, 222, 240–243, 370,
    387–389
decision-making study, 383. *See also* noise
    audit
decomposition *See* mediating assessments
    protocol
delayed holistic judgment, 309–310
Delphi method, forecasting, 262
denial of ignorance, 144–146
deontological ethics, 88
desirability bias, 169
deterrence
  criminal sentencing and, 74
  risk aversion and, 346
developmental review, performance
    evaluation, 290, 297
*Diagnostic and Statistical Manual of
    Mental Disorders,* 3rd edition
    (DSM-III) guidelines, 284
*Diagnostic and Statistical Manual of
    Mental Disorders,* 4th edition
    (DSM-IV) guidelines, 284
*Diagnostic and Statistical Manual of
    Mental Disorders,* 5th edition
    (DSM-5) guidelines, 285
diagnostic variability
  breast cancer, 276, 278
  endometriosis, 277
  heart disease, 277
  melanoma, 278
  pathology, 278
  radiology, 275–277
  tuberculosis, 278

dialectical bootstrapping, 84–85
disability matrix, 355–356
disagreement
  diversity and, 20–21
  expectation of bounded disagreement,
    44, 52, 362
  interjudge disparities, 14–18, 20–21
  medical decisions, 273–279
discrimination. *See also* bias
  algorithms and, 334–336
  in criminal sentencing, 14–15, 53, 71, 132
diversity
  absence of consensus and, 20–21
  unwanted variability vs., 27–29
divide-and-conquer principle, decision
    hygiene, 372
DNA analysis, 7
dollar awards, 194–197
Dreyfus, Alfred, 247
Dror, Itiel, 248–252

E
education, for overcoming biases, 238–239
employment interviews *See* job interviews
endometriosis, diagnostic variability for, 277
equal-weight model (improper linear
    model), 124–127
error. *See also* bias; noise
  costs of errors, 357–359
  forensic science and, 245–246, 253–255
  lap duration exercise, 40
  least squares method, 59–62
  mean squared error, 59–66, 68, 363–364
  noise reduction and, 331–334
  role of noise in, 40–41
  scoring verifiable judgments, 48–49
error equations, 62–66
  error in a single measurement, 62
  evaluative judgment, 67
  overall error, 62–66
estimate-talk-estimate method
  forecasting, 262
  mediating assessments protocol, 319, 323
evaluative judgment, 51–52, 362
  decision making and, 67–68
  error equation, 67
  expectation of bounded disagreement, 52
  multiple options and trade-offs, 51
  noise in, 52–53
  predictive vs., 52

ex ante debiasing, 237–240
  boosting, 238–239
  nudges, 237–238
excessive coherence, 171–173
  defined, 372
  noise and bias, 174
expectation of bounded disagreement, 44, 52, 362
Expert Political Judgment (Tetlock), 140
experts. *See also* criminal sentencing
  interjudge disparities, 14–18, 20–21
  noise audit, 380–381
  respect-experts, 226–235
    actively open-minded thinking, 234
    cognitive style, 232–235
    confidence, 228
    experience, 228
    intelligence, 228–232
    overview, 226–227
    professional doctrine, 227–228
  superforecasters, 142, 225–226, 265–267

F
Facebook
  Community Standards, 353–354
  Implementation Standards, 354
fatigue, as source of occasion noise, 89
Faulds, Henry, 246
fear of judging, 326
fingerprint analysis, 80, 91, 246–253
  ACE-V process, 247–248, 251
  cognitive bias, 256
  exclusion decision, 248
  exemplar prints, 247
  false positives, 253–254
  forensic confirmation bias, 249–253, 255–256, 258
  identification decision, 248
  latent prints, 247
  noise audit, 248–252
  noise in, 7
  occasion noise, 248–249
  overview, 246–248
fluid intelligence, 229
footbridge problem, 88–89
forced ranking system, 292, 294–296
forecasting, 80–81. *See also* performance prediction
  actively open-minded thinking, 267
  aggregation, 271–272

  averaging, 261
  Delphi method, 262
    estimate-talk-estimate, 262
    prediction markets, 261–262
  between-person noise, 260
  bias in, 267–270
  BIN model, 269
  decision hygiene, 271–272
  diversity vs. unwanted variability, 28
  Good Judgment Project, 262–266
  improving, 260–262
  noise in, 6, 267–270
  occasion noise, 260
  overconfidence, 259–260
  overview, 259–260
  perpetual beta, 266–267
  psychological biases, 270
  selection, 261, 268, 270–272
  short-term vs. long-term, 141–142
  statistical bias, 270
  superforecasters, 142, 225–226, 265–267
  teaming, 268, 270
  training, 268, 269–270
forensic confirmation bias, 249–253, 255–256
forensic science, 80
  error and, 245–246, 253–255
  fingerprint analysis
    cognitive bias, 256
    forensic confirmation bias, 249–253, 255–256
    occasion noise, 248–249
    overview, 246–248
  noise in, 7
  sequencing information, 256–258
Forgas, Joseph, 86–87
Fragile Families and Child Wellbeing Study, 149–152
frame-of-reference training, performance evaluation, 297–298
Frankel, Marvin, 14–15, 21, 51, 53, 70–71, 134, 325
Frankfurt, Harry, 87
free throws, variability in, 79–80
frugal models (simple rules), 127–128
fundamental attribution error, 218

G
Galton, Francis, 83, 246–247
Gambardi problem, 44–49, 163, 166–167, 177, 183, 266–267

gambler's fallacy, 90
gaming the system, 344–345
Gates, Bill, 231
Gauss, Carl Friedrich, 59–62
Gaussian (normal) distribution, 56
GMA (general mental ability), 229–231
Goldberg, Lewis, 117–122
Good Judgment Project, 262–266
GoodSell noise reduction example, 56–59,
    64–66
Google, interview practices
    aggregation, 307
    backdoor references, 309
    structuring complex judgments
        delayed holistic judgment, 309–310
        independent assessment, 308
        mediating assessments protocol, 307–308
Green Book, The, 237
group dynamics and decision making, 94–106
    group polarization, 103–106
    informational cascades, 100–102, 106
    music downloads study, 95–97
    political positions, 97–98
    referenda proposals, 97
    self-reinforcing nature of popularity,
        95–98
    social influences, 96, 103
    website comments, 98
    wisdom-of-crowds effect
        independence and, 98–99
        occasion noise, 83–85
group polarization, 103–106
guidelines See rules vs. standards
gullibility, mood and, 87–88
gut feeling See internal signal of judgment
    completion

H
halo effect, 172, 291, 293–294
Halpern Critical Thinking Assessment, 233
Haran, Uriel, 234
Havel, Václav, 332
heart disease, diagnostic variability for, 277
Hertwig, Ralph, 84–85
Herzog, Stefan, 84–85
heuristics and biases approach
    affect heuristic, 170
    anchoring effect, 170–171
    availability heuristic, 167
    conclusion biases, 168–171, 174

defined, 161
    excessive coherence, 171–173, 174
    heuristics and biases program, 161
    similarity vs. probability, 164–168
    substitution biases, 164–168, 173–174
hierarchical categorization, 184
hindsight, 155–156, 218
hiring See job interviews
Hirschman, Albert, 331
Hoffman, Paul, 117
Howard, Philip, 348
Human Rights First (Lawyers Committee
    for Human Rights), 14

I
ignorance See objective ignorance
illusion of agreement, 29–33, 202
illusion of validity, 115–116, 180
imperfect information, 138
improper linear model (equal-weight
    model), 124–127
incapacitation, criminal sentencing and, 74
independent assessments, 308, 317–318, 373
individualized treatment See case-by-case
    judgment
informal operations, 46
informational cascades, 100–102, 106
Innocence Project, 253
insurance industry, 8
    claims adjusters, 24–27
    illusion of agreement, 29–33
    naive realism, 31
    noise audit, 24–27
    overview, 23–24
    system noise, 27–29
    underwriters, 24–27
    unwanted variability, 27–29
intelligence
    crystallized intelligence, 229
    fluid intelligence, 229
    respect-experts, 228–232
intensity scales
    labels vs. comparisons, 184–186
    limitations of absolute judgment, 183–184
    matching intensities, 178–179
internal signal of judgment completion, 48–49
    objective ignorance and, 137–138, 144–146
    predictive judgment, 367
interrater reliability, 47, 173, 276, 279
interview guide, psychiatry, 285

interview-performance correlation, 138–139, 302. *See also* job interviews

intuition, 392–393. *See also* internal signal of judgment completion

J

job interviews
  aggregation, 307–308
  dangers of, 301–302
  Google's interview practices, 307
  informational cascades, 100–102
  noise in, 7, 302–304
  noise reduction, 300–311
  overview, 300–301
  persistence of an illusion, 311
  psychology of interviewers, 304–306
  structured behavioral interviews, 308–309
  structured judgment, 306–311
    delayed holistic judgment, 309–310
    independent assessment, 308
    mediating assessments protocol, 307–308
  work sample tests, 309

Jobs, Steve, 231

Journal of Applied Psychology, 301

judge-by-case interaction, 76

judges. *See also* criminal sentencing
  interjudge disparities, 14–18, 20–21
  noise audit, 380–381
  respect-experts, 226–235
    actively open-minded thinking, 234
    cognitive style, 232–235
    confidence, 228
    experience, 228
    intelligence, 228–232
    overview, 226–227
    professional doctrine, 227–228
  superforecasters, 142, 225–226, 265–267

judgment. *See also* criminal sentencing; evaluative judgment; predictive judgment
  comparative judgments, 184–186
  comparing to outcome, 49–51
  confidence in, 202–203
  defined, 39–40, 112
  evaluating process of, 49–51
  expectation of bounded disagreement, 44, 362
  Gambardi task, 44–49
  goal of, 39–40

illusion of agreement, 29–33

interjudge disparities, 14–18, 20–21

internal signal of judgment completion, 48–49, 137–138, 144–146, 367

judgment call, 362

judicial discretion, 13–14

limitations of absolute judgment, 183–186

lotteries, 24–27

matters of, 43–44

measurement analogy, 39–41

mechanical prediction vs., 114–116

medical decisions, 143–144

nonverifiable, 49–51, 362

opinion and taste vs., 43–44

professional judgments, 362

steps in complex judgment processes, 45–46

system noise, 21

thinking vs., 361

unwanted variability, 27–29

verifiable, 47–51, 362

within-person vs. between-person reliability, 47

judgment call, 362

jury deliberations, 103–105, 187–198
  comparing outrage, punitive intent, and damage awards, 192–194
  dollar awards, 194–197
  Joan Glover v. General Assistance example, 187–191, 193–197
  outrage hypothesis, 190–193
  punitive damages, 190–194

jury nullification, 356

K

Kadi justice, 359

Kahana, Michael, 91–92

Kahneman, Daniel, 189

Kant, Immanuel, 88

kappa statistic, 276

Kasdan, Lawrence, 168–169

Kennedy, Edward M., 17–18

Keynes, John Maynard, 264

Kuncel, Nathan, 32, 121–122

L

LaFleur, Jo Carol, 342

lap duration exercise, 40

Lawyers Committee for Human Rights (Human Rights First), 14

least squares method, 59–62

level errors, 73–74
level noise, 74, 78, 193
   criminal sentencing, 332
   defined, 365–366
   measuring, 212–217
   performance evaluation, 294
Lewis, Michael, 134
Lieblich, Samuel, 284
life trajectories
   causal thinking, 153–154, 157
   correlation vs. causation, 152–153
   Fragile Families and Child Wellbeing
      Study, 149–152
   hindsight, 155–156
   overview, 148–149
   statistical thinking, 153–154, 157
   understanding, 152–153, 154–156
linear regression models *See* simple models
linear sequential unmasking, 256–257
loan approvals, 90
lottery
   criminal sentencing, 72, 76
   free throws, 79–80
   insurance industry, 24–27
   occasion noise as product of second
      lottery, 80–81, 206
   system noise as product of first lottery,
      81, 206
Lucas, George, 168–170

M
machine learning models
   algorithms
      algorithm aversion, 135
      algorithmic bias, 334
      defined, 128–133
      predictive policing, 335–336
   bail decisions, 130–133, 143
   broken-leg principle, 129
   fairness, 132–133
   life trajectories, 150
   medical decisions, 144, 280
   predictive judgment, 128–133
Macy, Michael, 97
"Magical Number Seven, The" (Miller), 183
MAP *See* mediating assessments protocol
Mapco acquisition of Roadco example
   deciding on approach, 312–315
   decision meeting, 318–321
   estimate-talk-estimate method, 319, 323

independent assessment, 317–318
   outside view, 316–317
   sequencing information, 315–316
   transparency, 318
Mashaw, Jerry, 356
matching, 176–186
   Bill, the jazz-playing accountant example,
      176–177
   coherence and, 176–178
   defined, 176
   Julie's GPA example, 179–183
   matching intensities, 178–179
   matching predictions
      bias of, 179–183
      corrected predictions vs., 391–392
      defined, 391
   noise in, 183–186
Mayfield, Brandon, 245–246, 251
McLanahan, Sara, 148–149
mean absolute difference, 72–73
mean squared error (MSE), 59–66, 68, 211,
      363–364
measurement
   defined, 39
   judgment and, 39–41
mechanical prediction. *See also* rule-based
      approaches
   clinical judgment vs., 114–116
   defined, 113
   simple models, 113, 117–122, 129, 150
median, 60
mediating assessments protocol (MAP),
      312–321
   base rate, 316
   defined, 372
   job interviews, 307–308
   main steps of, 323
   Mapco acquisition of Roadco example
      deciding on approach, 312–315
      decision meeting, 318–321
      estimate-talk-estimate method, 319, 323
      independent assessment, 317–318
      outside view, 316–317
      sequencing information, 315–316
      transparency, 318
   recurrent decisions, 321–322
   reference class, 316
medical decisions, 273–286
   between-person noise, 276, 279
   clinical judgment, 143–144

diagnosing heart attacks, 143–144
diagnostic variability, 80
   breast cancer, 276, 278
   endometriosis, 277
   heart disease, 277
   melanoma, 278
   pathology and radiology, 275–279
   tuberculosis, 278
fatigue and prescription of opioids, 89
kappa statistic, 276
machine learning models, 144
noise in, 6
noise reduction, 274–275, 279–283
   algorithms, 280
   Apgar score, 280–282
   BI-RADS, 283
   Centor score, 282–283
   occasion noise, 278–279
   psychiatry, 283–286
   second opinion, 274
   white coat syndrome, 273–274
Meehl, Paul, 114–116, 134
melanoma, diagnostic variability for, 278
Mellers, Barbara, 142, 234, 262–266, 268–270
memory performance, 91–92
Merchant of Venice (Shakespear), 340
mindless consistency, 122
mini-Delphi method
   forecasting, 262
   mediating assessments protocol, 319, 323
model-of-the-judge, 118–122
Moneyball (Lewis), 134
mood and mood manipulation, 86–89, 173
Moore, Don, 262–266
moral values, 341–344
morale, 9, 292, 347
Morewedge, Carey, 238
MSE (mean squared error), 59–66, 68, 211, 363–364
Muchnik, Lev, 98–99
Mullainathan, Sendhil, 130–131, 143–144
multiple regression technique, 113
music downloads study, 95–97

N
naive realism, 31
Nash, Steve, 79
National Basketball Association, 79
negotiations
   anchoring and, 171

mood and, 87
noise. *See also* occasion noise; system noise
   bias vs., 4–6, 8, 53
   components of, 210
   conclusion biases and, 174
   contribution to error, 55–56, 62–66
   defined, 3–5
   effect of, 364–365
   equality with bias, 58
   excessive coherence, 174
   general discussion, 6–10
   importance of recognizing, 5
   job interviews, 302–304
   lap duration exercise, 40
   level noise, 74, 78, 193
   matching, 183–186
   measuring, 53–54, 363–364
   obscurity of, 369
   optimal noise, 9
   overall error equation, 62–66
   pattern noise, 74–77, 193, 203–204
   predictive judgment, 8
   response scales, 192–194
   shooting range metaphor, 3–5, 53
   substitution biases, 173–174
   types of, 365–367
noise audit, 53, 379–385
   administering, 383–384
   analyses and conclusions, 384–385
   asset management firm, 28–29
   clients, 380
   criminal sentencing, 15–17, 19–20, 69–76
   defined, 364
   fingerprint analysis, 248–252
   function of, 370
   GoodSell noise reduction example, 56–59, 64–66
   insurance, 25–27
   judges, 380–381
   prelaunch meeting, 382–383
   project manager, 381
   project team, 380
   simulation, 381–382
   standard deviation, 57–58
noise reduction. *See also* decision hygiene
   actively open-minded thinking, 370
   costs of, 329–337
      bias, 334–337
      error prone, 331–334
      overview, 329–331

noise reduction *(cont.)*
  debiasing, 222, 236–244, 370, 387–389
  forecasting, 260–262
  GoodSell noise reduction example, 64–66
  job interviews, 300–311
    aggregation, 307–308
    dangers of, 301–302
    delayed holistic judgment, 309–310
    independent assessment, 308
    mediating assessments protocol, 307–308
    noise, 302–304
    overview, 300–301
    psychology of interviewers, 304–306
    structured behavioral interviews,
      308–309
    structuring complex judgments,
      306–311
    work sample tests, 309
  medical decisions, 274–275, 279–283
    algorithms, 280
    Apgar score, 280–282
    BI-RADS, 283
    Centor score, 282–283
  noise audit, 370
  objections to, 327–328
  overall error equation, 63–66
  performance evaluation
    aggregation, 291–292
    behaviorally anchored rating scales,
      297–298
    case scales, 297–298
    forced ranking system, 292, 294–296
    frame-of-reference training, 297–298
    ranking, 294
    structuring, 293–294
    360-degree rating systems, 291–292
  with rules and guidelines, 21
nonregressive errors, 182
nonverifiable judgments, 49–51, 362
normal (Gaussian) distribution, 56
nudges, ex ante debiasing, 237–238
number scales, 46

O
Obama, Barack, 35
Obermeyer, Ziad, 143–144
objective ignorance
  clinical-versus-mechanical debate,
    142–144
  denial of ignorance, 144–146
  imperfect information, 138
  internal signal of judgment completion,
    137–138, 144–146
  intractable uncertainty, 139–140
  overconfidence, 140–142, 144–145
  performance prediction and, 138
  political pundits, 140–142
  predictive judgment, 367
  short-term vs. long-term forecasting,
    141–142
occasion noise, 8, 77–78, 366–367
  crowd within, 84–85
  dialectical bootstrapping, 84–85
  fingerprint analysis, 248–249
  free throw example, 79–80
  inner causes of, 91–93
  measuring, 81–82, 212–217
  medical decisions, 278–279
  order of cases as source of, 90
  pattern noise and, 203–204
  as product of second lottery, 80–81, 206
  size relative to system noise, 90–91
  sources of, 86–90
  substitution biases, 173
  wisdom-of-crowds effect, 83–85, 98–99, 223
OMB Circular A-4 document, 242
On Bullshit (Frankfurt), 87–88
O'Neal, Shaquille, 79
O'Neil, Cathy, 334–335
optimal noise
  case-by-case judgment, 339–348
    creativity, 346
    deterrence, 346
    gaming the system, 344–345
    moral values and, 341–344
    morale, 347
    overview, 339–340
    risk aversion, 346
  costs of noise reduction, 329–337
    bias, 334–337
    level of error, 331–334
    overview, 329–331
  overview, 325–328
  rules vs. standards, 350–360
    airline industry, 355
    bias, 353, 360
    bureaucratic justice, 356
    costs of decisions, 357–359
    costs of errors, 357–359
    disability matrix, 355–356

eliminating noise, 359–360
ignorance and, 352–353
jury nullification, 356
Kadi justice, 359
overview, 350–351
social and political divisions, 352
social media, 353–354
order of cases, as source of occasion noise, 90
outliers, 395
outside view, 153–154, 157, 219–220, 369
corrected predictions, 393
decision hygiene, 371–372
error prevention and, 167
mediating assessments protocol, 316–317
overconfidence, 239–240
forecasting, 259–260
objective ignorance and, 140–142, 144–145

P
Pashler, Harold, 83–85
patent grants, 7, 213
pathology, diagnostic variability in, 275–279
pattern errors, 75, 205–206, 212
defined, 203
transient and permanent factors, 203
transient error and, 203
pattern noise, 74–77, 193, 206, 209, 366
judge-by-case interaction, 76
measuring, 212–217
occasion noise and, 203–204
psychiatry, 284
sources of, 204–205
stable pattern noise, 203–204
patterns
illusion of agreement, 202
Julie's GPA example, 200–206
multiple, conflicting cues, 200–202
personality analogy, 207–208
stable pattern noise, 203–204, 206
PCAST (President's Council of Advisors on
Science and Technology), 253–254
Pennycook, Gordon, 87
percent concordant (PC)
defined, 108
interview-performance correlation, 139,
302
performance evaluation, 287–299
absolute ratings, 292–296
developmental review, 290, 297
halo effect, 291, 293–294

noise in, 7
noise reduction in, 291
aggregation, 291–292
behaviorally anchored rating scales,
297–298
case scales, 297–298
forced ranking system, 292, 294–296
frame-of-reference training, 297–298
ranking, 294
structuring, 293–294
360-degree rating systems, 291–292
questioning value of, 298–299
relative ratings, 292–296
system noise, 289–290
performance prediction
clinical judgment, 112, 114–116
mechanical prediction, 113–116
multiple regression technique, 113
objective ignorance and, 138
overview, 111–112
random linear model, 121–122
simple models, 113, 117–122
standard statistical method, 112–113
perpetual beta, forecasting, 266–267
personality analogy, 207–209
Big Five model, 207
joining of situation and, 207–208
personnel decisions. See also job interviews;
performance evaluation
informational cascades, 100–102
noise in, 7
planning fallacy, 162
political positions, 97–98
political pundits, 140–142
prediction markets, 261–262
predictive judgment, 8. See also
performance prediction
as-if model, 118
bias in, 162
defined, 362
evaluative vs., 52
illusion of validity, 115–116
internal signal of judgment completion, 367
model-of-the-judge, 118–122
noise in, 52
nonverifiable, 47–48, 362
objective ignorance, 367
performance prediction
clinical judgment, 112
mechanical prediction, 113–116

predictive judgment *(cont.)*
   multiple regression technique, 113
   overview, 111–112
   simple models, 113
   standard statistical method, 112–113
  psychological biases, 367–368
  rule-based approaches, 123–135
   frugal models, 127–128
   improper linear model, 124–127
   machine learning models, 128–133
   overview, 123–124
   superiority over human judgment, 133–135
  verifiable, 362
predictive policing, 335–336
prejudgments *See* conclusion biases
prelaunch meeting, noise audit, 382–383
President's Council of Advisors on Science and Technology (PCAST), 253–254
preventive debiasing, 237–240
  boosting, 238–239
  nudges, 237–238
Price, Mark, 79
Principles of Forecasting (Armstrong), 260
probabilistic thinking, 38
professional doctrine, respect-experts, 227–228
professional judgments, 362. *See also* respect-experts
project manager, noise audit, 381
project team, noise audit, 380
ProPublica, 335
psychiatry
  DSM-5 guidelines, 285
  DSM-III guidelines, 284
  DSM-IV guidelines, 284
  interview guide, 285
  noise in, 6
  pattern noise, 284
psychological biases
  causal thinking and, 218–219
  conclusion biases, 168–171, 174
  diagnosing, 162–164
  excessive coherence, 171–173, 174
  forecasting, 270
  fundamental attribution error, 218
  hindsight, 218
  planning fallacy, 162
  predictive judgment, 367–368
  scope insensitivity, 163
  statistical bias and, 161–162
  substitution biases, 164–168, 173–174
Pythagorean theorem, 62–63

R
racial discrimination, 71, 132, 337. *See also* bias
radiology, diagnostic variability in, 275–279
Ramji-Nogales, Jaya, 90–91
random linear model, performance prediction, 121–122
ranking, performance evaluation, 292, 294–296
ratio scales, 195
recruiting interviews *See* job interviews
recurrent decisions
  defined, 34
  singular decisions vs., 35–36
referenda proposals, 97
regression to the mean, 182, 392
regulating behavior, 350–360
rehabilitation, criminal sentencing and, 74
relative judgments, 374
relative ratings, 292–296
respect-experts, 369
  actively open-minded thinking, 234
  cognitive style, 232–235
  confidence, 228
  experience, 228
  intelligence, 228–232
  overview, 226–227
  professional doctrine, 227–228
response scales, 189
  ambiguity in, 189, 199
  comparing outrage, punitive intent, and damage awards, 192–194
  dollar awards, 194–197
  noise, 192–194
  outrage hypothesis, 190–193
  punitive damages, 190–194
  ratio scales, 195–196
Return of the Jedi (film), 168–169
Rhetoric of Reaction, The (Hirschman), 331
risk aversion, 346
Ritov, Ilana, 234
Rosenzweig, Phil, 219
rule-based approaches
  frugal models, 127–128
  improper linear model, 124–127
  machine learning models, 128–133

overview, 123–124
superiority over human judgment,
 133–135
rules vs. standards, 350–360
 airline industry, 355
 bias, 353, 360
 bureaucratic justice, 356
 costs of decisions, 357–359
 costs of errors, 357–359
 disability matrix, 355–356
 eliminating noise, 359–360
 ignorance and, 352–353
 jury nullification, 356
 Kadi justice, 359
 overview, 350–351
 social and political divisions, 352
 social media, 353–354

S
Salganik, Matthew, 95–97, 148–149
Salikhov, Marat, 269–270
Satopää, Ville, 268–270
Save More Tomorrow plans, 237
Schkade, David, 189
scope insensitivity, 163
second opinion, medical decisions, 274
select-crowd strategy, forecasting, 261
selection, forecasting, 260, 261, 268,
 270–272
selective attention and recall, 46
self-reinforcing nature of popularity, 95–98
Sellier, Anne-Laure, 239
Sentencing Reform Act of 1984, 18
sequencing information
 decision hygiene, 373
 forensic science, 256–258
 mediating assessments protocol, 315–316
shared norms, respect-experts, 227–228
"Shared Outrage and Erratic Awards"
 (Kahneman, Sunstein, Schkade), 194
shooting range metaphor, 3–5, 53, 162–163
Simonsohn, Uri, 90
simple models, 113, 117–122
 broken-leg principle, 129
 life trajectories, 150
simple rules (frugal models), 127–128
simulation, noise audit, 381–382
singular decisions, 34–38
 counterfactual thinking, 37–38
 decision hygiene and, 374

noise in, 36–38
noise reduction, 38
overview, 34–35
recurrent decisions vs., 35–36
response to COVID-19 crisis, 37–38
response to Ebola threat, 34–35, 36
Slovic, Paul, 170
social influences, 96, 103
social media, 353–354
stable pattern noise, 206, 212–217, 366
standard deviation, 41, 57, 72
standard statistical method, performance
 prediction, 112–113
standards See rules vs. standards
statistical bias, 173
 defined, 161
 forecasting, 270
 psychological bias and, 161–162
statistical thinking See outside view
status quo bias, 240
Stevens, S. S., 195–197
Stith, Kate, 20, 326
stress, as source of occasion noise, 89
structured behavioral interviews, 308–309
structuring complex judgments, 306–311
 delayed holistic judgment, 309–310
 independent assessment, 308
 mediating assessments protocol,
  307–308
 performance evaluation, 293–294
substitution biases
 Bill, the jazz-playing accountant example,
  164–166
 noise, 173–174
 substitution of easy judgment for hard,
  167–168, 181–182
 substitution of one question for the other,
  164–167
Sunstein, Cass R., 189
superforecasters, 142, 225–226, 265–267
suppression of alternative interpretations,
 202
System 1 thinking
 conclusion biases, 169
 defined, 161
 matching, 184
 matching predictions, 180, 182
System 2 thinking
 conclusion biases, 169
 matching predictions, 182

system noise, 21, 69
   components of, 78
   decomposition into system and pattern
      noise, 76
   defined, 78, 363
   inconsistency, 53
   jury deliberations, 193
   level noise, 74, 78, 193
      criminal sentencing, 332
      defined, 365–366
      measuring, 212–217
      performance evaluation, 294
   noise audit of insurance company,
      25–27
   occasion noise, 366–367
   pattern noise, 74–77, 193, 206, 209,
      366
      judge-by-case interaction, 76
      measuring, 212–217
      occasion noise and, 203–204
      psychiatry, 284
      sources of, 204–205
      stable pattern noise, 203–204
   performance evaluation, 289–290
   as product of first lottery, 206
   stable pattern noise, 366
   unwanted variability, 27–29

T
TB (tuberculosis), diagnostic variability for,
   278
teaming, forecasting, 268, 270
test-retest reliability, 82
Tetlock, Philip, 140–142, 262–266,
   268–270
Thinking, Fast and Slow (Kahneman), 161,
   309
360-degree rating systems, performance
   evaluation, 291–292
three-strikes policy, 332, 356
Todorov, Alexander, 214
training
   forecasting, 268, 269–270
   frame-of-reference training, 297–298
   respect-experts, 227–228
transparency, mediating assessments
   protocol, 318

tuberculosis (TB), diagnostic variability for,
   278

U
uncertainty, 139–140
understanding
   hindsight and, 155–156
   prediction and, 152–153
underwriters, insurance, 24–27, 31–32
Universal Declaration of Human Rights,
   352, 359–360
US Sentencing Commission, 18, 19
utilitarian calculation, 88

V
valley of the normal, 154–158, 217
verifiable judgment, 47–51, 362
   evaluating, 50–51
   scoring, 48–49
Vul, Edward, 83–85

W
Wainer, Howard, 126
Weapons of Math Destruction (O'Neil),
   334–335
weather, as source of occasion noise, 89–90
Weber, Max, 359
website comments, 98
Welch, Jack, 292
white coat syndrome, 273–274
Williams, Thomas, 16
wine competitions, 80
wisdom-of-crowds effect, 225
   forecasting, 223, 261, 271
   independence and, 98–99
   occasion noise, 83–85
within-person reliability, 47
Woodson v. North Carolina, 333
Work Rules! (Bock), 307
work sample tests, job interviews, 309

Y
Yang, Crystal, 20
Yu, Martin, 121–122

Z
Zuckerberg, Mark, 231

About the Authors

Daniel Kahneman is an emeritus professor of psychology and public affairs at Princeton University and the winner of the 2002 Nobel Prize in Economic Sciences and the 2013 Presidential Medal of Freedom. Kahneman is a member of the American Academy of Arts and Sciences and the National Academy of Sciences. He is a fellow of the American Psychological Association, the American Psychological Society, the Society of Experimental Psychologists, and the Econometric Society. He has been the recipient of numerous awards, among them the Distinguished Scientific Contribution Award of the American Psychological Association, the Warren Medal of the Society of Experimental Psychologists, the Hilgard Award for Career Contributions to General Psychology, and the Award for Lifetime Contributions to Psychology from the American Psychological Association. He is the author of *New York Times* bestseller *Thinking, Fast and Slow.* He lives in New York City.

———

Olivier Sibony is a professor of strategy at HEC Paris and an associate fellow at Saïd Business School, Oxford University. Previously, he spent twenty-five years in the Paris and New York offices of McKinsey & Company, where he was a senior partner. Sibony's research on improving the quality of strategic decision making has been featured in many publications, including *Harvard Business Review* and *MIT Sloan Management Review*. He is a graduate of HEC Paris and holds a PhD from Université Paris Sciences et Lettres. He is the author of *You're About to Make a Terrible Mistake!* He lives in Paris. Twitter: @siboliv

———

Cass R. Sunstein is the Robert Walmsley University Professor at Harvard, where he is founder and director of the Program on Behavioral Economics and Public Policy. From 2009 to 2012, he was administrator of the White House Office of Information and Regulatory Affairs. From 2013 to 2014, he served on President Obama's Review Group on Intelligence and Communications Technologies. Winner of the 2018 Holberg Prize from the government of Norway, Sunstein is the author of many articles and books, including two *New York Times* bestsellers: *The World According to Star Wars* and *Nudge* (with Richard H. Thaler). His other books include *How Change Happens* and *Too Much Information*. Twitter: @casssunstein